Financial
valuation
workbook

Second Edition

Step-by-Step Exercises and
Tests to Help You Master
Financial Valuation

JAMES R. HITCHNER

and

MICHAEL J. MARD

D1379690

WILEY

John Wiley & Sons, Inc.

To my mother and father, Earle and Virginia Hitchner, my sister, Deborah Hitchner, who left this world too early for me to get to know her, and my godmother, Aunt Thelma, whose positive attitude inspires me.

To Pam, Seph, Joe and Shelley, Laura and Jacob, and my mom and dad, Geneva and Joe Mard. And to Derick, we miss you.

contents

James R. Hitchner, CPA/ABV, ASA is the managing director of the Financial Valuation Group (FVG) in Atlanta, GA. FVG is a national financial advisory services firm specializing in valuation and litigation services. Mr. Hitchner is a founding member and current president of the Financial Consulting Group, L.C. (FCG). FCG is a national association of professional services firms dedicated to excellence in valuation, financial, and litigation consulting.

Mr. Hitchner has more than 28 years of professional experience, including 26 years in valuation services and two years in real estate development. He was with Phillips Hitchner Group, Inc. for seven years and was also partner-in-charge of valuation services for the southern region of Coopers & Lybrand (currently PricewaterhouseCoopers), where he spent more than nine years. He was also employed as a senior appraiser with the national appraisal firm American Appraisal Associates, in both the financial and industrial valuation groups.

Mr. Hitchner is co-author of the book *Valuation for Financial Reporting: Intangible Assets, Goodwill, and Impairment Analysis—SFAS 141 and 142*, editor/co-author of the book *Financial Valuation Applications and Models;* and co-author of the book *Financial Valuation Workbook,* all published by John Wiley & Sons. He is co-author of the American Institute of Certified Public Accountants (AICPA) three-part self-study video course series on SFAS 141 and 142 on business combinations, intangible assets, and goodwill impairment. He is editor in chief of *Financial Valuation and Litigation Expert,* a bi-monthly journal presenting views and tools from leading experts on valuation, forensic/fraud, and litigation services.

He has been recognized as a qualified expert witness and has provided testimony on valuations in numerous state and federal courts. In the valuation area he has co-authored over 20 courses, including the six-day AICPA Business Valuation Essentials courses and the three-day NACVA Advanced Business Valuation courses, all of which are based upon this book and *Financial Valuation Applications and Models.* Mr. Hitchner has taught over 50 courses, published over 50 articles and has made over 100 conference presentations including the American Institute of Certified Public Accountants, the American Society of Appraisers, the National Association of Certified Valuation Analysts, the Institute of Business Appraisers, and numerous state CPA societies. He has also been a faculty member teaching valuation courses for judges for the National Judicial College and the Flaschner Judicial Institute.

He is an inductee in the American Institute of Certified Public Accountants (AICPA) Business Valuation Hall of Fame and current member of the AICPA task force on Business Valuation Standards. Mr. Hitchner is past chairman of the Business Valuation Committee of the Georgia Society of CPAs, past member of the AICPA Business Valuation Subcommittee, past member of the AICPA ABV exam committee, past chairman of the ABV exam review course committee, contributing editor of AICPA *CPA Expert* newsletter, and a former member of The Appraisal Foundation Industry Advisory Council. He has a bachelor of science degree in engineering from the University of Pittsburgh and a masters of business administration degree from Rider University. He holds the AICPA Accreditation in Business Valuation (ABV) specialty designation, and also is an Accredited Senior Appraiser (ASA) with the American Society of Appraisers.

Michael J. Mard, CPA/ABV, ASA, The Financial Valuation Group, Financial Consulting Group, L.C.   Michael J. Mard is a managing director of The Financial Valuation Group (FVG) in Tampa, Florida. FVG is a national financial advisory firm specializing in valuation and litigation services. Mr. Mard was founding president of the Financial Consulting Group, a national association of professional service firms dedicated to excellence in valuation, litigation, and financial consulting.

Mr. Mard has been a full-time business appraiser and expert witness for over 21 years, specializing in intangible assets, specifically intellectual property. He has developed analyses that have been reviewed and accepted by the Securities and Exchange Commission (SEC), numerous accounting firms (including the Big Four), the Internal Revenue Service (IRS), and the courts. Mr. Mard has provided expert testimony in both Federal and state courts related to intangible assets, intellectual property, business damages, marital dissolution, shareholder disputes, and IRS matters.

Mr. Mard is lead author of *Driving Your Company's Value: Strategic Benchmarking for Value* and lead co-author of *Valuation for Financial Reporting: Intangible Assets, Goodwill, and Impairment Analysis—SFAS 141 and 142* and co-author of *Financial Valuation: Applications and Models*, all published by John Wiley & Sons. He is co-author of the American Institute of Certified Public Accountants (AICPA) three-part self-study video course series on SFAS 141 and 142 on business combinations, intangible assets, and goodwill impairment. He also co-authored the *AICPA Consulting Services Practice Aid 99-2: Valuing Intellectual Property and Calculating Infringement Damages*. Mr. Mard has co-authored 20 courses and published over 70 articles. He has been a presenter, speaker, and instructor over 80 times.

Mr. Mard is very active at state and national levels with emphasis on business valuation standards and intellectual property valuations. He has served on numerous committees and task forces of the AICPA, Florida Institute of Certified Public Accountants, American Society of Appraisers, and the Financial Accounting Standards Board (FASB). Mr. Mard continues to serve on two FASB task forces: Disclosure About Intangible Assets and Business Combination/Purchase Method Procedures.

He has received the AICPA Business Valuation Volunteer of the Year Award and been inducted into the AICPA Business Valuation Hall of Fame. He has been published in the Marquis Who's Who in Finance Industry and the International Who's Who of Professionals. He has a bachelor of science degree in accounting and a masters of accounting from the University of South Florida. He holds the AICPA Accreditation in Business Valuation (ABV) specialty designation, and is an Accredited Senior Appraiser (ASA) with the American Society of Appraisers.

acknowledgments

Several people were instrumental in preparing this book. Thank you Faye Danger and Deanna Muraki of The Financial Valuation Group in Tampa, Florida, and Karen Warner of The Financial Valuation Group in Atlanta, Georgia. You were great.

We would also like to thank Jim Alerding, CPA/ABV, ASA, CVA, of Clifton Gunderson in Indianapolis, Indiana for helping with the case study, and all the co-authors of *Financial Valuation: Applications and Models* for submitting the ValTips in Chapter 4: Mel H. Abraham, CPA/ABV, ASA, CVA; R. James Alerding, CPA/ABV, ASA, CVA; Terry Jacoby Allen, CPA/ABV, ASA; Larry R. Cook, CPA/ABV, CBA; Michael A. Crain, CPA/ABV, ASA, CFE, CFA; Don M. Drysdale, CPA/ABV; Robert E. Duffy, CPA/ABV, ASA, CFA; Edward J. Dupke, CPA/ABV; Nancy J. Fannon, CPA/ABV, ASA, MCBA; John R. Gilbert, CPA/ABV, ASA, Cr. FA; Chris Hamilton, CPA, CFE, CVA, DABFA; Thomas E. Hilton, CPA/ABV, ASA, CVA; Steven D. Hyden, CPA/ABV, ASA, CM+AA; Gregory S. Koonsman, CFA; Mark Kucik, CPA, CVA, CM+AA; Eva M. Lang, CPA/ABV, ASA; Derald L. Lyons, MT, CPA, CVA; Harold G. Martin, Jr., CPA/ABV, ASA, CFE; Michael Mattson; Edward F. Moran, MBA, CPA, ABV, CVA, CBA; Raymond E. Moran, ASA; James S. Rigby, Jr., CPA/ABV, ASA; Ronald L. Seigneur, MBA, CPA/ABV, CVA; Robin E. Taylor, CPA/ABV, CBA, CFE, CVA; Linda B. Trugman, CPA/ABV, ASA, MCBA; Samuel W. Wessinger; Donald P. Wisehart, ASA, CPA/ABV, CVA; and Kevin Yeanoplos, CPA/ABV, ASA.

The Financial Valuation Workbook (FVW) contains both educational exercises that guide the reader through a complete business valuation and valuation tools that professionals can use in preparing business valuations. It also contains detailed information on how to run a successful valuation practice. It is structured to be used on a stand-alone basis. It is also a companion text to *Financial Valuation: Applications and Models* (FV) (John Wiley & Sons), where the subject matter contained in the workbook is expanded upon. This workbook contains basic, intermediate, and advanced topics on valuing businesses conveyed in a series of easily understandable exercises with comprehensive answers.

FVW is targeted to the following professionals and groups who are typically exposed to financial valuation issues:

- Appraisers
- Appraisal Associations and Societies
- Actuaries
- Attorneys
- Bankers
- Business Brokers
- Business executives including CEOs, CFOs, and tax directors
- Business owners
- CPAs
- Estate and Gift Planners
- Financial Analysts
- Government agencies including the IRS, SEC, and DOL
- Insurance Agents
- Investment Advisors
- Investment Bankers
- Judges
- Pension Administrators
- Stockbrokers

FVW contains eight chapters, each with a different purpose.

Chapter 1 contains more than 75 exercises that have been placed throughout excerpts of an actual business valuation report presenting numerous valuation topics, including rates of return, the capitalized cash flow method of the income approach, and the guideline company transaction and guideline public company methods of the market approach.

Chapter 2 contains comprehensive answers to the exercises in Chapter 1.

Chapter 3 includes over 300 exercises that are a companion piece and correlate to the relevant chapters of *Financial Valuation Applications and Models,* 2nd editon. These exercises/tests can be used to prepare for business valuation certification exams or for university professors in the academic field or as reinforcement to learn the material.

Chapter 4 includes over 400 ValTips that are extracted from the companion book FV. This summary of ValTips can serve professionals as a quick reference source of important concepts, application issues, and pitfalls to avoid.

Chapter 5 presents a Valuation Process Flowchart to allow professionals to follow a more structured process in applying and documenting the income approach.

Chapter 6 highlights strategies for marketing, managing, and making money in a valuation services practice. It discusses risk management in regard to reports and engagement letters, and gives examples of each. This chapter also includes a bibliography of print and digital resources for the valuation professional. It advises how to keep up technically; find, train, and retain staff; and delegate authority.

Chapter 7 includes guidelines for practice management workflow procedures, which starts with the initial prospective client call, highlights checking points through the valuation analysis, then moves on to draft and final record, then to file retention and engagement closure.

Chapter 8 includes over 35 checklists that can be used by professionals in documenting their valuations. It can also be used by less experienced professionals as a guide in applying valuation concepts.

*   *   *   *   *   *   *

Financial valuations are very much affected by specific facts and circumstances. As such, the views expressed in these written materials do not necessarily reflect the professional opinions or positions that the authors would take in every business valuation assignment, or in providing business valuation services in connection with an actual litigation matter. Every situation is unique and differing facts and circumstances may result in variations of the applied methodologies. Furthermore, valuation theory, applications, and methods are continually evolving and, at a later date, may be different from what is presented here.

Nothing contained in these written materials shall be construed to constitute the rendering of valuation advice; the rendering of a valuation opinion; the rendering of an opinion as to the propriety of taking a particular valuation position; or the rendering of any other professional opinion or service.

Business valuation services are necessarily fact-sensitive particularly in a litigation context. Therefore, the authors urge readers to apply their expertise to particular valuation fact patterns that they encounter, or to seek competent professional assistance as warranted in the circumstances.

*   *   *   *   *   *   *

Disclaimer Excluding Any Warranties: This book is designed to provide guidance to analysts, auditors, management, and other professionals, but is not to be used as a substitute for professional judgment. Procedures must be altered to fit each assignment. The reader takes sole responsibility for implementation of material from this book. The implied warranties of merchantability and fitness of purpose and all other warranties, whether expressed or implied, are excluded from this transaction, and shall not apply to this book. None of the authors, editors, reviewers, or publisher shall be liable for any indirect, special, or consequential damages.

CHAPTER 1

Valuation Case Study Exercises

INTRODUCTION

The purpose of this chapter is to highlight and discuss important concepts in valuation through a series of exercises. These exercises have been intermittently placed in excerpts of a valuation report. You should attempt to complete these exercises as you read the report with reasoning and emphasis on an explanation of your conclusion. The authors' solutions to these exercises can be found in Chapter 2.

The following case presents selected excerpts from a business valuation report that, in its entirety, was in full compliance with the Uniform Standards of Professional Appraisal Practice. This report format is one of many that analysts can use in presenting business valuations. All schedules have been omitted as they are not necessary for the exercises. Some of the terms, numbers, sources, and other data have been changed for ease of presentation.

THE VALUATION REPORT

August 20, 20X6

Mr. Tom Profit
LEGGO Construction, Inc.
123 Builders Drive
Anycity, Anystate 54321

Dear Mr. Profit:

The objective of this valuation report is to estimate the fair market value of 100 percent of the common stock in LEGGO Construction, Inc. (LEGGO or the Company), on a nonmarketable, control interest basis, as of December 31, 20X5, for management purposes and internal planning. (A more informative term could be marketable illiquid [see Chapter 8 of *Financial Valuation Applications and Models, Second Edition*].) Assume for this case that nonmarketable for a 100 percent control interest means illiquid.

EXERCISE 1: The purpose of the valuation of LEGGO is to assist management in internal planning. What other purposes are there?

_____

_____

_____

_____

EXERCISE 2:   Which of the following is the "as of" date for valuation?

a. Anytime within one year
b. "As of" a single point in time
c. "As of" a single point in time or six months later
d. Date that the report is signed

In our opinion, the fair market value of 100 percent of the common stock in LEGGO, on a nonmarketable, control interest basis, as of December 31, 20X5, for management purposes, is (rounded):

$$\$6,300,000$$

EXERCISE 3:   Valuation conclusions can be presented as:

a. A range of values
b. A single value
c. An estimate of value
d. All of the above

EXERCISE 4:   This valuation is being done on a nonmarketable, control interest basis. It is also on a control stand-alone basis. Name the four traditional levels of value that are considered in a valuation.

1._____

2._____

3._____

4._____

The standard of value used in this appraisal report is fair market value. *Fair market value* is:

The price, expressed in terms of cash equivalents, at which property would change hands between a hypothetical willing and able buyer and a hypothetical willing and able seller, acting at arms length in an open and unrestricted market, when neither is under compulsion to buy or sell and when both have reasonable knowledge of the relevant facts.[1]

---

[1] International Glossary of Business Valuation Terms (The C.L.A.R.E.N.C.E. Glossary Project comprised of the following professional organizations: American Institute of Certified Public Accountants, American Society of Appraisers, Canadian Institute of Chartered Business Valuators, National Association of Certified Valuation Analysts, and The Institute of Business Appraisers, 2001).

EXERCISE 5: Which of these are standards of value?

  a. Fair market value, fair value financial reporting, investment value
  b. Fair value investment reporting, fair value state actions, intrinsic value
  c. Investment value, intrinsic value, equal value
  d. Fair market value, equal value, investment value

Valuation is based on relevant facts, elements of common sense, informed judgment, and reasonableness. Our scope was unrestricted and our methodology and analysis complied with the Uniform Standards of Professional Appraisal Practice. In addition, this valuation report and the values determined herein cannot be utilized or relied on for any purpose other than for internal management planning.

The enclosed narrative valuation report, as well as all documents and schedules in our files, constitute the basis on which our opinion of fair market value was determined. Statements of fact contained in this valuation report are, to the best of our knowledge and belief, true and correct. In the event that facts or other representations relied on in the attached valuation report are revised or otherwise changed, our opinion as to the fair market value of the common stock of the Company may require updating. However, Valking LLP has no obligation to update our opinion of the fair market value of the common stock of the Company for information that comes to our attention after the date of this report.

No partner or employee of Valking LLP has any current or contemplated future interest in the Company or any other interest that might tend to prevent them from making a fair and unbiased opinion of fair market value. Compensation to Valking LLP is not contingent on the opinions or conclusions reached in this valuation report.

We wish to express our appreciation to you and the management of the Company for your cooperation in making available to us financial data and other pertinent information necessary for the preparation of the report.

Very truly yours,

Valking LLP
Val Dude, CPA/ABV, ASA, CBA, CVA

INTRODUCTION

Description of the Assignment

Valking LLP was retained by Mr. Tom Profit to determine the fair market value of 100 percent of the common stock in LEGGO Construction, Inc. (LEGGO or the Company) on a marketable, control interest basis, as of December 31, 20X5, for management purposes.

Summary Description and Brief History of the Company

The Company was incorporated in 1978 in the state of Anystate. The Company is a closely held subcontractor whose revenues are predominantly earned from sewer and water-line construction, primarily in central Anystate. The Company's customers generally consist of area contractors, developers, and local governments. The Company is now legally structured as an S corporation.

EXERCISE 6: Valuation of S corporations is one of the most controversial issues in business valuations today. The main issue is whether to and how to tax affect S corporation income. What four options are there in valuing S corporations?

1. _____

2. _____

3. _____

4. _____

The Company obtains most of its business through bidding competitively with general contractors. Management believes that customers contract with the Company due to its solid reputation and competitive bids; its customers have remained loyal. The two largest customers are XYZ General Contractors and the city of Anycity.

Employee relations have been harmonious with minimal turnover. All employees of the Company are unionized with the exception of several office workers. Currently, the economic climates in the market and industry are good. The Company has six competitors that are similar in size and nature.

Ownership and Capital Structure of the Company

The Company is legally structured as a closely held S corporation. As of the date of valuation, there were 5,000 shares of common stock outstanding, structured as follows:

Name	Shares Owned	Percentage of Ownership
Tom Profit	4,250	85%
Gary Profit	250	5%
Susan Profit	250	5%
Michelle Profit	250	5%
Total	5,000	100%

EXERCISE 7: We are valuing a 100 percent controlling interest in LEGGO. The percentage of ownership of individual shareholders is not an issue here. However, assume we are valuing the 85 percent of Tom Profit as opposed to the 100 percent in LEGGO. The value of an 85 percent interest in LEGGO would be based on 85 percent of the 100 percent control value in LEGGO.

a. True
b. False

Standard of Value

The standard of value used in this report is fair market value. Fair market value is defined as:

> *The price, expressed in terms of cash equivalents, at which property would change hands between a hypothetical willing and able buyer and a hypothetical willing and able seller, acting at arms length in an open and unrestricted market, when neither is under compulsion to buy or sell and when both have reasonable knowledge of the relevant facts.*[2]

Among other factors, this valuation report considers elements of appraisal listed in the Internal Revenue Service's Revenue Ruling 59-60, which "outline[s] and review[s] in general the approach, methods, and factors to be considered in valuing shares of the capital stock of closely held corporations."[3] Specifically, Revenue Ruling 59-60 states that the following factors should be carefully considered in a valuation of closely held stock:

EXERCISE 8: Revenue Ruling 59-60 is only applicable to estate, gift, and income tax valuations.

    a. True
    b. False

---

1. *The nature of the business and history of the enterprise from its inception.* The Company was incorporated in 1978. It is engaged primarily as a sewage and water-line subcontractor. The Company has grown since its inception, and its customers have remained loyal.
2. *The economic outlook in general and condition and outlook of the specific industry in particular.* The consideration of the economic outlook on a national level, as well as on a regional and local level, is important in performing a valuation. How the economy is performing has a bearing in part on how the Company performs. Overall, the Company outlook is positive.
3. *The book value of the stock and the financial condition of the business.* The Company has a relatively strong balance sheet with a majority of its assets in three categories: cash, contract receivables, and fixed assets. The fixed assets consist primarily of construction equipment and vehicles.
4. *The earning capacity of the company.* The Company's compound growth rate in revenues from 20X1 to 20X5 was approximately 4 percent. The Company has demonstrated a good ability to generate profits.
5. *The dividend-paying capacity of the company.* The Company has made distributions equal to the amount of the shareholders' respective tax liabilities in the recent past and will likely continue this trend into the future.
6. *Whether the enterprise has goodwill or other intangible value.* It is generally acknowledged that goodwill is often measured by the earnings' ability of an enterprise being valued. Goodwill can be broadly defined as characteristics that

---

[2] Ibid.
[3] Internal Revenue Service, Revenue Ruling 59-60, Section 1.

induce customers to continue to do business with the Company and to attract new customers.

7. *Sales of the stock and size of the block to be valued.* There have been no sales of stock of the Company that would provide an indication of value during the period being analyzed.

8. *The market prices of stock of corporations engaged in the same or a similar line of business having their stocks actively traded in a free and open market, either on an exchange or over the counter.* The market approach was considered in this valuation. A search for guideline companies that are similar in nature and size to the Company was performed.[4]

EXERCISE 9:   These are the only eight tenets of value in Revenue Ruling 59-60 that need to be considered.

    a. True
    b. False

Sources of Information

Sources of information used in this appraisal include:

1. Audited financial statements for the years ended March 31, 20X1 through December 31, 20X5
2. *Stocks, Bonds, Bills, and Inflation, Yearbook*, published by Ibbotson Associates
3. *The Federal Reserve Bank* for the 20-year maturity rate on 30-year bonds as of December 31, 20X5
4. *20X1/20X5 editions of Benchmark Statistics and Ratios* (fictitious)
5. *The National Economic Review*, published by Mercer Capital Management, Inc. Fourth Quarter 20X5.
6. *The Beige Book* published by the Federal Reserve Bank
7. *www.xls.com* website for public company information
8. *www.hoovers.com* website for public company information
9. *Pratt's Stats* Online Comparable Transactions Database
10. *IBA* Comparable Transactions Database

Valking LLP has relied on these sources but has not provided attest services in regard to any of the sources. Val Dude, a financial analyst with Valking LLP, interviewed management of the Company.

NATIONAL ECONOMIC OUTLOOK

In conjunction with the preparation of our opinion of fair market value, we have reviewed and analyzed the economic conditions as of December 31, 20X5, the date

---

[4] Ibid., Section 4.

of valuation. This report includes summary discussions and analysis of the national economy for the fourth quarter of 20X5. These discussions are based on a review of current economic statistics, articles in the financial press, and economic reviews found in current business periodicals. The purpose of the review is to provide a representative "consensus" review of the condition of the national economy and its general outlook at the end of the fourth quarter of 20X5.

General Economic Overview

According to preliminary estimates released by the Department of Commerce's Bureau of Economic Analysis (BEA) real Gross Domestic Product (GDP), the output of goods and services produced by labor and property located in the United States, increased at an annualized rate of 5.8 percent during the fourth quarter of 20X5. Revised growth in GDP for the third quarter of 20X5 was 5.7 percent, which is higher than the preliminary estimated annualized growth rate of 4.8 percent. Increases in personal consumption expenditures, government spending, inventory investment, and exports were major contributors to the increase in GDP. These components were partially offset by an increase in imports. Annual growth in GDP for 20X5 was 4.0 percent, modestly lower than the 4.3 percent growth rate reported for 20X4. The U.S. economy is expected to continue expanding in the year 20X6 at approximately a 3 percent to 4 percent growth rate.

The Composite Index of Leading Economic Indicators (the government's primary forecasting gauge) increased 0.4 percent in December after rising 0.1 percent in October and 0.3 percent in November. The composite index attempts to gauge economic activity six to nine months in advance. Multiple consecutive moves in the same direction are said to be indicative of the general direction of the economy. In December, nine of the ten leading economic indicators rose. The most significant increases were money supply, interest rate spread, manufacturers' new orders of nondefense capital goods, stock prices, and manufacturers' new orders of consumer goods and materials. During the six-month span through December, the leading index rose 0.9 percent, and seven of the ten components advanced. According to the Conference Board's report, "the leading indicators point to a continuation of the [economic] expansion during 20X6."[5]

Stock markets ended the year at record levels. Broad market and blue chip stock indices turned in 20 percent to 25 percent annual gains, while the NASDAQ gained an unprecedented 85.6 percent during 20X5. The Federal Reserve (the "Fed") increased the Federal funds rate in mid-November in an effort to slow economic growth and thus curb inflation. The Fed is attempting to cool the robust economic engine before it produces excessive inflationary pressure. Additional rate tightening is expected during the early part of 20X6. Despite a midquarter respite in bond price declines, bond yields reached their highest levels of the year in December, with the 30-year Treasury bond averaging a yield to maturity of 6.35 percent.

Inflation results for 20X5 reflect very low core price growth but high growth in energy prices. The Consumer Price Index (CPI) rose 2.7 percent for the year. Tight labor markets and strong economic activity may produce inflationary pressures, however, pricing data continue to suggest that gains in productivity and limited pricing power are keeping inflation in check. The inflation rate is expected to continue

---

[5] *The National Economic Review,* published by Mercer Capital Management, Inc.

at approximately 2.5 percent to 3.0 percent in the first half of the year 20X6, but increasing fuel prices are posing a significant threat to future price stability.

Consumer Spending and Inflation

According to the Bureau of Labor Statistics (BLS), the CPI was unchanged at 168.3 in December (CPI: all urban consumers, 1982-1984 = 100, before seasonal adjustment). Excluding food and energy, this rate increased at a seasonally adjusted 0.1 percent in December, following an increase of 0.2 percent in November. The seasonally adjusted annual rate of inflation for the fourth quarter was 2.2 percent, compared to 4.2 percent, 2.9 percent, and 1.5 percent, respectively, for the prior three quarters. The inflation rate for 20X5 was 2.7 percent, higher than the 1.6 percent rate of 20X4, which was the smallest annual increase since a 1.1 percent rise in 19XX. The acceleration in 20X5 was largely due to an upturn in petroleum-based energy prices. The energy index, which declined 8.8 percent in 20X4, increased 13.4 percent in 20X5. Following a 15.1 percent decline in 20X4, petroleum-based energy costs increased 29.5 percent in 20X5, the largest annual advance since 20XX.

The Producer Price Index (PPI), generally recognized as predictive of near-term consumer inflation pressure, increased 0.3 percent in December (PPI for finished goods, seasonally adjusted) following a 0.2 percent increase in November and a 0.1 percent decline in October. For the year, the PPI increased 3.0 percent and reflected the dramatic impact of energy costs on producer costs. The PPI was flat in 20X4, reflecting the aforementioned energy price declines. Core PPI in 20X5 increased only 0.9 percent and mirrored the same underlying pattern in the CPI regarding productivity enhancements and limited wholesale pricing power.

According to the Census Bureau of the Commerce Department, the increase in retail sales for the October to November period was 1.1 percent, higher than the 0.9 percent originally reported. The advance estimate for December retail sales (adjusted for seasonal, holiday, and trading day differences) reflected an increase of 1.2 percent from November and a 9.7 percent increase over December 20X4 sales. Total sales for 20X5 were $3.0 trillion, 8.9 percent higher than 20X4. Personal consumption spending represents approximately two-thirds of total economic activity and is generally the primary component of economic growth. Real personal consumption spending increased 5.3 percent in the fourth quarter, following a 4.9 percent increase in the third quarter. Durable goods purchases increased 11.8 percent in the fourth quarter, after an increase of 7.7 percent in the third quarter of 20X5.

The Financial Markets

Stock markets began the fourth quarter with a volatile October amid speculations of an interest rate increase. Equity markets plunged during the third week of October before rebounding on investor hopes that the U.S. economy was slowing. The National Association of Securities Dealers Automated Quotations (NASDAQ) showed breathtaking gains in November and December, while the Dow Jones Average (Dow) and Standard and Poor's (S&P) 500 faltered several times before finishing with a strong December. The Dow, the S&P 500, and the NASDAQ finished the year at record levels. For the Dow and the S&P 500, it was the fifth straight year of double-digit growth. However, blue chip stocks were overshadowed by the NASDAQ's phenomenal 85.6 percent growth for the year.

The Dow Jones Industrial Average (DJIA) closed the fourth quarter at 11497.12, an increase of 11 percent for the quarter. The DJIA gained 25.2 percent in 20X5 after a 16 percent gain in 20X4. The S&P 500 closed the quarter at 1469.25, a 14.5 percent increase for the fourth quarter, following much the same pattern as the Dow. The S&P 500 gained almost 20 percent in 20X5 after a 27 percent gain in 20X4. The NASDAQ composite index, generally consisting of smaller and more technology-oriented issues, increased 48.2 percent during the quarter to close at 4069.31. The NASDAQ surpassed its almost 40 percent gain in 20X4 with an 85.6 percent gain in 20X5. More than half of the NASDAQ's 20X5 gain came after the index crossed 3000 on November 3. The broad-market Wilshire 5000 index closed at 13812.67, reflecting a quarterly gain of 18 percent. The Wilshire 5000 gained 22 percent in 20X5 following similar growth in 20X4.

The monthly average yield to maturity on the 30-year Treasury bond during the fourth quarter of 20X5 was 6.26 percent, 6.15 percent, and 6.35 percent, respectively, for October, November, and December. Bond prices are negatively correlated with their respective yields, which can shift abruptly on investor reactions to major variances in reported economic data versus market expectations (i.e., expected inflation, growth, monetary policy and other Fed action, etc.). With few exceptions, yields have generally risen throughout the year. Oddly, the November Fed rate hike did not result in a dramatic repricing, but in tandem with the Fed's lack of action at its later December meeting, bond prices fell abruptly in expectation of high growth and the possibility of impending action by the Fed to slow the economy.

Interest Rates

After leaving interest rates unchanged at its October 5 meeting, the Federal Reserve Open Markets Committee (FOMC) raised interest rates by a quarter of a percentage point, the third increase in a three-month span. The change was made to "markedly diminish the risk of rising inflation going forward." Although the FOMC remained idle at its December 21 meeting, it remains concerned "with the possibility that over time increases in demand will continue to exceed the growth in potential supply." Such trends could foster inflationary imbalances that would undermine the economy's performance. Nonetheless, the FOMC decided to adopt a symmetric directive in order to indicate that the focus of policy in the intermeeting period must be to ensure a smooth transition into the year 20X6.[6]

EXERCISE 10: What types of industries would most likely be affected by anticipated changes in interest rates?

_____

_____

_____

_____

---

[6] Ibid.

Construction, Housing, and Real Estate

Home building is generally representative of overall economic activity because new home construction stimulates a broad range of industrial, commercial, and consumer spending and investment. According to the U.S. Commerce Department's Bureau of the Census, new privately owned housing starts were at a seasonally adjusted annualized rate of 1.712 million units in December, 7 percent above the revised November estimate of 1.598 million units, but 2 percent below the December 20X4 rate. Single-family housing starts in December were 1.402 million, 8 percent higher than the November level of 1.299 million units. An estimated 1.663 million privately owned housing units were started in 20X5, 3 percent above the 20X4 figure of 1.617 million.

The seasonally adjusted annual rate of new housing building permits (considered the best indicator of future housing starts) was 1.611 million units in December, similar to the revised November rate of 1.612 million and 6 percent below the December 20X4 estimate of 1.708 million.

Unemployment

According to the Labor Department's Bureau of Labor Statistics, unemployment levels during the fourth quarter remained historically low. The unemployment rate for October, November, and December was 4.1 percent, slightly lower than the September rate of 4.2 percent. This marked the 30th consecutive month that the unemployment rate was below 5 percent. The unemployment rate for all of 20X5 was approximately 4.2 percent, down from 4.5 percent in 20X4. Tight labor markets remain a theme of Federal Reserve concerns regarding inflation. Productivity enhancements and relatively constant levels of workers' hours are believed to be mitigating historically inflationary conditions.

Summary and Outlook

Economic growth, as measured by growth in GDP, accelerated to 5.8 percent in the fourth quarter of 20X5, after registering a revised 5.7 percent annualized rate in the third quarter. Annual growth in GDP for 20X5 was 4.0 percent. Stock markets finished the year at record levels. Both the Dow and S&P 500 experienced double-digit growth for the fifth straight year, while the NASDAQ posted an 85.6 percent gain in 20X5. Bond prices generally declined throughout the year but showed particular weakness on rising yields late in the fourth quarter. Fourth-quarter inflation reflected a seasonally adjusted annualized rate of 2.2 percent, representing a decrease from the third-quarter rate of 4.2 percent. The rate of inflation for 20X5 was 2.7 percent, higher than the 1.6 percent rate for 20X4. After leaving interest rates unchanged at its October meeting, the Federal Reserve Open Markets Committee raised interest rates by a quarter of a percentage point at its November meeting. No change was made at the December meeting. Economic growth is expected to moderate somewhat from recent levels, but should remain historically favorable with GDP growing at 3 percent to 4 percent. Inflation is expected to remain relatively mild at below 3 percent, but increasing fuel prices are posing a significant threat to future price stability.

EXERCISE 11: What two economic indicators are probably the most important in valuation?

    a. Unemployment levels and Gross Domestic Product (GDP)
    b. Dow Jones Industrial Average and Producer Price Index
    c. GDP and inflation
    d. Inflation and unemployment levels

National Economic Impact on Valuation

Analyzing the national economy is an important step in performing a valuation because it helps to identify any risk that the economy may have in relation to the Company. In this case, the economy appears to be performing well.

EXERCISE 12: In valuing a small geographically concentrated business, which of these types of economic data should be considered?

    a. International, national, regional, local
    b. National, regional, local
    c. Regional, local
    d. Local only

REGIONAL ECONOMIC DATA (AS OF DECEMBER 8, 20X5)

The economy remained strong in October and early November, but was expanding more slowly than earlier in the year. Reports on consumer spending were mixed, with some noting strong sales' growth for the first weekend of the 20X5 holiday shopping season.

Construction activity generally was strong, despite softening on the residential side. Overall manufacturing output remained strong, but conditions were varied across industry segments. Lenders reported conditions similar to those noted in the last report and reports no signs of surges in inventory borrowing or cash demand. The labor markets remained much tighter than the rest of the nation, and seasonal demand put additional strain on some sectors of the market. The fall harvest was complete, as was the planting of winter wheat. A survey of agricultural bankers indicated that slow farm loan repayments continued to be a problem.

Consumer Spending

Reports on consumer spending activity were mixed. Prior to the Thanksgiving weekend, sales were well below most merchants' expectations. However, several retailers reported double-digit sales gains from a year ago for the Thanksgiving weekend and most merchants expected a strong holiday sales season. Most retailers' reports cited unusually warm weather as contributing to lackluster pre-Thanksgiving sales results, especially for cold-weather apparel. By contrast, sales of appliances, electronics, and lawn and garden goods continued to be strong. Retailers reported that inventories for most goods were in line with their planned levels, but inventories of winter merchandise were high. They also noted that they had not changed their promotional activity from a year earlier. Auto dealers reported that lighter floor traffic and a slowdown in light vehicle sales continued through October and into mid-November. One large auto group noted that service activity was also down and that used-car prices weakened considerably.

Construction and Real Estate

Overall real estate and construction activity was robust but softer than earlier in the year. Demand for both new and existing homes continued to ease in October and early November, but most reports described the market as strong. Those realtors contacted indicated that sales in October and early November were down about 10 percent from very strong results a year earlier. Home builders' reports appeared to be more positive than realtors' reports, with most reports indicating new home sales were unchanged or down slightly. Conditions in the nonresidential sector remained strong and steady for the most part, according to most reports.

Development of light industrial space was steady to down slightly, as was the development of infrastructure projects. A report from one of the largest metro areas suggested that a few large office projects that have recently broken ground might be the last of the current downtown office expansion. Some contractors noted that many customers had changed strategies, preferring to hire the contractor viewed as most likely to complete the job on schedule rather than going with the low bidder.

Manufacturing

The manufacturing sector generally remained strong, although activity varied by industry segment. According to most automakers, orders for light vehicles remained strong nationwide. Inventories were generally in good shape, although they were reportedly lean for select models. Despite these conditions, the pricing environment remained soft, with an increase in incentive spending noted by some analysts. Producers of agricultural and heavy construction equipment reported further softening in output in recent weeks, and most planned to reduce inventories further next year, although not as aggressively as this year. Reports expected domestic demand would be relatively soft in the coming year, while foreign demand was expected to pick up. Wallboard producers indicated that demand remained very strong and factories continued to run near capacity. With new capacity coming on stream, however, price increases were expected to moderate in the coming months. A large manufacturer of telecommunications equipment noted that orders continued to recover from weak sales early in the year, due in large part to strengthening demand in Asian markets.

Banking and Finance

Lending activity continued to be mixed in October and early November. Business lending remained robust, and most bankers suggested that growth was steady. A few reports indicated that overall asset quality on commercial loans might have deteriorated slightly, since intense competition for customers led some lenders to relax standards slightly. Some bankers appeared to be less optimistic about the near-term commercial lending outlook than they had been in recent months. Household loan demand softened further, according to most lenders, as new mortgage and refinancing activity continued to slow. Reports noted that asset quality on consumer loans improved as existing bank and store credit-card balances were paid down, delinquencies slowed, and personal bankruptcies decreased. A report from one large money center bank attributed this improvement to a lagged effect from strong refinancing activity earlier in the year, and as a result, did not expect the improvement to endure. None of the bankers contacted noted any unusual borrowing by businesses that would indicate an inventory buildup ahead of the year 20X6 rollover, nor was there any noticeable increase in the demand for cash by consumers.

Labor Markets

Labor markets remained very tight in October and early November, and worker shortages appeared to intensify as the holiday hiring season began. Retailers and others who increase hiring for the holidays were finding it particularly difficult to staff positions this year. According to one report, many traditional seasonal workers (such as students, homemakers, etc.) were already employed elsewhere, either part- or full-time, as a result of overall strength in the economy. Some retailers reportedly had gone to extraordinary lengths to attract seasonal hires by offering, among other things, increased wages, steeper in-store discounts, and even tuition reimbursement for part-time workers.

Demand for workers in most other sectors remained strong as well. Temporary help firms in some metro areas reported increasing demand for manufacturing workers, while there were a few reports of slackening demand for financial service professionals, partly as a result of slowing mortgage applications. On balance, reports suggested that overall wage pressures had not intensified further in recent weeks. Staffing services reports indicated that wages were increasing fastest in the administrative/clerical occupations while a slowdown in wage growth was noted for information technology professionals. Reports from a large trucking firm noted the continued shortage of drivers was especially serious during high seasonal demand for transporting goods. Most reports continued to argue that worker shortages were hampering the economic expansion.

Agriculture

The fall corn and soybean harvest was essentially complete in surrounding states. Storage space for corn and soybeans was reported to be tight in some areas, due to strong yields and a quick harvest pace that caused grain deliveries to bunch up at elevators. Winter wheat planting was finished and most of the crop had emerged, but its condition had deteriorated in some areas due to dry weather. A survey of agricultural bankers indicated that farmland values were steady to weak during the third quarter in several states, with rising values in only two states. Bankers also indicated that slow farm loan repayments continued to be a problem, and a majority believed there would be an increase in the incidence of financially stressed farmers selling assets during the fall and winter.

Regional Economic Impact on Valuation

The regional economy should also be analyzed in performing a valuation to help to determine specific risks associated with the particular region in which the Company operates. In this instance, the regional economy is performing very well in many areas.

LOCAL ECONOMY

Anycity, Anystate was founded in 1810. It has an estimated population of 670,000 citizens and is approximately 326 square miles in area. The economy is made up primarily of trade, services, and manufacturing. Anycity has the 12th strongest economy in the nation, according to a 20X4 economic analysis. The analysis studied factors such as employment, per capita personal income and construction, and retail employment.

According to a 20X4 study, Anycity, Anystate was one of the top ten metropolitan areas in the nation as a hot spot for starting and growing young companies. The survey measured the number of significant start-up firms created during the last ten years and the number of ten-year-old firms that grew substantially during the last four years. Also, in November 20X3, a national magazine named Anycity one of the top ten "most improved cities" for business in the United States. Anystate was ranked seventh based on cost of living, educational opportunities, quality of life, and business issues. Construction activity also remained good.

Local Economic Impact on Valuation

The local economy is another important aspect to consider when performing a business valuation. The local economy represents the immediate environment in which the Company operates. The economy of Anycity, Anystate appears to be doing very well. Thus, in our opinion, there is little risk associated with the local economy that will affect the Company.

INDUSTRY OUTLOOK: WATER AND SEWER SYSTEMS

Water supply construction increased 5 percent in 20X4, while sewerage construction was about the same as the level in 20X3. Both of these construction categories did well in the mid-20XXs, reflecting high levels of building construction as well as work on long-deferred projects. The strong construction market expected in 20X6 will help both categories do well. In the longer term, waterworks probably will be one of the more rapidly growing categories of public construction. The aqueduct systems of most older cities are so old that extensive replacement work must be done each year. The current level of construction in the United States is much lower than that needed to replace waterworks every 50 years, which is the recommended practice. Most water utilities are in a good position to raise the needed capital, so a steady increase in replacement construction is likely through 20X6.

The Safe Drinking Water Act requires numerous upgrades and replacements of water supply facilities. The Water Resources Act has expanded the role of the

Federal government in municipal water supply and appears to have facilitated increased Federal funding for water supply construction. After 20X5, sewerage construction probably will continue to increase, although at a growth rate lower than that of the overall economy. Federal spending may not keep up with inflation, but the state and local share will increase steadily. A growing market factor is the need to repair, modernize, and replace the sewage treatment plants that were built during the boom of the 1970s. The sustained recovery in building construction also will support sewerage construction.

Impact on Valuation

The outlook for this industry is good. The Company is a subcontractor that does mainly water-line and sewer work. The water and sewer portion of the construction sector appears to be growing and is expected to grow in the next few years. The fact that there is a need of repairs and modernization of sewage treatment plants that were built a few decades ago also provides a positive outlook for the Company.

EXERCISE 13: Which industry outlook factors are generally the most important in supporting valuation assumptions?

    a. Growth rates, profit margins, and risk
    b. Regulatory and legal issues
    c. Unemployment figures
    d. Minority discounts and/or control premiums

HISTORICAL FINANCIAL ANALYSIS AND OVERVIEW OF THE COMPANY

Financial statement amounts labeled "Dec-X4" represent the nine-month period, April 1, 20X4 through December 31, 20X4, due to change of year end.

EXERCISE 14: What is the most important use of historical financial data?

    a. To determine how the company has performed
    b. To assist in supporting anticipated performance
    c. To highlight profitability
    d. To determine average profits

EXERCISE 15: Analysts typically spread five years of financial statements because:

    a. Revenue Ruling 59-60 requires five years.

b. Uniform Standards of Professional Appraisal Practice requires five years.
c. An economic cycle is often captured in five years.
d. Most business plans are based on five years of projections.

Income Statements

REVENUES

Revenues are generally the first component to be reviewed by financial analysts. All other things equal, trends in revenues will translate into trends in profit margins, as well as the Company's ultimate fate. Increases in revenues, all things equal, should lead to higher profitability as the Company's fixed costs are spread over a wider revenue base, leading to lower fixed costs per dollar of revenue. Table 1.1 represents the actual revenues of the Company for each year and the growth trend associated with each year.

Table 1.1: Actual Revenues and Growth Trend						
	Mar-X1	Mar-X2	Mar-X3	Mar-X4	Dec-X4	Dec-X5
Revenues	$12,198,433	$11,345,938	$10,726,214	$11,558,858	$12,278,556	$14,819,373
% Change		-7.0%	-5.5%	7.8%	N/A	20.7%

As can be seen, the Company's revenues have increased toward the latter part of the analysis period. The revenues for the nine-month period ending December 20X4 were higher than any of the previous 12-month periods. Over the period 20X1 to 20X5, the compound growth rate in revenues was approximately 4 percent.

COST OF GOODS SOLD

To compare the Company to the industry, we used the 20X5/20X6 Benchmark Studies (fictitious). We believe that the appropriate industry classification for the Company is Standard Industrial Classification Code 1623: Construction: Water, Sewer, Pipeline, Communication and Power Line—General Contractors. According to the Benchmark Studies, the cost of goods sold averaged 78.2 percent. As presented in Table 1.2, the Company's cost of goods sold as a percentage of revenues was 78.8 percent in 20X5, which is comparable to the industry average.

Table 1.2: Cost of Goods Sold and Percentage of Revenues						
	Mar-X1	Mar-X2	Mar-X3	Mar-X4	Dec-X4	Dec-X5
Cost of Goods Sold	$9,774,937	$9,301,970	$8,193,650	$8,804,580	$8,868,450	$11,676,380
% of Sales	80.1%	82.0%	76.4%	76.2%	72.2%	78.8%

OPERATING EXPENSES

According to the *Benchmark Studies*, operating expenses as a percentage of sales for companies in this industry were approximately 14.2 percent in 20X5. As presented in Table 1.3, the Company's operating expense as a percentage of sales was approximately 8.1 percent in 20X5, significantly lower than that of the industry average.

Table 1.3: Operating Expenses and Percentage of Revenues						
	Mar-X1	**Mar-X2**	**Mar-X3**	**Mar-X4**	**Dec-X4**	**Dec-X5**
Operating Expenses	$1,135,984	$818,233	$1,213,537	$1,563,721	$872,841	$1,202,237
% of Sales	9.3%	7.2%	11.3%	13.5%	7.1%	8.1%

Balance Sheets

ASSETS

Current assets usually consist of cash and cash equivalents, accounts receivable, inventory, and other current assets, which usually consist of prepaid expenses.

ASSET MIX

Over the period, the majority of the Company's assets has been in fixed assets and contract receivables. Table 1.4 illustrates the Company's asset mix as a percentage of total assets:

Table 1.4: Asset Mix Percentages							
	Mar-X1	**Mar-X2**	**Mar-X3**	**Mar-X4**	**Dec-X4**	**Dec-X5**	**Benchmark**
Cash and Equivalents	13.8%	9.0%	10.2%	10.5%	1.7%	4.6%	11.2%
Contract Receivables	19.6%	15.8%	12.6%	10.1%	39.3%	34.3%	39.9%
Inventories	0.2%	0.2%	0.3%	0.2%	0.1%	0.6%	1.0%
Other Current Assets	5.8%	8.9%	14.2%	22.3%	9.7%	5.9%	7.7%
Net Fixed Assets	54.4%	58.8%	59.6%	55.3%	47.9%	53.3%	33.5%
Other Assets	6.2%	7.1%	3.3%	1.6%	1.3%	1.3%	6.7%

As shown in Table 1.4, the Company's asset mix was stable for the most part. The contract receivables increased significantly in 20X4 and 20X5 due to the change in the reporting periods. The contract receivables tend to be higher at the December 31 year-end than they were at the March 31 year-end. The Company also has a much higher percentage of net fixed assets than the industry average. The Company maintained a lower cash balance than the industry in the past few years, but that again is mainly due to the change in the fiscal year-ends.

LIABILITIES

The majority of the liabilities consisted of long-term debt, including the current portion. Table 1.5 illustrates the Company's liabilities mix as a percentage of total liabilities and stockholders' equity.

Table 1.5: Liability Mix Percentages							
	Mar-X1	**Mar-X2**	**Mar-X3**	**Mar-X4**	**Dec-X4**	**Dec-X5**	**Benchmark**
Short-Term Notes	2.2%	2.5%	2.4%	2.9%	8.7%	2.9%	3.4%
Current Portion of LTD	0.0%	0.0%	0.0%	0.0%	3.9%	6.8%	4.8%
Accounts Payable	3.2%	7.4%	3.1%	4.3%	6.3%	7.7%	15.2%
Other Current Liabilities	12.9%	6.2%	4.1%	15.9%	4.3%	5.9%	12.8%
Long-Term Debt	10.4%	12.6%	14.5%	13.4%	6.7%	4.1%	12.9%
Equity	71.3%	71.3%	75.9%	63.5%	70.0%	72.6%	50.9%

The liability section of the balance sheet was also stable. The largest liabilities were the accounts payable and the long-term debt. The equity as a percent is much higher than the industry average.

EQUITY

Stockholders' equity refers to the difference between the book value of a company's assets and its liabilities. The stockholders' equity increased each year over the period analyzed. During the entire period from March 20X1 to December 20X5, the stockholders' equity grew 109.8 percent.

Financial Ratio Analysis

Ratios for the nine-month period ending December 31, 20X4, are not presented.

> **EXERCISE 16:**   The main drawbacks of publicly available benchmark financial ratios are:
>
> a. There are very few SIC codes.
> b. They calculate the ratios incorrectly.
> c. The companies that make up the data cannot be used to determine pricing ratios or capitalization rates.
> d. The information is from public companies.

The industry statistics used in the ratio analysis were taken from *Benchmark Studies*. The median statistics are for businesses whose primary Standard Industrial Classification Code 1623: Construction: Water, Sewer, Pipeline, Communication and Power Line—General Contractors.

Ratios are divided into four groups, each representing an important aspect of the Company's financial position. The groups are liquidity, activity, leverage, and profitability.

LIQUIDITY RATIOS

Liquidity analysis assesses the risk level and ability of a company to meet its current obligations. It represents the availability of cash and the company's ability to eventually be converted into cash.

CURRENT RATIO

The current ratio compares current assets to current liabilities. It measures the margin of safety a company has for paying short-term debts in the event of a reduction in current assets. It also gives an idea of a company's ability to meet day-to-day payment obligations. Generally, a higher ratio is better.

Table 1.6: Current Ratios					
	Mar-X1	**Mar-X2**	**Mar-X3**	**Mar-X4**	**Dec-X5**
Company	2.3	2.1	3.9	1.9	2.0
Industry	1.4	1.2	1.2	1.5	1.5

The Company's current ratio was consistantly above the industry average over the period, as shown in Table 1.6. The Company's ratio is higher than the industry due to lower current liabilities.

Quick Ratio

The quick ratio adds accounts receivables to cash and short-term investments and compares the sum to current liabilities. The resulting ratio measures a company's ability to cover its current liabilities without having to convert inventory to cash. Generally, a higher ratio is better.

Table 1.7: Quick Ratios					
	Mar-X1	**Mar-X2**	**Mar-X3**	**Mar-X4**	**Dec-X5**
Company	1.9	1.5	2.4	0.9	1.7
Industry	1.1	1.0	1.0	1.2	1.2

As shown in Table 1.7, the Company's ratios fluctuated over the period. The basic difference between the current and quick ratio is that the quick ratio includes only cash and receivables as the numerator. Thus, inventory is not included. As can be seen from the table, the industry averages contained a larger inventory base due to the lower ratio. The Company carried a minimal inventory of materials and supplies. In 20X4, the Company's ratio was lower than the industry average due to a large increase in current liabilities in that year. Other than that year, the Company has been very liquid and could easily cover its current maturities.

Conclusion of Liquidity Ratios

The Company appears to have lower risk than that of the industry. The current ratio and the quick ratio are above the industry average for the most part. Thus, the

Company would have little difficulty covering its obligations when compared to other companies within the industry.

ACTIVITY RATIOS

Activity ratios, also known as "efficiency ratios," describe the relationship between the Company's level of operations and the assets needed to sustain the activity. The higher the ratio, the more efficient the Company's operations, as relatively fewer assets are required to maintain a given level of operations. Although these ratios do not measure profitability or liquidity directly, they are ultimately important factors affecting those performance indicators.

Collection Period Ratio

The collection period ratio, also known as the "days' sales in receivables," multiplies accounts receivable at year end by 365, then divides the result by net sales for the year. This ratio measures how much control a company has over its accounts receivable, and indicates how many days, on the average, it takes that company to convert accounts receivable to cash. Generally, the smaller the number of days, the better.

Table 1.8: Collection Period Ratios					
	Mar-X1	Mar-X2	Mar-X3	Mar-X4	Dec-X5
Company	19	19	16	16	58
Industry	55	54	59	63	60

Compared to the industry, the Company was better at collecting receivables. For the years represented in Table 1.8, the Company converted its accounts receivable to cash more quickly than the other companies within the industry. The Company's collection period ratio was higher in 20X5 due to exceptional circumstances concerning two accounts.

Fixed Assets Activity Ratio

The fixed assets activity ratio compares net sales to fixed assets. It indicates a company's ability to generate net sales from the use of its fixed assets. Largely depreciated fixed assets or a labor-intensive operation may cause a distortion of this ratio. Generally, a higher ratio is better.

Table 1.9: Fixed Assets Activity Ratios					
	Mar-X1	Mar-X2	Mar-X3	Mar-X4	Dec-X5
Company	6.9	5.2	4.7	4.1	4.1
Industry	5.8	6.2	6.1	6.9	6.4

The Company appears worse than the industry average during the period, as demonstrated in Table 1.9. The Company appears to have not utilized its fixed assets in generating revenues as effectively as the industry. However, the Company owns all of its equipment and machinery, as opposed to renting. Thus, the higher amount of fixed assets causes the ratio to be low as opposed to the industry figures. Most companies of this nature do not own all of their equipment. The industry averages most likely represent companies that both rent and own their respective equipment and machinery.

Asset Management Ratio

The asset management ratio compares net sales to total assets. It measures a company's ability to generate sales volume using its assets. It is useful in comparing companies within specific industry groups on their effective employment of assets. Generally, a higher ratio is better.

Table 1.10: Asset Management Ratios					
	Mar-X1	Mar-X2	Mar-X3	Mar-X4	Dec-X5
Company	3.7	3.0	2.8	2.3	2.2
Industry	2.1	2.0	1.9	2.4	2.2

The Company's average decreased each year. The Company's trend (as shown in Table 1.10) was worse than the industry the most recent two years. The Company is not generating sales volume using its assets as effectively as in the past, but is comparable to other companies in the industry currently.

Conclusion of Activity Ratios

The Company seems to be doing better and worse than the industry in this category. The Company does collect its receivables quicker than other companies within the industry, for the most part. However, the Company is not as effective as other companies within the industry with fixed assets, but this may be affected by the large level of owned fixed assets.

LEVERAGE RATIOS

Leverage ratios measure the relative exposure of the creditors versus the shareholders of a business. Leveraged companies accrue excess returns to their shareholders as long as the rate of return on the investments financed by debt is greater than the cost of debt. However, financial leverage brings additional risks primarily in the form of fixed costs that would adversely affect profitability if revenues decline. Additionally, the priority of interest and debt can have a severe negative impact on a company when adversity strikes. The inability to meet these obligations may lead to default and possibly bankruptcy.

Net Fixed Assets to Equity

The net fixed-assets-to-equity ratio divides net fixed assets by a company's equity. It measures a company's ability to support the acquisition of fixed assets by using the original investment plus retained earnings. Generally, a low ratio is better.

Table 1.11: Net Fixed Assets to Equity Ratios					
	Mar-X1	**Mar-X2**	**Mar-X3**	**Mar-X4**	**Dec-X5**
Company	0.8	0.8	0.8	0.9	0.7
Industry	0.7	0.8	0.7	0.8	0.6

Overall, the Company is close to the industry averages. The Company's ratio was pretty stable over the period, as shown in Table 1.11. Generally, the Company would have no problem supporting the acquisition of fixed assets with retained earnings.

Total Debt to Equity Ratio

The debt-to-equity ratio compares a company's total liabilities to its net worth. It expresses the degree of protection provided by the owners for the creditors. Generally, a lower ratio is better.

Table 1.12: Debt to Equity Ratios					
	Mar-X1	**Mar-X2**	**Mar-X3**	**Mar-X4**	**Dec-X5**
Company	0.4	0.4	0.3	0.6	0.4
Industry	1.3	1.2	1.0	1.1	1.0

The Company's ratio has been better than the industry averages for every year. A lower ratio indicates less debt in relation to equity. As presented in Table 1.12, the Company had less debt than the industry.

Conclusion of Leverage Ratios

The Company is leveraged and contains some debt and related interest expense, but its debt is still not as high as the industry averages. The Company should have little trouble supporting the purchase of fixed assets with retained earnings. The Company also has the capacity to take on some long-term debt if necessary.

PROFITABILITY RATIOS

Profitability ratios measure the ability of a company to generate returns for its stockholders.

Return on Equity

The return on equity ratio compares pretax income to equity. It measures a company's ability to generate a profit on the owner's investment. Generally, a higher ratio is better.

Table 1.13: Return on Equity Ratios					
	Mar-X1	**Mar-X2**	**Mar-X3**	**Mar-X4**	**Dec-X5**
Company	54.9%	47.3%	46.8%	41.4%	40.3%
Industry	30.5%	32.7%	31.9%	28.8%	31.2%

Although the Company's return-on-equity ratio has deteriorated during the period under analysis, it is still higher than the industry average, as presented in Table 1.13.

Return on Assets Ratio

The return on asset ratio is calculated by dividing pretax income by total assets. This ratio expresses the pretax return on total assets and measures the effectiveness of management in employing available resources. Generally, a higher ratio is better.

Table 1.14: Return on Asset Ratios					
	Mar-X1	Mar-X2	Mar-X3	Mar-X4	Dec-X5
Company	39.7%	33.7%	35.5%	26.3%	29.3%
Industry	21.2%	26.2%	19.8%	23.2%	19.9%

Table 1.14 shows the Company's ratio was better than the industry average for each year in the analysis period.

Conclusion of Profitability Ratios

The Company is profitable and appears to be outperforming the industry, although there is a recent decrease in the margins.

EXERCISE 17: Indicate whether you believe that LEGGO is a better or worse performer based on the financial ratios previously presented.

_____

_____

_____

APPRAISAL OF FAIR MARKET VALUE

Valuation Approaches

Conventional appraisal theory provides several approaches for valuing closely held businesses. The asset approach looks to an enterprise's underlying assets in terms of either its net going concern or its liquidation value. The income approach looks at an enterprise's ongoing cash flows or earnings and applies appropriate capitalization or discounting techniques. Finally, the market approach derives value multiples from guideline company data or transactions.

EXERCISE 18: All three approaches to value must be applied in all valuations.

a. True
b. False

Asset Approach

ADJUSTED BOOK VALUE METHOD

The adjusted book value method consists of determining the fair market value of a company's assets and subtracting the fair market value of its liabilities to arrive at the fair market value of the equity. Both tangible and intangible assets are valued. Appraisals are used to value certain assets, and the remaining assets and liabilities are often included at book value, which is often assumed to approximate fair market value. This method does not provide a strong measure of value for goodwill or other intangible assets, which are more reasonably supported through the Company's income stream. In this case, the value under the adjusted book value method was less than the values calculated under the income and market approaches. Thus, the adjusted book value method was not utilized in the determination of a conclusion of value for the Company.

EXCESS CASH FLOW METHOD

The excess cash flow method, which is sometimes referred to as the excess earnings or formula method, is based on the excess cash flow or earnings available after a percentage return on the tangible assets used in a business have been subtracted. This residual amount of cash flow is capitalized at a percentage return for intangible assets of the business to derive the intangible asset value. This method is commonly used for very small businesses and in marital dissolution proceedings. The Internal Revenue Service's position on this method is that it should only be used when no better method exists.[7] It was not used in the valuation of LEGGO since more appropriate methods were available.

EXERCISE 19: In what type of valuation setting is the excess cash flow method most often used?

  a. ESOPs (Employee stock ownership plans)
  b. Estate tax
  c. Dissenting rights
  d. Marital dissolution

EXERCISE 20: On which Revenue Ruling is the excess cash flow method based?

  a. Revenue Ruling 59-60
  b. Revenue Ruling 83-120
  c. Revenue Ruling 68-609
  d. Revenue Ruling 77-287

---

[7] Revenue Ruling 68-609.

Income Approach

CAPITALIZED CASH FLOW METHOD (PREDEBT/INVESTED CAPITAL BASIS)

The capitalized cash flow method determines the value of a Company as the present value of all of the future cash flows that the business can generate to infinity. An appropriate cash flow is determined, then divided by a risk-adjusted capitalization rate, here the weighted average cost of capital. In this instance, control cash flows were used. This method was used to determine the Company's indicated value. The value is stated on a marketable, control-interest basis.

EXERCISE 21: Which method(s) is(are) considered valid under the income approach?

 a. Guideline public company method
 b. Discounted cash flow method
 c. Capitalized cash flow method
 d. Excess cash flow method

EXERCISE 22: In which situation(s) would a capitalized cash flow method be more applicable?

 a. When a company's future performance is anticipated to change from its prior performance
 b. In litigation settings
 c. When a single historical or pro forma amount of cash flow is anticipated to be earned with a constant growth in the future
 d. When valuing very small businesses

EXERCISE 23: List the two main bases when using the capitalized cash flow (CCF) or discounted cash flow (DCF) methods of the income approach.

 1._____

 2._____

Determination of Appropriate Control Cash Flow

Under the capitalized cash flow method, we used a predebt/invested capital basis for our calculation. This is due, in part, to the fact that the interest being valued is on a control-interest basis. This control interest can influence the amount of debt held by the Company. We began our analysis with the adjusted pretax earnings at the date of valuation and for the five years prior to the date of valuation. The adjustments that were made to arrive at adjusted pretax earnings include an adjustment to officers' compensation, a control adjustment. We then made adjustments for interest expense, nonrecurring items, and items that are not reflective of operations to the pretax earnings.

EXERCISE 24:   Under the direct equity basis, what are the components of net cash flow?

_____

_____

_____

_____

EXERCISE 25:   For the invested capital basis of the income approach, list the components of net cash flow.

_____

_____

_____

_____

EXERCISE 26:   What is the difference between minority cash flows and control cash flows?

_____

_____

_____

_____

EXERCISE 27:   Which adjustment(s) are made when valuing both minority and control cash flows?

  a. Nonrecurring items
  b. Nonoperating assets
  c. Excess compensation
  d. Perquisites
  e. Taxes

EXERCISE 28: Assume the company does not have any control adjustments and the company is run to the benefit of all shareholders without any shareholders taking out cash flow over or above what they are entitled. Is this value control or minority?

_____

_____

_____

_____

The first adjustment was to add back the depreciation expense. This is a noncash expense and should be added back to arrive at an appropriate cash flow. The adjustment for the gains and losses on the sale of marketable securities was made because the marketable securities are considered an excess/nonoperating asset. All income and expenses related to excess/nonoperating assets are taken out of the income stream, because the total value of these assets is unrelated to the indicated value of operations. The reason for the adjustments to dividend income, income from the investment in a partnership, and unrealized gains on marketable securities is the same. These assets relate to excess/nonoperating assets and must be taken out of the income stream. The second adjustment was an adjustment to the interest income.

EXERCISE 29: List some of the nonoperating/excess assets that are sometimes encountered in a business valuation.

_____

_____

_____

_____

EXERCISE 30: In valuing a *controlling interest* in a corporation, most analysts agree that the nonoperating and/or excess assets of the business must be removed out of the operating business, then added back at fair market value.

a. True
b. False

EXERCISE 31: In valuing a *minority interest* of a company, most analysts agree that the nonoperating and/or excess assets of the business must be removed out of the operating business, then added back at fair market value.

a. True
b. False

The resulting amount for each year (adjusted income before income tax) was then averaged. We believe a straight average is appropriate due to the cyclical nature of the Company. However, the Company changed year ends in 20X4. Since we have nine months of data at December 31, 20X4, an adjustment was made accordingly.

EXERCISE 32: In the valuation of LEGGO, the analyst decided to use a straight average of the adjusted income before income taxes for five historical years. Besides a straight average, what other method(s) can be used to determine the appropriate cash flow to be capitalized into perpetuity?

a. Weighted average
b. Most recent fiscal year
c. Most recent trailing 12 months
d. Trend line analysis/next year's budget
e. DCF average of next three years

EXERCISE 33: Analysts will generally use a straight historical average where the earnings and cash flows are more volatile.

a. True
b. False

The next step was to deduct an estimated ongoing depreciation expense in order to calculate state and Federal taxes. In this instance, the ongoing depreciation expense was estimated to be $650,000 based on estimated future capital expenditures. After the ongoing depreciation was deducted, state and Federal taxes were calculated at a combined rate of 40 percent and deducted. The amount that resulted was adjusted income predebt and after-tax.

EXERCISE 34: Which situation is most appropriate when adjusting cash flows for depreciation and capital expenditures?

a. Capital expenditures should exceed depreciation.
b. Depreciation should exceed capital expenditures.
c. Depreciation and capital expenditures should be similar.
d. The actual unadjusted amounts should be capitalized.

EXERCISE 35: Assuming taxes are to be deducted, what two choices are there in making the tax adjustments?

a. Tax each year historically, then determine the average.
b. Taxes should never be deducted in the value of an S corporation.
c. Make all adjustments in the historical period pretax, determine the average, then deduct for taxes.

Three further adjustments were then made to the predebt and after-tax income. The ongoing depreciation that was deducted to calculate taxes was added back because it is not a cash expense. The estimated future capital expenditures were then deducted. In this case, it was estimated that future capital expenditures would approximate $650,000 per year based on historical trends. The final adjustment was a working capital adjustment. The formula for this adjustment is based on industry data, as shown in Table 1.15. After making these final three adjustments, predebt and after-tax cash flow resulted. We believe that this cash flow is representative of future operations. The cash flow was then divided by a risk-adjusted capitalization rate using weighted average cost of capital, which is discussed below, to derive a value of the operations.

Table 1.15: Working Capital Adjustment Formula					
Current Year Revenue	X	Expected Growth Rate	=	Projected Revenue
Projected Revenue	–	Current Year Revenue	=	Change in Revenue
Change in Revenue	÷	Sales to Working Capital Ratio	=	Working Capital Adjustment

EXERCISE 36: Which economic benefit stream(s) can be used for cash flow in a capitalized cash flow method?

   a. After-tax income
   b. Pretax income
   c. Net cash flow
   d. EBITDA (Earnings before interest, taxes, depreciation, and amortization)
   e. Revenues
   f. Debt-free net income
   g. Debt-free cash flow

DETERMINATION OF WEIGHTED AVERAGE COST OF CAPITAL

EXERCISE 37: When using the direct equity basis instead of the invested capital basis, assumptions of capital structure can be avoided.
   a. True
   b. False

There are a number of steps involved in calculating the weighted average cost of capital (WACC). These steps involve calculating the cost of equity, the cost of debt, and the determination of an optimal capital structure for the Company using industry averages. The WACC formula is:

$$\text{WACC} = \text{We(Ke)} + \text{Wd}(K_{dpt})(1 - t)$$

Where

$\quad$ We $=$ Percentage of equity in the capital structure (at market value)
$\quad$ Ke $=$ Cost of equity
$\quad$ Wd $=$ Percentage of debt in the capital structure (at market value)
$\quad$ K_{dpt} $=$ Cost of debt, pretax
$\quad$ t $=$ Tax rate

EXERCISE 38: When using the invested capital basis to determine a control value, you should always use an optimal capital structure in the weighted average cost of capital.

   a. True
   b. False

Cost of Equity

EXERCISE 39: Name the two methods most often used to derive a cost of equity in the income approach.

1._____

2._____

EXERCISE 40: When using the modified capital asset pricing model (MCAPM) to derive an equity cost of capital for a controlling interest, it is sometimes necessary to adjust beta for differences between the capital structure of the public companies and the capital structure of the subject company being valued. This is not necessary if the capital structure is assumed to be the same. Given the following information, and if the MCAPM was used for LEGGO, calculate the unlevered and relevered beta.

a. Average beta of guideline public companies = 1.4

   Tax rate = 40%

   Market value capital structure = 35% debt, 65% equity

   The formula for unlevered beta is:

      $Bu \quad = \quad Bl / (1 + (1 - t)(Wd / We))$

   Where

      Bu = Beta unlevered

      Bl = Beta levered

      t = Tax rate for the company

      Wd = Percentage of debt in the capital structure (at market value)

      We = Percentage of equity in the capital structure (at market value)

b. Assuming that LEGGO has a capital structure of 25% debt and 75% equity and that the MCAPM can be used, what would be the beta?

   The formula to relever the beta is:

      $Bl \quad = \quad Bu (1 + (1 - t)(Wd / We))$

EXERCISE 41: Should build-up method and MCAPM rates of return be applied to income or cash flow?

_____

_____

_____

_____

EXERCISE 42: Which of these rates of return are derived using Ibbotson data?

    a. Minority rates of return
    b. Control rates of return
    c. Both
    d. Neutral

We used a build-up method to calculate the cost of equity. The first step was to begin with the risk-free rate of return, represented by the yield on long-term (20-year) constant maturity U.S. Treasury Coupon Bonds of 4.7 percent, as reported in the *Federal Reserve Bulletin* at the date of valuation.

EXERCISE 43: Why are long-term 20-year U.S. Treasury coupon bonds most often used for the risk-free rate of return in both the build-up method and the MCAPM?

_____

_____

_____

_____

The second and third steps are to add the common stock equity risk premium of 7.2 percent and the small stock risk premium of 6.4 percent (10th decile), both calculated in Ibbotson Associates *SBBI Yearbook*.

EXERCISE 44: The common stock equity risk premium was 7.2 percent as of the valuation date from the *SBBI Yearbook*. What benchmark is this return based on?

    a. S&P 500
    b. New York Stock Exchange
    c. Dow Jones Industrial Average
    d. Russell 5000

EXERCISE 45: In applying a small-stock risk premium, what are the choices that analysts can make using the Ibbotson data?

   a. 10th decile annual beta
   b. 10th decile monthly beta
   c. 10th decile sum beta
   d. 10A monthly beta
   e. 10B monthly beta
   f. Micro-cap annual beta
   g. Micro-cap monthly beta
   h. Micro-cap sum beta
   i. All of the above

The final step is to add a company-specific premium that takes into account additional risks specific to the Company. These additional risks include:

- *Company's depth of management.* The Company appears to have sufficient depth of management.
- *The importance of key personnel to the Company.* The Company does have several key employees whose loss would have a negative impact on the Company.
- *The growth potential in the Company's market.* The water and sewer portion of the construction sector appears to be growing and is expected to grow in the next few years. (See earlier discussion on the industry outlook section.)
- *The stability of the Company's earnings and gross profits.* The Company has a consistent history of generating profits.
- *The Company's bidding success rates.* The Company has had good bidding success. In addition, the Company has maintained good profit margins. This indicates that the Company's bidding success is not due to underpricing contracts.
- *The financial structure of the Company.* The Company is financially sound.
- *The geographic location of the Company.* The Company is located in Anycity, Anystate. (See earlier discussion on the local economy.)
- *The Company's order backlogs.* The Company has a sufficient amount of contract backlogs.
- *The diversification of the Company's customer base.* The majority of the Company's revenue is generated from only a few customers. The Company could be negatively impacted should any of these customers be lost.

After considering the financial ratio analysis and these risk factors, plus the size of the company as compared to the Ibbotson companies, it is our opinion that a company-specific premium of 4 percent is appropriate for the Company.

EXERCISE 46: A list of risk factors was previously presented for LEGGO to calculate the specific risk premium. Discuss the different methods for determining what the actual specific risk premium should be.

_____

_____

EXERCISE 47: Specific company risk premiums can be determined from Ibbotson data.

   a. True
   b. False

EXERCISE 48: Using the information in the text, calculate the cost of equity for LEGGO.

Rs	=	Risk-free rate of return	=	____
RPm	=	Risk premium common stock	=	____
RPs	=	Risk premium small stock	=	____
RPu	=	Company-specific risk premium	=	____
Ke	=	Cost of equity	=	____

The total of these four factors provides a net cost of equity, which is also called the equity rate, of 22 percent (rounded).

Cost of Debt

Next, we determined the cost of debt. To calculate this rate, we began by determining the Company's actual borrowing rate at the date of valuation. The borrowing rate of the Company at the date of valuation was at prime. We also added a risk premium of 1 percent to the prime rate. The prime rate at December 31, 20X5 was 7 percent. Therefore, the Company's borrowing rate was 8 percent. To this rate, which is called the debt rate, a 40 percent tax rate is deducted. The result is the after-tax cost of debt of approximately 5 percent (rounded).

EXERCISE 49: Which of these factors causes the cost of debt to be tax-affected?

   a. Debt principal is tax deductible.
   b. Interest expense is tax deductible.
   c. It should not be tax-affected since equity is not tax-affected.
   d. Debt and interest are tax deductible.

Weighted Average Cost of Capital

Finally, we determined the WACC using the debt and equity rates that were already calculated. The equity discount rate is multiplied by an equity percentage, and the debt discount rate is multiplied by a debt percentage as determined based on average capital structure for a company in this industry. In this instance, a 75 percent equity multiple and a 25 percent debt multiple were determined from industry averages. The percentages were then multiplied by the equity and debt discount rates calculated earlier and then summed to arrive at the WACC discount rate. This rate was calculated to be 17.75 percent.

EXERCISE 50:   Using the information in the text, calculate the weighted average cost of capital for LEGGO.

_____

_____

_____

_____

EXERCISE 51:   Which methods can be used to determine the weights in the weighted average cost of capital?

   a. Iterative process
   b. Guideline public companies
   c. Aggregated public industry data
   d. Risk Management Associates
   e. Troy
   f. Book values
   g. Anticipated capital structure

EXERCISE 52:   Explain the iterative process for determining the weights in the weighted average cost of capital.

_____

_____

_____

_____

EXERCISE 53:   Changing the amount of debt in the capital structure of the company has no effect on the return on equity.

   a. True
   b. False

EXERCISE 54: When valuing a controlling interest in a company, should you use the optimal capital structure based on public data or the capital structure anticipated to be employed by the owner of the company?

_____

_____

_____

_____

From this amount, a 3 percent growth factor is deducted to arrive at a net cash flow capitalization rate for the next year. The 3 percent growth factor is a long-term inflationary component used to adjust the capitalization rate. The rate derived after deducting the 3 percent was divided by 1 plus the growth rate to arrive at a net cash flow capitalization rate for the current year. In this instance, the rate amounts to 14 percent (rounded).

EXERCISE 55: Calculate the capitalization rate from the information in the text (apply to historical cash flow).

_____

_____

_____

_____

EXERCISE 56: Items used to support growth rates in the capitalized cash flow method of the income approach include:

a. Inflation
b. Nominal Gross Domestic Product
c. Industry growth rate
d. Actual historical company growth rate
e. All of the above

Capitalized Cash Flow Method Conclusion of Value on a Marketable, Control Interest Basis

The indicated value of the Company's invested capital determined under this method was $7,149,743, which was stated on a marketable, control-interest basis. The final step was to add nonoperating/excess assets and subtract any structured debt that the Company possessed at the date of valuation. In this instance, the Company possessed excess/nonoperating assets of $388,580. These assets included marketable securities, an investment in a partnership, other receivables, and life insurance premiums receivable. The Company also held structured debt of $918,121. Thus, after adding the nonoperating assets and subtracting the interest-bearing debt, a value of $6,620,202 is derived, as shown in Table 1.16.

Table 1.16: Income Approach—Capitalized Cash Flow Method	
	Calculated Values
Invested Capital	$7,149,743
Add: Nonoperating Assets	388,580
Less: Interest-Bearing Debt	(918,121)
Value on a Marketable, Control Interest Basis	$6,620,202

DISCOUNTED CASH FLOW METHOD

EXERCISE 57: When is it more appropriate to use a discounted cash flow method instead of a capitalized cash flow method?

_____

_____

_____

_____

The discounted cash flow method is a multiple period valuation model that converts a future series of economic income or cash flow into value by reducing it to present worth at a rate of return (discount rate) that reflects the risk inherent therein. The income might be pretax, after-tax, debt-free, free cash flow, or some other measure deemed appropriate and adjusted by the analyst. Future income or cash flow is determined through projections provided by the Company. However, no such projections were available or attainable. Furthermore, given the trends and growth prospects of the Company, the capitalized cash flow method was deemed more appropriate.

Market Approach

GUIDELINE COMPANY TRANSACTIONS METHOD

The guideline company transactions method values a company by finding acquisitions of similar companies in the marketplace and applying the multiples at which those companies sold to the subject company data to derive a value. In this instance, we researched various databases and found applicable transactions in two of them: Pratt's Stats and IBA (Institute of Business Appraisers). The transactions discovered within these databases are considered relevant.

EXERCISE 58: Which of these are general transaction databases used by analysts in valuing companies?

   a. Pratt's Stats
   b. RMA
   c. Ibbotson Associates
   d. Institute of Business Appraisers
   e. Done Deals
   f. Bizcomps
   g. Mergerstat Review

EXERCISE 59: What is one of the most significant problems when using transaction data?

_____

_____

_____

_____

Pratt's Stats Database

Pratt's Stats database provides a list of transactions of companies in various industry sectors. In this instance, we researched the water, sewer, and pipeline construction sector and found nine sale transactions that took place from 20X2 to the date of valuation. Using this database, we calculated values based on gross revenues and net income, as shown in Table 1.17.

Table 1.17: Pratt's Stats Database Values	
	Calculated Values
Sales Price to Gross Revenue	$6,915,495
Sales Price to Net Income	6,974,419
Average = Value on Nonmarketable, Control Interest Basis	$6,944,957

IBA Database

The IBA database provides a list of transactions of companies in various industry sectors. In this instance, we researched the water, sewer, and pipeline construction sector and found four transactions that took place from 20XX to the date of valuation. Using this database, we calculated values based on gross revenues and discretionary cash flows. To each value, however, we added and deducted some balance sheet items. The multiples derived from the IBA database apply only to the value of fixed assets, inventory, and intangibles. Thus, to get to a total-entity value, all current assets must be added and all liabilities must be deducted. The values using this database are presented in Table 1.18.

Table 1.18: IBA Database Values	
	Calculated Values
Sales Price to Gross Revenue	$4,630,801
Sales Price to Discretionary Cash Flows	3,267,016
Average	3,948,908
Add: Current Assets (Less Inventory)	3,090,597
Less: Total Liabilities	(1,864,359)
Value on Nonmarketable, Control-Interest Basis	$5,175,146

Database Conclusion of Value on a Nonmarketable, Control Interest Basis

Table 1.19 presents the conclusions of value for each database after adding the nonoperating assets that the Company possesses.

Table 1.19: Database Conclusions of Value		
	Pratt's Stats	**IBA**
Nonmarketable, Control Interest Value	$6,944,957	$5,175,146
Add: Non-Operating Assets	388,580	388,580
Total Indicated Value of LEGGO on a Nonmarketable, Control Interest Basis	$7,333,537	$5,563,726

> **EXERCISE 60:** Is a controlling interest nonmarketable?
>
> _____
>
> _____
>
> _____
>
> _____

GUIDELINE PUBLIC COMPANY METHOD

A market approach using guideline public companies requires estimates of a capitalization rate (or multiple) derived from publicly traded guideline companies and ongoing earnings (or a variation thereof, such as EBIT) for the subject entity.

Search for Guideline Public Companies

Guideline public companies provide a reasonable basis for comparison to the relevant investment characteristics of a company being valued. They are most often publicly traded companies in the same or similar business as the valuation subject.

However, if there is insufficient evidence in the same business, it may be necessary to consider companies with an underlying similarity of relevant investment characteristics such as markets, products, growth, cyclical variability, and other salient factors.

Our procedure for deriving group guideline companies involves:

- Identifying the industry in which the Company operates
- Identifying the Standard Industrial Classification Code for the industry in which the Company operates
- Using Internet search tools to search filings with the SEC for businesses that are similar to the subject company
- Screening the initial group of companies to eliminate those that have negative earnings, those with a negative long-term debt to equity ratio, and those whose stock price could not be obtained
- Reviewing in detail the financial and operational aspects of the remaining potential guideline companies and eliminating those whose services differ from the subject company

Based on these criteria, our search identified two publicly traded companies that we believe are similar to the Company. The companies selected were:

1. *Kaneb Services, Inc.: headquartered in Richardson, Texas.* This company provides on-site services such as sealing under-pressure leaks for chemical plants, pipelines, and power companies.
2. *Infracorps, Inc.: headquartered in Richmond, Virginia.* This company specializes in the installation and renovation of water, wastewater, and gas utility pipelines. The company is now focusing on trenchless technology to repair subsurface pipelines.

EXERCISE 61: Size is often a consideration in selecting guideline public companies. General criterion for using size as a selection parameter is:

    a. Two times
    b. Five times
    c. Ten times
    d. None of the above

EXERCISE 62: In the valuation of LEGGO, only one company, Infracorps, was comparable by both industry and size. Given that fact, which option would probably result in the best presentation of the GPCM in the valuation of LEGGO?

    a. Only use Infracorps.
    b. Use both Infracorps and Kaneb.
    c. Reject the guideline public company method.
    d. Use both companies but only as a reasonableness test for the other approaches.

EXERCISE 63:   Guideline public company methods are not applicable to smaller businesses such as LEGGO.

   a. True
   b. False

EXERCISE 64:   Which selection criteria are generally used by analysts in choosing guideline public companies?

   a. Size
   b. Return on equity
   c. Profit margin
   d. Industry similarity
   e. Similar products and services
   f. Growth rates
   g. Investors' similarities

We have chosen to use four multiples to value the Company: earnings before interest and taxes (EBIT), revenues, assets, and equity. We believe that the asset and equity multiples are appropriate because construction companies tend to be asset intensive. We also believe that the EBIT and revenue multiples are appropriate because the Company has a strong income statement and is profitable. We have calculated both one-year and three-year multiples due to the cyclical nature of the industry. No adjustments have been made to the financial statements of the guideline companies as we believe none are necessary.

EXERCISE 65:   Which of these are commonly used guideline public company valuation multiples?

   a. Price/earnings
   b. Invested capital/revenues
   c. Price/gross profits
   d. Invested capital/book value of equity
   e. Invested capital/EBITDA
   f. Invested capital/EBIT
   g. Price/assets
   h. Invested capital/debt-free net income
   i. Invested capital/debt-free cash flow

EXERCISE 66:   When using the guideline public company method, at what point in time are the prices of the public companies' stock?

   a. 30-day average
   b. As of valuation date

c. Six-month average

d. Three-year average

EXERCISE 67:   What type of value is the result of the application of the guideline public company method?

a. Control

b. Minority

c. Neutral

Guideline Public Company Method Conclusion of Value on a Marketable, Control-Interest Basis

Applying multiples to the one- and three-year averages of the Company's EBIT, revenues, assets, and equity provides the values shown in Table 1.20. We have not applied any size premiums to the Company or fundamental discounts to the guideline company multiples in this case. We also put more weight on the income measures of value. As mentioned previously, we must add the nonoperating assets to the value to arrive at a total indicated value.

Table 1.20: Total Selected Values—Guideline Public Company Method		
	One-year Values	Three-year Values
Selected Value	$5,000,000	$6,000,000
Add: Nonoperating Assets	388,580	388,580
Value on Marketable, Control Interest Basis	$5,388,580	$6,388,580

EXERCISE 68:   In selecting multiples from guideline public companies for application to a subject company such as LEGGO, what options do analysts typically have?

a. Mean average of the multiples

b. Median average of the multiples

c. Individual guideline company multiples

d. Average multiples with a fundamental discount

e. All of the above

EXERCISE 69:   Which of these time periods can be used to derive valuation multiples from publicly traded companies?

a. Most recent four quarters

b. Most recent fiscal-year end

c. Three-year average
d. Five-year average
e. One-year projected
f. Three-year future average

LACK OF MARKETABILITY DISCOUNT

EXERCISE 70:   Discounts for lack of marketability/liquidity can be applied to 100 percent controlling interests in a company such as LEGGO.

a. True
b. False

EXERCISE 71:   Which discounts for lack of marketability studies and/or data are typically relied on in determining discounts?

a. Mergerstat Review
b. Restricted stock studies
c. IPO studies
d. Court cases
e. Flotation costs
f. CAPM
g. Ibbotson Associates
h. Quantitative Marketability Discount Model (QMDM)

EXERCISE 72:   Although we are valuing a 100 percent controlling interest in LEGGO, there are numerous other levels of ownership interests that can exist in a closely held company. Provide some examples of other levels of ownership.

_____

_____

_____

_____

_____

A marketability/liquidity discount is intended, among other things, to account for the issues a controlling owner must face as he or she begins to liquidate his or her controlling interest in the company. There are a number of studies and cases over the years that have attempted to identify this discount.

EXERCISE 73: A discount for lack of marketability/liquidity should be applied to all of the valuation methods used in the valuation of LEGGO.

   a. True
   b. False

Selection of Applicable Discount for Lack of Marketability/Liquidity

To quantify the discount for lack of marketability/liquidity applicable to the control, marketable ownership interest in the Company, we considered these factors to have an impact on the magnitude of the discount:

- Uncertain time horizon to complete the offering or sale
- Cost to prepare for and execute the offering or sale
- Risk concerning eventual sale price
- Noncash and deferred transaction proceeds
- Liquidity implied in underlying valuation methodology

Based on our analysis of the factors we consider to affect the lack of marketability/liquidity discount, it is our opinion that the appropriate discount for lack of marketability/liquidity is 5 percent for a control interest as of December 31, 20X5.

CORRELATION OF VALUES

To reach a final conclusion for the value of the stockholders' equity on a nonmarketable, control-interest basis, the methods used were subjectively weighted according to their merits as indicators of value, as shown in Table 1.21. In this instance, we believe that the capitalized cash flow method provides the best indication of value because of the discernible trends of the company. This value is supported by the guideline company transactions method (GCTM) (Pratt's Stats and IBA Databases) and the guideline public company method (GPCM) (one-year and three-year). The guideline company transaction method was not chosen as the best indication of value due to the age of some of the transactions and the lack of detailed knowledge of the terms of the transactions. The guideline public company method was also not chosen as the best indication of value since there were only two companies, and one was larger and not as good a fit based on the industry description.

Table 1.21: Value Indications			
Method	Marketable Control Interest Basis	Discount for Lack of Liquidity	Nonmarketable Control Interest Basis
Capitalized Cash Flow Method	$6,620,202	5%	$6,289,192
GCTM Pratt's Stats Database			7,333,537
GCTM IBA Database			5,563,726
GPCM — One-year	5,388,580	5%	5,119,151
GPCM — Three-year	6,388,580	5%	6,069,151

EXERCISE 74:   Which method can be used to correlate and reconcile value?

   a. Straight average of the indications of value
   b. Numerical weights assigned to each of the value indications
   c. Qualitative judgment in selection of value
   d. All of the above

TOTAL CONCLUSION OF VALUE ON A NONMARKETABLE, CONTROL INTEREST BASIS

In our opinion, the fair market value of 100 percent of the common stock of LEGGO, on a nonmarketable, control interest basis, as of December 31, 20X5, for management purposes and internal planning, is approximately (rounded):

$6,300,000

ADDENDUM: DISCOUNT CASE STUDY EXERCISES

Exercise A

Assume that we are determining the fair market value of a minority nonmarketable interest in a company for gift-tax purposes. The minority marketable value derived by various methods is $100 per share. We are in a state where you need over 50 percent for full control. What is the relative discount for lack of marketability (DLOM) in these situations?

a. Value of a 10 percent interest with one 90 percent owner

_____

_____

_____

b. Value of a 10 percent interest with nine other 10 percent owners

_____

_____

_____

c. Value of a 50 percent interest with one other 50 percent owner

_____

_____

_____

d. Value of a 33.33 percent interest with two other 33.33 percent owners

_____

_____

_____

e. Value of a 2 percent interest with two 49 percent owners

_____

_____

_____

Exercise B

Again, assume we are determining the fair market value of a company for gift tax purposes. In this case study we are valuing a 100 percent controlling interest on a stand-alone basis in a closely held company. What is the discount for lack of marketability in these situations where the prediscount value is determined by using:

a. P/E ratios from control transactions information (i.e., Pratt's Stats)

b. P/E ratios from guideline public companies

c. Discounted cash flow (DCF) with a discount rate determined using Ibbotson information

d. Capitalized cash flow method

e. Asset approach

CHAPTER 2

Valuation Case Study Exercises: Solutions and Explanations

EXERCISE 1: The purpose of the valuation of LEGGO is to assist management in internal planning. What other purposes are there?

ANSWER: Valuations are used for a variety of purposes including estate tax, income tax, gift tax, ESOPs, marital dissolution, buying companies, selling companies, shareholder oppression cases, dissenting rights cases, financial reporting, reorganization and bankruptcy, minority stockholder disputes, various types of litigation, and internal planning.

EXERCISE 2: Which of the following is the "as of" date for valuation?

    a. Anytime within one year
    b. "As of" a single point in time
    c. "As of" a single point in time or six months later
    d. Date that the report is signed

ANSWER: b. "As of" a single point in time

The valuation date is always as "of a" single point in time, typically a day. Valuation of a business is a dynamic, not static, exercise. Values can change constantly, such that a value today may be very different from the value a year from now or even just a few months from now. In the estate tax area, valuations are as of the date of death or six months later. However, this is only for estate tax. The date that the analyst signs the report usually does not coincide with the "as of" date. The signature date is most often after the valuation date.

EXERCISE 3: Valuation conclusions can be presented as:

    a. A range of values
    b. A single value
    c. An estimate of value
    d. All of the above

ANSWER: d. All of the above

Value conclusions can be presented in a variety of formats. Most often it is either a single value or a range of values. Values are always estimates, since subjective judgment is applied.

EXERCISE 4:   This valuation is being done on a nonmarketable, control-interest basis. It is also on a control stand-alone basis. Name the four traditional levels of value that are considered in a valuation.

ANSWER: 1. Control synergistic/strategic
              2. Control stand-alone (liquid or nonliquid)
              3. Minority marketable
              4. Minority nonmarketable

Control synergistic/strategic value reflects the synergies and attributes in a deal between two companies. It is usually investment value. Control stand-alone value is the value of a company that reflects the management philosophies and strategy of the current owners and management team. Minority marketable value is the value of a single share of public company stock, an often-used starting point when valuing private companies. Minority nonmarketable value is the value of a minority interest in a private company that reflects the lack of control and lack of marketability of the interest.

   This valuation is also prepared on a nonmarketable controlling interest basis. Some analysts believe that there is no such thing as a nonmarketable controlling interest. Their point is that 100 percent controlling interest is as marketable as any company of like kind that wants to be sold. Other analysts believe that a company can be nonmarketable controlling depending on the underlying valuation methodologies used. For example, when valuing a 100 percent controlling interest in a private company, the methodologies used typically rely on public company stock data that reflect the fact that the public company interest can be sold in a very short amount of time. If the public company data are applied to determine a controlling interest in a company, the same level of marketability and liquidity would be implied. You cannot sell an entire company in just a few days as you can with public stock. As such, some discount may be appropriate. A controlling interest in a company may be marketable but it is not liquid.

EXERCISE 5:   Which of these are standards of value?

   a. Fair market value, fair value financial reporting, investment value
   b. Fair value investment reporting, fair value state actions, intrinsic value
   c. Investment value, intrinsic value, equal value
   d. Fair market value, equal value, investment value

ANSWER: a. Fair market value, fair value financial reporting, investment
              value

There are five standards of value: fair market value, investment value, intrinsic value, fair value financial reporting, and fair value state actions.

EXERCISE 6: Valuation of S corporations is one of the most controversial issues in business valuations today. The main issue is whether to and how to tax affect S corporation income. What four options are there in valuing S corporations?

ANSWER:
1. Tax affect at the corporate rate
2. Tax affect at the personal rate
3. Do not tax affect at all
4. A combination or hybrid of the other options including factors in the new S corporation models

Most analysts agree that S corporation should be tax affected when valuing a controlling interest. For example, there is no evidence that valuation multiples in deals for companies is any different if the company is a C corporation or an S corporation. There is still some controversy in the valuation of minority interests in S corporations. It is based on the facts and circumstances in each situation and is based in part on the distribution policy of the S corporation. It is also based on the factors considered in the Treharne, Mercer, Grabowski, and Van Vleet models.

EXERCISE 7: We are valuing a 100 percent controlling interest in LEGGO. The percentage of ownership of individual shareholders is not an issue here. However, assume we are valuing the 85 percent of Tom Profit as opposed to the 100 percent in LEGGO. The value of an 85 percent interest in LEGGO would be based on 85 percent of the 100 percent control value in LEGGO.

a. True
b. False

ANSWER: b. False

An 85 percent interest in the company may not be equal to 85 percent of the 100 percent controlling interest value. The sum of the parts may not equal the whole. Although Tom still controls the corporation with his 85 percent interest, there is the possibility of a nuisance value attributable to the other three 5 percent interests. Tom does not have complete control and could be exposed at some time in the future to a dissenting rights action or shareholder oppression action. As such, 85 percent interest would probably be worth somewhat less than a proportional amount of the 100 percent controlling interest value in LEGGO.

EXERCISE 8: Revenue Ruling 59-60 is only used in estate, gift, and income tax valuations.

a. True
b. False

ANSWER: b. False

Technically, Revenue Ruling 59-60 should be followed when valuing interests for estate, gift, and income taxes. However, Revenue Ruling 59-60 is often relied on and quoted for other valuations as well. It has withstood the test of time.

EXERCISE 9: These are the only eight tenets of value in Revenue Ruling 59-60 that need to be considered.

a. True
b. False

ANSWER: b. False

Although there are eight main tenants of value contained in Revenue Ruling 59-60, there is a multitude of other important factors contained in the Revenue Ruling that must also be considered. Other factors include key person discounts, operating versus holding companies, acceptable approaches and methods, and types of historical information.

EXERCISE 10: What types of industries would most likely be affected by anticipated changes in interest rates?

ANSWER: Residential housing
Banking
Auto
Manufacturing

Although all industries are ultimately affected by changes in interest rates, these industries would be impacted more because changes in interest rates change both supply and demand as well as profit margins.

EXERCISE 11: What two economic indicators are probably the most important in valuation?

a. Unemployment levels and Gross Domestic Product (GDP)
b. Dow Jones Industrial Average and Producer Price Index
c. GDP and inflation
d. Inflation and unemployment levels

ANSWER: c. GDP and inflation

Although all economic indicators can be important, typically the two most important ones are historical and anticipated changes in GDP, which measures the real growth of the U.S. economy, and inflation, typically measured through changes in the Consumer Price Index. These two factors affect all industries and can be critical in choosing growth rates in both the discounted cash flow and capitalized cash flow methods of the income approach.

EXERCISE 12: In valuing a small geographically concentrated business, which of these types of economic data should be considered?

a. International, national, regional, local
b. National, regional, local

c. Regional, local

d. Local only

ANSWER: b. National, regional, local

Although a small geographically concentrated business would most likely be affected by local and regional data, the national outlook should also be analyzed in preparing the business valuation. It is true that there are often differences in both the local and regional economy versus the national economy. However, in many industries, what is happening at the national level will eventually trickle down to the regional and local levels. There are exceptions to this rule and each valuation can be different. It is highly unlikely that the international economic situation would impact a small local business.

EXERCISE 13: Which industry outlook factors are generally the most important in supporting valuation assumptions?

a. Growth rates, profit margins, and risk

b. Regulatory and legal issues

c. Unemployment figures

d. Minority discounts and/or control premiums

ANSWER: a. Growth rates, profit margins, and risk

When applicable and available, the industry data should tie to the assumptions used in the valuation for growth rates, profit margins, and risk factors. Regulatory and legal issues and unemployment figures are also important but only to the extent that they affect growth, profits, and risks. Discounts and premiums are separate issues.

EXERCISE 14: What is the most important use of historical financial data?

a. To determine how the company has performed

b. To assist in supporting anticipated performance

c. To highlight profitability

d. To determine average profits

ANSWER: b. To assist in supporting anticipated performance

All of the items listed above are important components of a historic review of financial data. However, when applicable, the main purpose of the historical review is to support anticipated performance and the assumptions in the valuation models. The analysis of the historical operating performance of a company also indicates how well the management team is performing overall and can lead to information concerning trends.

Alternatively, history may not repeat itself and/or history may not be indicative of future performance. For example, the company may not have performed well in the past due to such factors as loss of a key person or litigation. The absence of those items going forward would indicate better performance. The analysis of the historic information should also be made in light of the local, regional, and national economy, as well as the industry outlook. All these items can be used to support assumptions in the valuation models.

EXERCISE 15:   Analysts typically spread five years of financial statements because:

   a. Revenue Ruling 59-60 requires five years.
   b. Uniform Standards of Professional Appraisal Practice requires five years.
   c. An economic cycle is often captured in five years.
   d. Most business plans are based on five years of projections.

ANSWER: c. An economic cycle is often captured in five years.

There is no magic to looking at five years of data. In some industries only the most recent year or just a few years are relevant. In other industries five to ten years may be more appropriate. The underlying theme is that it captures enough financial information to indicate trends, the performance of the company, and an economic cycle. Although Revenue Ruling 59-60 suggests that five years of data be reviewed, it is not required. USPAP does not have any requirements concerning the number of years of financial information. Although it may be true that many projections include five years of data, this has no real relevance in terms of a historical review of information.

EXERCISE 16:   The main drawbacks of publicly available benchmark financial ratios are:

   a. There are very few SIC codes.
   b. They calculate the ratios incorrectly.
   c. The companies that make up the data cannot be used to determine pricing ratios or capitalization rates.
   d. The information is from public companies.

ANSWER: c. The companies that make up the data cannot be used to determine pricing ratios or capitalization rates.

Most of the national databases do have fairly extensive amounts of information by SIC code, and the ratios typically are calculated properly. Most of the information is from closely held companies.

   The main drawback of the data is that none of it is tied to pricing ratios or valuation multiples such as price to earnings or invested capital to EBITDA. There is also no tie to any type of discount or capitalization rate. Therefore, some analysts believe that these types of comparisons are less meaningful. Alternatively, when using the guideline public company method of the market approach, ratios can be tied to valuation multiples. You can take a look at how the subject company compares to the various ratios of the public companies, then make adjustments to the public company multiples to reflect those differences. This cannot be done when using public benchmark data that again have no references or ties to valuation multiples or capitalization rates. However, they can help in a general risk assessment.

It is also important to recognize that many of the ratios are calculated differently and that consistency is important when comparing the subject company being valued to the ratios in the benchmark data.

EXERCISE 17: Indicate whether you believe that LEGGO is a better or worse performer based on the financial ratios previously presented.

ANSWER: Although each ratio is important, some are more useful than others. For example, profit margins and leverage ratios are typically more important than other ratios. In general, it appears that LEGGO is more liquid. In terms of activity ratios, it appears that they are under-performing based on fixed assets, but this may be due to owning more of their fixed assets as opposed to leasing them. In terms of leverage, it appears that the Company uses less debt than its industry counterparts and could add additional debt if it chooses. The Company's return-on-equity ratio and return-on-assets ratio are much higher, indicating that it may be generating higher profit margins than the industry. Overall, it appears that LEGGO is outperforming its peers based on the benchmark data presented.

EXERCISE 18: All three approaches to value must be applied in all valuations.

   a. True
   b. False

ANSWER: b. False

Although it is true that all three approaches to value should be considered in each valuation, they need not all be applied in every valuation. Most analysts do not use the full asset approach (tangible and intangible assets) in valuing an operating company because increases in the accuracy of the appraisal, if any, are not worth the time and expense of having all the assets valued. The value of all the aggregated assets, including intangible assets, is considered in the value derived from the income and market approaches. The asset approach is often the primary approach in valuing investment or holding companies.

EXERCISE 19:   In what type of valuation setting is the excess cash flow method most often used?

a. ESOPs (Employee stock ownership plans)
b. Estate tax
c. Dissenting rights
d. Marital dissolution

ANSWER: d. Marital dissolution

Although the excess cash flow method can be used in any valuation, it is most often seen in marital dissolutions. Analysts may use this method because the court in a jurisdiction is familiar with it. In some situations, exclusion of the excess cash flow method could be perceived as an omission.

EXERCISE 20:   On which Revenue Ruling is the excess cash flow method based?

a. Revenue Ruling 59-60
b. Revenue Ruling 83-120
c. Revenue Ruling 68-609
d. Revenue Ruling 77-287

ANSWER: c. Revenue Ruling 68-609

The excess cash flow method, sometimes referred to as the formula method or the excess earnings method, was first discussed in ARM 34, which was used to determine goodwill in breweries due to prohibition. This eventually led to Revenue Ruling 68-609. Revenue Ruling 59-60 contains the basic tenants and procedures for valuing closely held businesses. Revenue Ruling 83-120 deals with valuation of preferred stock. Revenue Ruling 77-287 deals with the valuation of restricted securities.

EXERCISE 21:   Which method(s) is(are) considered valid under the income approach?

a. Guideline public company method
b. Discounted cash flow method
c. Capitalized cash flow method
d. Excess cash flow method

ANSWER: b. Discounted cash flow method, and
              c. Capitalized cash flow method

Discounted cash flow and capitalized cash flow are the two main methods under the income approach. There are variations of these two methods. The guideline public company method is a market approach, and the excess cash flow method is a hybrid of the income and asset approaches.

EXERCISE 22: In which situation(s) would a capitalized cash flow method be most applicable?

    a. When a company's future performance is anticipated to change from its prior performance

    b. In litigation settings

    c. When a single historical or pro forma amount of cash flow is anticipated to be earned with a constant growth in the future

    d. When valuing very small businesses

ANSWER: c. When a single historical or pro forma amount of cash flow is anticipated to be earned with a constant growth in the future, and

              d. When valuing very small businesses

Capitalized cash flow methods are most often used when future performance is anticipated to be at a steady rate based on either a historical figure, such as an average or recent year, or a pro forma single figure. Discounted cash flow is most often used when future performance is anticipated to be different from the past. Both discounted cash flow and capitalized cash flow methods are used in litigation, although some analysts believe that the capitalized cash flow method is more supportable because it is easier to explain. Capitalized cash flow methods are most often seen in valuations of small businesses, since that is how they are often bought and sold.

EXERCISE 23: List the two main bases when using the capitalized cash flow (CCF) or discounted cash flow (DCF) methods of the income approach.

ANSWER: 1. Direct equity
                2. Invested capital

There is much debate in the valuation community about whether to use direct equity methods of valuation in which interest expense and debt principal are included, or to use invested capital methods in which interest expense and debt principal are excluded. Theoretically, the use of both models should give you a similar result. Both methods can be used in most valuations. However, in certain circumstances, one method may be better than the other. For example, the invested capital method may be used in control valuations where the capital structure of the company is anticipated to change. Alternatively, in a minority valuation, some analysts believe that the direct equity method is more appropriate, since the minority shareholder cannot change the capital structure of the company. It is often a matter of preference.

EXERCISE 24: Under the direct equity basis, what are the components of net cash flow?

ANSWER: Net income after tax
                        Plus   Depreciation and noncash charges
                       Minus   Capital expenditure requirements
                  Plus/minus   Working capital requirements
                        Plus   New debt principal paid in
                       Minus   Debt principal paid out

EXERCISE 25: For the invested capital basis of the income approach, list the components of net cash flow.

ANSWER: Net income after tax
                        Plus   Interest expense times 1 minus the tax rate
                        Plus   Depreciation and noncash charges
                       Minus   Capital expenditure requirements
                  Plus/minus   Working capital requirements (debt-free)

EXERCISE 26: What is the difference between minority cash flows and control cash flows?

ANSWER: The difference between control cash flows and minority cash flows is normalization adjustments. Normalization adjustments for control include excess compensation and perquisites. When such amounts are added back, it is considered a control value. When such amounts are left in as expenses, it is considered a minority value, since the minority shareholder cannot change the policies of the control owner.

EXERCISE 27: Which adjustment(s) are made when valuing both minority and control cash flows?

  a. Nonrecurring items
  b. Nonoperating assets
  c. Excess compensation
  d. Perquisites
  e. Taxes

ANSWER: a. Nonrecurring items,
                b. Nonoperating assets, and
                e. Taxes

The goal of normalizing cash flows is to determine what a normalized amount would be into perpetuity. Nonrecurring items are typically removed from the cash flows. Most analysts will also adjust the P&L for the effect of removing nonoperating assets from the balance sheet. For example, there may be an adjustment for interest and dividend income associated with excess marketable securities, as is the situation here with LEGGO. Excess compensation and perquisites are only adjusted in control cash flows. When using after-tax rates of return, taxes are typically an expense in minority and control cash flows.

EXERCISE 28: Assume the company does not have any control adjustments and the company is run to the benefit of all shareholders without any shareholders taking out cash flow over or above what they are entitled. Is this value control or minority?

ANSWER: The value would clearly be control stand-alone, since the capitalized cash flow is the cash flow of the entire company reflecting the benefits to all shareholders. Since the current owner of the company is operating to the benefit of all shareholders, it becomes a minority value as well. However, it is minority value only to the extent that the current owners continue their policies. Policies can change and/or new owners can come in, which increases the risk such that a discount for a lack of control or minority interest may still be appropriate. A possible adjustment for lack of control may be appropriate to reflect the risk of potential future changes in either the owner or the policies or both.

EXERCISE 29: List some of the nonoperating/excess assets that are sometimes encountered in a business valuation.

ANSWER: Marketable securities
Cash
Inventory
Working capital
Land
Buildings
Condominiums
Boats

EXERCISE 30: In valuing a *controlling interest* in a corporation, most analysts agree that the nonoperating and/or excess assets of the business must be removed out of the operating business, then added back at fair market value.

   a. True
   b. False

ANSWER: a. True

The rate of return requirements for excess assets and/or nonoperating assets are often less than the cost of capital of the company. As such, including the income and expenses of the nonoperating/excess assets in the P&L, and capitalizing such amounts at a higher rate of return, will undervalue the company. There are also situations where there are nonoperating assets that generate no income. The capitalization of cash flow without adjustment would result in a zero value for those assets. This is why these types of assets are typically removed from the balance sheet with appropriate P&L adjustments, then added back to the operating value of the business.

EXERCISE 31:   In valuing a *minority interest* of a company, most analysts agree that the nonoperating and/or excess assets of the business must be removed out of the operating business, then added back at fair market value.

　　a. True
　　b. False

ANSWER: a. True

Although this is true for most analysts, there are still differences of opinions. Some analysts believe that the same methodology should be employed as in valuing a controlling interest; that is, value the nonoperating or excess assets separately and make the related P&L adjustments. They would then take a discount for lack of control and a discount for lack of marketability from the nonoperating asset value before they added it to the company's discounted operating value. Other analysts believe that a minority stockholder has no access to these types of assets and the P&L should be as it is, reflecting the way the company operates. The assets are not separately valued and added back. Again, this can create a situation where the value of nonoperating/ excess assets may be zero, which is difficult to defend.

EXERCISE 32:   In the valuation of LEGGO, the analyst decided to use a straight average of the adjusted income before income taxes for five historical years. Besides a straight average, what other method(s) can be used to determine the appropriate cash flow to be capitalized into perpetuity?

　　a. Weighted average
　　b. Most recent fiscal year
　　c. Most recent trailing 12 months
　　d. Trend line analysis/next year's budget
　　e. DCF average of next three years

ANSWER: a. Weighted average,
　　　　　　　b. Most recent fiscal year,
　　　　　　　c. Most recent trailing 12 months, and
　　　　　　　d. Trend line analysis/next year budget

The first four items can be considered in valuing and determining how cash flow should be capitalized. An example of a weighted average is (3,2,1), which would be used for a three-year average, with the most recent year given the weight of 3, the second year 2, and the most distant year 1. Some analysts will use (5,4,3,2,1) for five years of data. The weighted average is typically used when the analyst believes there may be an increasing trend but wants to reflect the possibility that there could be some underperforming years. Fiscal year end and trailing 12 months are typically used when there is anticipation that the most recent information is indicative of the future. Some analysts will use an estimate of next year's budget if they believe it is more indicative of the potential performance of the company. DCF is typically used when historical information is not anticipated to continue. DCF and capitalized cash flow methods do not average future years, only historical years.

EXERCISE 33: Analysts will generally use a straight historical average where the earnings and cash flows are more volatile.

  a. True
  b. False

ANSWER: a. True

This is the situation with LEGGO. Although there is some trend upward for LEGGO, the construction industry is fairly cyclical such that a straight historical average is more appropriate here. The other methods are often more appropriate where there is more of a trend in the historical results.

EXERCISE 34: Which situation is most appropriate when adjusting cash flows for depreciation and capital expenditures?

  a. Capital expenditures should exceed depreciation.
  b. Depreciation should exceed capital expenditures.
  c. Depreciation and capital expenditures should be similar.
  d. The actual unadjusted amounts should be capitalized.

ANSWER: c. Depreciation and capital expenditures should be similar.

A common mistake made in business valuation is to capitalize cash flow into perpetuity where the depreciation greatly exceeds the future capital expenditure requirements. This is obviously an impossible situation, since future capital expenditures have to be made in order to generate future depreciation. Many analysts will normalize depreciation and capital expenditures by making them equal or similar. This equalization process is a simplifying assumption, since capital expenditures would slightly exceed depreciation due to the inflationary pressure in a stable business. However, this usually (but not always) has a nominal effect on value. There are situations in which depreciation/amortization can exceed capital expenditures within a definite period of time. This occurs when there is a previous purchase of a long-life asset such as a building, or where goodwill or other intangible assets are amortized over a longer period of time. In those situations, it may be appropriate to have depreciation exceed capital expenditures.

EXERCISE 35: Assuming taxes are to be deducted, what two choices are there in making the tax adjustments?

    a. Tax each year historically, then determine the average.
    b. Taxes should never be deducted in the value of an S corporation.
    c. Make all adjustments in the historical period pretax, determine the average, then deduct for taxes.

ANSWER: a. Tax each year historically, then determine the average, and
            c. Make all adjustments in the historical period pretax, determine the average, then deduct for taxes.

Some analysts will go back and compute taxes in each of the years used in the average income as opposed to making all the adjustments pretax, calculating the average, then adjusting for taxes. When the tax rates are the same, this will not have an impact. However, in C corporations, where taxes may differ for each year due to certain types of planning, an average of five years after-tax income may be different from the average of five years pretax, which is aggregated with one tax amount applied to it. There may be years when the taxes would be less than the marginal rate. As such, some analysts believe that an average tax-affected rate is more appropriate. Other analysts believe that the company will eventually end up paying close to the marginal rate into perpetuity, and that would be the more appropriate rate.

EXERCISE 36: Which economic benefit stream(s) can be used for cash flow in a capitalized cash flow method?

    a. After-tax income
    b. Pretax income
    c. Net cash flow
    d. EBITDA (Earnings before interest, taxes, depreciation, and amortization)
    e. Revenues
    f. Debt-free net income
    g. Debt-free cash flow

ANSWER: a. After-tax income
            b. Pretax income
            c. Net cash flow
            f. Debt-free net income
            g. Debt-free cash flow

Cash flow is often used in many business valuations. However, there are circumstances, particularly with small businesses, when income is capitalized both on an after-tax and a pretax basis. Debt-free net income is used in the invested capital basis and is after-tax income with interest expense added back. Debt-free cash flow is debt-free net income with depreciation added back. Although theoretically EBITDA could be a capitalizeable amount, it is more often used in the market approach than the income approach. Revenues are seldom capitalized in the income approach, although they can be capitalized through the market approach.

There is some debate in the valuation industry concerning the use of either cash flow or income when performing the income approach. However, this is frequently a moot point because analysts often equalize depreciation and capital expenditures. The only other real adjustment would be incremental working capital. Not all businesses require incremental working capital, particularly cash businesses or businesses whose receivables are turned quickly. As such, and particularly in small businesses, cash flow and income may be equal or similar. However, there are many businesses that require working capital to fund growth. In those situations, working capital should be considered as a cash outflow. Cash flow in a growing business would typically be less than income in those businesses with working capital needs. Debt would also have to be normalized in terms of debt principal in and debt principal out. However, again, if they are normalized, they net out to net income.

EXERCISE 37: When using the direct-equity basis instead of the invested-capital basis, assumptions of capital structure can be avoided.

   a. True
   b. False

ANSWER: b. False

One of the reasons often given for using the direct equity basis is that the analyst can avoid making assumptions of capital structure, that is, what percent debt and what percent equity a company will use. However, in a direct equity basis there needs to be assumptions of debt principal in and debt principal out, and they need to be normalized. Anytime you normalize the amount of debt that is used in a company, you are explicitly assuming a capital structure. As such, debt is a consideration in using the direct-equity basis.

EXERCISE 38: When using the invested capital basis to determine a control value, you should always use an optimal capital structure in the weighted average cost of capital.

   a. True
   b. False

ANSWER: b. False

Although many analysts will use an optimal capital structure, often deter-mined based on a review of public company capital structures or other means, it is not always the basis to use for control value. If the management of a company decides to operate with a different capital structure, it would still be a control value on a stand-alone basis reflecting the current policies of management.

EXERCISE 39:   Name the two methods most often used to derive a cost of equity in the income approach for a smaller business.

ANSWER: 1. Modified capital asset pricing model (MCAPM)
              2. Build-up method

There is controversy in the valuation industry about whether the MCAPM should be used to value small businesses. Some analysts believe that MCAPM should not be used to value even large businesses. The only difference between the MCAPM and the build-up method is the use of beta. It is often difficult to find betas for small publicly traded companies that could be applicable to small private companies. There are many different sources of betas and many different ways to calculate betas. Betas can also differ for the same public company at the same point in time.

   Betas are sometimes available that could be used in a MCAPM for small companies. There are industries where there are large numbers of public small companies where betas may be available. However, if there are no reasonably similar companies whose betas could be used as a proxy for the small closely held company, then the build-up method may be the best method to use. However, if the betas are reasonable and can be used, then the MCAPM may be considered as well. Each of these situations is fact- and circumstance-specific and could differ depending on the type of company, the industry of the subject company, and the size of the company.

EXERCISE 40:   When using the MCAPM to derive an equity cost of capital for a controlling interest, it is sometimes necessary to adjust beta for differences between the capital structure of the public companies and the capital structure of the subject company being valued. This is not necessary if the capital struc-ture is assumed to be the same. Given the following information, and if the MCAPM was used for LEGGO, calculate the unlevered and relevered beta.

   a. Average beta of guideline public companies = 1.4
      Tax rate = 40 percent
      Market value capital structure = 35 percent debt, 65 percent equity

      The formula for unlevered beta is:
         $B_u = B_l / (1 + (1 - t)(W_d / W_e))$

Where

Bu	=	Beta unlevered
Bl	=	Beta levered
t	=	Tax rate for the company
Wd	=	Percentage of debt in the capital structure (at market value)
We	=	Percentage of equity in the capital structure (at market value)

b. Assuming that LEGGO has a capital structure of 25 percent debt and 75 percent equity and that the MCAPM can be used, what would be the beta?

The formula to relever the beta is:

$$Bl = Bu (1 + (1 - t) (Wd / We))$$

ANSWER: a. $\begin{aligned} Bu &= 1.4 / (1 + (1 - .40)(.35 / .65)) \\ &= 1.4 / 1 + .6 (.54) \\ &= 1.4 / 1.32 \\ &= 1.06 \end{aligned}$

b. $\begin{aligned} Bl &= 1.06 (1 + (1 - .40)(.25 / .75)) \\ Bl &= 1.06 (1 + (.6) (.33)) \\ Bl &= 1.06 (1.20) \\ Bl &= 1.27 \end{aligned}$

EXERCISE 41:   Should build-up method and modified capital asset pricing model (MCAPM) rates of return be applied to income or cash flow?

ANSWER: The current general consensus is that these are cash flow rates of return. They are also rates of return after corporate tax but before personal investor tax. The rates of return are based on dividends and capital appreciation. Dividends are paid after tax by public corporations, and capital appreciation is also after-tax due to retained earnings used to grow the business. However, these returns are pretax to an individual investor. Ibbotson agrees that traditional rates of return derived using their data, whether MCAPM or build-up method, should be applied to after-tax cash flows.

EXERCISE 42:   Which of these rates of return are derived using Ibbotson data?

a. Minority rates of return
b. Control rates of return
c. Both
d. Neutral

ANSWER: d. Neutral

There is some controversy concerning whether the rates of return derived using Ibbotson data are minority rates of return or control rates of return. However, Ibbotson is very clear in stating that it believes they are not minority returns even though the data are based on returns of shares of stock that are on a minority basis. Ibbotson believes the returns are neutral. Most analysts today believe that control or minority features are in the cash flows to be capitalized versus the discount or capitalization rate. A controlling shareholder in a public company would not necessarily be able to maximize or increase the returns over and above what the minority shareholders are experiencing. The management and board of directors of publicly traded companies must maximize returns for all shareholders regardless of how the company is held, supporting the concept of a neutral return.

EXERCISE 43:   Why are long-term 20-year U.S. Treasury coupon bonds most often used for the risk-free rate of return in both the build-up method and the MCAPM?

ANSWER: Most analysts use a 20-year risk-free rate of return from a U.S. Treasury bond because this is the basis from which Ibbotson derives its risk premiums. There is no such thing as an original issue 20-year bond. Analysts and Ibbotson use 30-year Treasury bonds that have 20 years remaining.

EXERCISE 44:   The common stock equity risk premium was 7.2 percent as of the valuation date from the *SBBI Yearbook*. What benchmark is this return based on?

a. S&P 500
b. New York Stock Exchange
c. Dow Jones Industrial Average
d. Russell 5000

ANSWER: The risk premium used in this report is from the S&P 500. This is the most commonly used benchmark for determining equity premiums for the marketplace.

EXERCISE 45:   In applying a small stock risk premium, what are the choices that analysts can make using the Ibbotson data?

a. 10th decile annual beta
b. 10th decile monthly beta
c. 10th decile sum beta
d. 10A monthly beta

> e. 10B monthly beta
> f. Micro-cap annual beta
> g. Micro-cap monthly beta
> h. Micro-cap sum beta
> i. All of the above

ANSWER: i. All of the above

In the valuation of LEGGO, the analysts decided to use the 10th decile monthly beta. All of these small stock premiums are the premiums in excess of CAPM that Ibbotson uses to derive small stock risk premium. Some analysts will use the 10th decile, whereas others will use the micro-cap strata, which is the 9th and 10th deciles. There are also differences of opinion as to which small stock premiums should be used based on the type of beta. It could be monthly betas, annual betas, or sum betas. Monthly and annual betas are based on the timing of the calculation. Sum betas are sometimes referred to as lagged betas and reflect the fact that small stock market reactions may lag the market by a certain amount of time. Some analysts use a micro-cap small stock risk premium because the average includes more companies. In 20X5, the micro-cap risk premium was 4.0 percent versus the 6.4 percent used for the 10th decile. The 10B decile risk premium was 9.9 percent. Although the 10B decile risk premium is based on smaller companies, it is also based on a lower number of companies that make up the average. There is currently no clear requirement for selecting small stock risk premiums, and the controversy continues about whether to use the 10th decile, micro-cap, or 10B strata, as well as the type of beta on which the information is based. Many analysts are also using risk premium data from Duff & Phelps, LLC.

EXERCISE 46:   A list of risk factors was previously presented for LEGGO to calculate the specific risk premium. Discuss the different methods for determining what the actual specific risk premium should be.

ANSWER: In this valuation the analyst made a subjective selection of an aggregate 4 percent risk premium. This was based on the analyst's judgment concerning the additional risk of the previously described items. This is a common method of selecting specific risk premiums. Other methods that can be used are some type of numerical system placed on the categories (i.e., -3, -2, -1, 0, 1, 2, 3). However, this sometimes implies accuracy that may not exist and may be difficult to defend in a litigation setting. Other analysts use a plus and minus system to determine the potential amount of specific risk.

EXERCISE 47:   Specific company risk premiums can be determined from Ibbotson data.

> a. True
> b. False

ANSWER: b. False

Specific company risk premium data are not included in the Ibbotson *SBBI yearbooks*. In fact, there are no empirical studies indicating specific risk premiums. This is a subjective area for the analyst.

EXERCISE 48: Using the information in the text, calculate the cost of equity for LEGGO.

Rs	=	Risk-free rate of return	=	____
RPm	=	Risk premium common stock	=	____
RPs	=	Risk premium small stock	=	____
RPu	=	Company-specific risk premium	=	____
Ke	=	Cost of equity	=	____

ANSWER: 4.7% + 7.2% + 6.4% + 4.0% = 22% (rounded)

EXERCISE 49: Which of these factors causes the cost of debt to be tax-affected?

    a. Debt principal is tax deductible.
    b. Interest expense is tax deductible.
    c. It should not be tax-affected since equity is not tax-affected.
    d. Debt and interest are tax deductible.

ANSWER: b. Interest expense is tax deductible

Principal is never tax deductible for a corporation (ESOP exception). Since interest expense is a cost of debt and is tax deductible, there is an adjustment for taxes. Equity returns derived by using Ibbotson data are already on an after-tax basis, so no adjustments need to be made to equity returns.

EXERCISE 50: Using the information in the text, calculate the weighted average cost of capital for LEGGO.

ANSWER: 75% (22%) + 25% (5%) = 17.75%

EXERCISE 51: Which methods can be used to determine the weights in the weighted average cost of capital?

    a. Iterative process
    b. Guideline public companies

    c. Aggregated public industry data
    d. Risk Management Associates
    e. Troy
    f. Book values
    g. Anticipated capital structure

ANSWER: a. Iterative process
                 b. Guideline public companies
                 c. Aggregated public industry data
                 g. Anticipated capital structure

Both guideline public company information and aggregated public industry data are often viewed as optimal capital structures with the idea that public companies use an optimal amount of debt to lower their weighted average cost of capital. Iterative processes can be used for both minority and controlling interests but are more typically used in minority valuations. Clients will often have an anticipated capital structure that can also be employed. Risk Management Associates, Troy, and book value information are all based on book values, not fair market values. The weights to be used in the weighted average cost of capital are fair market value weights, not book value weights.

EXERCISE 52:   Explain the iterative process for determining the weights in the weighted average cost of capital.

ANSWER: The analyst will choose the capital structure to value the company, then determine the percent of debt based on that value using the actual debt of the company. If it is different, then you redo the capital structure until it iterates to the proper capital structure that is in existence. This is easily accomplished by the use of spreadsheets.

EXERCISE 53:   Changing the amount of debt in the capital structure of the company has no effect on the return on equity.

    a. True
    b. False

ANSWER: b. False

As you change the capital structure of the company through an iterative process, the increases in debt may increase the rates of return on equity as well. The more debt the company takes on, the higher the return on equity. This can be reflected directly through the use of MCAPM by levering and unlevering betas based on the different debt levels. If the build-up method is used, the adjustment is more subjective.

EXERCISE 54: When valuing a controlling interest in a company, should you use the optimal capital structure based on public data or the capital structure anticipated to be employed by the owner of the company?

ANSWER: This answer depends on the type of valuation being performed. The valuation could be from the perspective of a sale to an owner that could employ a different capital structure. The company may be valued on a stand-alone basis, and the owners may want to know what it is worth to them with the existing or anticipated capital structure. In the valuation of LEGGO, the Company was valued using industry capital weights.

EXERCISE 55: Calculate the capitalization rate from the information in the text (apply to historical cash flow).

ANSWER: $(17.75\% - 3\%)/1.03 = 14.32\%$

$$= 14\% \text{ rounded}$$

EXERCISE 56: Items used to support growth rates in the capitalized cash flow method of the income approach include:

   a. Inflation
   b. Nominal Gross Domestic Product
   c. Industry growth rate
   d. Actual historical company growth rate
   e. All of the above

ANSWER: e. All of the above

The selection of the growth rate can have a tremendous impact on the value conclusion. Value is very sensitive to growth. Many analysts use the inflation rate as the perpetual growth rate in the capitalized capital cash flow method, which is used here for LEGGO. Others use the average nominal (real and inflation) growth of the GDP of the United States which has been 6 to 6.5 percent when measured from 1926 to the present. Still other analysts use what they believe to be the anticipated or long-term industry growth rate. Economic and industry information can be helpful in supporting the growth rate. A company's historical growth is also a consideration.

EXERCISE 57: When is it more appropriate to use a discounted cash flow method instead of a capitalized cash flow method?

ANSWER: If a company anticipates growing at a steady rate in the future, it is unnecessary to prepare a discounted cash flow method. A capitalized cash flow method, as used here in the valuation of LEGGO, is sufficient. Discounted cash flow methods are typically used when short-term growth is anticipated to be different from long-term growth and/or the company's cash flow has not reached a stabilized or normalized period that can be capitalized into perpetuity.

EXERCISE 58: Which of these are general transaction databases used by analysts in valuing companies?

　a. Pratt's Stats
　b. RMA
　c. Ibbotson Associates
　d. Institute of Business Appraisers
　e. Done Deals
　f. Bizcomps
　g. Mergerstat Review

ANSWER:　a. Pratt's Stats
　　　　　　d. Institute of Business Appraisers
　　　　　　e. Done Deals
　　　　　　f. Bizcomps
　　　　　　g. Mergerstat Review

Ibbotson does not provide any transaction information. RMA provides book value ratios of companies.

EXERCISE 59: What is one of the most significant problems when using transaction data?

ANSWER: One of the common mistakes made in the application of transaction multiples is to aggregate the transactions from the different databases. This will result in an inaccurate valuation, since each of the databases collects and presents its data in a different format. Some of the databases use invested capital multiples, some use equity multiples, some include working capital, some include debt, some include inventory, and so on. When using these databases, if they are different, it is recommended that information from each database be used and applied separately to the subject company's earnings parameters, as it was done here in LEGGO. This will avoid any possible inaccuracies.

EXERCISE 60: Is a controlling interest nonmarketable?

ANSWER: Some analysts believe that the term *nonmarketable*, as it applies to a controlling interest, is inappropriate. However, the price of the transaction should reflect some reasonable amount of time to sell the company such that marketability issues are included in the value. The marketability, or lack thereof, is already reflected in the transaction price.

EXERCISE 61: Size is often a consideration in selecting guideline public companies. General criterion for using size as a selection parameter is:

    a. Two times
    b. Five times
    c. Ten times
    d. None of the above

ANSWER: d. None of the above

There is really no general criterion for selecting guideline public companies based on size. A rule of thumb used by some analysts is no greater than ten times revenue. However, this is not always applicable. The reason analysts adjust for size is not so much because the guideline public companies are larger but because size typically indicates that the company is more diversified both in product lines and geography. Furthermore, larger companies tend to have more management depth.

EXERCISE 62: In the valuation of LEGGO, only one company, Infracorps, was comparable by both industry and size. Given that fact, which option would probably result in the best presentation of the GPCM in the valuation of LEGGO?

    a. Only use Infracorps
    b. Use both Infracorps and Kaneb
    c. Reject the guideline public company method
    d. Use both companies but only as a reasonableness test for the other approaches

ANSWER: d. Use both companies but only as a reasonableness test for the other approaches.

Kaneb's revenue is 30 times as large as LEGGO, whereas Infracorps' revenue is twice as large. Some analysts would eliminate Kaneb because it is so much larger than LEGGO. Furthermore, it does not operate in the same industry. Infracorps seems to be a better fit in terms of size as well as the types of construction services it provides. Some analysts would have eliminated Kaneb and only relied on Infracorps. That would result in reliance on one guideline public company, a presentation that may be more difficult to defend. Other analysts would completely reject the guideline public company method as it applies to LEGGO. Given the lack of good guideline companies, the analyst here decided to use the guideline public company method only as a reasonableness test for the income approach.

EXERCISE 63: Guideline public company methods are not applicable to smaller businesses such as LEGGO.

   a. True
   b. False

ANSWER: b. False

Some analysts do believe that guideline public companies are not applicable to small businesses. However, some of these analysts may be surprised by the number of potential publicly traded companies that are similar in size in certain industries. At the very least, in valuing a small company, a cursory review of public companies should be undertaken to determine if there are any similar companies.

EXERCISE 64: Which selection criteria are generally used by analysts in choosing guideline public companies?

   a. Size
   b. Return on equity
   c. Profit margin
   d. Industry similarity
   e. Similar products and services
   f. Growth rates
   g. Investors' similarities

ANSWER: a. Size
               d. Industry similarity
               e. Similar products and services

Analysts typically screen initially by industry similarity, including similar products and services and then by size. Once an initial selection of companies is made, they will often look at profit margins, return on equity, and growth rates. However, these are typically not looked at in the initial screening. Some analysts will also look at similarity in terms of investor preferences. They believe that the selection process for guideline public companies can be expanded outside the particular industry in which the company operates. They will look for similar investment characteristics such as growth, return on equity, profit margin, and so forth. Their belief is that a prudent investor would invest in companies that have similar characteristics regardless of industry. Generally, the courts have been reluctant to accept companies outside the subject company's industry that are not at least somewhat similar in product, market, and so on.

EXERCISE 65: Which of these are commonly used guideline company valuation multiples?

   a. Price/earnings
   b. Invested capital/revenues
   c. Price/gross profits
   d. Invested capital/book value of equity
   e. Invested capital/EBITDA
   f. Invested capital/EBIT
   g. Price/assets
   h. Invested capital/debt-free net income
   i. Invested capital/debt-free cash flow

ANSWER: a. Price/earnings
                b. Invested capital/revenues
                e. Invested capital/EBITDA (widely used)
                f. Invested capital/EBIT
                h. Invested capital/debt-free net income
                i. Invested capital/debt-free cash flow

There are a variety of multiples that can be used to value a company. In the valuation of LEGGO, the analysts used invested capital to EBIT, invested capital to revenue, invested capital to assets, and price to equity. This is a subjective area, and the analyst should consider all potential multiples and decide which ones may be the best fit. It is preferable for the numerator and denominator to be similar. For example, if price of equity is in the numerator, then the earnings' parameters should be the earnings available to equity in the denominator. If the numerator is invested capital, then the denominator should be the earnings' parameters available for invested capital. Price/gross profit, invested capital/book value of equity, and price to assets would not be the best multiples to use here.

EXERCISE 66:   When using the guideline public company method, at what point in time are the prices of the public companies' stock?

   a. 30-day average
   b. As of valuation date
   c. Six-month average
   d. Three-year average

ANSWER: b. As of valuation date

There has been some recent controversy due to the current volatility of the stock market. Since stock prices in P/E multiples can change rapidly, some analysts believe that some type of average stock price or P/E multiple should be used as opposed to a P/E multiple based on a particular point in time. However, traditional valuation theory holds that the value should be at a single point in time, typically as of a single day. They believe that whatever the day the valuation is, that is the day the stock price should be used. In addition, some analysts use the current price divided by a projected income or cash flow figure. They believe that this is a better fit of the price of the stock to the anticipated performance of the company.

EXERCISE 67: What type of value is the result of the application of the guideline public company method?

   a. Control
   b. Minority
   c. Neutral

ANSWER: c. Neutral

This is a controversial area. Those that believe it is a minority value argue that the underlying stocks are minority such that the application of a valuation multiple would result in a minority value. Others argue that the valuation multiples are nothing more than inverted capitalization rates derived from the public market. As such, the underlying theory about minority/control being in the cash flows for the income approach should also apply to the market approach. If that is true, then the application of valuation multiples would be neutral and control/minority would, like the income approach, be an adjustment to the earnings' parameter to which the valuation multiples are applied.

EXERCISE 68: In selecting multiples from guideline public companies for application to a subject company such as LEGGO, what options do analysts typically have?

   a. Mean average of the multiples
   b. Median average of the multiples
   c. Individual guideline company multiples
   d. Average multiples with a fundamental discount
   e. All of the above

ANSWER: e. All of the above

Some analysts use an average of multiples to derive a value. Some use a mean average that is the sum of the indications divided by the number of indications. Others believe that the median average is a better fit because it excludes outliers since it is the midpoint. Still other analysts believe that you should look at each guideline company separately, decide which ones are more comparable, and rely on those multiples rather than an average of the multiples. Some analysts will use averages, then take a fundamental discount from the average to reflect the subject company's differences. This fundamental discount is often used to adjust for size and/or other factors.

EXERCISE 69:   Which of these time periods can be used to derive valuation multiples from publicly traded companies?

    a. Most recent four quarters
    b. Most recent fiscal year-end
    c. Three-year average
    d. Five-year average
    e. One-year projected
    f. Three-year future average

ANSWER: a. Most recent four quarters
              b. Most recent fiscal year-end
              c. Three-year average
              d. Five-year average
              e. One-year projected

Analysts must decide whether the multiples derived from publicly traded companies should be the most recent multiples, typically based on an annual fiscal year-end or four-quarter trailing figure or a multiple of some average earnings such as a three-year or five-year average. If it is believed that an average multiple would be more indicative of future performance of a company, then that may be more appropriate. Many analysts use both—the most recent period as well as a historical period—and weight them according to what they think would be most indicative of the future value and performance of the company. Some analysts also use a multiple based on a one-year projected annual earnings' parameter typically forecasted by investing banking houses that follow the company.

EXERCISE 70:   Discounts for lack of marketability/liquidity can be applied to 100 percent controlling interests in a company such as LEGGO.

    a. True
    b. False

ANSWER: a. True

There is continuing controversy about whether discounts for lack of marketability/liquidity should be applied to controlling interests, particularly 100 percent controlling interests as we have in LEGGO. Some analysts believe that a 100 percent interest is marketable and no discount would apply. Other analysts believe that it depends on the underlying methodology used to derive the prediscount value. For example, when using valuation multiples or rates of return derived from public company data, the rates of return, or multiples, reflect the fact that the public stock can be sold in a very short amount of time, typically receiving cash within three days. You cannot sell a company and receive cash within three days. These analysts believe that the underlying method assumes such marketability or liquidity, which does not exist in a controlling interest in a private company. Thus, some level of discount may be appropriate. There are no known studies to determine discounts for lack of marketability/liquidity of a 100 percent controlling interest in a business. Many analysts rely on discount for lack of marketability studies for minority interests and subjectively reduce the discount to reflect the 100 percent control.

EXERCISE 71: Which discounts for lack of marketability studies, models or data are typically relied on in determining discounts?

    a. Mergerstat Review
    b. Restricted stock studies
    c. IPO studies
    d. Court cases
    e. Flotation costs
    f. MCAPM
    g. Ibbotson Associates
    h. Quantitative Marketability Discount Model (QMDM)

ANSWER: b. Restricted stock studies
              c. IPO studies
              e. Flotation costs
              h. QMDM

Analysts typically rely on restricted stock studies, which compare restricted or letter stocks to their publicly traded counterparts, and to IPO studies, which look at the value of companies within a few months of when they went public. Flotation costs are sometimes looked at when valuing much larger companies. However, they assume that the company is an IPO candidate. QMDM is the Quantitative Marketability Discount Model, which looks at holding periods for investments for minority interests in closely held companies. It is a present-value technique that has gained increased acceptance at the current time, although usually in conjunction with other studies. *Mergerstat Review* reports control premiums; MCAPM is the model for deriving discount rates; and Ibbotson contains data for calculating risk premiums. Court cases will indicate discounts for lack of marketability, but they are very fact- and circumstance-specific and should seldom be relied on in determining discounts. Knowledge of court cases can be important, but they should not be used as the primary method for discounts.

EXERCISE 72: Although we are valuing a 100 percent controlling interest in LEGGO, there are numerous other levels of ownership interests that can exist in a closely held company. Provide some examples of other levels of ownership.

ANSWER: 100 percent ownership
              Less than 100 percent ownership but greater than majority
              Majority interest
              Operating control
              Two 50 percent interest

Largest minority block of stock
Minority with swing vote
Minority can elect board member
Pure minority (no control rights)

Each of these may have a different discount for lack of control and/or lack of marketability/liquidity.

EXERCISE 73: A discount for lack of marketability/liquidity should be applied to all of the valuation methods used in the valuation of LEGGO.

    a. True
    b. False

ANSWER: b. False

As previously mentioned, the Capitalized Cash Flow Method and the Guideline Public Company Method are based on securities that can be sold with cash received within three days. This does not exist for LEGGO. As such, a small discount for lack of marketability/liquidity, subjectively derived and based on judgment, may be appropriate. In the application of the transaction databases, the transaction prices already reflect any potential discount for lack of marketability. No discount is applied. A 100 percent control interest may be marketable but it is not liquid.

EXERCISE 74: Which method can be used to correlate and reconcile value?

    a. Straight average of the indications of value
    b. Numerical weights assigned to each of the value indications
    c. Qualitative judgment in selection of value
    d. All of the above

ANSWER: d. All of the above

In correlating and reconciling values, many analysts simply average all of the indications of value. This implies that each method has equal weight, validity, and accuracy. This is seldom the case in a business valuation, including the situation here with LEGGO. Other analysts will assign weights to each of the methods, such as 0.5 to the income approach, 0.2 to the guideline public company approach, 0.1 to transactions, and so on. However, this may again imply accuracy that does not exist. Also, if you are only putting a 10 percent weight on a method, you may be indicating that the method may not be very accurate. In the valuation of LEGGO, the analyst looked at each one of the methodologies and decided that the income approach was the most relevant. The analyst believes that the other methods support that value.

ADDENDUM: DISCOUNT CASE STUDY EXERCISES

EXERCISE A: Assume that we are determining the fair market value of a minority nonmarketable interest in a company for gift tax purposes. The minority marketable value derived by various methods is $100 per share. We are in a state where you need over 50 percent for full control. What is the relative discount for lack of marketability (DLOM) in these situations?

    a. Value of a 10 percent interest with one 90 percent owner
    b. Value of a 10 percent interest with nine other 10 percent owners
    c. Value of a 50 percent interest with one other 50 percent owner
    d. Value of a 33.33 percent interest with two other 33.33 percent owners
    e. Value of a 2 percent interest with two 49 percent owners

ANSWER: a. This is a typical minority ownership with very few rights. The 90 percent owner has full control, and, absent any shareholder oppression or dissenting rights issues, can pretty much do what he or she wants concerning the direction of the company, including selling the company and distributions. The 10 percent owner is almost completely at the mercy of the 90 percent owner.

      b. This is a much better situation than "a," since no one has control. A 10 percent owner would need to team up with five other owners to control the company. As such, they have more potential for influence than the situation in "a."

      c. In owning a 50 percent interest with one other 50 percent owner, each owner possesses veto power. Although he or she cannot do anything without agreement of the other owner, he or she can veto anything the other owner does. This is a better situation than in "a" or "b." There would still be a discount for lack of control and marketability, but not as great as in "a" and "b."

      d. In this situation there is more ability to influence the company since a one-third owner would only have to team up with another one-third owner. There is some risk that two one-third owners could collaborate on the direction of the company.

      e. This is the classic situation of swing value. Each one of the owners may be willing to couple with the 2 percent owner to direct the company. However, there are many situations where there are two major owners of a company with a small minority share where the two major owners collaborate. This may not necessarily be to the benefit of the small minority owner. The value of a 2 percent interest may go up when the two 49 percent owners are in a dispute.

EXERCISE B: Again, assume we are determining the fair market value of a company for gift tax purposes. In this case study we are valuing a 100 percent controlling interest on a stand-alone basis in a closely held company. What is the discount for lack of marketability in these situations where the prediscount value is determined by using:

a. P/E ratios from control transactions information (i.e., Pratt's Stats)
b. P/E ratios from guideline public companies
c. Discounted cash flow (DCF) with a discount rate determined using Ibbotson information
d. Capitalized cash flow method
e. Asset approach

ANSWER: a. Many analysts believe that the application of control transaction information results in a value that already reflects the marketability of the company. This is because most control transactions are of private companies.

b. Many analysts believe that when using P/E ratios from public companies, the marketability and liquidity of the public company stocks are inherent in the multiples when applied to a private company. That level of liquidity does not exist, even for a 100 percent interest. In those situations, many analysts will take a discount for lack of marketability based on the DLOM studies for minority interests, which are then subjectively reduced.

c. This is similar to "b." Since the discount rate is determined using Ibbotson information based on publicly traded company rates of return, they too, reflect much greater marketability and liquidity than exists in a 100 percent controlling interest in a private company. Some subjectively determined level of discount may be appropriate.

d. Same situation for capitalized cash flow as for DCF when using Ibbotson information.

e. When valuing a company through an asset approach, the marketability of the asset is included in the individual values of those assets. A discount for lack of marketability may be appropriate, since selling an entire company may be more difficult than selling individual assets. Some analysts will apply some level of discount, again usually based on DLOM studies based on minority interests reduced for the 100 percent controlling interest being valued.

Financial Valuation: Applications and Models, Companion Exercises and Test Questions

This chapter comprises exercise and test questions taken from the book, *Financial Valuation: Applications and Models, Second Edition.* You should read the book, answer the questions, and then proceed to the Answer Grid of this chapter. Good luck! The reader should note that questions are grouped according to chapter and similar subject matter but do not necessarily follow the chapter order of *FVAM*.

CHAPTER 1: INTRODUCTION TO BUSINESS VALUATION

Note: Select the best answer(s) from the list of multiple choice questions. Some multiple choice questions have only one correct answer and some have several correct answers. Do not assume each question has only one correct answer. Circle the correct answer(s) for each question.

1. Which of the following is/are a purpose of a valuation?
   a. Income tax
   b. Divorce
   c. Corporate planning
   d. Litigation
   e. Going-concern value
   f. Fair market value

2. Which of the following is/are considered a type of interest in a business that can be valued?
   a. 100% control
   b. 50% interest with one other 50% owner
   c. Minority
   d. Majority without control
   e. Minority with control

3. Articles of incorporation and bylaws are seldom useful in determining value.
   a. True
   b. False

4. Name the five organizations that have adopted the International Glossary of Business Valuation Terms.

   1. _____

   2. _____

   3. _____

   4. _____

   5. _____

5. Relying on the wrong standard of value can result in a very different value.
   a. True
   b. False

6. Which of the following is/are considered standards of value?
   a. Investment value
   b. Actual value
   c. Intrinsic value
   d. Going-concern value
   e. Fair market value
   f. Fair value (state rights)
   g. Fair value (financial reporting)
   h. Liquidation value

7. Treasury regulations and Revenue Rulings define fair market value.
   a. True
   b. False

8. Which of the following is/are components of the fair market value definition?
   a. Willing buyer
   b. Most probable price
   c. Not under compulsion
   d. Control
   e. Willing seller
   f. Knowledge of relevant facts
   g. Normalization adjustments
   h. Lack of marketability

9. Fair market value is the standard of value in divorce.
   a. True
   b. False

10. Investment value is the value:
    a. To a particular investor
    b. To a hypothetical investor
    c. In the marketplace
    d. In tax valuations

11. SFAS 141 and 142 require which standard of value?
    a. Fair market value
    b. Fair value (financial reporting)
    c. Fair value (state rights)
    d. Investment value

12. All states have the same definition of fair value (state rights).
    a. True
    b. False

13. The SEC sets the standard of value for financial reporting.
    a. True
    b. False

14. Which of the following statements is/are true?
    a. Fair value (financial reporting) assumes a hypothetical buyer and seller.
    b. Fair market value assumes a hypothetical buyer and seller.
    c. Fair value (state rights) assumes a hypothetical buyer and seller.

15. Investment value always assumes that the investor has control.
    a. True
    b. False

16. Which of the following is/are considered a premise of value?
    a. Intrinsic value
    b. Going-concern value
    c. Orderly-liquidation value
    d. Depreciated value
    e. Fair market value
    f. Fair value
    g. Forced-liquidation value

17. The intangible elements that result from factors such as having a trained work-force, an operational plant, and the necessary licenses, systems, and procedures in place is/are considered in what premises of value?
    a. Fair value (financial reporting)
    b. Fair market value
    c. Orderly-liquidation value
    d. Going-concern value

18. Investment value and intrinsic value are the same.
    a. True
    b. False

19. Forced liquidation value assumes an instant sale on the date of the valuation.
    a. True
    b. False

20. Which of the following statements is/are true?
    a. Price and cost equal value.
    b. Value is based on what a business's profits and cash flows are historically.
    c. Value is forward-looking, so a discounted cash flow method using expected projected cash flows must be used.

21. The valuation date is/are which of the following?
    a. The date the report is signed.
    b. The date the analysis is finished.
    c. The effective date of the valuation.
    d. The date the report is sent to the client.

22. Which of the following is/are approaches to value?
    a. Guideline public company
    b. Transactions
    c. Discounted cash flow
    d. Capitalized cash flow
    e. Excess cash flow
    f. Income
    g. Market
    h. Asset

23. Which of the following statements is/are true?
    a. All valuation approaches must be considered.
    b. All valuation approaches must be applied.
    c. All valuation methods must be applied.
    d. Indications of value should be averaged.
    e. There are four main approaches to value.

24. The income approach is always the preferred approach in valuing a business.
    a. True
    b. False

25. In valuing a business, most analysts agree that only facts known or knowable at the valuation date should be considered.
    a. True
    b. False

CHAPTER 2: RESEARCH AND ITS PRESENTATION

Note: Select the best answer(s) from the list of multiple choice questions. Some multiple choice questions have only one correct answer and some have several correct answers. Do not assume each question has only one correct answer. Circle the correct answer(s) for each question.

1. Which of the following statements concerning research is/are true?
    a. Analysts should start with a plan.
    b. 10-Ks of public companies are good sources of industry information.

    c. The author and publisher of information is not important as long as the information is good.

    d. Trade associations are poor sources of information since they are biased.

2. Name five major sources of information for business financial databases.

    1. _____

    2. _____

    3. _____

    4. _____

    5. _____

3. Which of the following is/are external factors that can affect value?
    a. Interest rates
    b. Inflation
    c. Management competence
    d. Product or service diversification
    e. Technological changes
    f. Dependence on natural resources
    g. Inventory controls
    h. Legislation

4. The green book contains economic information through reports from interviews with key business professionals, economists, and so on.
    a. True
    b. False

5. Which of the following is/are important considerations in industry research?
    a. Growth prospects
    b. Dominant economic traits
    c. Competitive forces
    d. Potential change
    e. Profitability
    f. Regulations

6. Which of the following is/are sources for transaction information?
    a. Pratt's Stats
    b. Public company 10-Ks
    c. RMA
    d. Bizcomps
    e. Done Deals
    f. S & P Compustat
    g. Troy
    h. IBA
    i. Mergerstat

7. EDGAR stands for electronic disclosure government analysis and retrieval.
    a. True
    b. False

8. Which of the following statements concerning EDGAR is/are true?
   a. Contains information on thousands of companies.
   b. Includes more private companies than public companies.
   c. Established by the department of justice.
   d. All eligible companies must file on EDGAR unless they receive hardship exemption.

9. Industry and economic research is informative but is seldom relied on in actually supporting values.
   a. True
   b. False

10. A "canned" management questionnaire should not be used in a valuation.
    a. True
    b. False

CHAPTER 3: FINANCIAL STATEMENT AND COMPANY RISK ANALYSIS

Note: Select the best answer(s) from the list of multiple choice questions. Some multiple choice questions have only one correct answer and some have several correct answers. Do not assume each question has only one correct answer. Circle the correct answer(s) for each question.

1. Which of the following is/are considered elements of valuation analysis?
   a. An estimation of the amount of future economic benefit
   b. Assessment of risk
   c. An assessment of the probability that projected future economic benefits will be realized

2. Which of the following is/are steps in financial statement analysis?
   a. Industry comparisons
   b. Ratios
   c. Common sizing
   d. Spreading
   e. Normalizing
   f. Key-person discount
   g. Excess compensation
   h. Perquisites
   i. Nonoperating assets
   j. Taxes
   k. Customer concentration

3. Only audited statements can be relied on in a valuation.
   a. True
   b. False

4. CPA analysts must take responsibility for the financial statements relied on in a valuation even if they did not prepare them.
   a. True
   b. False

5. Analysts should spread five years of historical financial statements.
   a. True
   b. False

6. Which of the following statements concerning financial statement adjustments is/are true?
   a. Historical statements are used to help predict future performance.
   b. Historical statements should not be adjusted if they are GAAP statements.
   c. Historical statements help analysts understand a company but are not helpful in projecting future performance.
   d. Adjustments are made to better reflect true operating performance.
   e. Historical statements should enable a company to compare itself over time.
   f. Historical statements should enable a company to compare to industry peer data.

7. Which of the following is/are considered normalization adjustments?
   a. Unusual items
   b. Lack of marketability
   c. Nonoperating assets
   d. Control
   e. Nonconformance with GAAP
   f. Extraordinary items
   g. Change in accounting principles
   h. Nonrecurring items

8. Which of the following is/are considered unusual, nonrecurring, or extraordinary items?
   a. Gain or loss on a sale of a business unit or assets
   b. Losses
   c. High profits
   d. Interest income on operating cash
   e. Capital expenditures exceeding depreciation in any one year

9. Which of the following is/are typical nonoperating assets?
   a. Excess compensation
   b. Boat
   c. Condo
   d. Excess working capital
   e. Raw land not currently used
   f. Art
   g. Excess cash

    h. Planes

    i. Autos used in the business

    j. Antiques

    k. Cash reserves for bonding

10. Changing from LIFO to FIFO is normal so it is not considered a change in accounting principles.

    a. True

    b. False

11. The *Gross, Heck, Adams,* and *Wall* tax court cases opined that:

    a. You tax affect S corporations.

    b. You do not tax affect S corporations.

    c. Facts and circumstances dictate whether you tax affect S corporations or not.

    d. You tax affect S corporations because the IRS Appeals Officer Manual says to do so.

12. A change to a company's capital structure is considered a control adjustment.

    a. True

    b. False

13. Which of the following is/are true concerning common sizing normalized financial statements?

    a. They provide insight into a company's historical operating performance.

    b. They facilitate an assessment of relationships between and among certain accounts.

    c. They identify trends or unusual items.

    d. They can be used to make comparisons to public companies or industry data.

14. Review Exhibits 3.4 through 3.9 and comment on any perceived trends for Ale's. Also, review these schedules and comment on any factors that may need to be considered in a valuation of Ale's.

_____

_____

_____

_____

_____

_____

_____

_____

_____

15. Which of the following statements is/are true regarding financial ratios and ratio analysis?
    a. They are the most commonly used tools in financial analysis.
    b. They do little to help us understand the future prospects of a company.
    c. They include such groupings of ratios as liquidity, performance, profitability, leverage, and growth.
    d. They provide a quantitative method for calculating rates of return.
    e. Risk Management Association (RMA) calculates ratios based on year-end versus average beginning- and ending-year balances.
    f. Time series analysis compares a specified company's ratios to other companies or industry benchmarks.
    g. Cross-sectional analysis compares a company's ratios over a specified historical time period.

16. It doesn't matter whether you compare year-end ratios with information based on average beginning- and ending-year data.
    a. True
    b. False

17. Analysts should be familiar with how benchmark industry ratios are calculated, their scope as well as limitations in the data.
    a. True
    b. False

18. Review Exhibits 3.10 through 3.12 and comment on any perceived trends for Ale's. Also, review these schedules and comment on any factors that may need to be considered in a valuation of Ale's.

    _____

    _____

    _____

    _____

    _____

    _____

    _____

    _____

    _____

19. Which of the following is/are considered specific company risk assessment models?
    a. Porter
    b. McKinsey 7-S
    c. Macroenvironmental

    d. SWOT
    e. Normalization
    f. Ibbotson
    g. Mergerstat
    h. RMA

20. The DuPont model considers which factors?
    a. Current ratio
    b. Working capital turnover
    c. Growth
    d. Profit margins
    e. Asset turnover
    f. Leverage

CHAPTER 4: INCOME APPROACH

Note: Select the best answer(s) from the list of multiple choice questions. Some multiple choice questions have only one correct answer and some have several correct answers. Do not assume each question has only one correct answer. Circle the correct answer(s) for each question.

1. The income approach is probably the most widely recognized approach in business valuation.
    a. True
    b. False

2. An investment in the equity of a company will compensate the investor for which of the following factors?
    a. The time the funds are committed
    b. Inflation
    c. Uncertainty
    d. Risk
    e. The time value of money

3. The income approach has a numerator and a denominator.
    a. True
    b. False

4. Which of the following statements is/are true concerning the income approach?
    a. It is forward looking.
    b. Value is equal to future cash flow discounted at the opportunity cost of capital.
    c. Economic benefit is always cash flow.
    d. Investor expectations include the real rate of return, inflation, and risk.
    e. Net cash flow is net income after tax plus depreciation.

5. Name the three income approach methods.
   1. _____
   2. _____
   3. _____

6. The excess cash flow method is a hybrid of both the income approach and the asset approach.
   a. True
   b. False

7. CPA analysts must attest to and verify any financial information they rely on.
   a. True
   b. False

8. Normalizing adjustments result in a control value when using the income approach.
   a. True
   b. False

9. Which of the following categories is/are considered normalizing adjustments in the income approach?
   a. Ownership characteristics
   b. Taxes
   c. Marketability
   d. Key person
   e. Extraordinary, nonrecurring, and unusual items
   f. Nonoperating assets and liabilities
   g. Synergies if applicable
   h. Trapped capital gains taxes
   i. Information access and reliability

10. Which of the following, when applicable, is/are considered control adjustments?
    a. Excess fringe benefits
    b. Nonbusiness expenses
    c. Related-party transactions at arm's length
    d. Purchases from a sister company owned by the same person
    e. Perquisites

11. The discount rate determines whether the application of the income approach results in a minority or control value.
    a. True
    b. False

12. Normalization adjustments are typically made pretax.
    a. True
    b. False

13. Which of the following is/are examples of potential nonoperating assets?
    a. Plane
    b. Boat
    c. Expensive cars
    d. Adjacent vacant land with no plans for future use
    e. Unsold and unused excess plant facilities

14. There is no adjustment to the income statement for unused raw land since it does not produce income.
    a. True
    b. False

15. Fair market should always include synergistic value.
    a. True
    b. False

16. In many small companies, income and cash flow are the same or similar.
    a. True
    b. False

17. Only cash flow can be discounted or capitalized in the income approach.
    a. True
    b. False

18. Concerning net cash flow, which of the following statements is/are true?
    a. It is the most common measure of future economic benefit.
    b. It is equivalent to dividends or distributions paid.
    c. It is the measure that most rate-of-return data is based on.
    d. It should be used only in the direct equity method, not the invested capital method.

19. List the six components of net cash flow to equity.
    1. _____
    2. _____
    3. _____
    4. _____
    5. _____
    6. _____

20. Net cash flow direct to equity is a debt-inclusive model.
    a. True
    b. False

21. List the five components of net cash flow to invested capital.
    1. _____
    2. _____
    3. _____

　　4. _____

　　5. _____

22. Net cash flows to invested capital include interest expense and debt principal.
　　a. True
　　b. False

23. List the five most common methodologies by which to estimate future economic benefits from historical data.
　　1. _____
　　2. _____
　　3. _____
　　4. _____
　　5. _____

24. Company A has the following historical normalized cash flows: 20x5(most recent year) $500,000; 20x4 $480,000; 20x3 $400,000; 20x2 $200,000; 20x1 $380,000. Calculate the simple average, a weighted average, and the trend line-static method. Which result gives the best indication of anticipated future cash flows? Explain your answer.
　　a. Simple average _____
　　b. Weighted average _____
　　c. Trend line-static method _____
　　d. Current cash flow _____
　　e. Best indication _____
　　f. Explanation _____

　　_____

　　_____

　　_____

　　_____

　　_____

　　_____

　　_____

　　_____

　　_____

25. Discounted cash flow (DCF) models should use five years of projections.
　　a. True
　　b. False

26. In a DCF model, the period beyond the projected discrete period is called the explicit period.
　　a. True
　　b. False

27. Which of the following statements concerning DCF models is/are true?
    a. For companies that have fairly even cash flows throughout the year, the midyear convention is generally preferred.
    b. Some analysts believe that the end-of-year convention better reflects when dividends/distributions are paid.
    c. The midyear convention may not be as applicable in a seasonable business.
    d. The midyear convention generally results in a value similar to discounting monthly cash flows.

28. The terminal value in a DCF model is often the majority of the value.
    a. True
    b. False

29. The Gordon Growth model can be used in a capitalized cash flow (CCF) model or a DCF model.
    a. True
    b. False

30. Which of the following statements is/are true regarding the excess cash flow model?
    a. The return on net tangible assets should be the debt rate after tax.
    b. Revenue Ruling 68–609 states that the excess earnings method should always be used in valuing a business.
    c. There is no direct method for determining the cap rate to capitalize excess cash flow into intangible asset/goodwill value.
    d. The cap rate developed in the capitalized cash flow method can be used to check the values and returns in the excess cash flow method.

CHAPTER 5: COST OF CAPITAL AND RATES OF RETURN

Note: Select the best answer(s) from the list of multiple choice questions. Some multiple choice questions have only one correct answer and some have several correct answers. Do not assume each question has only one correct answer. Circle the correct answer(s) for each question.

1. The cost of capital is an expected rate of return that the market requires to attract funds to a particular investment.
   a. True
   b. False

2. The cost of capital depends on the investor, not the investment.
   a. True
   b. False

3. Which of the following statements concerning cost of capital is/are true?
   a. It is an opportunity cost.
   b. It involves the principle of substitution.
   c. It is investor-driven.

    d. It is market-driven.
    e. It includes risk.
    f. It includes a real rate of return.
    g. It excludes inflation.
    h. Cost of capital equals discount rate.
    i. It equals expected rate of return, which is expected dividends/distributions plus expected capital appreciation.

4. Which of the following is/are cost of capital methods?
    a. Buildup
    b. Modified capital asset pricing model
    c. Capital asset pricing model
    d. Weighted average cost of capital
    e. Price-to-earnings
    f. Excess earnings
    g. Specific company risk

5. Discount rate equals capitalization rate plus growth.
    a. True
    b. False

6. Long-term growth rates are used in both the DCF and CCF models.
    a. True
    b. False

7. Which of the following factors is/are typically considered in determining growth rates?
    a. Subject company historical growth
    b. Subject company projected growth as prepared by management
    c. Industry growth
    d. Inflation
    e. Gross domestic product
    f. Analyst judgment

8. Which of the following factors is/are considered a risk category in the cost of capital?
    a. Maturity risk
    b. Lack of marketability
    c. Minority
    d. Systematic
    e. Unsystematic

9. Systematic risk can be captured by beta.
    a. True
    b. False

10. Investors cannot diversify unsystematic risk away.
    a. True
    b. False

11. The calculation of unsystematic risk is subjective.
    a. True
    b. False

12. Which of the following factors is/are primary sources of unsystematic risk?
    a. Size
    b. Lack of marketability
    c. Minority
    d. Industry (non beta)
    e. Specific company attributes

13. Which of the following resources is/are sources of size equity risk premiums for a discount rate?
    a. Mergerstat
    b. Ibbotson
    c. Duff & Phelps
    d. Emory
    e. FMV Opinions

14. Which of the following is/are considered macroenvironmental forces?
    a. Economic
    b. Technological
    c. Company strengths
    d. Company weaknesses
    e. Company opportunities
    f. Company threats
    g. Sociocultural
    h. Demographic
    i. International
    j. Political

15. Name the five main industry-related risk factors according to Michael E. Porter.
    a. Threat of new entrants
    b. Bargaining power of suppliers
    c. Bargaining power of customers
    d. Company strengths
    e. Industry strengths
    f. Threat of substitutes
    g. Company threats
    h. Rivalry among existing firms

16. Which of the following factors is/are considered potential risks particular to a small business?
    a. Key person
    b. Thin management
    c. Access to financing
    d. Industry
    e. Economic
    f. Lack of marketability

g. Minority

h. Lack of diversification

17. List the four components of a buildup method formula for computing equity returns for a small private company. Include the formula inputs and the actual name. Exclude the industry risk premium.

a. _____

b. _____

c. _____

d. _____

18. The risk-free rate is typically based on a 10-year U.S. treasury bond.

a. True

b. False

19. Which of the following size premiums and/or type of data can be considered based solely on Ibbotson information?

a. Micro-cap NYSE and equivalent ASE and NASDAQ companies

b. 10th decile NYSE and equivalent ASE and NASDAQ companies

c. Ten A NYSE and equivalent ASE and NASDAQ companies

d. Ten B NYSE and equivalent ASE and NASDAQ companies

e. Based on in excess of CAPM with a monthly beta

f. Based on in excess of CAPM with an annual beta

g. Based on in excess of CAPM with sum beta

h. Average return on the market (large stocks) minus the average return on micro-cap stocks since 1926

20. Some analysts include the Ibbotson industry risk premium in the modified CAPM but not the buildup model.

a. True

b. False

21. Ibbotson and Duff & Phelps data can be used to determine specific company risk.

a. True

b. False

22. Which of the following statements concerning Ibbotson data is/are the general position of Ibbotson concerning its data?

a. It is based on after-tax cash flows from the entities.

b. It is based on minority returns.

c. Discount rates are neutral as to minority or control.

d. Going back to 1926 is more preferable than shorter periods.

e. It is based on earnings' returns.

f. Industry risk premiums can be used in MCAPM but not CAPM.

23. In a perfect world, all securities would fall on the securities market line and the return reflects risk (beta).

a. True

b. False

24. Which two components is/are in the MCAPM but not the CAPM?
    1. _____
    2. _____

25. What is the only difference between MCAPM and buildup?
    a. _____

26. All betas are calculated the same so it doesn't matter which source of betas you use.
    a. True
    b. False

27. Given the formula for unlevering a beta (Bu) and using the following information, calculate the levered beta for the subject company.
    From guideline public company data:
    - Levered beta is 1.4.
    - Tax rate is 40 percent.
    - Market value capital structure is 35 percent debt, 65 percent equity.
    For the subject company:
    - Tax rate is 36 percent.
    - Market value capital structure is 20 percent debt, 80 percent equity.
    - $Bu = Bl / [1 + (1-t) (Wd/We)]$.

28. Given the following information, calculate the weighted average cost of capital (WACC) for the subject company.
    Wd = 30%
    We = 70%
    Rf = 6%
    RPm = 7%
    RPs = 6%
    RPu = 3%
    Relevered beta = 1.2
    Tax rate = 40%
    Kd/pt = 8%

29. Which of the following factors concerning the price-to-earnings (P/E) method is/are true?
    a. It is based on public company multiples.
    b. It is pretax.
    c. When inverted, the P/E ratio is a capitalization rate.
    d. The capitalization rate is an earnings rate, not a cash flow rate.
    e. It includes assumptions of growth.

30. Which of the following statements concerning the Duff & Phelps (formerly Standard & Poors and PricewaterhouseCoopers) is/are true?
    a. It includes eight different measures of size.
    b. It allows for 25 magnitudes of size for the companies in the data.
    c. It includes both public and private company data.

d. It goes back to 1963, not 1926 like Ibbotson.
e. It includes risk measures including operating margin, coefficient of variation in operating margin, and coefficient of variation of return on equity.

CHAPTER 6: MARKET APPROACH AND SUPPLEMENTAL STATISTICS

Note: Select the best answer(s) from the list of multiple choice questions. Some multiple choice questions have only one correct answer and some have several correct answers. Do not assume each question has only one correct answer. Circle the correct answer(s) for each question.

1. The use of statistics in valuation replaces qualitative judgment.
    a. True
    b. False

2. Statistics can be used in the following areas of valuation:
    a. Calculation of market multiples of public companies
    b. Picking market multiples of public companies
    c. Determining the effect of one variable on another variable
    d. Determining averages

3. Which of the following is/are considered an average?
    a. Mean
    b. Mode
    c. Median
    d. Correlation
    e. Regression
    f. R squared

4. Which of the following statements is/are true?
    a. Correlation analysis summarizes the strength of the relationship between factors.
    b. Correlation coefficients (r) are between 0 and 1.
    c. An (r) of 0 denotes no relationship.
    d. Regression analysis (linear) shows how to predict one of the variables using the other one.
    e. Coefficient of determination says how much of the variability of Y is explained by X.
    f. R squared stands for regression analysis.

5. Guideline companies generally have the following traits in the market approach:
    a. They are in the same or similar industry.
    b. They are the same in size.
    c. They should not be more than 10 times the revenue size of the subject company.
    d. They should have similar capital structures.
    e. They should have similar profit margins.

    f. They must be publicly traded.

    g. Sufficient information should exist for the guideline company for it to be used as a primary value indicator.

6. Which of the following is/are market approach methods?
   a. Guideline public companies
   b. Guideline company transactions
   c. Excess earnings
   d. Rules of thumb
   e. Subject company transactions
   f. Subject company acquisitions

7. Guideline company transactions are control values.
   a. True
   b. False

8. The application of the guideline public company method results in a control value.
   a. True
   b. False

9. Which of the following statements is/are true concerning the guideline company transaction method?
   a. It results in a nonmarketable value.
   b. It results in a liquid value.
   c. It results in a nonliquid value.
   d. The result is a value assuming the marketability of the guideline companies that were acquired.

10. Which of the following statements is/are true concerning the guideline public company method?
    a. It results in a marketable value.
    b. It results in a nonmarketable value.
    c. It results in a liquid value.
    d. It results in a nonliquid value.
    e. The result is a value assuming the marketability of the guideline public companies' stock.

11. The application of the market approach includes intangible assets and goodwill to the extent they exist.
    a. True
    b. False

12. The market approach is forward looking.
    a. True
    b. False

13. The price of a public company stock includes anticipated growth.
    a. True
    b. False

14. Name the five major sources of transaction data.
    1. _____
    2. _____
    3. _____
    4. _____
    5. _____

15. Which of the following statements is/are true concerning the guideline company transaction method?
    a. It generally relies on numerous known details about the transactions.
    b. It can include acquisitions of both public and private companies.
    c. Only P/E multiples are valid.
    d. Noncompete agreements are excluded.
    e. All the expenses are normalized.
    f. It is important to distinguish whether the transaction is an asset or stock deal.

16. The guideline company transaction method is generally a better method than the guideline public company method when valuing very small businesses.
    a. True
    b. False

17. You should always consider the guideline public company method when valuing any company.
    a. True
    b. False

18. The level of detailed information is the same for the guideline public company method and the guideline company transaction method.
    a. True
    b. False

19. Which of the following statements concerning the guideline public company method is/are correct?
    a. The prices of the stocks should be on or near the valuation date.
    b. The financial statement data of the public companies must match the date of the stock prices.
    c. Only audited statements of the public companies should be used.

20. 10-Ks and 10-Qs of public companies are audited.
    a. True
    b. False

21. Which of the following statements is/are true concerning the selection process for guideline public companies?
    a. Management of the subject company is often a good source for companies.
    b. Management often thinks its company is unique.
    c. If a small division of a diversified public company is the only part of that public company that is similar to the subject company, it should be used as a guideline company.

    d. Industry publications and websites can be good sources for potential guideline companies.

    e. After industry similarities, size is often the next most important selection criteria.

22. Low volume and/or infrequent trades may indicate that a public company's stock price may not be indicative of value.
    a. True
    b. False

23. It is better to have a larger number of guideline public companies that are only somewhat similar than a small number that are more similar.
    a. True
    b. False
    c. Based on facts and circumstances

24. Examine Exhibit 6.10 and determine the comparability of the subject company to the guideline public companies. Assume all are similar in terms of the industry. Decide how you would apply multiples based on these comparisons: specific companies, mean, median, percentiles, averages with fundamental discount, and so on. Write your comments below.

_____

_____

_____

_____

_____

_____

_____

_____

_____

25. Which of the following financial information periods can be used in calculating guideline public company multiples?
    a. Trailing four quarters
    b. Most recent fiscal year end
    c. Three-year average
    d. Five-year average
    e. One-year forecast

26. List the two main numerators for deriving market multiples:

_____

_____

27. Which of the following multiples is/are correct?
    a. MVEq/net income after tax
    b. MVEq/pretax income
    c. MVIC/net income after tax
    d. MVIC/pretax income
    e. MVEq/book value of equity
    f. MVIC/EBITDA
    g. MVIC/EBIT
    h. MVIC/revenue
    i. MVIC/debt-free net income after tax

28. Rules of thumb are often a primary method for determining value.
    a. True
    b. False

29. Negative multiples should be relied on.
    a. True
    b. False

30. Based on your comparisons from Exhibit 6.10, choose multiples and values for the subject company based on the multiples presented in Exhibits 6.11 and 6.12. Again, assume all the guideline companies are equally similar based on the industry. Write your results below.

_____

_____

_____

_____

_____

_____

_____

_____

_____

CHAPTER 7: ASSET APPROACH

Note: Select the best answer(s) from the list of multiple choice questions. Some multiple choice questions have only one correct answer and some have several correct answers. Do not assume each question has only one correct answer. Circle the correct answer(s) for each question.

1. Which of the following statements is/are true concerning the asset approach?
   a. Book value equals fair market value.
   b. Book value balance sheets are often the starting point for the asset approach.

c. The asset approach does not include intangible assets.

d. Book value seldom equals fair market value.

2. Some asset book values on the balance sheet are often similar to fair market value.
   a. True
   b. False

3. Unless purchased as part of a transaction, intangible assets are usually not on the books.
   a. True
   b. False

4. Which of the following statements concerning the asset approach is/are true?
   a. The asset approach should be considered in every business valuation.
   b. The asset approach is more commonly applied in valuing operating companies that sell products and/or services.
   c. The asset approach is more commonly used in valuations for financial reporting purposes.
   d. The book value of real estate is usually pretty close to fair market value.
   e. The asset approach is sometimes used in valuing very small companies and/or professional practices where there is little or no company or practice intangible assets and goodwill value.
   f. When valuing a business, valuing intangible assets in an operating company is common and provides increased accuracy for the valuation conclusion.

5. Revenue Ruling 59–60 ignores the asset approach.
   a. True
   b. False

6. Control and minority issues are not a concern in applying the asset approach.
   a. True
   b. False

7. Notes to financial statements can contain useful information about contingent liabilities.
   a. True
   b. False

8. Which of the following statements is/are true concerning real estate and equipment appraisal?
   a. Market value equals fair market value in real estate appraisal.
   b. The income approach is often used in real estate but not equipment appraisal.
   c. The cost approach is the most common approach in real estate appraisal.

9. As in business valuation, there are three approaches to value for real estate and equipment appraisal.
   a. True
   b. False

10. Economic obsolescence reflects the fact that an asset is not earning a required rate of return.
    a. True
    b. False

CHAPTER 8: VALUATION DISCOUNTS AND PREMIUMS

Note: Select the best answer(s) from the list of multiple choice questions. Some multiple choice questions have only one correct answer and some have several correct answers. Do not assume each question has only one correct answer. Circle the correct answer(s) for each question.

1. The two main discounts are the discount for lack of marketability (DLOM) and the discount for lack of control (DLOC).
    a. True
    b. False

2. The DLOC and the minority discount are the same.
    a. True
    b. False

3. When applying the DLOM and the DLOC, you should add them together and then apply the aggregated discount.
    a. True
    b. False

4. DLOCs are derived from control premium studies.
    a. True
    b. False

5. Which of the following statements is/are true concerning discounts and premiums?
    a. They are either entity-level or shareholder-level.
    b. They must all be applied sequentially.
    c. DLOMs and DLOCs are applied to all valuation methods.

6. Control premiums:
    a. Are based on public company acquisitions.
    b. Include synergistic or strategic premiums when present.
    c. Quantify the value of controlling the destiny of a company.

7. Which of the following statements is/are true?
    a. Control often means a lesser or no DLOM.
    b. DLOMs for control and minority are the same since a DLOM only reflects the lack of marketability of the entire company.
    c. There is no relationship between DLOCs and DLOMs.

8. Control adjustments to earnings/cash flow:
   a. Should be made in every valuation.
   b. Are often made when valuing a controlling interest.
   c. Are made before applying a control premium.

9. A 50 percent/50 percent ownership arrangement contains which of the following rights?
   a. Swing vote
   b. Cumulative voting
   c. Veto power
   d. Right of first refusal

10. All other things being equal, in the same company, which of the following 25 percent interest is worth relatively more (i.e., would have lesser discounts)?
    a. Four–25 percent interests
    b. One–25 percent interest with one 75 percent interest
    c. Two–25 percent interests with one 50 percent interest
    d. 25 percent interests with no other shareholder holding more than 10 percent

11. A greater than 50 percent interest always gives full control.
    a. True
    b. False

12. When the interest being valued represents a minority position, nonvoting stock is generally valued the same or slightly less than voting stock.
    a. True
    b. False

13. Minority and lack of control discounts is/are derived from which of the following sources?
    a. Court cases
    b. Mergerstat Review data
    c. Thin air
    d. Restricted stock studies

14. The formula for calculating a DLOC from control premium data is:
    a. 1 divided by control premium
    b. 1 divided by (1 + control premium)
    c. 1 minus {1 divided by (1 + control premium)}
    d. (1 divided by control premium) times 100

15. Mergerstat data allows the analyst to segregate the pure control premium and the synergistic/acquisition premium.
    a. True
    b. False

16. Which of the following valuation methodologies result(s) in a control value where the cash flows have been adjusted for control items?
    a. Discounted cash flow method
    b. Guideline company transaction method

    c. Guideline public company method
    d. Capitalized cash flow method

17. Which of the following statements is/are true?
    a. Public stock is marketable.
    b. Public stock is liquid.
    c. Minority stock is marketable.
    d. Minority stock is liquid.
    e. 100 percent control is marketable.
    f. 100 percent control is liquid.

18. There is direct empirical evidence supporting a DLOM for a controlling interest.
    a. True
    b. False

19. Which of the following studies can be relied on when selecting DLOMs?
    a. Restricted stock
    b. Quantitative marketability discount model (QMDM)
    c. Initial public offering
    d. Emory
    e. Willamette
    f. Hitchner
    g. Revenue Ruling 77–287
    h. Revenue Ruling 50–60

20. Which of the following statements is/are true concerning the Emory studies?
    a. They include transactions of a company within 12 months of an IPO.
    b. They include failed IPOs.
    c. They include only stock option transactions.
    d. They are adjusted to reflect the rise or fall of a company's stock price after the IPO.
    e. Discounts have typically been in the range of 60 percent to 65 percent.

21. Which of the following statements is/are true concerning restricted stock studies?
    a. They include only publicly traded companies.
    b. They are based on control transactions of a company's stock.
    c. Stocks are restricted for two years in all the studies.
    d. Recent studies have resulted in lower average discounts.

22. Which restricted stock study reports results by major SIC?
    a. Management Planning
    b. Silber
    c. FMV Opinions
    d. Columbia Financial Advisors

23. Which of the following factors is/are considered in the QMDM?
    a. Control value of the stock
    b. Expected holding period

   c. Required rate of return over the holding period

   d. Expected dividend payments

24. Name at least five factors that can affect the marketability of a minority interest in a private business.

   1. _____

   2. _____

   3. _____

   4. _____

   5. _____

25. Which of the following tax court cases is/are famous for the method used to select a DLOM?

   a. *Branson*

   b. *Mandelbaum*

   c. *Sheffield*

   d. *Weinberger*

26. Some discounts are applied after the prediscount value is determined, and some are incorporated into the cost of capital in the income approach or the multiples in the market approach.

   a. True

   b. False

27. Which of the following is/are discounts that can be considered in a valuation?

   a. Key person

   b. Restrictive agreement

   c. Information access and reliability

   d. Trapped capital gains

   e. Blockage

   f. Market absorption

   g. Small company

   h. Lack of diversification

28. It is generally acceptable to take the average of various DLOM studies and apply that average to the subject company.

   a. True

   b. False

29. Dr. Mukesh Bajaj et al. have provided further support for the typical averages in the IPO and restricted stock DLOM studies.

   a. True

   b. False

30. A private company that pays substantial dividends/distributions would generally have a lesser DLOM than the same company that pays little or no dividends/distributions.

   a. True

   b. False

CHAPTER 9: REPORT WRITING

Note: Select the best answer(s) from the list of multiple choice questions. Some multiple choice questions have only one correct answer and some have several correct answers. Do not assume each question has only one correct answer. Circle the correct answer(s) for each question.

1. Reports must be prepared for every valuation.
   a. True
   b. False

2. Reports must contain sufficient detail to allow another qualified analyst to re-create or replicate the work.
   a. True
   b. False

3. Which of the following factors should be included in a report?
   a. What the analyst was asked to do
   b. The fee
   c. Standard of value
   d. Information relied on
   e. Names of all people who worked on the engagement
   f. Procedures that were performed
   g. Assumptions and limiting conditions
   h. Conclusion and reconciliation

4. Which of the following types of reports is/are allowed by the Uniform Standards of Professional Practice (USPAP) for a business valuation?
   a. Appraisal report
   b. Summary appraisal report
   c. Restricted use appraisal report
   d. Limited appraisal report
   e. Other appraisal report

5. All valuation analysts are required to adhere to the reporting requirements of USPAP in every engagement.
   a. True
   b. False

6. Outside of USPAP, analysts generally produce two types of reports, complete and other.
   a. True
   b. False

7. Which of the following sections is/are generally included in a complete valuation report?
   a. Summary
   b. Introduction

   c. Sources of information
   d. Analysis of the business
   e. Economic conditions
   f. Industry conditions
   g. International economic and industry outlook
   h. Relationships amongst the owners
   i. Financial statement analysis

8. Revenue Ruling 59–60 contains detailed reporting requirements.
   a. True
   b. False

9. Which of the following factors is/are often considered in the analysis of industry conditions section of a report?
   a. Identity of the industry
   b. Description of the industry
   c. Suppliers
   d. Government regulations
   e. Marketability of the companies that make up the industry
   f. Key person issues
   g. Risks

10. The financial statement analysis should include at least five years of financial statement information.
   a. True
   b. False

11. Reports should include a quantitative method of reconciling various values derived by different valuation methods.
   a. True
   b. False

12. The AICPA requires CPA valuation analysts to attach a valuation certification.
   a. True
   b. False

13. Which of the following statements is/are true concerning disclosure in a report?
   a. Analysts should report on assurance services provided.
   b. If assurance services were not provided, the analyst must present a limited appraisal and summary report.
   c. It is improper to rely on financial statements provided by others.

14. Summary or letter reports should not be relied on by clients.
   a. True
   b. False

15. Which of the following statements concerning assumptions and limiting conditions is/are true?
    a. They can reduce the risk to the analyst.
    b. They inform the reader of what the analyst did and did not do.
    c. They should not be provided in valuation reports prepared in a litigation setting.

CHAPTER 10: BUSINESS VALUATION STANDARDS

Note: Select the best answer(s) from the list of multiple choice questions. Some multiple choice questions have only one correct answer and some have several correct answers. Do not assume each question has only one correct answer. Circle the correct answer(s) for each question.

1. Name the four major U.S. associations that grant certifications in valuation:
   a. AICPA, ASA, IBA, CFA
   b. AICPA, ASA, CFE, CFA
   c. AICPA, NACVA, IBA, ASA
   d. AICPA, IBA, NACVA, CFA

2. CPAs are required to follow the Uniform Standards of Professional Practice (USPAP).
   a. True
   b. False

3. The IRS has recently adopted USPAP.
   a. True
   b. False

4. Name the two operating boards of the Appraisal Foundation.
   a. Appraiser Ethics
   b. Appraiser Qualifications
   c. Appraiser Examinations
   d. Appraiser Standards
   e. Appraiser Sanctions
   f. Appraiser Education

5. Which of the following organizations has/have adopted the International Glossary of Business Valuation Terms?
   a. AICPA
   b. AIMR
   c. NACVA
   d. IBA
   e. CICBV
   f. IRS
   g. ASA
   h. Appraisal Foundation

6. Business valuation appraisers must abide by the specific standards for real estate and personal property in their business valuations.
   a. True
   b. False

7. USPAP Standard Rule 3, Review Appraisal, is applicable only to real estate and personal property appraisers.
   a. True
   b. False

8. Which of the following statements concerning USPAP is/are true?
   a. There are 10 standards rules.
   b. Statements on Appraisal Standards are only for explanatory purposes and do not have the weight of a standards rule.
   c. Advisory opinions are for explanatory purposes only and do not have the weight of a standards rule.
   d. Standards 9 and 10 address development and reporting for business valuation.
   e. The preamble, ethics rule, competency rule, departure rule, jurisdictional exception rule, and the supplemental standards affect business appraisers.

9. The IRS has business valuation guidelines.
   a. True
   b. False

10. The SEC has issued SFAS 141 and 142 for financial reporting purposes in regard to allocations of purchase price, business combinations, and goodwill impairment.
    a. True
    b. False

CHAPTER 11: VALUATION ISSUES IN PASS-THROUGH ENTITIES

and

CHAPTER 24D: VALUATION ISSUES IN PREFERRED STOCK

and

CHAPTER 24E: RESTRICTED STOCK VALUATION

and

CHAPTER 24G: STOCK OPTIONS

Note: Select the best answer(s) from the list of multiple choice questions. Some multiple choice questions have only one correct answer and some have several correct answers. Do not assume each question has only one correct answer. Circle the correct answer(s) for each question.

1. The biggest issue in valuing pass-through entities is taxes.
   a. True
   b. False

2. Which of the following Tax Court cases disallowed the application of taxes at the entity level?
   a. *Gross*
   b. *Wall*
   c. *Mandelbaum*
   d. *Jelke*
   e. *Adams*
   f. *Heck*

3. There is less controversy concerning the application of taxes in control valuations versus minority valuations.
   a. True
   b. False

4. In valuing a pass-through entity, the level of distributions can affect value.
   a. True
   b. False

5. Valuing a pass-through entity by capitalizing pretax cash flows at a pretax capitalization rate results in an after-tax value.
   a. True
   b. False

6. Which of the following statements concerning preferred stock is/are true?
   a. It is a hybrid security.
   b. Dividend rate is the yield rate.
   c. It can be cumulative or noncumulative.
   d. If redeemable, it is considered solely as an equity security.
   e. Preferred stock is never voting since it is not common stock.
   f. It can be convertible into common stock.
   g. It can contain put options or features.

7. Which of the following Revenue Rulings directly address(es) the valuation of preferred stock?
   a. 59-60
   b. 68-609
   c. 83-120
   d. 93-12
   e. 77-287

8. Which of the following factors should be considered when valuing preferred stock?
   a. Yield
   b. Lack of control
   c. Lack of marketability

    d. Dividend coverage

    e. Liquidation preferences

9. Given the following information, calculate the value of the preferred stock using the dividend discount model:

    Par value = $100

    Stated rate = $6

    Required yield = 10%

    _____

    _____

    _____

10. Employee stock options can be incentive stock options or nonqualified stock options.

    a. True

    b. False

11. Options that can be exercised only on the expiration date are called American options.

    a. True

    b. False

12. Which of the following statements is/are true concerning stock options?

    a. Call options give the holder the right to buy the stock.

    b. Put options give the holder the right to sell the stock.

    c. Exercise price typically changes over time.

    d. "In the money" occurs when an option's strike price is less than the current price of the underlying stock.

    e. "Out of the money" options can never have value.

13. Name the two best-known option models.

    1. _____

    2. _____

14. There is never a discount for lack of marketability of a stock option in a private company.

    a. True

    b. False

15. Which of the following factors is/are considered when applying the Black-Scholes option model?

    a. Underlying stock price

    b. Lack of control

    c. Exercise price

    d. Volatility

    e. Time to expiration

    f. Risk-free rate

16. Volatility has a great impact on the value of a stock option.
    a. True
    b. False

17. Binomial models are sometimes referred to as lattice models.
    a. True
    b. False

18. Which of the following Revenue Rulings directly address(es) the valuation of restricted stock?
    a. 59-60
    b. 68-609
    c. 83-120
    d. 93-12
    e. 77-287

19. Restricted stocks are typically stocks in public companies that are restricted from public trading for a period of time.
    a. True
    b. False

20. Which of the following statements is/are true concerning restricted stocks?
    a. All the companies in the restricted stock studies had a two-year holding period.
    b. Rule 144 restrictions no longer apply.
    c. Volume limitations under Rule 144 include a restriction that no more than 1.0 percent of the outstanding shares of stock can be sold during any three-month period.
    d. Volume limitations under Rule 144 include a restriction that no more than the average weekly market trading volume in such securities during the four calendar weeks preceding a sale of stock can be sold during any three-month period.
    e. Dribble-out periods should be considered in valuing restricted stock.

CHAPTER 12: ESTATE, GIFT, AND INCOME TAX VALUATIONS

Note: Select the best answer(s) from the list of multiple choice questions. Some multiple choice questions have only one correct answer and some have several correct answers. Do not assume each question has only one correct answer. Circle the correct answer(s) for each question.

1. Revenue Ruling 59-60 is applicable only to tax valuations.
    a. True
    b. False

2. Revenue Ruling 59-60 addresses the concept of a key person.
    a. True
    b. False

3. Which of the following statements is/are included in Revenue Ruling 59-60?
   a. Use common sense, judgment, and reasonableness.
   b. Valuation must be based on the facts available at the required date of appraisal.
   c. Consider at least five years of income statements and two years of balance sheets.
   d. Valuation of securities is a prophecy as to the future.
   e. Valuation reflects the degree of optimism or pessimism of investors.
   f. The appraiser should include subsequent events after the appraisal date.

4. Which of the following statements is/are true regarding fair market value for tax purposes?
   a. Assumes a hypothetical buyer only
   b. Assumes a hypothetical seller only
   c. Assumes both a hypothetical buyer and seller
   d. Assumes specific buyers and sellers
   e. Assumes the most likely buyer and seller

5. Revenue Ruling 59-60 does not address excess compensation and its potential effect on value.
   a. True
   b. False

6. Which of the following statements concerning Revenue Ruling 59-60 is/are true?
   a. It requires reliance on historical averages of earnings.
   b. It is silent concerning intangible assets and goodwill and their value.
   c. It addresses the concept of control and minority.
   d. It gives consideration to the value of similar publicly traded company stock.

7. Revenue Ruling 59-60 presents standard capitalization rates.
   a. True
   b. False

8. Name the four main Revenue Rulings in valuation.
   a. 48-220
   b. 83-120
   c. 77-287
   d. 98-254
   e. 59-60
   f. 93-12
   g. 69-609

9. The IRS has adopted USPAP.
   a. True
   b. False

10. Which of the following statements concerning the definition of fair market value is/are true?
    a. Most likely buyer
    b. Willing buyer

    c. Willing seller

    d. Same knowledge of relevant facts

    e. No compulsion

11. Which of the following statements is/are most true regarding court cases?

    a. They can be used to determine discounts.

    b. They should not be used to determine discounts.

    c. They are informative only as to the court's view on discounts.

    d. They should be quoted in valuation reports.

12. Revenue Ruling 59-60 supports the use of the asset approach for valuing investment or holding companies.

    a. True

    b. False

13. Averaging the values from different methods is endorsed by Revenue Ruling 59-60.

    a. True

    b. False

14. Which of the following statements is/are true regarding Revenue Ruling 77-287?

    a. It can be used to determine discounts for lack of marketability for closely held stock.

    b. It can be used to value restricted stock.

    c. It can be used to value preferred stock.

    d. It replaces Revenue Ruling 68-609.

15. Revenue Ruling 93-12 addresses family attribution for gift and estate tax.

    a. True

    b. False

16. What is the single most important court case dealing exclusively with discounts for lack of marketability?

    a. *Lappo*

    b. *Mandelbaum*

    c. *Jelke*

    d. *Perachio*

17. The IRS has business valuation guidelines.

    a. True

    b. False

18. Which of the following statements is/are true regarding Revenue Ruling 83-120?

    a. It expands on Revenue Ruling 59-60.

    b. It discusses yield, dividend coverage, and liquidation preferences.

    c. It addresses "freeze" transactions.

    d. It applies only to public companies.

    e. It is no longer relevant with the issuance of Revenue Ruling 93-12.

19. The IRS has regulations regarding the valuation of charitable contributions of closely held stock, including a definition of a qualified appraiser.
    a. True
    b. False

20. Which was one of the first tax court cases to allow a reduction in value due to trapped-in capital gains taxes?
    a. *Lappo*
    b. *Mandelbaum*
    c. *Jelke*
    d. *Davis*

CHAPTER 13: VALUATION OF FAMILY LIMITED PARTNERSHIPS

and

CHAPTER 24B: VALUATION ISSUES IN BUY-SELL AGREEMENTS

Note: Select the best answer(s) from the list of multiple choice questions. Some multiple choice questions have only one correct answer and some have several correct answers. Do not assume each question has only one correct answer. Circle the correct answer(s) for each question.

1. Which of the following statements is/are true concerning family limited partnerships (FLPs)?
    a. Discounts can be taken for more than 50 percent limited partner interests.
    b. Discounts can be taken only for less than 50 percent limited partner interests.
    c. The general partner interest can never be discounted.
    d. The partnership agreement is not considered in setting discounts.
    e. Discounts cannot be taken if there are high cash distributions.
    f. No discounts can be taken if the FLP holds only liquid marketable public securities.

2. The partnership agreement provisions concerning limited partner rights are not allowed to be considered in valuing an interest in an FLP.
    a. True
    b. False

3. Which of the following factors is/are included in Chapter 14?
    a. Taxation of certain transfers of corporate and partnership interests
    b. Sections 2701, 2702, 2703, and 2704
    c. Impact of buy-sell agreements
    d. Lapsing rights
    e. Applicable restrictions

4. Which of the following statements concerning section 2703 and buy-sell agreements is/are true?
    a. They are bona fide business arrangements.
    b. They must include a formula for valuation.

    c. They are not devices to transfer property for less than full and adequate consideration.

    d. Terms are comparable to similar arrangements entered into by persons in arm's-length transactions.

5. FLPs are typically valued using the asset approach.
    a. True
    b. False

6. FLPs that hold marketable securities are discounted using mutual fund data.
    a. True
    b. False

7. Which of the following is/are typically relied on when determining discounts for limited partner interests in an FLP that holds marketable securities and real estate?
    a. Revenue Ruling 59-60
    b. The Partnership Spectrum
    c. Morningstar closed-end funds
    d. Restricted stock studies
    e. Pre-IPO studies

8. Closed-end fund information is always used to determine the DLOM of a limited partner interest in an FLP.
    a. True
    b. False

9. There is some marketability in the sales of partnerships from Partnership Profiles.
    a. True
    b. False

10. There is instant marketability/liquidity when using closed-end fund data.
    a. True
    b. False

11. In tax valuations, values in buy-sell agreements are:
    a. Determinative of value for gift tax purposes
    b. Determinative of value for estate tax purposes
    c. Only a consideration for gift and estate tax purposes
    d. Determinative for value for estate tax purposes and a consideration of value for gift tax purposes

12. What are the names of the three types of buy-sell agreements?
    a. Restrictive, hybrid, cross-purchase
    b. Hybrid, restrictive, repurchase
    c. Hybrid, repurchase, cross-purchase
    d. First refusal, restrictive, hybrid

13. Buy-sell agreements should be customized for each company.
    a. True
    b. False

14. Which of the following statements is/are true concerning buy-sell agreements?
    a. The greater the selling restrictions, the greater the possible impact on a DLOM.
    b. They should include the standard of value and a definition of the standard of value.
    c. Discounted values are not acceptable for tax purposes.
    d. Funding of a buyout should be excluded.

15. Buy-sell agreements are not typically legal agreements under state law.
    a. True
    b. False

CHAPTER 15: SHAREHOLDER DISPUTES

and

CHAPTER 16: VALUATION ISSUES IN ESOPS

Note: Select the best answer(s) from the list of multiple choice questions. Some multiple choice questions have only one correct answer and some have several correct answers. Do not assume each question has only one correct answer. Circle the correct answer(s) for each question.

1. For dissenting stockholder suits, the standard of value and its definition are the same for each state.
    a. True
    b. False

2. Which of the following is/are typically shareholder disputes under state statutes?
    a. Dissenting shareholder
    b. Gift tax
    c. Estate tax
    d. Minority oppression
    e. Income tax
    f. ESOPs

3. Which of the following standards of value is/are the standard(s) of value for shareholder disputes under state statutes?
    a. Fair market value
    b. Investment value
    c. Intrinsic value
    d. Fair value
    e. Going concern value
    f. Orderly liquidation value

4. Fair value equals fair market value.
    a. True
    b. False

5. Which state(s) is/are the most influential in the area of dissenting rights nationally?
   a. Pennsylvania
   b. Texas
   c. Delaware
   d. Rhode Island
   e. California
   f. Georgia

6. In the dissenting shareholder area, all states do not allow discounts for minority interest and lack of marketability.
   a. True
   b. False

7. The ultimate responsibility for obtaining an accurate valuation in an ESOP is the appraiser.
   a. True
   b. False

8. Every valuation in an ESOP must fulfill the regulations of both the IRS and the Department of Labor.
   a. True
   b. False

9. Which of the following statement(s) is/are true regarding ESOPs?
   a. Adequate consideration is the fair market value of the asset as determined in good faith by the trustee or named fiduciary.
   b. The analyst preparing the valuation must be independent of all parties to the transaction.
   c. ESOPs create greater liquidity for an ownership interest in a closely held company.
   d. ESOPs can own stock in C corporations only.
   e. Adequate consideration means that the ESOP cannot pay less than fair market value.
   f. Most ESOPs have put provisions that allow greater liquidity.
   g. ESOPs provide favorable tax treatment.
   h. Discounts for lack of marketability are not allowed because of put provisions.

10. Analysts should consider repurchase liabilities when considering the value of a company's shares pursuant to an ESOP.
    a. True
    b. False

CHAPTER 17: VALUATION IN THE DIVORCE SETTING

and

CHAPTER 18: VALUATION ISSUES IN SMALL BUSINESSES

and

CHAPTER 19: VALUATION ISSUES IN PROFESSIONAL PRACTICES

Note: Select the best answer(s) from the list of multiple choice questions. Some multiple choice questions have only one correct answer and some have several correct answers. Do not assume each question has only one correct answer. Circle the correct answer(s) for each question.

1. Fair market value is the standard of value in all states in divorce actions.
   a. True
   b. False

2. Which of the following statements is/are true concerning goodwill in a divorce valuation?
   a. All states allow goodwill value.
   b. All states allow entity goodwill but not personal goodwill.
   c. Generally, state case law will determine whether personal goodwill is considered a marital asset.
   d. Personal goodwill is usually more difficult to transfer than entity goodwill.
   e. In many professional practices and very small businesses, it is not unusual that personal goodwill makes up the majority of goodwill value.

3. Noncompete agreements completely protect the transfer of personal goodwill.
   a. True
   b. False

4. Which of the following is/are considered factors about the professional that can be considered in determining the amount of personal goodwill in a professional practice?
   a. Age and health
   b. Reputation
   c. Types of clients and services
   d. Source of new clients
   e. Location and demographics

5. Divorce courts never aggregate family interests since this violates the concept of hypothetical buyer and seller.
   a. True
   b. False

6. Small businesses tend to be highly dependent on their owner.
   a. True
   b. False

7. Which of the following is/are generally characteristics of small businesses?
   a. They have less access to capital.
   b. Their cost of borrowing is higher.
   c. There is a need for personal guarantees by owner.
   d. They have audited financial statements.

   e. They contain discretionary owner items.

   f. Only the guideline company transaction method of the market approach is valid.

   g. They have a higher failure rate.

   h. They may not contain any entity goodwill value.

   i. Guideline public company method of the market approach is never a valid method.

   j. Rules of thumb, particularly from business brokers, should be rejected for consideration.

8. Discretionary earnings are usually defined as earnings before interest, taxes, depreciation, and amortization and one owner's compensation.
   a. True
   b. False

9. In preparing a reasonableness test for the value of a small business, which of the following is/are typical financing assumptions?
   a. 25 percent to 30 percent down payment.
   b. Seller financing.
   c. Repayment over 10 years.
   d. Owner must stay for at least three years.
   e. All-cash deals.

10. Analysts should consider all three approaches to value when valuing an interest in a professional practice.
    a. True
    b. False

CHAPTER 21: VALUATION OF INTANGIBLE ASSETS

Note: Select the best answer(s) from the list of multiple choice questions. Some multiple choice questions have only one correct answer and some have several correct answers. Do not assume each question has only one correct answer. Circle the correct answer(s) for each question.

1. Goodwill is an intangible asset.
   a. True
   b. False

2. The standard of value for the valuation of intangible assets is fair market value.
   a. True
   b. False

3. Intangible assets receiving legal protection are often referred to as intellectual property.
   a. True
   b. False

4. Which of the following is/are major categories of intangible assets as defined by the Financial Accounting Standards Board (FASB)?
   a. Marketing related
   b. Customer related
   c. Artistic related
   d. Contract based
   e. Technology based
   f. Assembled workforce

5. Rates of return on many intangible assets are generally higher than rates of return on tangible assets.
   a. True
   b. False

6. Fair value is the same for financial reporting and dissenting rights actions.
   a. True
   b. False

7. SFAS 141 addresses business combinations including allocating the purchase price to intangible assets.
   a. True
   b. False

8. SFAS 142 addresses the treatment of intangible assets and goodwill and how to test them for impairment.
   a. True
   b. False

9. Goodwill must be amortized over its estimated life.
   a. True
   b. False

10. Indefinite-life intangibles cannot be valued separately and are included in goodwill.
    a. True
    b. False

11. Which of the following statements is/are true regarding goodwill impairment?
    a. If necessary, it is a two-step process.
    b. Step 2 requires the valuation of all intangible assets as if the reporting unit was just acquired and purchase accounting applied.
    c. There is no impairment if carrying value is less than fair value.
    d. Fair value assumes a market participant in a hypothetical transaction.
    e. It is calculated after SFAS 144 impairments.

12. Intangible assets are generally valued after tax.
    a. True
    b. False

13. The amortization tax benefit recognizes the value of the tax shield as a result of the 15-year tax amortization of most intangible assets and goodwill.
    a. True
    b. False

14. Goodwill typically has the highest rate of return assigned to it.
    a. True
    b. False

15. Which of the following statements is/are true regarding the valuation of intangible assets for financial reporting?
    a. Net cash flows attributable to a specific intangible assets must be after returns on other contributory assets, both tangible and intangible.
    b. Returns on contributory assets are pretax.
    c. FASB Concept 7 presents two present-value approaches, the expected cash flow approach and the traditional approach.
    d. IPR&D is not an intangible asset since it is written off, not amortized.

16. The amount of value to be allocated under SFAS 141 is the purchase price paid for the invested capital of a business.
    a. True
    b. False

17. Where applicable and feasible, the income approach is often the preferred approach in valuing intangible assets.
    a. True
    b. False

18. The three approaches to value should be applied in the valuation of any intangible asset.
    a. True
    b. False

19. Internally used software not for resale is often valued using the cost approach.
    a. True
    b. False

20. Individual returns on assets can be reconciled to the company's weighted average cost of capital.
    a. True
    b. False

CHAPTER 1: INTRODUCTION TO BUSINESS VALUATION

1. a, b, c, d
2. a, b, c, d
3. b
4. American Institute of Certified Public Accountants
   American Society of Appraisers
   Canadian Institute of Chartered Business Valuators
   Institute of Business Appraisers
   National Association of Certified Valuation Analysts
5. a
6. a, c, e, f, g
7. a
8. a, c, e, f
9. b
10. a
11. b
12. b
13. b
14. b
15. b
16. b, c, g
17. d
18. b
19. b
20. none
21. c
22. f, g, h
23. a
24. b
25. a

CHAPTER 2: RESEARCH AND ITS PRESENTATION

1. a, b
2. Bloomberg
   Dialog Corporation PLC
   Factiva
   Lexis Nexus
   OneSource
3. a, b, e, f, h
4. b

5. a, b, c, d, e, f
6. a, b, d, e, h, i
7. b
8. a, d
9. b
10. b

CHAPTER 3: FINANCIAL STATEMENT AND COMPANY RISK ANALYSIS

1. a, b, c
2. a, b, c, d, e
3. b
4. b
5. b
6. a, d, e, f
7. a, c, d, e, f, g, h
8. a
9. b, c, d, e, f, g, h, j
10. b
11. b
12. a
13. a, b, c, d
14. –total assets, total liabilities, and total equity have increased each year
    –they have made capital expenditures each year
    –revenues and gross profit up each year
    –EBITDA and operating income up each of last 4 years with a dip from the first to second year
    –officers compensation up 500,000 or one-third increase over the 5 year period
    –steady use of liabilities
    –gross margin steady
    –some fluctuation in operating income margin (low of 2.5 percent to high of 4.5 percent; however, margin up each of last 4 years)
    –Ale's seems to be growing although down from year one to two in margin and profits
15. a, c, e
16. b
17. a
18. See addendum of Chapter 3 of *Financial Valuation Applications and Models, Second Edition* for detailed explanation
19. a, b, c, d
20. d, e, f

CHAPTER 4: INCOME APPROACH

1. a
2. a, b, c, d, e
3. a
4. a, b, d

5. discounted cash flow
   capitalized cash flow
   excess cash flow
6. a
7. b
8. b
9. a, b, e, f, g
10. a, b, d, e
11. b
12. a
13. a, b, c, d, e
14. b
15. b
16. a
17. b
18. a, c
19. net income after tax
   plus: depreciation amortization and other noncash charges
   less: incremental working capital needs
   less: incremental capital expenditure needs
   plus: new debt principal in
   less: repayment of debt principal
20. a
21. net income after tax
   plus: interest expense (tax affected)
   plus depreciation amortization and other noncash charges
   less: incremental "debt-free" working capital needs
   less: incremental capital expenditure needs
22. b
23. current earnings
   simple average
   weighted average
   trend line–static
   formal projection
24. a. $392,000
   b. $426,667
   c. $496,000
   d. $500,000
   e. $500,000
   f. 20x2 seems like an aberration. The last three years show growth as well. A management interview would help make the proper selection. A simple average doesn't recognize the upward trend. If an average was used, the weighted average would be better. The trend line-static method recognizes the trend but is based on only five periods. May be okay, though.
25. b
26. b
27. a, b, c, d
28. a
29. a
30. c, d

CHAPTER 5: COST OF CAPITAL AND RATES OF RETURN

1. a
2. b
3. a, b, d, e, f, h, i
4. a, b, c, d, e
5. a
6. a
7. a, b, c, d, e, f
8. a, d, e
9. a
10. b
11. a
12. a, d, e
13. b, c
14. a, b, g, h, i, j
15. a, b, c, f, h
16. a, b, c, h
17. a. Rf risk-free rate
    b. RPm risk premium in the market
    c. RPs risk premium for size
    d. RPu risk premium for unsystematic (specific company) risk
18. b
19. a, b, c, d, e, f, g
20. b
21. b
22. a, b, c, d
23. a
24. 1. Rps
    2. Rpu
25. a. Beta (sometimes RPi—industry risk premium)
26. b
27. 1.23
28. MCAPM = 6% + (1.2 × 7%) + 6% + 3% = 23.4%
    WACC = .3(1−.40) 8% + .7 (23.4%)
    WACC = 17.8%
29. a, c, d, e
30. a, b, d, e

CHAPTER 6: MARKET APPROACH AND SUPPLEMENTAL STATISTICS

1. b
2. b, c, d
3. a, b, c
4. a, c, d, e
5. a, g
6. a, b, d, e, f
7. a
8. b

9. c, d
10. a, c, e
11. a
12. a
13. a
14. Bizcomps
    Done Deals
    Institute of Business Appraisers (IBA)
    Mergerstat
    Pratt's Stats
15. b, f
16. a
17. a
18. b
19. a
20. b
21. a, b, d, e
22. a
23. c
24. See explanation in Chapter 6 of *Financial Valuation Applications and Models, Second Edition*
25. a, b, c, d, e
26. equity, invested capital
27. a, b, e, f, g, h, i
28. b
29. b
30. See explanation in Chapter 6 of *Financial Valuation Applications and Models, Second Edition*

CHAPTER 7: ASSET APPROACH

1. b, d
2. a
3. a
4. a, c, e
5. b
6. b
7. a
8. b
9. a
10. a

CHAPTER 8: VALUATION DISCOUNTS AND PREMIUMS

1. a
2. b
3. b
4. a
5. a
6. a, b, c
7. a

8. b
9. c
10. d
11. b
12. a
13. b
14. c
15. b
16. a, b, c, d
17. a, b, e
18. b
19. a, c, d, e, f
20. none
21. a, d
22. c
23. b, c, d
24. dividend policy
    stock restrictions
    redemption policy
    number of shareholders
    size of block of stock
    state law
25. b
26. a
27. a, b, c, d, e, f, g, h
28. b
29. b
30. a

CHAPTER 9: REPORT WRITING

1. b
2. b
3. a, c, d, f, g, h
4. a, c
5. b
6. a
7. a, b, c, d, e, f, i
8. b
9. a, b, c, d, g
10. b
11. b
12. b
13. a
14. b
15. a, b

CHAPTER 10: BUSINESS VALUATION STANDARDS

1. c
2. b

3. b
4. b, d
5. a, c, d, e, g
6. b
7. b
8. a, c, d, e
9. a
10. b

CHAPTER 11: VALUATION ISSUES IN PASS-THROUGH ENTITIES

and

CHAPTER 24D: VALUATION ISSUES IN PREFERRED STOCK

and

CHAPTER 24E: RESTRICTED STOCK VALUATION

and

CHAPTER 24G: STOCK OPTIONS AND OTHER SHARE-BASED COMPENSATION

1. a
2. a, b, e, f
3. a
4. a
5. a
6. a, c, f, g
7. c
8. a, b, c, d, e
9. $6 \div .10 = $60
10. a
11. b
12. a, b, d
13. Black-Scholes
    Binomial
14. b
15. a, c, d, e, f
16. a
17. a
18. e
19. a
20. c, d, e

CHAPTER 12: ESTATE, GIFT, AND INCOME TAX VALUATIONS

1. b
2. a
3. a, b, c, d, e

4. c
5. b
6. c, d
7. b
8. b, c, e, f
9. b
10. b, c, e
11. b, c
12. a
13. b
14. a, b
15. b
16. b
17. a
18. a, b, c
19. a
20. d

CHAPTER 13: VALUATION OF FAMILY LIMITED PARTNERSHIPS

and

CHAPTER 24B: VALUATION ISSUES IN BUY-SELL AGREEMENTS

1. a
2. b
3. a, b, c, d, e
4. a, c, d
5. a
6. b
7. a, b, c, d, e
8. b
9. a
10. a
11. c
12. c
13. a
14. a, b, c
15. b

CHAPTER 15: SHAREHOLDER DISPUTES

and

CHAPTER 16: VALUATION ISSUES IN ESOPS

1. b
2. a, d
3. d
4. b

5. c
6. b
7. b
8. a
9. a, b, c, f, g
10. a

CHAPTER 17: VALUATION IN THE DIVORCE SETTING

and

CHAPTER 18: VALUATION ISSUES IN SMALL BUSINESSES

and

CHAPTER 19: VALUATION ISSUES IN PROFESSIONAL PRACTICES

1. b
2. c, d, e
3. b
4. a, b, c, d, e
5. b
6. a
7. a, b, c, e, g, h
8. a
9. a, b
10. a

CHAPTER 21: VALUATION OF INTANGIBLE ASSETS

1. a
2. b
3. a
4. a, b, c, d, e
5. a
6. b
7. a
8. a
9. b
10. b
11. a, b, c, d, e
12. a
13. a
14. a
15. a, c
16. b
17. a
18. b
19. a
20. a

CHAPTER 4

ValTips

INTRODUCTION

In the companion book, *Financial Valuations: Applications and Models (FV)*, there are numerous ValTips throughout the chapters of the text that are used to highlight important concepts, application issues, and pitfalls to avoid. We have re-created these ValTips in this chapter with certain modifications to make them presentable on a stand-alone basis. These ValTips are organized and identified by the chapter/section in *FV*.

CHAPTER 1: INTRODUCTION TO FINANCIAL VALUATION

1. Relying on the wrong standard of value can result in a very different value, and, in a dispute setting, the possible dismissal of the value altogether.
2. Although many states use the term *fair market value* in their marital dissolution cases, the definition of fair market value may vary from state to state and will not necessarily be the same definition as in the tax area.
3. Some companies are worth more dead than alive. It is important for the analyst, particularly when valuing an entire company, to determine if the going-concern value exceeds the liquidation value. For a minority interest, there are situations where the going-concern value is less than liquidation value. However, the minority shareholder cannot force a liquidation if the controlling shareholder desires to continue the business as a going concern.
4. Price and cost *can* equal value but do not necessarily *have to* equal value. Furthermore, value is future-looking. Although historical information can be used to set a value, it is the expectation of future economic benefits that is the primary value driver. Investors buy tomorrow's cash flow, not yesterday's or even today's.

CHAPTER 2: RESEARCH AND ITS PRESENTATION

1. Because of the complexity of the data-assembling process, most analysts use checklists that detail the types of information they are seeking. Chapter 8 of this workbook contains many useful checklists. The use of these tools can help ensure that the valuation analyst covers the necessary bases in gathering information.

2. Before looking for information, valuation analysts should have a plan.

3. 10-Ks of public companies often have detailed analyses of the industry.

4. The major information services provide one-stop sources for business and financial data. These services, which include Dialog, Lexis-Nexis, Factiva, OneSource, and Bloomberg, offer extensive collections of periodicals, legal information, and financial data available.

5. If you are looking for a one-stop source for business and financial data, consider one of the major information services. These services, which include such names as Dialog, Lexis-Nexis, Factiva, OneSource, Alacra, Proquest, and Bloomberg, offer the most extensive collections of periodicals, legal information, and financial data available.

6. The analyst will need to consider the key external factors that affect value, such as interest rates, inflation, technological changes, dependence on natural resources, and legislation.

7. The *Beige Book* contains information on current economic conditions in each district, gathered through reports from interviews with key business professionals, economists, and market experts.

8. *Investext Industry Insider™ Trade Association Research* (available online through <u>Investext</u>), is currently the only online collection of trade association research. It includes industry-specific information such as statistics, economic indicators, analyses, trends, forecasts, and surveys.

9. The EDGAR database contains information on thousands of public companies.

10. A common mistake made by inexperienced valuation analysts is to wait until the last minute to do the industry and economic analysis, then drop it into the text without any discussion of how it relates to the valuation conclusion.

CHAPTER 3:   FINANCIAL STATEMENT AND COMPANY RISK ANALYSIS

1. The CPA-analyst must take special care to set expectations in both the engagement letter and the valuation report regarding the degree of responsibility assumed regarding financial statements presented within the report because of accounting standards for attestations, reviews, and compilations.

2. The valuation report should provide substantive commentary regarding methods and ratios chosen and results of the comparative analysis.

3. Analysts should not mix year-end data with beginning and ending year average data when preparing comparisons of the subject company to industry benchmark data and ratios.

4. To use benchmark industry ratios appropriately, analysts must be familiar with their scope and limitations, as well as differences among them regarding data presentation and computation methods.

CHAPTER 4:   INCOME APPROACH

1. Failure to develop the appropriate normalizing adjustments may result in a significant overstatement or understatement of value.

2. By choosing to make certain adjustments to the future economic benefit (i.e., the numerator), the analyst can develop a control or noncontrol value.

3. Normalization adjustments affect the pretax income of the entity being valued. Consequently, the control adjustments will result in a corresponding modification in the income tax of the entity, if applicable.

4. Adjustments to the income and cash flow of a company are the primary determinants of whether the capitalized value is minority or control.

5. When there are controlling interest influences in the benefit stream or operations of the entity and a minority interest is being valued, it may be preferable to provide a minority value directly by not making adjustments. This will avoid the problems related to determining and defending the application of a more general level of minority discount.

6. Depending on the situation, statements prepared on a "tax basis" or "cash basis" may have to be adjusted to be closer to GAAP and/or normalized cash flow.

7. As with the control-oriented adjustments, extraordinary, nonrecurring, or unusual item adjustments affect the profit or loss accounts of a company on a pretax basis. Therefore, certain income tax–related adjustments may be necessary. These types of adjustments are made in both minority and control valuations.

8. Valuing nonoperating assets may involve the expertise of someone who specializes in the valuation of these particular assets, such as a real estate appraiser. Engagement letters should clearly set out these responsibilities and the related appraisal expenses.

9. Synergistic value is investment value, which may not be fair market value.

10. In many small companies, income and cash flow are the same or similar.

11. Cash flows for financial statement purposes are generally not used in business valuations. Because cash flows are normalized to estimate cash flows in perpetuity, specific changes in current assets and liabilities, specific purchases, and specific borrowings and repayments are ignored.

12. There are only four types of analyses for application of the traditional income approach.

	Direct Equity	Invested Capital
CCF	1	2
DCF	3	4

13. Regardless of the method employed, dialogue or information from management can provide critical insight into future projections.

14. Theoretically, the length of the explicit period in the discounted cash flow (DCF) is determined by identifying the year when all the following years will change at a constant rate. Practically, however, performance and financial position after three to five years is often difficult to estimate for many companies. Lesser periods are sometimes used as well.

15. There are circumstances where the past is not indicative of the future. In these situations, care must be exercised in analyzing projected performance. There has to be adequate support for the assumptions on which the projections are based.

16. The valuation analyst uses normalized historical data, management insights, and trend analysis to analyze formal projections for the explicit period of the DCF. These projections may take into account balance sheet and income statement items that affect the defined benefit stream and may involve not only projected income statements but also projected balance sheets and statements of cash flow.

17. The more certain the future streams of cash flow are in a DCF, the more valuable the asset or entity is.

18. The terminal value of a DCF is critically important, since it often represents a substantial portion of the total value of an entity.

19. The value driver method for terminal year calculations can result in a lower terminal value than the Gordon Growth Model.

20. Property (i.e., real estate) also may be segregated from operating tangible assets at the outset and added back later. Rent expense is properly substituted for real estate–related expenses if the decision is to separately value the operating real estate.

21. If the control excess cash flow method is used and a minority value is the interest that is being valued, a discount for lack of control must be determined and applied.

22. Assets that are normally considered operating assets may in reality be non-operating. For example, excess cash and cash equivalents are actually non-operating assets and can be isolated from the operating assets during normalization.

23. The company's lending rate may be different if personal guarantees are required from the company's owners, officers, and depending on the types of assets.

24. Whatever rate of return is used for goodwill in the excess cash flow method, the aggregate return on all assets should approximate the weighted average cost of invested capital for the entity.

CHAPTER 5:   COST OF CAPITAL/RATES OF RETURN

1. Identifying the value drivers of an enterprise and developing action steps to limit or reduce controllable (i.e., internally oriented versus external) risks can be of great benefit to many closely held businesses in terms of their increasing value.

2. The value of a company can be expressed as the present value of all of the future economic benefits that are expected to be generated by the company.

3. Values are reflections of the future, not the past or even the present.

4. In valuing a company, analysts need to estimate sustainable growth into perpetuity, not just short-term growth.

5. Since 1926, the U.S. economy has been able to sustain a nominal growth rate of approximately 6.5 percent over time. This is a combination of the real growth rate and inflation.

6. Overall, the deciding factor in determining how to reflect growth in the rates of return will be informed professional judgment.

7. For publicly held companies, systematic risk is captured by a measurement referred to as the *beta* of the enterprise.

8. It is common to assume a privately held company's beta as 1.0 and develop separate risk factors to include in its overall rate of return calculations, or to use a beta for an industry group or from guideline public companies.

9. The estimation of unsystematic risk is one of the more difficult aspects of calculating rates of return.

10. Every business enterprise will have its own unique attributes and risks, which can be incorporated into the rate of return.

11. There is no direct source for returns on 20-year Treasury bonds. Analysts can consult the *Wall Street Journal* to find the quoted market yields on 30-year bonds with approximately 20 years of maturity left. Another source for this data is the St. Louis branch of the Federal Reserve Bank, which maintains an extensive inventory of historical yield rates on all types of government securities, including a continuing proxy for the 20-year constant maturity Treasury bond. This can be found online at www.stls.frb.org/fred/data/irates/gs20.

12. Lists of small-company risk factors can be used to analyze the attributes of a specific subject company and to select the level of adjustment for size and unsystematic risk. It is important, however, to avoid a double counting, since adjustments for size can often implicitly include adjustments for other operating attributes.

13. The authors note that the Ibbotson industry risk data for specific industries, as presented in Chapter Three of the *SBBI* appears to change significantly between annual editions, and therefore, caution that the direct application of an added or subtracted component to the BUM for industry risk remains questionable. An alternate approach is to evaluate the risk premia provided for SIC codes related to the valuation target under consideration and then use such information inferentially to adjust the unsystematic risk component under the premise that industry risk is an element thereof. This is also an important distinction, as well, as when using the industry data directly it is important to eliminate any consideration of industry risks within the unsystematic adjustment.

14. While the amount of industry risk premia data available from Ibbotson Associates is expected to grow over time, many analysts in the valuation community are not yet comfortable with the direct application of industry risk premia adjustments. However, analysts can consider this new empirical evidence where the subject falls within one of the Ibbotson-defined industries and there is a need to assess industry risk that may not be captured in the build-up method.

15. Caution should be used whenever a methodology assigns specific numerical adjustments to various categories of specific company risks in the build-up or CAPM rate. Due to the subjective nature of the numerical assignments for each category, one can easily get trapped upon cross-examination in testimony as to whether it might be considered reasonable for each of the factors to be, say, half a percent higher or lower, thereby causing a significant change in the resulting capitalization or discount rate being developed.

16. The format and content of an analytical framework for analyzing unsystematic risk will vary considerably depending on the nature of the assignment and the depth of analysis required. However, the articulation of the analyst's thought process by use of diagnostic tools can be a means of competitive differentiation, whether the tools are included in the final report or only in engagement work papers.

17. The betas published by different sources can display different results due to differing time periods, methodologies, and adjustments. Therefore, care should be exercised.

18. A good source of information for determining industry capital structures can be found in the Ibbotson Associates *Cost of Capital* publications. If the guideline public company method is being used, the public companies can be a source of capital structure components.

19. Since traditionally derived discount and capitalization rates are cash flow rates, not earnings rates, an upward subjective adjustment would have to be made to convert the rate for application to earnings.

20. It is important to recognize the increasingly "noisy" nature of public company reported valuation multiples including P/E. As indicated in the August 21, 2001, *Wall Street Journal*,[1] many public companies have moved away from using GAAP earnings for the E of the P/E. They may instead utilize other earnings measures, such as operating earnings before extraordinary items, core earnings, and even pro forma earnings. Each of these revised definitions of earnings allows reporting entities to exclude certain one-time, exceptional, special, or noncash expenses, and, in turn, the net income of the enterprise is higher. According to the *Wall Street Journal* article, more than 300 of the 500 entities making up the S&P 500 now exclude some ordinary expenses as defined by GAAP from the operating earnings numbers provided to investors and analysts.

21. Arbitrage pricing theory (APT) is not widely used in business valuation assignments for cost of capital determinations due to the unavailability of usable data for the components of the model.

22. There has been much debate over the merits of the build up summation model. Many analysts have determined that the suggested source of rate adjustments is not empirically grounded and can be misleading, especially with regard to the perceived accuracy of the presentation. However, the detailed list of questions for the various factors can be very useful as an analytical tool and for work paper support.

23. The value from the excess cash flow method should approximate that derived from the capitalized cash flow method since the two rates used with ECF methods should reasonably tie to the rate used in the CCF method.

CHAPTER 6:   MARKET APPROACH

1. The prices paid for businesses and business interests reflect investor expectations. Consequently, any valuation methods that use stock or sale prices of businesses, such as the market approach, must necessarily be prospective in nature.

2. The values derived from both the market and income approaches implicitly include all assets, both tangible and intangible.

3. Implicit in the prices of publicly traded companies and transactions is some assumption about growth. Generally, the higher the expected growth, the higher the value, all else being equal.

4. There are two distinct pools from which guideline company information can be drawn: (1) actual transactions and (2) publicly traded companies.

---

[1] Jonathan Weil, "What's the P/E Ratio? Well, Depends on What Is Meant by Earnings," *Wall Street Journal*, August 21, 2001.

Understanding the value implications of using these different types of data is crucial in properly applying the market approach.

5. When using the market approach to value a very small business and with the right data, the guideline company transaction method may be a better method than guideline publicly traded company analysis.

6. Because detailed information is often not available for transactions, it is difficult to know the structure of the transactions or the motivation of the buyer or seller.

7. Detailed financial statements of acquired companies are usually not available for transactions. Therefore, it is impossible to make certain adjustments to the data underlying the pricing ratios, assuming such adjustments are necessary.

8. When using electronic sources of public company data, the analyst may have to consult the individual companies' filings for the underlying detail. This is not to suggest that adjustments do not have to be made to either of the values to make them truly comparable; rather, the point is that the values in these electronic databases are usually good starting points.

9. There is the perception that public companies are much too large to be used as comps in many situations. While this may be true for the smallest of subject companies, such as mom-and-pop operations, small professional practices, or sole proprietors, there is usually enough size variation among public companies that they should be considered at least for most other valuations.

10. In a recent study of all publicly held companies, 19 percent had sales of $10 million or less for the last 12 months.

11. 14 percent of all public companies have assets of $10 million or less.

12. In a recent study, one-quarter of all public companies have market capitalizations of $36 million or less.

13. Almost one-third of all publicly traded companies lost money for the last 12 months on a net income (after-tax) basis. Only about 30 percent of all U.S. companies had net income profit margins of more than 10 percent.

14. Examining detailed business descriptions of the possible guideline companies is an essential step in the guideline public company analysis. Some data vendors provide good descriptions of a company's business(es); however, they are never more detailed than the data found in a company's 10-K filing.

15. One challenge involved with showing a list of potential guideline public companies to management is that they will often not view any of the companies as comparable, since they believe their company is truly unique. It is unlikely that the market niche into which the subject company fits really appreciates some of the nuances that make the subject truly unique. Unless these nuances result in prospects for the subject that are substantially different from those of the potential guideline companies, these companies can usually be used.

16. One of the most important of comparative indicators is size. Size can be expressed in terms of sales, total assets, or market capitalization. Numerous studies have indicated that smaller companies have lower pricing multiples than larger companies. The main reason is that smaller companies typically have more business and financial risk than large companies.[2]

17. Expected growth is much more important in the determination of value than historical growth.

---

[2] More risk means investors will require a higher rate of return on their investment, and the way to get this is by lowering the price.

18. Another issue is whether trading of a guideline company's stock is sufficiently large to give meaningful and realistic values for that company. While companies with low trading volumes may be very similar to the subject in terms of business and financial characteristics, if their stocks' prices are questionable, there is no point in using the valuation ratios that are based on these prices.

19. The analysts may have to choose between (a) a very small group of companies whose business descriptions are very similar to that of the subject and (b) a larger group of companies with some of the companys' descriptions not as good a match with the subject.

20. Many analysts believe that valuation multiples should not be adjusted for differences in profit margins between the guideline public companies and the subject company. They believe that there may be a double effect by adjusting the multiple downward to reflect the lower margins of the subject company and then applying those lower multiples to that lower profit. They believe the more important criteria is the anticipated growth of those profits.

21. The debt number used in the market approach should be its market value; however, on a practical basis, most analysts simply use the book value of the debt as a proxy for market value.

22. Using percentiles of valuation multiples rather than simple averages or composites has the advantage of providing a range of values and protecting the information from the effects of outliers.

23. It should be noted that when using transactions, there is much less data available. In particular, usually there is no data on which to compute growth rates or long-term margins. This lack of information might limit the confidence in the results obtained from this method.

24. Excess working capital can be determined by comparing the working capital ratio of the subject with those of the guideline companies, or by using industry norms.

25. Making certain adjustments can change the character of the resulting value—many times from a minority to a controlling value.

26. The quality and quantity of publicly traded company information will affect the confidence in the results from the market approach.

27. Whether to use the Market Value of Equity or Market Value of Invested Capital will be a function of the purpose of the valuation, the capital structures of the subject and guideline companies, and the analyst's preference.

28. The term *capital structure* refers to the relationship between the market values of debt and equity—never the book value of equity.

29. In theory, the best denominator to use in a valuation multiple would be one based on expectations—that is, using next year's expected revenues or income. It is an appropriate match with the numerator, since the value of equity or invested capital is a prospective concept, containing the market's best assessment of the prospects for the future.

30. Overall, EBITDA and EBIT multiples tend to be frequent indicators across many industries.

31. Although rules of thumb should seldom be used as the sole way of valuing a business, they do provide some good industry knowledge and investor insight.

32. Negative valuation multiples, which usually arise from losses, are not meaningful and should be ignored.

33. The final determination of which particular pricing multiple(s) to use must be based on an understanding of how the subject compares to the guideline com-

panies in terms of the important factors (i.e., growth, size, longevity, profitability, etc.).

34. The application of market multiples from different databases results in varying types of value (e.g., with or without inventory or working capital).

35. Sometimes large differences between values derived from the income approach and the market approach can be explained by differences in growth assumptions.

CHAPTER 7: ASSET APPROACH

1. *Book value*, which pertains to cost basis accounting financial statements, is not fair market value.

2. The asset approach is sometimes used in the valuation of very small businesses or professional practices where there is little or no goodwill.

3. Although the asset approach can be used in almost any valuation, it is seldom used in the valuation of operating companies. The time and costs involved in valuing individual tangible and intangible assets typically is not justified, because there is little if any increase in the accuracy of the valuation. The value of all tangible and intangible assets is captured, in aggregate, in the proper application of the income and market approaches. In many valuations there is no real need to break out the amount of value associated with individual assets, including goodwill.

4. If the net asset/cost approach is used in valuing a minority interest of a closely held company, the value indication derived will usually have to be adjusted from control to minority and from a marketable to a nonmarketable basis.

5. The notes of the financial statements often contain useful information concerning contingent liabilities.

CHAPTER 8: VALUATION DISCOUNTS AND PREMIUMS

1. Two of the fundamental tools used by valuation professionals are discounts, which reduce the value of interests in closely held businesses, and premiums. which increase the value of those interests.

2. Discounts and premiums may be classified as entity-level or shareholder-level depending on whether the driver for the premium or discount affects the entity as a whole (such as an environmental discount), or whether the driver reflects the characteristics of a specific ownership interest.

3. Control premiums *quantify the value of controlling the destiny of the company*. Acquisition or strategic premiums *quantify the incremental value of a particular investment as viewed by a specific investor*. There is empirical evidence of the size of combined control and strategic premiums. However, these data do not separate the two types of premiums.

4. Lack of control and liquidity are not necessarily separate and distinct entities. A majority shareholder may be able to affect liquidity in ways that a minority shareholder cannot. Pursuing a sale, a merger, or an initial public offering are examples of such situations. Thus, the two discounts should be considered in conjunction with each other.

5. From the point of view of the minority shareholder, the majority shareholder's ability to control gives the majority shareholder the ability to reduce or eliminate the return on the minority shareholder's investment.

6. The quantification of the amount of the minority discount or the discount for lack of control is difficult due to the lack of empirical evidence in this area.

7. The Mergerstat data includes synergistic and acquisition premiums along with the control premium. Segregation of these premiums is difficult.

8. The use of minority cash flows in the income approach produces a minority interest value. Minority cash flows are those cash flows without any adjustments for controlling shareholders, actions such as excess compensation, rent payments, or perquisites.

9. Consistency is important. Whether you start with control cash flows or minority cash flows, it is important to consistently apply this methodology throughout the minority value engagement.

10. Marketability is the term that expresses the relative ease and promptness with which a security or commodity may be sold when desired, at a representative current price, without material concession in price merely because of the goal of a prompt sale.

11. While some experts support a discount, there remains no generally accepted empirical evidence to support a discount for the lack of marketability/liquidity for a controlling interest. Remember that all the initial public offering and restricted stock studies deal with minority interests and not controlling interests.

12. DLOM studies are usually based on two types of analyses:
    1. Studies based on the difference between the initial public offering (IPO) price of a company and transactions in the same company's stock prior to the IPO. These are referred to as IPO studies.
    2. Studies that measure the difference between the private price of a restricted security and the publicly traded stock price of the same company. These are referred to as restricted stock studies.

13. The IRS, in Revenue Ruling 77-287, dealt with the issue of valuing restricted stocks. It was issued ". . . to provide information and guidance to taxpayers, Internal Revenue Service personnel, and others concerned with the valuation, for Federal tax purposes, of securities that cannot be immediately resold because they are restricted from resale pursuant to Federal securities laws."

14. The QMDM represents continued theoretical development of the concept of the marketability discount. Some appraisers have adopted some form of the framework for analyzing discounts that Mercer has presented, but most agree that if used, it should be in conjunction with the use of traditional discount studies.

15. In addition to the discounts for lack of control and marketability, there are several other potential discounts. Some analysts consider these discounts in the calculation of a discount or capitalization factor, while others separately quantify and apply the discounts.

16. Restrictions under certain agreements limit the ability to sell or transfer ownership interests.

17. In valuing a closely held company, an adjustment for information access and reliability may be in order.

18. An ongoing disagreement between the IRS and many tax practitioners revolves around the treatment of the costs related to liquidating the assets in estates.

19. A key person or thin management entity-level discount would be appropriate in the valuation of a closely held company where an owner or employee is responsible for generating a significant portion of the business's sales or prof-

its. This key person may be a revenue generator, possess technical knowledge, or have close relationships with suppliers, customers, banks, and so forth.

20. Blockage discounts are based on the theory that a large block of publicly traded stock cannot ordinarily be sold as readily as a few shares of stock.

21. Blockage or market absorption discounts also can be considered when valuing other assets, such as real estate. In the valuation of a closely held real estate investment holding company, a discount for potential market absorption should be considered.

22. When a smaller closely held company is being compared to a larger publicly traded company, an adjustment for size may be appropriate.

23. Small companies often have limited access to capital, limited ability to weather a market downturn, limited resources to develop and market new products, and so forth. Smaller companies can also have a higher cost of capital than larger companies.

24. Care should be exercised to avoid overlaps or "double discounting" with thin management discounts, small-company risk discounts, lack-of-diversification discounts, or others.

CHAPTER 9: REPORT WRITING

1. A full written report should provide the detail necessary to permit another qualified analyst to use similar information to replicate the work done and the valuation conclusion reached.

2. Although many analysts often comply with the Uniform Standards of Professional Appraisal Practice (USPAP) as a general rule, most of the analysts' report writings are not conducted under the services specified by USPAP for compliance.

3. There are two primary types of valuation reports produced by analysts: "complete" and "other."

4. In certain engagements, such as litigation, the analyst might not be granted access to the facilities. In that event, the introduction section can explain this, and what was done to obtain the knowledge normally gained during a site visit.

5. Financial statement adjustments may be of two different types. Normalizing adjustments convert the statements into economic financial statements. Control adjustments reflect prerogatives of control and adjust the statement to conditions only the control interest may realize.

6. Analysts usually do not audit or perform reviews or any other assurance procedures on the historical financial information provided by the entity. They often accept the information as accurate and state this in the assumptions.

7. Some analysts include the assumptions and limiting conditions in the engagement letter as well as the report.

CHAPTER 10: BUSINESS VALUATION STANDARDS

1. The Internal Revenue Service has not officially adopted USPAP.

2. Terminology used in USPAP standards is not uniform across the professions doing appraising work. For example, USPAP Standard 3 discusses the "review" of other appraisers' work. To certified public accountants (CPAs) doing busi-

ness valuation, the term *review* carries a meaning that is unique to the accounting profession and represents a level of service related to financial statements.

3. The pertinent sections of USPAP for the business appraiser include the preamble, the ethics rule, the competency rule, the departure rule, the jurisdictional exception, and the supplemental standards. Standard 9 covers development of a business appraisal, Standard 10 covers reporting, and Standard 3 covers appraisal review.

4. For CPAs, the word *certify* has special meaning concerning attestation of financial information. Some CPAs will add a sentence in their reports that they are not certifying any financial information but are adhering to the appraisal certification requirements of USPAP. In the proposed business valuation standards of the AICPA, the word *certification* is replaced with *representation*.

5. The FASB provides guidance for how to measure fair value of financial and nonfinancial assets and liabilities under authoritative accounting pronouncements. This fair value measurement is for financial statement purposes and is not to be confused with fair value in dissenting shareholder cases, which are determined according to state laws and court decisions in the respective states.

CHAPTER 11: VALUATION OF PASS-THROUGH ENTITIES

1. The analyst should be aware that there may be differences when approaching the valuation of a controlling versus a minority interest in a pass-through entity. In some circumstances the approach may be the same or at least similar, while other circumstances will dictate a different approach. After taking into consideration the rights and interests being valued, given different ownership rights, analysts may use entirely different approaches. This makes intuitive sense.

2. The vast majority of the discussion of whether there is an S corporation premium or not is focused on the fair market value standard, within the context of estate and gift taxes. Invariably, this should be the same perspective as the marketplace, with a buyer who would consider the benefits that would flow to him or her from ownership of the interest.

3. If each model is applied diligently and with attention to the specific facts relating to the interest in mind, theoretically, one should not arrive at a dramatically different conclusion no matter which model is used.

4. A general trend has emerged from the models and the literature. The trend has been to value the shares from the perspective of the investor; that is, to follow the cash all the way into the investor's pockets. This makes intuitive sense, as we know that investors take taxes into consideration when pricing any investment.

5. Many, if not most, of the reasons why appraisers were saying they were deducting taxes were rejected by the Tax Court. Thus, if analysts are still providing these same reasons for the deduction of income taxes in their valuation reports, then they should either examine their reasoning or better explain why they believe such logic is to be well founded.

6. At the very least, the controlling interest studies initiated the debate about whether tax benefits create value and, if so, at what level. Nearly everyone agrees that tax benefits at the corporate level create shareholder value; however, whether tax benefits enjoyed at the election of the shareholder also create value has been the subject of much debate.

7. C corporations have a greater incentive to bonus-out earnings in order to lower their EBT relative to S corporations. For this reason, the sales multiple is the more reliable measure. Note further that C corporations generally bonus-out salaries, not pay dividends. Although this ability is limited by tax regulations on excessive compensations, this practice contributes to causing the notion of double tax to be more myth than reality.

8. When using market data for transaction pricing for either S or C corporations without understanding the basis for the data, analysts must be careful to consider, at a minimum:

   - Asset or stock sale
   - Assets transacted
   - S or C corporation
   - Size of the transaction
   - Capital structure and liabilities assumed

   Failure to take these factors into consideration when using market data to value a pass-through entity could result in inappropriate valuation conclusions.

9. There is no conclusive market transactional evidence that S corporation values are different from private C corporation values on a control basis. However, if the analyst has used publicly traded C corporation data to value the S corporation, the differences between the expectations of the investor in a public C corporation and a private S corporation should be considered.

10. Some analysts have interpreted Treharne's articles as recommending consideration of all three scenarios for each valuation project. However, Treharne presented the three scenarios solely for the purpose of emphasizing the possible range of value conclusions attributed to the three possible input scenarios. Typically, all three scenarios do not need to be considered in each valuation project.

11. It is important to note that there are still many analysts who prefer simpler, more qualitative methods to valuing S corporations than the models presented here. Assuming a well thought-out analysis, this is acceptable.

12. Each of the four theories considers these issues:

    - Amount and timing of distributions
    - Retained net income
    - Holding period and exit strategy
    - Tax rates—personal, corporate, and capital gains
    - Further effect of minority or marketability discounts
    - Possible ability to participate in step up of basis transaction

CHAPTER 12: ESTATE, GIFT, AND INCOME TAX VALUATIONS

1. Use of an alternative date may help to minimize estate taxes. For example, if the decedent was the key person in a closely held business, then the business's financial performance may decline during the period subsequent to death. The actual financial results will serve to support the proposition that the business was dependent on the decedent.

2. Often events that would otherwise affect a subject company's value occur subsequent to the valuation date. Such events should generally not be considered

for purposes of estate and gift tax valuations. The key to determining what events should be considered is what facts were known or reasonably knowable as of the valuation date.

3. Many analysts make the mistake of focusing on a subject company's past historical performance as the primary determinant of value. It is the expectation of the company's future performance as of the valuation date that determines value. The past performance is only relative to the extent that it is indicative of the company's future performance.

4. Value is dependent on investors' expectations of a company's *future* earnings capacity. If an unprofitable operation can be discontinued without adversely affecting the company's other lines of business, then the future earnings' capacity (and hence the value) of the remaining lines of business may be materially greater than if the values of all operating lines were aggregated—that is, the sum of *some* of the parts may be greater than the whole.

5. This definition of dividend-paying capacity is equivalent to equity net cash flows—that is, *those cash flows available to pay out to equity holders (in the form of dividends) after funding operations of the business.*[3]

6. Many inexperienced appraisers fail to consider the use of the market approach/guideline public company methodology because they believe that publicly traded companies are too large to be truly comparable. While the size of many public companies may eliminate them as comparables, the sizes of many public companies may approximate that of the closely held company being valued, particularly in certain industries, such as high technology, for which there have been initial public offerings for companies with relatively small market capitalizations.

7. Revenue Ruling 59-60 does not specifically address the use of the market approach/guideline company transaction method in valuing closely held companies, as these data have only had widespread availability in recent years. However, the guidelines relating to comparability of the business lines and consideration of other relevant factors presented in Revenue Ruling 59-60 for the application of the guideline public company method may be applicable to the guideline company transaction method as well.

8. Revenue Ruling 59-60 supports the use of an asset approach for valuing investment or holding companies. Therefore, use of an asset approach when valuing family limited partnerships and limited liability companies with similar characteristics is considered reasonable in view of Revenue Ruling 59-60.

9. Inexperienced analysts often make the mistake of arbitrarily averaging each of the various valuation approaches/methodologies used in valuing a closely held company. For example, if three approaches are used, each approach may be assigned an equal one-third weighting. As noted in Revenue Ruling 59-60, such an approach would serve no purpose. Rather, each valuation is subject to particular facts and circumstances, which must be considered in selecting the most appropriate approach(es) and level of reliance when determining the final estimate of value.

---

[3] *International Glossary of Business Valuation Terms* (The C.L.A.R.E.N.C.E. Glossary Project comprised of the following professional organizations: American Institute of Certified Public Accountants, American Society of Appraisers, Canadian Institute of Chartered Business Valuators, National Association of Certified Valuation Analysts, and The Institute of Business Appraisers, 2001).

CHAPTER 13: VALUATION OF FAMILY LIMITED PARTNERSHIPS (FLPs)

1. Once a valuation analyst has a solid understanding of the bundle of rights, he or she is better prepared to determine how to capture the impact on value in the subject's benefit stream, rate of return, discount applied to enterprise value, or a combination of these. This will involve gaining a picture of not only the rights that exist but, more importantly, those rights that do not.

2. Term restriction is important from a valuation perspective because it defines the inability of the limited partners to receive a return on their investment prior to the completion of the partnership term.

3. This type of provision provides rights for limited partners in certain circumstances that may enable them to affect some operations of the partnership. As such, the impact of this type of provision is partially dependent on the size of the limited partnership interest being valued.

4. If the provisions in the agreement are anything other than fair market value among family members, the agreement may be disregarded under § 2703.

5. Most partnership agreements will have a clearly stated restriction on transferability of partnership interests. This is primarily to protect all partners from finding themselves legally bound to the partnership with individuals not of their choice. From a valuation perspective, such restrictions on transferability may have a material impact on the selection of the degree of discounts for lack of control and lack of marketability. However, if other provisions modify the transferability restrictions, they may provide a mitigating effect on the depth of the discounts.

6. All contributions are to be credited to the partners' accounts to avoid the "gift on formation" issue.

7. The provisions concerning amendments to the partnership agreement provide a substantial level of authority to the general partner with input by the limited partners. However, many partnership agreements provide for a "power of attorney" clause whereby the limited partners specifically provide the authority for the general partner to act on their behalf. In addition, a restriction on transferability provides some level of protection to the limited partners regarding possible changes in partnership management of the partnership. These restrictions as well as the general partner(s)' legally binding fiduciary responsibility toward the limited partners may allow for some level of discount for lack of control when valuing a general partner interest.

8. One of the benefits to a limited partnership structure is the protection afforded the limited partners from the debts and obligations of the partnership or of other partners.

9. Certain FLP provisions serve as the foundation for selecting appropriate discounts for lack of control and lack of marketability because:

   - A limited partner by definition does not have any right to manage or control the partnership, thus eliminating his or her ability to determine the amount and timing of any distributions or asset liquidations of the partnership. This effectively eliminates some of the sources of return on the partner's investment.

- The inability to readily transfer the interest or withdraw from the partnership eliminates the other avenue for a limited partner to receive a return on his or her investment.

10. In order to avoid the negative impact that Section 2704(a) can have on the estate tax value of a limited partnership interest, it is better if the limited partner does *not* own a general interest in the partnership at death. Alternatively, the limited partner can gift all of his or her limited interest before he or she dies. The GP can also be a separate entity.

11. If fair market value is the appropriate standard of value, factors influencing the pricing of partnership interests in secondary transactions may be considered.

12. Assets within a particular category may produce different impacts on value. For instance, if an FLP is holding undeveloped land instead of an income-producing property, its value will be influenced by the inability of the undeveloped land to generate a return to partners other than through ongoing appreciation and possible liquidation of the asset.

13. The closed-end funds to be used should match as closely as possible the specific portfolio structure of the FLP. For instance, if the FLP is holding only technology stock and some blue chips, the selected closed-end funds should have a similar asset mix so that the market perception of risk will be appropriately reflected for the type of portfolio being held by the FLP.

14. As a point of reference, publicly traded open-end mutual funds issue and redeem shares directly to and from the fund itself. Consequently, if the demand for an open-end fund increases, the fund issues more shares. An open-end mutual fund normally prices unit purchases and redemptions at the transaction cost-adjusted net asset value. Therefore, these types of funds will continually dilute and grow with purchases and shrink with sales. Typically, they do not experience the price fluctuations that closed-end funds do.

15. An analysis of closed-end funds with similar investment characteristics to the subject FLP can provide an indication of the adjustment to net asset value that the market would require.

16. Since closed-end funds are publicly traded, the difference between the trading price and net asset value has nothing to do with marketability. In addition, be aware that some funds are thinly traded and, as a result, are not good indicators of market dynamics.

17. The derived discount from net asset value (NAV) can be viewed in two ways. The first is as a discount:

$$\text{NAV} \times (1\text{–}D) = \text{Value} \quad \text{where D = Discount}$$
$$\text{NAV} - \$1,000,000 \times (1 - .20) = \$800,000$$

or it can be viewed as a market multiple:

$$\text{NAV} \times \text{Multiple} = \text{Value}$$
$$\$1,000,000 \times .80 \ = \ \$800,000$$

CHAPTER 15:   SHAREHOLDER DISPUTES

1. State statutes and judicial precedent control this area of valuation. Although analysts should not be acting as attorneys, it is important that they become

generally familiar with the statutes and case law in the jurisdiction where the lawsuit has been filed.

2. Shareholder dispute cases arise under two different state statutes, dissenting shareholder actions, and minority oppression (dissolution) actions.

3. In both dissenting and oppressed shareholder disputes, the statutes are clear—the standard of value is fair value.

4. Not only is the standard of value important in determining the methodology that will be performed and the discounts and premiums that will or will not be applied, but the courts have also shown that they do not equate fair value and fair market value.

5. When preparing a fair value analysis, the valuation analyst should consult the attorney on the engagement, who will consider the state statute to establish the valuation date.

6. The courts look to the valuation analyst to provide a well-reasoned, objective valuation to aid the court in its findings. This requires the analyst to maintain objectivity and independence.

7. Currently, the three approaches to value—market, income, and asset—are all acceptable in the shareholder dispute arena, although it is important to confer with the attorney in the particular jurisdiction. Methodologists (or preferred methods) vary from one jurisdiction to the other.

8. Various courts interpret methodologies differently and will refer to commonly known methods by other names.

CHAPTER 16: VALUATION ISSUES IN EMPLOYEE STOCK OWNERSHIP PLANS

1. Both private and publicly held corporations can establish employee stock ownership plans (ESOPs) to encourage their employees to think and act like owners.

2. Closely held companies and some thinly traded publicly held companies must be valued by an independent valuation analyst.

3. The ultimate responsibility for obtaining a reasonable valuation of a closely held company ESOP rests squarely with the plan trustee.

4. Every valuation must fulfill the regulations of both the Internal Revenue Service (IRS) and the Department of Labor (DOL).

5. The ESOP generally borrows funds to conduct such transactions from or through the sponsoring company, although the company can also simply contribute new shares of stock to an ESOP or contribute cash to buy existing shares.

6. Expounding on the DOL "adequate consideration" proposed regulations, the ESOP cannot pay more than fair market value for its shares or sell for less than FMV.

7. Plan provisions written at the time of the inception of the ESOP are very important and have an effect on when distributions will occur.

8. The greater the employee turnover, the higher the expected level of repurchase obligation. The higher the growth of stock value of the sponsoring company, the more the per-share distributions must be. The effect on the dollar amount of the repurchase obligation can be substantial.

9. It is important to understand and plan strategies for dealing with repurchases early in the life of an ESOP company.

10. By making loans through the ESOP, the company receives a number of tax benefits.
11. There is no limit on the term of an ESOP loan other than what lenders will accept. ESOP loans typically amortize over five to seven years. However, ESOP shares are released as collateral after 10 years.
12. The company measures compensation expense on the basis of the fair value (an accounting term not to be confused with fair market value) of the shares to be released, which can cause some dramatic fluctuations in recorded compensation expense.
13. ESOP valuations are usually those of a noncontrolling interest, unless compelling requisite relevant factors and empirical evidence are available to support a control value.
14. When valuing a minority block of stock of a closely held corporation, there is no range of discounts that will universally be applicable in any given circumstance.
15. A put right is the legal right, not the requirement, of a participant, under certain circumstances of plan termination, to convert sponsoring company stock held in individual accounts to cash under a detailed, time-specific formula.
16. It is difficult to forecast repurchase obligations much further than a few years and to estimate the present value of future repurchase obligations.
17. In order to comply with the requirements of the DOL, the analyst's conclusion of fair market value must be presented in a written document.
18. The valuation is generally made on at least an annual basis and may be used in several scenarios over which the analyst has little or no control.

CHAPTER 17:   VALUATION IN THE DIVORCE SETTING

1. The analyst must know the specific definition of value that is to be used in determining a value in a divorce setting. Failure to do so could result in the valuation being excluded, discounted, or ignored by the judge if challenged. The attorney should provide guidance on the law to the analyst.
2. The various definitions and components of goodwill often cause confusion. Therefore, it is important to fully understand the term's meaning in the context being used.
3. Since state laws are so diverse, the analyst must constantly be alert to not only the espoused standard of value in a particular jurisdiction, but also the variations imposed by judicial decisions. Consultation with an attorney is advised.
4. Personal goodwill is that goodwill that attaches to the personal efforts of the individual. It is generally considered to be difficult to transfer, if at all. Entity goodwill is the goodwill that attaches to the business enterprise.
5. If analysts present their case well and support the allocations with sound logic, the court will be more likely to accept their value conclusions as a reasonable approximation of the personal versus entity goodwill.
6. In the case of a law or accounting practice, location of the client might not be as important, except in smaller communities.
7. The analyst should consider the number of employees, the job titles and job descriptions, the pay scale, and the length of service in a goodwill review.
8. The issue of nonowner professionals and their impact on value is one that moves beyond the issue of separation of personal and entity goodwill. In determining

the fair market value of a professional practice, the issue of control of clients, patients, and customers is one that relates to the transferable value of the practice without just the consideration of personal and entity goodwill of the owner.

9. Notwithstanding the fact that compliance with USPAP is not a requirement for an acceptable value for divorce purposes, the cross-examining attorney can nevertheless use noncompliance as a tool for impeachment.

10. Noncompliance to standards does not necessarily invalidate the valuation report (that decision is up to the judge), but it can provide fodder for cross-examination.

CHAPTER 18:   VALUATION ISSUES IN SMALL BUSINESSES

1. Small businesses tend to have lower-quality financial statements. Outside accountants are less likely to have prepared the financial statements. Their statements tend to be tax-oriented rather than oriented to stockholder disclosure, as in larger companies.

2. For valuation assignments, where necessary, adjustments from cash-basis accounting to a more accrual-basis accounting are made among the smallest companies.

3. The characteristics of small businesses tend to result in overall higher risk than is found in larger businesses. Among small businesses, these characteristics can be extreme, and risk tends to increase as size decreases.

4. It may be necessary to make certain adjustments to improve comparability of the subject company to industry norms, publicly traded companies, or companies involved in market transactions considered in the valuation process.

5. When valuing a control interest in a small business, it is appropriate to adjust discretionary items. When valuing a minority interest, it may not be appropriate to adjust for discretionary items because the owner of a minority interest is not in a position to change these items. However, a minority shareholder may be in a position to force an adjustment as an oppressed shareholder.

6. Business brokers can provide insight into the qualitative factors being considered in a particular market.

7. Earnings in the latest 12 months and average earnings in recent years tend to be given the most weight in establishing prices for small businesses. Capitalization of earnings/cash flow is often an appropriate method for valuing these small businesses.

8. Many analysts assume that the guideline public company method is never applicable to small businesses. For the mom-and-pop, very small business, this is often a safe assumption. For other small businesses, this assumption is not always safe. There is a large number of publicly traded companies with market capitalization less than $50 million, putting them within reasonable range for some small businesses.

9. The valuation analyst must exercise caution using transaction databases because they define variables in different ways.

10. Revenue and discretionary earnings are two of the most common multiples used in the guideline company transaction method.

11. Value indications derived from the guideline company transaction method are on a control basis.

12. Although rules of thumb may provide insight on the value of a business, it is usually better to use them for reasonableness tests of the value conclusion.

13. The excess cash flow/earnings' method is widely used for small businesses, but analysts frequently misuse it.

CHAPTER 19: VALUATION ISSUES IN PROFESSIONAL PRACTICES

1. Many professional practices obtain most of their patients or clients through referrals, based on the reputation of specific professionals.

2. In some jurisdictions, an important issue in valuing professional practices is distinguishing between the goodwill that is solely attributable to the professional (and difficult to transfer) and the goodwill that is attributable to the practice.

3. Although professional practices are valued for the same reasons as other types of businesses, litigation (including disputes among principals and marital dissolutions) and transactions (including the sale of a practice, an associate buying in, and buy-sell formulas) account for a large portion of the valuation work.

4. Goodwill may be the primary intangible asset found in professional practices, but the definition of goodwill differs in different scenarios.

5. When a professional practice is being valued for transaction or litigation purposes (depending on state law and judicial precedent), it may be important to identify professional and practice goodwill separately and to discuss the likelihood that a portion of the professional goodwill can be transferred in a transaction.

6. Analysts should have a clear understanding of state law as it pertains to marital dissolution in divorce valuations.

7. It is important to be sure the professional's earnings and/or the practice's economic income have been calculated in the same manner as the comparative compensation data in a divorce valuation.

8. In a small professional practice, value may be greater if a successor for the key professional is in place. Bringing in an associate and introducing the associate to clients or patients may facilitate the transfer of some professional goodwill and may increase the price received by the exiting professional.

9. When valuing professional practices, it is important to analyze and make appropriate adjustments to the financial statements. The widespread use of cash-basis accounting may require a number of adjustments.

10. If the practice owns material amounts of nonoperating assets such as art collections and antiques in excess of what is customary in the decor of comparable offices, it may be necessary to value these assets separately from practice operations.

11. If the economic benefits stream being discounted or capitalized is pretax earnings or pretax earnings plus owners' compensation and benefits, the discount rate or the capitalization rate should be higher than if the benefits stream is after-tax net cash flow.

12. Guideline company transactions are often used as a reasonableness test of values obtained by other methods.

13. The usefulness of past transactions in the subject company is often limited by the way the transactions are structured. A substantial portion of the trans-

ferred practice value may be included through salary differentials, and it may be difficult to distinguish that portion of the salary differential attributable to the buyout of a practitioner. Prior transactions also sometimes reflect a punishment to the exiting practitioner for early withdrawal of capital and the practitioner's professional services.

14. Although rules of thumb may provide insight on the value of a professional practice, it is usually only appropriate to use them for reasonableness tests of the value conclusion.

CHAPTER 20: STRATEGIC BENCHMARKING FOR VALUE

1. The SBV process is a holistic approach that starts with identifying critical success factors and appropriate financial and nonfinancial performance measures. It then moves on to designing scorecards linking compensation to appropriate behavior and accomplishments. It finishes by putting it all together with a cost-effective, usable benchmarking/performance management system allowing management to drive its company's value.

2. Businesses utilize six types of capital. Organizational capital, financial capital, physical capital, and human capital are combined by the company's systems' capital, which are then converted into customer capital.

3. One of the simplest but perhaps most effective methods for executives to use in analyzing their company is to perform a SWOT analysis of the company. SWOT analysis gets its name from the four concepts it attempts to analyze: the company's strengths, weaknesses, opportunities, and threats. Using this simple framework will identify a company's strengths and determine where its greatest opportunities lie while at the same time requiring a company to address its weaknesses and new threats from competitors or technological advances.

4. Performance areas typically include:

   - Shipping
   - Advertising and public relations
   - Customer service
   - Manufacturing
   - Purchasing
   - Research and development
   - Warehousing
   - Information technology (the computer department)
   - Finance department
   - Other

5. *Activity measures* are defined as specific procedures or processes in a performance area. These measures are input items for a specific performance indicator and must be able to be measured consistently. To be an effective measure, the activity must be definable and documented and have a performance standard established.

6. Companies that get the most benefit from the scorecard-type performance systems generally have these key characteristics:

- They have developed the performance system to focus on the key points of the company's corporate strategy.
- They have a comprehensive system focused on the company as a whole and not a particular area of the company.
- Compensation and reward systems are tied to both individual and group performance.
- The performance measures are accepted and used by the employees.

7. CSFs have these characteristics, which management can consider when developing its own systems:

- They have a material impact on the bottom line and strategic effectiveness.
- They directly affect the successful competitive performance of the company.
- There usually are less than 10 factors in any one company.
- They most likely affect customer satisfaction, directly or indirectly.
- They must be related to the company's strategy.

8. KPIs have unique characteristics that management must consider when selecting them:

- They relate to a specific procedure or process.
- They are an input item for a specific performance indicator.
- They have consistency of measurement.
- They can be impacted by persons responsible for them.

9. The third step in the SBV process is actually the heart of applying strategic benchmarking throughout the company. Once management has identified the CSFs and the related KPIs, these elements need to be cascaded through various employee levels in the company, and the key employees need to be brought into the long-term value creation process. By establishing activity measures for employee groups that support the KPIs, all employees can be brought into the value creation process.

10. The formulation of strategy is an art. The communication of strategy is a responsibility. The execution of strategy is about practicing operational art. All of it is about leadership.

11. In SBV strategy alignment maps, we recognize four tiers of value dimensions: (1) Input and Outcome Relationships, (2) Customer Satisfaction, (3) the Value-Creating Process, and (4) Integration of Assets and Activities. Strategic intent is driven from top to bottom in the map; value creation is driven from bottom to top.

12. Strategic objectives should:

- Contextually fit in the cause-and-effect chain
- Add value in telling the strategy story
- Reflect logical and systems thinking
- Be actionable (verb + descriptor + result)
- Be measurable

13. The five dimensions of value are all related to growth and productivity within the company:

- Increase market share using a constant capital investment (Growth Dimension)
- Invest capital in projects that yield a higher economic return, such as a new product line (growth dimension)
- Increase profit through operating efficiencies while using a constant capital structure (productivity dimension)
- Maintain profit while using less capital through improved asset turnover (productivity dimension)
- Maintain or improve profit while lowering the weighted average cost of capital (WACC) (productivity dimension)

14. The SBV alignment model connects the dots among value and strategy execution, producing maximum economic profits through optimal growth and productivity. Today, the only sustainable source of competitive advantage any company has is its ability to execute strategy faster and more effectively than its competition.
15. The SBV Process presented includes:

- Determining a company's current state on a qualitative and quantitative basis
- Deciding where the company is to go in the future state
- Developing a workable strategy and executing it using strategic benchmarking keys, the focus of which then cascades through the company by following the paths of critical success factors and key performance indicators
- Aligning a company's systems and people to the defined strategy so that everyone is singing out of the same book

CHAPTER 21: VALUATION OF INTANGIBLE ASSETS

1. Intangible assets receiving legal protection are called intellectual property, which is generally categorized as patents, copyrights, trade names (-marks, -dress), trade secrets, and know-how.
2. More than three dozen FASB statements require consideration of fair value.[4]
3. Since return requirements increase as risk increases and since intangible assets are usually more risky for a company than are tangible assets, it is reasonable to conclude that the returns expected on intangible assets typically will be at or above the average rate of return (discount rate) for the company as a whole.
4. A principal difference between the two definitions is that *fair value* for the business enterprise considers synergies and attributes of the specific buyer and specific seller, while *fair market value* endeavors to be a more objective standard, contemplating a hypothetical willing buyer and a hypothetical willing seller.
5. Goodwill is the excess of the cost of an acquired entity over the net of the amounts assigned to assets acquired less liabilities assumed.[5]
6. Under SFAS No. 142, amortization of goodwill is not allowed. Instead, goodwill is tested annually for impairment.
7. A present-value technique is often the best available technique with which to estimate the fair value of a group of assets (i.e., a reporting unit).

---

[4] Michael Mard, *AICPA Task Force Report to Business Valuation Subcommittee* (2000).
[5] Financial Accounting Standards Board, Statement of Financial Accounting Standards No. 141, *Business Combinations* (June 2001), at 43.

8. The second step of the goodwill impairment test is triggered if the carrying value of the reporting unit, including goodwill, exceeds the fair value of the reporting unit.

9. IPR&D can be generally defined as a research and development project that has not yet been completed. Acquired IPR&D is an intangible asset to be used in R&D activities.

10. To be recognized as assets, IPR&D projects must have substance, that is, sufficient cost and effort associated with the project to enable its fair value to be estimated with reasonable reliability.[6] Further, the IPR&D must be incomplete; technological, engineering, or regulatory risks must remain.[7]

11. Including such tax effects in the valuation process is more common in the income and cost approaches but not typical in the market approach, since any tax benefit should be factored into the quoted market price.

12. The risk premium assessed to a new product launch should decrease as a project successfully proceeds through its continuum of development since the uncertainty related to each subsequent stage diminishes.

13. An acquiring company must record the fair value of the assets acquired in a business combination. SFAS No. 141 mandates such purchase accounting for all acquisitions.[8]

14. The appropriate rate of return in valuing the enterprise is the weighted average cost of capital, the weighted average of the return on equity capital, and the return on debt capital. The weights represent percentages of debt to total capital and equity to total capital. The rate of return on debt capital is adjusted to reflect the fact that interest payments are tax deductible to the corporation.

15. The formula for the amortization benefit is:

$$\text{AB} = \text{PVCF}*(n/(n - ((\text{PV}(Dr,n, - 1)*(1 + Dr)^{0.5}*T)) - 1)$$

Where:

AB	=	Amortization benefit
PVCF	=	Present value of cash flows from the asset
n	=	15-year amortization period
Dr	=	Discount rate
$\text{PV}(Dr,n, - 1)*(1 + Dr)^{0.5}$	=	Present value of an annuity of \$1 over 15 years, at the discount rate
T	=	Tax rate

16. Valuation of customer relationships: Cost versus Income. Valuation of customer relationships using the cost approach requires the identification of the selling costs associated with the generation of new customers. In this example, management indicated that the split in selling costs was roughly equivalent to the revenue split between new and existing customers. Thus, the valuation is based on that split. Depending on the nature of the business, this split between new and existing customers may vary greatly. Thus, the analyst will need to identify the costs associated with generating the new customers appropriately. This is probably most easily done based on an allocation of the sales team's

---

[6] Ibid., at 3.3.42.

[7] Ibid., at 3.3.55.

[8] Ibid., at 13.

time, such as 40 percent spent on finding new customers and 60 percent to handle existing ones. Or there may be certain sales or marketing people or departments that are devoted entirely to servicing existing accounts, while others spend all of their time prospecting for new ones. In such cases, the costs can be broken out on a departmental or individual level. For many smaller businesses, top executives also spend a large amount of time in the generation of new customers, so these costs must be considered in the analysis.

Use of the cost approach also assumes that the customers and selling effort required to obtain them are all relatively equivalent. If the company has few customers that make up the majority of its business, then the cost approach may not be appropriate to determine the value of the customer relationships.

The income approach is often recommended for valuing customer relationships. For many consumer products and old economy businesses, the customer relationship may have much higher value than the technology associated with the products being sold, since these products may be a commodity or near commodity that may be easily substituted with products from another vendor. The customer relationship may allow the sale of multiple products and services through the same sales channels. An income approach may be more appropriate in these cases.

17. SFAS No. 141 specifically prohibits the recognition of assembled workforce as an intangible asset apart from goodwill.[9]

18. Trade names and trademarks must be considered individually to determine their remaining useful life. Trade names and trademarks that are associated with a company name or logo (e.g., McDonald's) typically have indefinite lives. Many product trade names and trademarks also will have an indefinite life if no reasonable estimate can be made of the end of the product life (e.g., Coca-Cola). However, the analyst must be careful to find out whether there is a planned phase-out of a product or ascertain whether it can be estimated with reasonable certainty that a name will lose value or be abandoned over time. In such a case, a finite life is suggested and, therefore, an amortization period is warranted. Remember, for tax purposes, generally all intangibles are amortizable over a 15-year life.

19. In the valuation of a successful business enterprise, there are often intangible assets that cannot be separately identified. These intangible assets are generally referred to as goodwill. The term *goodwill*, however, is sometimes used to describe the aggregate of all of the intangible assets of a business. In a more restricted sense, goodwill is the sum total of only the qualities that attract future new customers to the business.

20. By its nature, goodwill is usually the riskiest asset of the group, and therefore it should require a higher return than the overall business return.

CHAPTER 22: MARKETING, MANAGING, AND MAKING MONEY IN A VALUATION SERVICES GROUP

1. Some practices whose revenues are primarily based on fixed fees make the mistake of failing to maintain or to evaluate time records and other information

---

[9] Ibid., at 39.

about efficiency and profitability that would indicate problem areas needing corrective action.

2. It is desirable that chargeable hours for engagements, on average, result in billings equal to 90% or more of the recorded hours.

3. On average, professionals in the practice should be charging billable hours to engagements for more than 70% of the standard hours available for them to work.

4. In spite of the higher rates offered by litigation services, some practitioners find that being an expert witness is disruptive to the processes needed to direct a practice that must deliver valuation reports on a regular basis.

5. Since a business valuation engagement is a consulting project, proactive planning and control is key to maximization of the efficiency, quality, and profitability of the work process and product.

6. Resource flexibility in staffing is a rich area for practice leaders to explore as they seek to smooth the peaks and valleys of the workflow.

7. Unless the practice has a culture toward quality and client value, there is less chance for good economics, at least for any sustained period of time.

8. Litigation service engagements especially need an organized and disciplined approach because so often the engagement objectives identified at the start are augmented and revised over the life of the project.

9. A practice may not want to accept engagements for individuals (as opposed to companies) as clients without substantial retainers being received.

10. In most situations, if you are good enough to be engaged, you are good enough to be partially paid in advance through retainers.

11. A work plan and budget provide a valuable tool to supervise and control the engagement team and are conducive to obtaining efficiency on the job.

12. Sometimes the best approach to take with an engagement that is going badly economically is to put the practice's best people on the job to finish.

13. An old adage, "People do what you inspect, not what you expect," applies here, since few team members will know or admit to the leader on a timely basis that they are off-track about the direction in which their work is headed.

14. A general rule of thumb for frequency of inspection by a practice leader or engagement manager is that the work of juniors/novices should be reviewed every two hours. The work of all other professionals should be inspected on a time interval of three hours for each year of their experience. This is highly affected by the type and complexity of the engagement.

15. Preparing a work plan and budget (whether written or oral) for known tasks and obtaining approval aid the client and attorney in understanding the likely fee levels required.

16. Nothing should be assumed with the client and the client's attorney without frequent, clear communication.

CHAPTER 23:   BUSINESS DAMAGES

1. Although financial experts are usually not attorneys and are not expected by their professional standards to know the law, attorneys frequently choose experts who have some knowledge of the law that applies to a particular litigation matter.

2. Establishing reasonable certainty involves rigorous analysis, of which the identification and testing of key assumptions may be an important part. Some of these key assumptions are commonly based on client representations.

3. Financial experts are sometimes requested by the attorney to opine on causation. The experts should evaluate whether they have the qualifications and foundation to render such an opinion.

4. Although *Daubert* involved a scientific expert, the court set forth four criteria by which a trial judge could evaluate the reliability of all expert testimony.[10]
   a. Whether a theory or technique can be (and has been) tested;
   b. Whether the theory or technique has been subjected to peer review and publication;
   c. The known or potential rate of error and the existence and maintenance of standards controlling the technique's operation; and
   d. Explicit identification of a relevant scientific community and an express determination of a particular degree of acceptance within that community.

5. In litigation, the financial expert can expect to be challenged regarding qualifications, the proper application of valuation theory, and the appropriateness of the underlying assumptions and facts.

6. One of the most challenging aspects of a lost profits calculation is determining how far into the future to project ongoing lost profits. The period of recovery largely depends on the facts and circumstances of the case, as well as the consideration of reasonable certainty and proximate cause.

7. In many jurisdictions, the law mandates the treatment for prejudgment interest, often by prescribing a statutory interest rate, generally based on simple rather than compound interest calculations.

8. The purpose of compensatory damages is to make the plaintiff whole—that is, the plaintiff should receive no more or no less than is necessary to make it whole.

9. In certain damage calculations, analysts will discount future *pretax* earnings by the appropriate *after-tax* discount rate, which may be different than in a business valuation.

CHAPTER 24:   OTHER VALUATION SERVICES AREAS

A. Valuations for Public Companies and/or Financial Reporting

1. The increasing importance of intangible assets and intellectual property to public companies' financial positions and strategic profiles also increases the need for valuation services.

2. Unlike most other valuation assignments, the need for public company valuation services is often dictated by GAAP.

3. The standard of value most often used in financial reporting valuations is fair value. This is different from the "fair value" used in shareholder disputes.

4. When engaged to provide an opinion regarding the fair value of a particular public company's assets or liabilities, it is important to confirm with the com-

---

[10] William Daubert, et ux, etc., et al., Petitioners v. Merrell Dow Pharmaceuticals, Inc. (113 S. Ct. 2786, 125 C. Ed., 2d 469 [1993]).

pany's auditor the exact definition (and interpretation) of fair value to be utilized and to clearly identify which items are to be valued.

5. While a public corporation's traded stock has a readily determinable value and the company may have publicly traded options, distinct differences between employee stock options and publicly traded stock options influence their value. Also, corporations may grant employee stock options on shares that are not publicly traded, including shares in subsidiaries and shares with voting rights different from the publicly traded stock.

6. In certain businesses, the lines are blurred between the intangible assets of the business and income-producing real estate. Some examples include: hotels, motels, hospitals, and skilled nursing centers, among others. By performing a purchase price allocation, the intangible assets can be separated from the real property and can then be amortized over a much shorter life.

7. The client will not typically be versed in the differences among standards of value, so early communication and active listening are the keys to a successful engagement.

B. Valuation Issues in Buy-Sell Agreements

1. Every closely held business owner should have a buy-sell agreement with his or her business partners/shareholders.

2. The battles that accompany triggering events often occur at a time when the company needs most to be projecting assurances to their employees and customers. This can disrupt operations and ultimately serve to reduce the very value the owners are at odds over.

3. A buy-sell agreement can set the ground rules for any matter the owners want to include. For this reason, there is no "one size fits all" when it comes to shareholder agreements. An owner who signs a "cookie-cutter" buy-sell agreement is practically assured of disagreement and misunderstanding down the road.

4. Most disputes that arise as a result of a triggering event do so because the agreement is either unclear or misunderstood by the parties involved. Unfortunately, this is also the worst time to try to resolve such a dispute; it is better to be in the position of making these decisions when the parties are amicable.

5. Rarely do formulas result in "easy" solutions when the time comes to put them into practice.

6. If a buy-sell agreement entered into after October 8, 1990 contains a clause that would value the stock at less than fair market value, it will be disregarded for tax purposes.

7. Shareholders who have signed agreements that value the company's stock at something less than fair market value may find themselves in the unfortunate position of having transferred the stock for the price set by the agreement only to find that the IRS values it at something greater. This may result in an unexpected tax liability.

C. Valuing Debt

1. The value of a convertible bond is closely tied to the value of the underlying common stock as long as the per share price multiplied by the conversion ratio

(i.e., the number of the shares represented by the convertible option) is greater than or equal to the par value of the bond. When the value of the common stock multiplied by the conversion ratio is substantially lower than the par value of the bond, the value of the bond more closely approximates the straight debt amount.

2. Since a bond with a long period until maturity is riskier than a bond that will mature in the near future, the bond with the longer term to maturity usually has a higher discount rate than the bond with the shorter term to maturity. Inverted yield curves can occur though.

3. Since there are significant public trading markets for debt securities, it is easy to determine the present value of a publicly traded debt security.

4. The best method to estimate the yield to maturity of a debt security of a closely held company is a guideline company analysis.

D. Valuation Issues in Preferred Stock

1. Preferred stock is a "hybrid" security with features similar to both common stock and bonds. Like common stock, it represents equity ownership and much like a bond (debt holder) it can receive fixed income distributions and preferential treatment.

2. The dividend rate is the predetermined rate an issuer promises to pay the preferred shareholder.

3. A company that has issued preferred stock with cumulative dividend terms has an obligation to make all accumulated dividend payments to the preferred stockholders before declaring and paying a dividend on common stock.

4. Shares of preferred stock with noncumulative features do not carry a guarantee of dividend payments and, as a result, carry more risk.

5. Convertible preferred stock gives the investor the option to exchange the security for common stock.

6. Revenue Ruling 83-120 is intended to amplify Revenue Ruling 59-60 and set out other considerations regarding the valuation of preferred and common stock for gift tax and recapitalization of private companies.

7. The fair market value of a share of preferred stock is equal to the present value of the future cash payments, discounted back to the present using a discount rate that embodies the risk associated with the investment.

E. Restricted Stock Valuation

1. *Restricted stock* is stock of a publicly traded corporation that is restricted from public trading for a specified period of time. Restricted stock is often identical to its publicly traded counterpart except that it is not freely tradeable.

2. The seminal IRS revenue ruling in this area, Revenue Ruling 77-287, provides guidance for the valuation of restricted stock.

3. The Longstaff analysis[11] indicates that the greater the volatility of the stock, the greater the discount, and that the marketability discount is not a linear

---

[11] Frances A. Longstaff, "How Much Can Marketability Affect Security Values?" *Journal of Finance,* Vol. 1, No. 5 (December 1995), pp. 1767–1774.

function of time because the greatest risks, and therefore the largest increases in the percentage discount, occur early in the restriction period.

F. Valuation of Early-Stage Technology Companies

1. To avoid excess compensation expense, companies often attempt to set the grant price of options equal to the underlying common stock's fair market value at the time of issuance.
2. A technology company's most important assets (intangibles) may not be recorded on the balance sheet.
3. The analyst may need to focus on when the company will attain sustainable profit margins and work backward to the valuation date.
4. As with more traditional companies, the largest impediment to properly using the guideline company transaction method in the technology arena is lack of information. Information on what bundle of assets and liabilities was acquired, what the true price and terms were, and whether strategic consideration was present is difficult to obtain.
5. Actual company transactions are the preferred market approach method if the analyst is fortunate enough to have a contemporaneous transaction in the subject company's securities.
6. Simultaneous gifts made by the same donor in the same security can have different fair market values.
7. Due to the potential for abnormally high growth in operations, revenue, and cash flows, the income approach discounted cash flow (DCF) method is usually the method used when valuing early-stage technology companies.
8. One of the first decisions the valuation analyst will face in implementing the income approach is whether to accept management projections as representing the most likely potential outcome or whether multiple scenarios should be projected and probability of occurrence assigned to each. In theory, the latter approach is best, but, due to practical considerations, projection risk is addressed most often in the discount rate and not through multiple-outcome scenarios.
9. Forecast losses that result from prerevenue phase expenditures (e.g., R&D and brand-building) should be discounted at a rate different from profits.
10. If venture capital rates of returns are referenced in selecting an appropriate discount rate, the valuation analyst may need to adjust the lack of marketability discount applied later because many venture capital discount rates are predicated on investments in nonmarketable securities.

G. Valuation Issues Related to Stock Options and Other Share-Based Compensation

1. Employee stock options (ESOs) can be attractive given the fact that cash is not normally involved. Vesting rights are often embedded in these ESOs to promote employee retention by rewarding longevity.
2. Employee stock options are classified as either incentive stock options or nonqualified stock options.
3. Options that can be exercised during and up to the expiration date are known as American options, whereas options that can be exercised only upon the expiration date are known as European options.

4. If not exercised before the expiration date, the option simply expires with no value.

5. As a result of dilution, the value of a warrant may vary somewhat from the value of a call option with identical terms.

6. Even without being "in the money," an option may have value. This value is created by the possibility that the option could be exercised profitably in the future. There are three factors that determine time value: the volatility of the stock underlying the option, the risk-free rate of interest over the option period, and the length of time before the option expires.

7. A key limitation of the Black-Scholes model is that it was developed to price European call options in the absence of dividends.

8. Warrants are often sold in connection with other financial instruments as a "sweetener" to enhance the attractiveness of the placement of the financial instrument they are bundled with or to get favorable terms on another financial instrument.

9. ESOs are characterized as incentive stock options or non-qualified stock options.

10. The causes driving the need for a valuation are fairly universal: litigation/divorce, management planning, tax-oriented (gift or estate), transaction-oriented, or financial reporting.

11. If the underlying stock is lightly traded or not publicly traded, then volatility can be estimated using a representative sampling of guideline companies or an industry benchmark.

12. If an intervening event is identified in the analysis, it may be appropriate to exclude it from the volatility.

13. The final consideration is the marketability of the option itself. There are no studies available regarding the lack of marketability of closely held stock options.

H. Real Option Valuations

1. The traditional DCF model may also fail to capture the existence of any flexibility that a financial executive maintains as the decision maker of a project or strategic initiative. Once an investment decision is initiated, a financial executive may expand it, shut it down, defer additional work until later and then restart it, or even switch the investment entirely into another strategic purpose.

2. The benefit of real-option analysis is its ability to apply a positive indication of value to uncertainty or volatility. Financial executives have many options in reacting to changes throughout the investment's economic life by adapting or revising their decisions in response to unexpected developments. This flexibility clearly provides companies with value, and the real option analysis assesses the value of this flexibility.

3. The analysis behind real option theory is the valuation of opportunities associated with management's flexibility and is derived from the relationship connecting the methods in valuing financial options and the methods in valuing flexibility.

4. Real options exist in most businesses and may be more representative of the manner in which businesses operate, although they are not always very readily identifiable.

5. Real-option analysis can become an important measurement tool in management's strategic decision making. Although many analysts still predominately

use DCF, real-option analysis, as it becomes better understood and properly applied, may be more prevalent in the future.

I. Maximizing Shareholder Value

1. The most notable metric that has attempted to better measure value creation and has become increasingly accepted by analysts is the concept popularized by Stern Stewart & Company, economic value added (EVA).
2. The EVA concept, which is a value-driven financial performance measure, attempts to charge earnings with an expense for the cost of capital employed. In other words, it is simply a measure of what is left to the shareholders over the cost of capital.
3. The principle behind the EVA concept is that if a corporation's net income is positive after applying a charge for the cost of capital employed, the corporation has added shareholder value. If a corporation's net income is negative after applying a charge for the cost of capital employed, the corporation has destroyed shareholder value.
4. Similar models, such as market value added (MVA), return on invested capital (ROIC), and cash flow return on investment (CFROI), are also value-based concepts that claim to parallel the interests of shareholders with management.
5. Value drivers can be identified in almost any company. Some of the more widely recognized value drivers are:

   - Sales growth
   - Key people
   - Optimal profit margins
   - Effective capital controls
   - Broad and varied customer base
   - Optimal cash flow

CHAPTER 25:   VALUATION OF HEALTHCARE SERVICE BUSINESSES

1. In the mergers and acquisition marketplace, the demand for business valuation services has shifted away from transactions involving physician practices toward other types of deals.
2. Reimbursement is a critical assumption in the financial projections of health-care organizations. Many analysts make the inaccurate assumption that reimbursement will continue to increase at the national inflation rates. Analysts must first understand the payor mix of the business being valued, including how specific payors reimburse for services and the prospect for future changes in that reimbursement.
3. The volatility of reimbursement for individual procedures can be very high. It is important to consider all prospective reimbursement changes when performing the valuation analysis.
4. Individual physicians exert a significant amount of control over the direction of patient referrals to healthcare service providers.

5. Valuation analysts should understand that the level of scrutiny may be very high when providing opinions of fair market value that could be subject to the anti-kickback laws. A very large number of transactions are subject to the anti-kickback regulations.

6. It is important to identify applicable situations and seek advice from healthcare attorneys on the fraud and abuse implications of valuations performed in the healthcare services industry.

7. It is important to note that violations of the anti-kickback law are subject to criminal fines and possible imprisonment, whereas violations of the Stark law are punishable only by civil penalties at this time.

8. Appropriately factoring the regulatory environment into the valuation is important when valuing healthcare businesses.

9. It may be necessary to consult a qualified tax lawyer in order to understand how to appropriately consider the tax laws when valuing a business that involves a tax-exempt enterprise.

10. If a valuation is being performed as a result of regulatory requirements, the valuation must apply the fair market value standard of value.

11. If a valuation is being performed as a result of regulatory requirements, the valuation must apply the fair market standard of value.

12. It is important to understand what is included in the revenue stream of the subject entity, since professional versus technical revenue generation involves different valuation dynamics.

13. A negative reimbursement trend for certain healthcare services is not uncommon. It may be erroneous to assume that reimbursement will increase at inflationary rates without having performed some level of reimbursement analysis.

14. One of the erroneous assumptions sometimes made in healthcare valuations is that variable expenses are always solely a function of revenue.

15. The net result of volatile reimbursement levels for some healthcare entities is declining margins, making it important for the valuation analyst to carefully track variable costs.

16. Historically, public healthcare companies have been acquisitive and have had high valuation multiples. As a result, the multiples generated by public companies are usually not comparable to those of private businesses.

17. Many analysts try to force the use of guideline transaction multiples. This can increase the risk of a flawed valuation. Unfortunately, it is rare when the information is at the level of detail necessary to perform a supportive guideline transaction analysis. However, they can sometimes be used as a general reasonableness test depending on the situation.

18. Some minority interests in healthcare businesses do not exhibit the characteristics that affect the magnitude of discounts in other closely held businesses.

19. The analyst should read the operating and/or partnership agreement in order to determine the level of minority or marketability discounts.

20. The regulatory and legal issues may pertain to the valuation of entities in many industry niches.

21. A common oversimplification is utilizing limited market transaction data without thoroughly understanding the transactions, potentially leading to faulty conclusions. They can be used as a reasonableness test.

22. When valuing a dialysis center, it is important to understand the center's relationship with the nephrologist. It is critical in assessing risk.

Case Study #1: Valuation of a Surgery Center

1. It is important to understand the underlying components in the case mix, since the reimbursement rates for each specialty are not homogeneous.
2. The analysis will want to ascertain the likelihood that the top 10 surgeons will continue to perform cases at a center, which affects the specialty growth rates used in the projections.
3. Some analysts obtain a sampling of the surgery center's explanation of benefits (EOBs) from the most recent surgical cases to understand the dynamics of the payor mix. An adequate sampling of 25 to 30 EOBs with the associated gross and net charges for that procedure will provide an understanding of the main procedures performed under each specialty as well as help assess the reasonableness of the facility's overall charge rates.

Case Study #2: Valuation of a Hospital

1. *Assets, limited as to use* and *investments*, are considered excess assets and therefore may be added back to the resulting DCF value to arrive at the total value. "Assets limited as to use" refers to those assets that are earmarked for specific activities (e.g., related future capital expenditures, etc.). "Investments" refers to cash/marketable securities.
2. Simply adding inpatient days plus outpatient cases would be erroneous, since patients who are treated on an outpatient basis in the hospital are not measured in terms of days. As a result, the hospital applies an outpatient conversion factor to convert the outpatient cases into outpatient days. This is necessary in order to arrive at adjusted patient days, the term for measuring a hospital's occupancy rate and capacity.

CHAPTER 26: SPECIAL INDUSTRY VALUATIONS

A. Construction

1. The U.S. market for construction contractors is approximately $500 billion. About 6,000 firms have revenues exceeding $10 million, just over 100 firms have revenues exceeding $500 million, and only a handful of firms have revenues in the billions of dollars.[12]
2. Construction contractors can engage in several different types of contracts that differ in the manner in which the contactor is compensated and the level of risk assumed. These contracts include fixed-price contracts, time and materials contracts, and unit-price contracts.
3. The three most common methods of accounting are the cash-basis method, the completed-contracts method, and the percentage-of-completion method.
4. The amount of retention is typically between 5 percent and 10 percent of each billing. Once a project is completed to the satisfaction of the customer, the

---

[12] Bureau of Labor Statistics.

retention will be released. The purpose of the retention is to provide an incentive to the contractor to complete a project to the satisfaction of the customer.

5. Many construction contractors have little, if any, goodwill value. This stems from the low margins that result from the competitive bidding process. Those with goodwill tend to have more negotiated contracts and may have a good reputation or good relationship with customers.

6. There are three types of surety bonds:

   - Bid bond—provides a financial guarantee that the bid has been submitted in good faith and that the bidder intends on entering into the contract at the bid price.
   - Performance bond—protects the owner of a project from financial losses if the contractor should fail to perform under the contract.
   - Payment bond—guarantees that the contractor will pay subcontractors.

7. General rules of thumb:[13]

   - Book value
   - Book value plus a multiple of backlog
   - 10 percent to 30 percent of annual revenues
   - 2 to 3.5 times cash flows

8. General contractors would tend to be on the low end. Specialty contractors would tend to be on the high end. Variations based on region, name recognition, financial strength, and other reasons can occur.

9. These rules of thumb are provided as a general benchmark from which reasonableness *may* be assessed. The facts and circumstances of each individual company should be considered in determining the value of that particular company.

B. Valuation in Auto Dealerships

1. Dealers are required to report their financial results to their respective manufacturers on a monthly basis, using the particular manufacturers' standardized accounting system. For the most part, the various accounting systems follow generally accepted accounting principles (GAAP).

2. Dealerships typically do not record liabilities for estimated future chargebacks, instead expensing them as incurred. Some dealers will establish a reserve to offset future chargebacks. The potential contingent liability for these charges can be significant, and the analyst may consider making an adjustment for the chargebacks.

3. Dealerships have a significant investment in inventory, whether new car, used car, or parts. New vehicles are generally purchased at cost from the respective manufacturer and are typically acquired subject to related dealership floor-plan financing. The related portion of the floor-plan liability is paid off each time a vehicle is sold. Used vehicles are often acquired through trade-in, and the purchase price is subject to negotiation between the parties.

---

[13] Internal Revenue Service.

4. A dealership's primary intangible asset is known as "blue sky," which is another name for the dealership's goodwill. The value of blue sky generally includes the value of the dealership's franchise agreement.

5. The analyst should consider these factors, among others, in adjusting the derived market multiples:

   - Import franchise versus domestic franchise
   - Urban location versus rural location
   - Local demographics
   - Level of competition
   - Local economy
   - Terms of the sale

6. *Terms of the Franchise Agreement.* Most dealership franchise agreements have language restricting the transfer of the franchise to a factory-approved buyer. As such, the transferability of franchise is restricted.

7. *Potential Impact of the Economy.* The automobile industry is significantly impacted by changes in the economy. For instance, recently the automobile industry has been affected by changes in interest rates, wars, severe weather affecting oil prices, and similar problems.

8. Rules of thumb:

   - In order to quantify the blue sky of a dealership, the industry generally considers normalized pretax earnings of the dealership times a multiple of the earnings. The multiple generally falls between one to three times the earnings, with the higher multiples for more desirable brands, more profitable lines, better locations, and similar characteristics.
   - Based on this industry formula, a particular dealership's total assets can be purchased for adjusted book value plus blue sky determined by using the aforementioned multiple.

C. Radio

1. The Communications Act prohibits the assignment of a license or the transfer of control of a licensee without prior approval of the FCC.

2. All commercial radio stations are required to have a license from the FCC in order to operate. This license represents the station's primary intangible asset. The station may also have purchased goodwill, due in large part to the significant number of acquisitions that have occurred in the industry.

3. As with any business valuation, it is desirable to obtain detailed financial information for the acquired business, the motives for the acquisition, the price and terms of the sale, information on the buyer, and other important qualitative information relating to the sale in order to perform a meaningful market analysis and comparison.

4. The motives for the acquisition are important to consider, as they can impact the price paid for a particular radio station. A radio station may have been acquired to take advantage of market synergies, to increase market share, or to expand into a particular geographic market.

5. Because of the high volume of transactions in the radio broadcasting industry subsequent to the adoption of the 1996 act, and the fact that there are a large

number of publicly traded radio companies, there is a sufficient amount of relevant industry transactional data to be able to use the guideline company method in most engagements. In addition, as radio broadcasting industry transactions are subject to regulatory approval, it is relatively straightforward to obtain relevant transaction documents.

D. Cable TV

1. The Communications Act prohibits the assignment of a license or the transfer of control of a licensee without prior approval of the FCC.
2. Cable systems are generally operated in accordance with nonexclusive franchises granted by a municipality or other state or local government entity in order to cross public rights-of-way. Cable franchises are generally granted for fixed terms and in many cases include monetary penalties for noncompliance. They may be terminable if the franchisee fails to comply with material provisions.
3. Significant intangible assets include FCC licenses, call letters, account lists, and audience growth potential. Accounting for license cost often includes the direct cost plus permits, as well as other costs to obtain permits for construction and expansion. This license represents the station's primary intangible asset.
4. As with any business valuation, it is desirable to obtain detailed financial information for the acquired business, the motives for the acquisition, the price and terms of the sale, information on the buyer, and other important qualitative information relating to the sale in order to perform a meaningful market analysis and comparison.
5. The motives for the acquisition are important to consider, as they can impact the price paid for a particular cable television company. A company may have been acquired to take advantage of market synergies, to increase market share, or to expand into a particular geographic market.

E. Restaurants

1. At first glance, restaurants appear similar and seemingly could all be treated the same. But in reality, each one is different and requires individual analysis.
2. A successful restaurant can make its owners wealthy; however, managing a restaurant is complex, and the failure rate is higher than most other businesses.
3. A major risk in restaurant valuation is the "risk of the unknown." Topping the list of unknowns is the risk of a competitor arriving shortly after a purchase.
4. Another potential unknown risk is the major reinvestment surprise.
5. Few restaurant managers know their break-even point, by year, by month, and by day.
6. This is the second secret of restaurant valuation. Variable expenses can fall dramatically as volume increases.
7. Management is the third secret of restaurant valuation.
8. Every restauranteur has a memorized rule of thumb. They are all different, and they seldom are correct. Readers of most valuation texts are certainly aware of all the problems, limitations, and flaws in the rule of thumb approach, if it can even be called that.

CHAPTER 5

Income Approach Valuation Process Flowchart

INTRODUCTION

The income approach is the most often used approach in valuing operating companies. It is the most direct approach in that it is based on the actual and/or anticipated earnings and cash flow parameters of a company, which are then directly correlated to a discount or capitalization rate that reflects the risk in achieving those earnings and cash flows. This is not to say it does not contain numerous subjective assumptions. It does. However, the data used to prepare this method continue to evolve and allow for more accurate valuations.

The purpose of the Income Approach Valuation Process Flowchart is to allow valuation analysts to follow a more structured process to determine how to apply the income approach properly. It also provides less experienced analysts with a roadmap to follow in selecting and supporting the various methods and assumptions used in the income approach. This guide also will provide all analysts with good documentation of the reasons the approach was applied in the manner ultimately determined.

The Income Approach Valuation Process Flowchart is presented in the form of an outline to allow easy adoption to a checklist for compliance. It also follows a series of questions to answer and concepts to consider when preparing the income approach. The cost of capital topic is not part of this guide.

INCOME APPROACH VALUATION PROCESS FLOWCHART

Business Name: _____

Date of Valuation: _____

Disclaimer Excluding Any Warranties: This Income Approach Valuation Process Flowchart is designed to provide guidance to analysts, auditors, and management, but is not to be used as a substitute for professional judgment. This guide does not include nor address all the considerations and assumptions in a valuation. These procedures must be altered to fit each assignment; the various factors listed in this flowchart may not be necessary for every valuation. The practitioner takes sole responsibility for implementation of this guide. The implied warranties of merchantability and fitness of purpose and all other warranties, whether express or implied, are excluded from this transaction and shall not apply to this guide.

I.   Input five years of financial statements or tax returns.

  A. If five years do not exist, number of years input _____

  B. Reason for inputting less than five years _____

II. Is a minority or control valuation being performed?

    _____ Minority   _____ Control

  A. Make all appropriate normalization adjustments including nonrecurring, nonoperating, and extraordinary items.

  B. If control value, list and explain all adjustments.

    1. Excess compensation

    2. Other perquisites

    3. Capital structure

    4. Other

III. Analyze historical trends and compare to industry information, economic information, and projected/anticipated performance.

  A. Revenue growth rates

    1. Investigate reasons for each year's growth.

    2. Explain all fluctuations.

      a. Generally upward

      b. Generally downward

      c. Erratic (up and down)

    3. Is historical growth in line with projected/anticipated performance? If not, explain the differences.

    4. Are historical growth and projected performance in line with industry and general economic growth rates? Explain.

  B. Gross margin

    1. Investigate reasons for each year's gross margins.

    2. Explain all fluctuations.

      a. Generally upward

      b. Generally downward

      c. Erratic (up and down)

    3. Is historical gross margin in line with projected/anticipated performance? If not, explain the differences.

    4. Are historical gross margin and projected performance in line with industry and general gross margins? Explain.

C. Selling, General and Administrative (S, G&A) expenses as a percent of revenue

    1. Investigate reasons for each year's expenses.

    2. Explain all fluctuations.

        a. Generally upward

        b. Generally downward

        c. Erratic (up and down)

    3. Are historical S, G&A expenses in line with projected/anticipated performance? If not, explain the differences.

    4. Are historical S, G&A expenses and projected performance in line with industry and general S, G&A expenses? Explain.

D. Operating income margin

    1. Investigate reasons for each year's operating income margin.

    2. Explain all fluctuations.

        a. Generally upward

        b. Generally downward

        c. Erratic (up and down)

    3. Are historical operating income margins in line with projected/anticipated performance? If not, explain the differences.

    4. Are historical operating income margins and projected performance in line with industry and general operating income margins? Explain.

E. Pretax income margin

    1. Investigate reasons for each year's pretax income margin.

    2. Explain all fluctuations.

        a. Generally upward

        b. Generally downward

        c. Erratic (up and down)

    3. Are historical pretax income margins in line with projected/anticipated performance? If not, explain the differences.

    4. Are historical pretax income margins and projected performance in line with industry and general pretax income margins? Explain.

F. Taxes

    1. Are taxes anticipated to change? _____ Yes _____ No

    2. Include both Federal and State taxes.

    3. If net operating losses exist, explain how they were handled.

G. Net income growth rates

   1. Investigate reasons for each year's net income growth.

   2. Explain all fluctuations.

      a. Generally upward

      b. Generally downward

      c. Erratic (up and down)

   3. Are historical net income growth rates in line with projected/antici-
      pated performance? If not, explain the differences.

   4. Are historical net income growth rates and projected performance in
      line with industry and general net income growth rates? Explain.

H. Working capital

   1. If using a debt-free discounted cash flow (DCF) method, make sure
      you are using debt-free working capital, which excludes short-term
      interest-bearing debt including notes and the current portion of long-
      term debt.

   2. Investigate reasons for each year's working capital.

   3. Explain all fluctuations.

      a. Generally upward

      b. Generally downward

      c. Erratic (up and down)

   4. Are historical working capital requirements in line with projected/
      anticipated performance? If not, explain the differences.

   5. Are historical working capital requirements and projected perfor-
      mance in line with industry and general working capital requirements?
      Explain.

I. Depreciation

   1. Investigate reasons for each year's depreciation.

   2. Explain all fluctuations.

      a. Generally upward

      b. Generally downward

      c. Erratic (up and down)

   3. Is historical depreciation in line with projected/anticipated perfor-
      mance? If not, explain the differences.

   4. Is historical depreciation and projected performance in line with indus-
      try and general depreciation? Explain.

J. Capital expenditures

1. Investigate reasons for each year's capital expenditures.

2. Explain all fluctuations.

a. Generally upward

b. Generally downward

c. Erratic (up and down)

3. Are historical capital expenditures in line with projected/anticipated performance? If not, explain the differences.

4. Are historical capital expenditures and projected performance in line with industry and general capital expenditures? Explain.

IV. Are there any nonoperating or excess assets? Explain why they are nonoperating or excess assets.

A. Identify all such assets, value separately, and make sure both income statement and balance sheet are adjusted both *historically* and *projected*. Remove the effect of nonoperating assets from the operating cash flows. Consider whether to discount nonoperating assets when valuing a minority interest.

1. Cars, boats, condos, houses

2. Real estate

3. Idle machinery and equipment

4. Working capital

5. Cash

6. Receivables

7. Inventory

8. Other

V. Are earnings and cash flow anticipated to continue consistent with past trends?

A. Yes

1. Consider using a capitalized cash flow (CCF) method instead of a DCF.

2. If using a CCF method, choose the period(s) and explain your choice.

a. Five-year straight average

b. Three-year straight average

c. Five-year weighted average

d. Three-year weighted average

e. Most recent 12 months trailing

    f. Most recent four quarters trailing

    g. Most recent fiscal year-end

    h. One-year forward

    i. Trend analysis

    j. Other _____

B. No

  1. If the future performance of the company is expected to change, consider using a DCF method. This usually means either growth rates or profit margins are anticipated to change, or a normalized level of cash flow has not been achieved currently. It may also mean that the business itself may be changing. Sometimes it may be appropriate or informative to use both methods of the income approach.

  2. Has the client prepared projections of future cash flows?
    _____ Yes _____ No

  3. If no, who prepared projections? _____

  4. Do projections include:

    a. Revenue

    b. Gross profits

    c. Depreciation

      (1) Book (remember to consider deferred taxes)

      (2) Tax (deferred taxes are not considered)

    d. S, G&A

    e. Operating income

    f. Other income/expenses

      (1) Interest expense

      (2) Interest income

      (3) Nonoperating income or expenses, such as real estate, securities

    g. Pretax income

    h. Net income after tax

    i. Capital expenditure needs

    j. Incremental working capital needs (Must be debt-free working capital if using a debt-free or invested-capital model. This means that all interest-bearing short-term debt is removed from the working capital calculation. This usually includes the current maturity of long-term debt.)

    k. Debt principal to be repaid

l. New debt principal in (Must be normalized in CCF and terminal year of DCF)

m. Deferred taxes if using book depreciation

n. Decide whether to use a debt-free or debt-inclusive model and explain your decision. _____ Debt-free _____ Debt-inclusive

o. Terminal-year value (What is your future anticipated perpetuity growth rate?)

VI. Is future growth rate greater than historical nominal Gross Domestic Product (GDP) growth of 6 to 6.5 percent? _____ Yes _____ No _____ Same Explain.

A. Is future growth rate greater than forecasted nominal GDP growth?

1. What is forecasted nominal GDP growth? _____

2. Explain.

B. Test growth rates in revenue versus earnings versus cash flow. If different, explain why.

C. Is there a large difference between the terminal-year growth rate and the growth rate in the last year of the discrete period? _____ Yes _____No

1. Explain.

2. Do not mix revenue growth rates with cash flow growth rates. They are often the same, but it is growth in normalized cash flow that is correct.

D. If using the Gordon Growth Model (GGM), apply the value in the terminal year as a multiple of EBITDA or EBIT. _____ EBITDA _____ EBIT

1. Is this consistent with the multiples used in the market approach?

a. EBITDA

b. EBIT

2. Explain. It is sometimes justified to test this against the market multiples adjusted downward to reflect the risk of projecting a multiple in future years.

E. Is the working capital assumption into perpetuity driven by the perpetuity growth rate? _____ Yes _____ No   Explain.

VII. Do capital expenditures and depreciation equal to each other (or similar) in the terminal year?

A. If yes, no further adjustment is necessary.

B. If no, normalize them to be equal or similar, or

1. If there is a material depreciation overhang, value it separately and add it to the value.

2. If there is a material capital expenditure overhang, value it separately and deduct it from the value.

VIII. Are projections and resultant value minority or control?
_____ Minority _____ Control

    A. Explain. If all discrete expenses have been added back—excess compensation, perquisites, capital structure—the value is on a control stand-alone value. If such expenses have not been added back, then the resultant value is on a minority stand-alone basis because the cash flows reflect the diminished cash flows and value. If the company has no discrete expenses to add back, then the value is the same for both minority and control. In this situation, some practitioners will take a smaller minority discount when valuing a minority interest to reflect the fact that, although the controlling stockholder is not taking cash out today, they could change that policy in the future, so there is added risk that diminishes value. Be careful using minority discounts derived from control premium studies (*Mergerstat Review* and Houlihan, Lokey, Howard and Zukin [HLHZ]) to discount for stand-alone minority value, since those studies reflect mostly synergized premiums paid by strategic buyers of public companies.

    B. Is the resultant value a marketable or liquid value? _____ Yes _____ No

        1. Explain. If using Ibbotson Associates data, the value is a marketable/liquid value and assumes a cash sale in less than three days. As such, a further discount for marketability/liquidity may be warranted for both a minority and control value. Some practitioners will discount minority interest at a greater amount than a controlling one. However, even a controlling interest cannot usually be sold in three days.

    C. Optional: Check terminal-year value using the Value Driver Formula (VDF)[1]

        1. VDF assumes that the company will always earn a return on new invested capital equal to its cost of capital and thus no increase in value. This is true regardless of the growth rate, since both returns on capital and the actual costs of new capital will grow at the same rate under this formula. VDF is sometimes used to check the individual components of the GGM for reasonableness.

        2. VDF = DFNI / WACC (DFNI is Debt-free Net Income)

        3. To check the components of GGM, we consider the value driver model:

            a. Continuing Value = FCF / (WACC − g) =
[NOPLAT (1 − g / r)] / (WACC − g)

                (1) FCF = Free cash flow, or (DFNI + Depr. − CAPEX − ΔW / C)

                (2) NOPLAT = Net operating profits less adjusted taxes (this is the same as DFNI)

---

[1] Copeland et al., *Valuation, Measuring and Managing the Value of Companies*, 4th ed. (John Wiley & Sons, Inc., 2005), pp. 271–290.

      (3) g = Growth rate in NOPLAT

      (4) r = Rate of return on new capital invested

  b. Using algebra, we deduce: FCF = NOPLAT $(1 - g / r)$, or FCF = DFNI $(1 - g / r)$

  c. Restating the formula:

      (1) DFNI + Depr. − CAPEX − ΔW / C = DFNI $(1 - g / r)$

      (2) As we know the individual components of the formula, we can test our conclusion of value by solving for g or r, such that:

         (a) g = r $[1 - ((\text{DFNI} + \text{Depr.} - \text{CAPEX} - \Delta W / C) / \text{DFNI})]$, and

         (b) r = g $/ [1 - ((\text{DFNI} + \text{Depr.} - \text{CAPEX} - \Delta W / C) / \text{DFNI})]$

      (3) If the calculated r is much greater or less than the discount rate used in your conclusion of value, maybe you need to reconsider your Depr., CAPEX, or ΔW / C growth, or even your discount rate.

4. What is VDF value?

  a. Is it higher or lower than GGM value?

      (1) If VDF is higher, then the company is destroying value by growing since the costs of capital must then be exceeding the return on capital.

      (2) If the VDF is lower, then the company is earning a return on capital higher than its cost of capital into perpetuity.

5. Conclusion: If used, correlate with other values derived from other valuation approaches/methods.

CHAPTER 6

Marketing, Managing, and Making Money in Valuation Services

Caveat: Most of the following information is presented in a best-case scenario where everything is almost perfect. It may not be possible or relevant to adopt all of these procedures, policies, and ideas. Each professional and firm should choose the resources that fit the firm/group, its philosophy, and its culture.

Disclaimer: For discussion and educational purposes only. Some topics may not be relevant to every practice. Valuation and litigation services are very much affected by specific facts and circumstances. As such, the views expressed in this chapter do not necessarily reflect the professional opinions or positions that the authors would take in every assignment or practice, or in providing valuation or litigation services in connection with an actual engagement, matter, or practice. Every situation and practice is unique, and differing facts and circumstances may result in variations of the information presented. Jim Hitchner, Financial Valuation Solutions LLC, The Financial Valuation Group LC, FVG Holdings, LC and FVG California partnership assume no responsibility for any errors in this information, use of this information, or reliance on the information. Use at your own risk.

SMART "MULTI-MARKETING": HOW TO LEVERAGE YOUR EFFORTS-SELLING AND NETWORKING BEYOND ONE ON ONE

The following point list is designed to assist the professional firm in planning an effective marketing strategy.

- Decide on target market you want to reach:
  - Attorneys;
  - Business owners;
  - CPAs;
  - Bankers; or
  - Other advisors.
- Publish an article:
  - Look back at last two years and do something different.
  - Court cases popular and very low risk.
  - Cap rates and discounts popular, but practice what you preach:
    - Remember, articles are discoverable.
  - Write on a subject that is leverageable and of interest to your target market.
  - Publishers are always in need of articles.

- Send a pitch letter.
- Tell them the subject has not been addressed in last two years.
- Call them.
- Get a commitment for article, assuming it is acceptable to the publisher and editor.
- Leverage the article:
  - Speak on the article:
    - Appraisal/Valuation Society meetings;
    - State CPA society meetings; and
    - National conferences.
  - Send article to clients.
  - Send article to prospects, for example, attorneys.
    - Invest in Martindale & Hubbell.
- Court case E-Flashes:
  - Very inexpensive except for initial setup of database.
  - E-mail.
  - Should come from practice leader.
  - Subject line important.
  - Court cases a good start.
  - Keep it simple and short.
  - Provide advertising:
    - A little up front (e.g., banners)(Appendix 6.1), and
    - A lot at the end.
  - Attached Adobe files can also be used.
    - See the Financial Valuation Group Sample (Appendix 6.2).
  - Sources:
    - AICPA;
    - ASA;
    - Financial Consulting Group (FCG);
    - Financial Valuation Group (FVG) (John Gilbert of FVG is the main source of FVG, FCG, AICPA, and ASA court case E-Flashes); and
    - Other local, state, or national society.
- Advertising:
  - Must be continuous;
  - Takes a while to be effective;
  - Must be classy;
  - Use color and images;
  - Stay away from clutter; and
  - See FVG Atlanta example (Appendix 6.3).
- Speeches:
  - Contact state CPA society groups;
  - Contact local appraisal/valuation chapters;
  - Contact bar associations;
  - Contact 1aw firms:
    - Breakfast and lunches at law firm good.
    - Cocktail parties at law firm or in same building good.
  - National conferences:
    - AICPA;

- ASA;
- NACVA; and
- IBA.
  - Industry associations:
    - All business owners interested in valuation.
    - Always looking for speakers.
    - Rules of thumb a big hook.
  - Make sure the participants learn at least two terrific new pieces of information as a take-away
- Teaching:
  - Volunteer for national BV organizations.
  - Teach what you are comfortable with.
  - Keeps you up to speed.
  - Good networking.
  - May be time consuming depending on the commitment.
  - Good for resume.
- Random thoughts:
  - The talk meter sales call.
    - Just the questions, man, just the questions (let the client talk).
  - Keep a manageable target list of prospects/clients.
    - Much work can come from a lesser number that you keep in constant contact with.
    - "Nifty Fifty" technique (50 main contacts).
  - Marketing is not a fancy word for selling.
  - Good work travels fast, bad work travels faster.
  - It's expensive to keep a client, but it's more expensive to gain a client.
  - Prospects who choose based on fee will continually choose on fee . . . hard to raise fees later.
  - Good work should be paid for.
  - Good work sometimes goes unnoticed.
  - Your bad work rarely goes unnoticed.
  - Love what you do and do what you love.
  - Get rid of difficult clients.
  - Do everything, well . . . almost everything, to keep "pay on time" clients.
  - Stay in front of clients . . . they sometimes forget about you.
  - Most of your competitors hate to market and sell.
  - The phone never rings unless you make it ring.
  - Cold calls are just that: cold.
  - Use warm-call techniques (get someone you know to help).
  - Be patient.
  - Be diligent.
  - Be different.
  - And always be good.

RISK MANAGEMENT: ENGAGEMENT LETTERS, REPORTS, AND TURNING DOWN WORK

The following list is intended to provide the professional with those items they should consider when establishing assignment guidelines and practices.

- Risk . . . not all purposes are created equal.
- Riskier engagements:
  - ESOPs;
  - Transactions;
  - 141/142 work for public clients;
  - Seat-of-the-pants valuations for any reason;
  - Any purpose without an engagement letter; and
  - Any purpose without the proper protection in an engagement letter.
- Engagement letters (see Engagement Letter and Report Language Examples section):
  - Must be written, bilateral, and signed.
    - One-way communication not a binding contract.
  - Restrictions on:
    - Who can see it.
    - Who can rely on it.
    - Purpose and use.
    - No other use.
    - Sometimes who is *not* allowed to see it.
    - Only good as of a single date.
    - Scope.
  - Protective language:
    - Indemnification.
    - Corporate/entity only without any liability to individuals.
    - Fees:
      - Retainer applied against last bill . . . stay ahead.
      - Client cannot sue unless fees paid up front.
      - Must be paid regardless of outcome of matter.
      - Must be paid regardless of what the court awards in fees.
      - Timing of billings and expected collections.
      - Interest on unpaid balances.
      - Can quit if not paid timely.
      - Caveat that you will inform client of higher fees due to unexpected events or information problems.
      - No report or testimony unless paid in full.
      - Require retainer before testimony.
    - Mediation/arbitration provision for disputes;
    - Disclaimers:
      - Not an attest service.
      - Reliability of data used.
    - Relationship check.
    - Form of work product/report.
    - Work paper retention policy.
    - Standards abided by:
      - USPAP, AICPA, NACVA, ASA, IBA.

- Confidentiality section:
  - May help in later litigation cases when asked about other clients.
- Other services and additional fees.
- Expiration date on engagement letter.
- Reports:
  - Type:
    - Detailed.
    - Summary.
    - Oral.
    - Other?
  - Protective language:
    - Repeat much of what is in engagement letter.
    - Belt and suspenders.
- Don't eat bad food.
  - When you're hungry you'll be tempted to eat anything . . . don't.
  - Signs of a possible difficult client:
    - Retainer resistance;
    - Fee or rate resistance;
    - Many suggested changes to engagement letter;
    - Unresponsive when you try to contact them;
    - Gruff and unpleasant;
    - Does not treat you with respect; and
    - Does not listen.
  - Bad jobs will:
    - Upset your staff;
    - Take a lot of energy;
    - Take away from your ability to work on good engagements and good clients;
    - Possibly cause billing and collection problems; and
    - Make you miserable.

ENGAGEMENT LETTER AND REPORT LANGUAGE EXAMPLES

Caution for Using Engagement Letter and Report Language Examples

This selected engagement letter and report language are to be adjusted to the facts and circumstances of each assignment/engagement. The language examples presented here are only a tool that is subordinate to the judgment of the valuation professional in charge of the engagement. This language should not be used unless the valuation professional understands each term and phrase in the language examples and has verified that the facts of an engagement were properly captured.

FVW readers and language example users MUST have an attorney review the terms of these engagement letter and report language examples to make sure that it reflects the particular needs of each firm. Jim Hitchner, Mike Mard, Financial Valuation Solutions LLC, The Financial Valuation Group, FVG Holdings, LC, FVG California Partnership, and The Financial Consulting Group, LC assume no responsibility for any errors in the language, use of the language, or reliance on the language. Use at your own risk.

Purpose and Objectives

The valuation is provided for the sole purpose of _____ planning.

The objective of the valuation is to provide an independent valuation analysis and report (OPTION: letter/summary report) to assist you in your determination of the fair market value of (a minority, a majority, a controlling interest, a __% interest) in (*COMPANY NAME*) ("_____" or "Company") as of _____.

Disclaimer

We will read and analyze, to the extent available and relevant, financial statements, income tax returns, contracts, agreements, property schedules, and such other records or other documents we deem appropriate. In addition, outside research sources and knowledgeable individuals will be consulted as necessary. Factual information provided will be relied upon as being true and correct. We will not perform an Audit, Review, or Compilation of financial statements in the capacity of certified public accountants under the standards promulgated by the American Institute of Certified Public Accountants ("AICPA"). Our work cannot be relied upon to discover errors, irregularities, or illegal acts including fraud or defalcations. As part of the valuation process, projections and/or forecasts of future operating results and related balance sheets may be utilized if deemed practical in the circumstances. If so, such projections and forecasts will be performed by management and represented as being management's best estimate of such future results and balance sheets. FIRM will not perform procedures prescribed by the AICPA that would otherwise be required were we to be engaged specifically to compile or examine such forecasts. Accordingly, the Company and its owners understand and accept that FIRM is not being employed in the capacity of examining certified public accountants and will not therefore express any form of comfort or assurance in the achievability of the forecasts or projections or the reasonableness of underlying assumptions.

Form of Work Product

(OPTION 1)

Our valuation will be presented in a complete report for your use. Our analysis and report will meet the development and reporting requirements of the Uniform Standards of Professional Appraisal Practice ("USPAP") of the Appraisal Foundation and the Business Valuation Standards of the American Society of Appraisers. (*Insert other association standards as appropriate, e.g., AICPA, NACVA, IBA.*) (Option) Our report will be subject to the Statement of Assumptions, Contingent and Limiting Conditions contained as Appendix B.

Fees and Billing

Our total fee for the valuation services and report will be $_____ to $_____, plus expenses. Expenses include travel and meals, document and report reproduction, telephone, mail, computer charges, research information, and related overhead.

An initial retainer fee is due upon acceptance of this contract. Accordingly, an invoice for our (nonrefundable) retainer fee of $_____ is attached. The retainer will be applied to the last invoice.

Following the receipt of the retainer and the commencement of work on this project, fees and expenses will be billed to you (INSERT TIME PERIOD—monthly, quarterly, etc.) and are due upon presentation of statements. Our final bill must be paid prior to issuing our final report. If for any reason the transaction is terminated prior to its consummation and FIRM is requested to terminate work, then FIRM's fee shall not be less than FIRM's total time and costs at the normal rate for such projects, plus out-of-pocket expenses.

Our fee is based on our knowledge of the facts and circumstances as of the date of this engagement letter. This fee is also contingent upon our receiving all data and information in a timely manner. Any changes that require additional professional time will be discussed before proceeding.

Any invoice not paid within thirty (30) business days following presentation shall bear interest at the rate of 1–1/2% compounded each month. Should it be necessary to refer any invoice for collection or arbitration, you shall be responsible for all costs of collection and arbitration, including attorney's fees. In the event that you disagree with or question any amount due under an invoice, you agree that you shall communicate such a disagreement to us in writing within thirty (30) days of the invoice date. Any claim not made within that period shall be deemed waived.

When initiated by the Client and as a condition precedent to mediation, arbitration, or suit, the parties agree that all invoices billed by FIRM shall be paid in full, including accrued but unpaid interest.

Arbitration Provision (Could Be Mediation Provision)

All claims, disputes, and other matters in question between FIRM and you, the client, arising out of, or relating to, this Representation and Engagement Letter, or its breach, shall be decided by arbitration at (CITY, STATE). Either FIRM or you may serve upon the other by certified mail a written demand that the dispute, explaining in detail its nature, be submitted to arbitration. Within ten (10) days after service of such demand, each of us shall appoint a neutral arbitrator from the approved list of mediators and arbitrators appointed by the (_____ _____ Court). If either of us fails within the specified time to appoint an arbitrator, the single arbitrator appointed will have the right to decide alone, and his decision will be binding on both of us. The two arbitrators appointed shall select and appoint an independent third arbitrator. The decision of two arbitrators in writing under oath shall be final and binding upon us. The arbitrators shall decide the total of the expenses, including reasonable attorney's fees, and award them to the prevailing party. If the two arbitrators appointed by us fail to agree upon a third arbitrator within ten (10) days after their appointment, then either of us may apply, upon notice to the other, to any court of competent jurisdiction in CITY, STATE for the appointment of a third arbitrator, and any such appointment shall be binding upon us. Judgment on the arbitrators' decision, including the decision on who is to pay expenses, may be entered by any court of competent jurisdiction in CITY, STATE.

(OPTION)

Representations

Our report will be subject to the Representations attached hereto as Appendix A. At the conclusion of the engagement, we may require you to sign an additional representation letter on these and various other assumptions and information relied upon in the valuation.

(OPTION)

Statement of Assumptions, Contingent, and Limiting Conditions

Our report will be subject to the Statement of Assumptions, Contingent, and Limiting Conditions or something similar to, as attached hereto as Appendix B.

Indemnity

(See your attorney and/or the AICPA guide on engagement letters. Highly recommended in certain types of valuations.) Also tie to *Daubert* challenges below.

Daubert Challenges

As "*Daubert* challenges" (or other similar challenges to the admissibility of an expert's testimony) have become an increasingly common means of contesting an opposing expert's opinions, you agree to compensate us for any time or out-of-pocket expenses incurred in defending such challenges. Additionally, should a trier-of-fact determine that the testimony to be offered by a member of our FIRM be excluded, you and your client agree to indemnify and hold harmless the FIRM and its personnel from any claims, liabilities, costs, and expenses arising from this exclusion, except to the extent it is finally determined that such exclusion resulted solely from the FIRM's gross negligence or willful misconduct. (See your attorney.)

Relationships

We have undertaken a limited review of our records to determine the professional relationships of FIRM with the persons and entities you identified in connection with this matter. We have not identified any such relationships at this time. (Option: We have relayed all such relationships to you.) While we will notify you immediately of any relationships that come to our attention, we cannot assure you that all such relationships will come to light.

Confidentiality and Work Papers

We agree to hold in strict confidentiality all proprietary information provided by you in connection with this project. We agree not to share any confidential information with persons outside FIRM. The working papers for this engagement will be retained in our files and are available for your reference. We would be available to support our valuation conclusion(s), should this be required. Those services would be performed for an additional fee. (Option: The ownership of schedules, information, and other work papers developed during the assignment by FIRM or supplied by the Company are the sole property of FIRM and are not subject to examination or production to the client at any time during or after the engagement.)

Termination

Failure to make the payments required by this agreement, or failure by you to comply with the terms of this agreement, will release FIRM from this agreement.

Other Services

If FIRM is called upon to render services, give testimony, produce documents, answer depositions or interrogatories, or otherwise become involved in connection with any administrative or judicial proceedings, investigations, or inquiries relating to the engagement, the Company will pay, in addition to other fees here, for the time reasonably required to be expended by any officers or employees of FIRM, at their standard hourly rates as then in effect, plus out-of-pocket expenses relating thereto. Professional fees for such services are independent of this engagement.

Corporate Obligation

The obligations of FIRM are solely corporate obligations, and no officer, principal, director, employee, agent, shareholder, or controlling person shall be subjected to any personal liability whatsoever to any person or entity, nor will any such claim be asserted by or on behalf of any other party to this agreement or any person relying upon the opinion.

Distribution of Analysis, Conclusions, and Report

Our analysis, conclusions, and report, which are to be used only in their entirety, are for the use of the Company, their accountants and attorneys, solely to assist them in their determination of the value of the Company for (INSERT PURPOSE). They are not to be used for any other purpose, or by any other party for any purpose, without our express written consent. (Option) Our report may be furnished to the (example—Internal Revenue Service). No third parties are intended to be benefited.

Any summary of, or reference to, the opinion, any verbal presentation with respect thereto, or other references to FIRM in connection with the transaction will be, in each instance, subject to FIRM's prior review and written approval, except as may be required by a governmental agency or court. The opinion will not be included in, summarized, or referred to in any manner in any materials distributed to the public without FIRM's express prior written consent.

Acceptance

If this engagement letter is satisfactory to you, please indicate approval of the terms set forth above and attached hereto by signing and dating the engagement letters and returning one of the originals. Retain the other original for your file. This offer for engagement will expire if not accepted within ____ days.

ASSUMPTIONS AND LIMITING CONDITIONS EXAMPLES

Caution for Using Assumptions and Limiting Conditions Language Example

This selected assumptions and limiting conditions language is to be adjusted to the facts and circumstances of each assignment/engagement. The language example presented here is only a tool that is subordinate to the judgment of the valuation professional in charge of the engagement. This language should not be used unless the valuation professional understands each term and phrase in the language example and has verified that the facts of an engagement were properly captured.

FVW readers and language example users MUST have an attorney review the terms of this assumptions and limiting conditions language example to make sure that it reflects the particular needs of each firm. Jim Hitchner, Financial Valuation Solutions, LLC, The Financial Valuation Group, FVG Holdings, LC, FVG California Partnership and The Financial Consulting Group, LC assume no responsibility for any errors in the language, use of the language, or reliance on the language. Use at your own risk.

Language Examples

The primary assumptions and limiting conditions pertaining to the value estimate conclusion(s) stated in this report are summarized below. Other assumptions are cited elsewhere in this report.

The valuation may not be used in conjunction with any other appraisal or study. The value conclusion(s) stated in this appraisal is based on the program of utilization described in the report and may not be separated into parts. The appraisal was prepared solely for the purpose, function, and party so identified in the report. The appraisal report may not be reproduced, in whole or in part, and the findings of the report may not be utilized by a third party for any purpose, without the express written consent of FIRM.

No change of any item in any of the appraisal report shall be made by anyone other than FIRM, and we shall have no responsibility for any such unauthorized change.

Unless otherwise stated in the appraisal, the valuation of the business has not considered or incorporated the potential economic gain or loss resulting from contingent assets, liabilities, or events existing as of the valuation date.

The working papers for this engagement are being retained in our files and are available for your reference. We would be available to support our valuation conclusion(s), should this be required. Those services would be performed for an additional fee.

Neither all nor any part of the contents of the report shall be disseminated or referred to the public through advertising, public relations, news or sales media, or any other public means of communication, or referenced in any publication, including any private or public offerings, including but not limited to those filed with the Securities and Exchange Commission or other governmental agency, without the prior written consent and approval of FIRM.

Management is assumed to be competent and the ownership to be in responsible hands, unless noted otherwise in this report. The quality of business management can have a direct effect on the viability and value of the business.

Unless otherwise stated, no effort has been made to determine the possible effect, if any, on the subject business due to future federal, state, or local legislation, including any environmental or ecological matters or interpretations thereof.

Events and circumstances frequently do not occur as expected, and there will usually be differences between prospective financial information and actual results, and those differences may be material. Accordingly, to the extent that any of the information used in this analysis and report requires adjustment, the resulting fair market value would be different.

Any decision to purchase, sell, or transfer any interest in the COMPANY, or its assets, shall be your sole responsibility, as well as the structure to be utilized and the price to be accepted.

The selection of the price to be accepted requires consideration of factors beyond the information we will provide or have provided. An actual transaction involving the subject business might be concluded at a higher value or at a lower value, depending upon the circumstances of the transaction and the business, and the knowledge and motivations of the buyers and sellers at that time.

All facts and data set forth in our report are true and accurate to the best of the appraiser's knowledge and belief.

No investigation of legal fees or title to the property has been made, and the owner's claim to the property has been assumed valid. No consideration has been given to liens or encumbrances that may be against the property except as specifically stated in the valuation report. We assume that the COMPANY is a legitimate corporation.

All recommendations as to fair market value are presented as the appraiser's conclusion based on the facts and data set forth in this report.

During the course of the valuation, we have considered information provided by management and other third parties. We believe these sources to be reliable, but no further responsibility is assumed for their accuracy.

This valuation study is intended solely for use by the owners of interests in the COMPANY and their accountants and attorneys, for gift tax (OTHER PURPOSE), and should not be used for any other purpose or distributed to third parties, in whole or in part, without the express written consent of FIRM. This report may be provided to the Internal Revenue Service (OTHER USERS).

We have no responsibility or obligation to update this report for events or circumstances occurring subsequent to the date of this report.

Our report is based upon historical and/or prospective financial information provided to us by management and other third parties. This information has not been audited, reviewed, or compiled by us, nor has it been subjected to any type of audit, review, or compilation procedures by us, nor have we audited, reviewed, or compiled the books and records of the subject company. Had we audited, reviewed, or compiled the underlying data, matters may have come to our attention that would have resulted in our using amounts that differ from those provided; accordingly, we take no responsibility for the underlying data presented or relied upon in this report.

We have relied upon the representations of the owners and other third parties concerning the value and useful conditions of all equipment, real estate, investments used in the business, and any other assets or liabilities except as specifically stated to the contrary in this report. We have not attempted to confirm whether or not all assets of the business are free and clear of liens and encumbrances, or that the COMPANY has good title to all assets.

Our valuation judgment, shown herein, pertains only to the subject business, the stated value standard (fair market OR OTHER), as at the stated valuation date, and only for the stated valuation purposes (gift tax reporting OR OTHER).

The various estimates of value presented in this report apply to the valuation report only and may not be used out of the context presented herein.

In all matters that may be potentially challenged by a Court, Internal Revenue Service, Securities and Exchange Commission, or other regulatory or governmental body, we do not take responsibility for the degree of reasonableness of contrary positions that others may choose to take, nor for the costs or fees that may be incurred in the defense of our recommendations against challenge(s). We will, however, retain our supporting work papers for your matter(s) and will be available to assist in the defense of our professional positions taken at our then-current rates, plus direct expenses at actual, and according to our then-current Standard Professional Agreement.

LIBRARY RESOURCES

The following list is intended to provide a basic list of library resources for the professional firm. It is not all inclusive.

Books

Cimasi, CBI, CBC, Robert James. *A Guide to Consulting Services for Emerging Healthcare Organizations.* Hoboken, NJ: John Wiley & Sons, 1999.

Cook, Larry. *Financial Valuation of Employee Stock Ownership Plan Shares.* Hoboken, NJ: John Wiley & Sons, 2005.

Dietrich, Mark O. *Medical Practice Valuation Guidebook 2001/2002.* San Diego, CA: Windsor Professional Information, LLC, 2001.

Dunn, Robert L. *Recovery of Damages for Lost Profits,* 6th edition. Westport, CT: Lawpress Corporation, 2005.

Fishman, Jay E., Shannon P. Pratt, and J. Clifford Griffith. *PPC's Guide to Business Valuations,* 16th edition. Fort Worth, TX: Practitioners Publishing Company, 2006.

Hitchner, James R., ed. *Financial Valuation Applications and Models,* 2nd Edition. Hoboken, NJ: John Wiley & Sons, 2006.

Hitchner, James R., and Michael J. Mard. *Financial Valuation Workbook,* 2nd Edition. Hoboken, NJ: John Wiley & Sons, 2006.

Koller, Tim, Marc Goedhart, and David Wessels. *Valuation: Measuring and Managing the Value of Companies,* 4th edition. Hoboken, NJ: John Wiley & Sons, 2005.

Lang, Eva, and Jan Tudor. *Best Websites for Financial Professionals, Business Appraisers, and Accountants,* 2nd edition. Hoboken, NJ: John Wiley & Sons, 2003.

Laro, David, and Shannon P. Pratt. *Business Valuation and Taxes: Procedure, Law and Perspective.* Hoboken, NJ: John Wiley & Sons, 2005.

Mard, Michael M., Robert R. Dunn, Edi Osborne, and James S. Rigby, Jr. *Driving Your Company's Value: Strategic Benchmarking for Value.* Hoboken, NJ: John Wiley & Sons, 2004.

Mard, Michael J., James R. Hitchner, and Steven D. Hyden. *Valuation for Financial Reporting: Fair Value Measurement, Intangible Assets and Goodwill,* Second Edition. Hoboken, NJ: John Wiley & Sons (to be published 2007).

Mercer, Z. Christopher. *Valuing Enterprise and Shareholder Cash Flows: The Integrated Theory of Business Valuation.* Memphis, TN: Peabody Publishing, LP, 2004.

Pratt, Shannon P. *Cost of Capital: Estimation and Applications,* 2nd edition, Hoboken, NJ: John Wiley & Sons, 2002.

Pratt, Shannon P. *Business Valuation Discounts and Premiums.* Hoboken, NJ: John Wiley & Sons, 2001.

Pratt, Shannon P. *The Market Approach to Valuing Businesses,* 2nd edition, Hoboken, NJ: John Wiley & Sons, 2005.

Pratt, Shannon P., *Valuing a Business: The Analysis and Appraisal of Closely Held Companies,* 5th edition. New York: McGraw-Hill (to be published 2007).

Pratt, Shannon P., Reilly, Robert F., and Robert P. Schweihs. *Valuing Small Businesses and Professional Practices.* New York: McGraw-Hill, 1998.

Reilly, Robert F. and Robert P. Schweihs. *Valuing Intangible Assets.* New York: McGraw-Hill, 1999.

Reilly, Robert F. and Robert P. Schweihs. *The Handbook of Business Valuation and Intellectual Property Analysis.* New York: The McGraw-Hill Companies, 2004.

Slee, Robert T. *Private Capital Market: Valuation, Capitalization, and Transfer of Private Business Interests.* Hoboken, NJ: John Wiley & Sons, 2004.

Smith, Gordon V., and Russell L. Parr. *Intellectual Property: Valuation Exploitation and Infringement Damages.* Hoboken, NJ: John Wiley & Sons, 2006.

Smith, Gordon V. and Russell L. Parr. *Valuation of Intellectual Property and Intangible Assets,* 3rd edition. Hoboken, NJ: John Wiley & Sons, 2000.

Trugman, Gary R. *Understanding Business Valuation: A Practical Guide to Valuing Small to Medium-Sized Businesses,* 2nd edition. New York: American Institute of Certified Public Accountants, 2002.

Weil, Roman L., Michael J. Wagner, Christian W. Hughes, and Peter B. Frank. *Litigation Services Handbook: The Role of the Financial Expert,* 4th edition. Hoboken, NJ: John Wiley & Sons, 2006.

West, Tom, *The 2006 Business Reference Guide: The Essential Guide to Pricing a Business,* 16th edition. Worcester, MA: Business Brokerage Press, 2006.

West, Thomas L. and Jeffrey D. Jones. *Handbook of Business Valuation,* Second Edition. Hoboken, NJ: John Wiley & Sons, 1999.

Data Sources

ASA Business Valuation E-Letter
ASA Fast Read
Business Valuation Resources (www.bvlibrary.com)
The Financial Valuation Group (www.fvginternational.com)
Ibbotson Associates (www.ibbotson.com)
Institute of Business Appraisers (www.go-iba.org)
JT Research (www.jtresearch.com)
Mercer Capital Management (www.bizval.com)
Morningstar Principia (www.morningstarprincipia.com)
National Association of Certified Valuation Analysts (www.c-e-i-r.com)
Partnership Profiles, *Direct Investments Spectrum* (formerly *The Partnership Spectrum*), Dallas, TX: Partnership Profiles, Inc. (www.partnershipprofiles.com)

Periodicals

ASA Professional, published by the American Society of Appraisers, www.appraisers
    .org
Business Appraisal Practice, published by the Institute of Business Appraisers, www.go-iba.org
Business Valuation Review, published quarterly by the Business Valuation Committee of the American Society of Appraisers, www.appraisers.org
CPA Consultant, published quarterly by The American Institute of Certified Public Accountants (AICPA), www.cpa2biz.com
CPA Expert, published quarterly by The American Institute of Certified Public Accountants (AICPA), www.cpa2biz.com
Financial Valuation and Litigation Expert, published bimonthly by Valuation Products & Services, LC, www.valuationproducts.com
National Litigation Consultants' Review, Litigation Consultants, LLC, www .litigationconsultantsllc.com
Business Valuation Update, Published monthly by Business Valuation Resources, L.L.C., www.BVResources.com
Valuation Case Digest, Valuation Information, Inc., www.valuationinformation.com
Valuation Strategies, published bimonthly by Warren, Gorham & Lamont, a division of RIA, www.thomson.com
Value Examiner, published bimonthly by the National Association of Certified Valuation Analysts (NACVA), www.nacva.com

---

KEEPING UP TECHNICALLY

The following list is intended to provide the professional with resources and suggestions for maintaining their professional designation(s) and keeping up to date with the valuation industry.

- Attend one or two national conventions per year.
- Attend all local events.
- Join state CPA society valuation/litigation sections or local ASA, IBA, NACVA chapters:
  - Good information/resources.
  - Good for mentoring.
- Read:
  - At least two to four different periodicals per year.
  - At least one valuation book per year.
  - Organization E-Flashes or Alerts:
    - The Financial Valuation Group.
    - Financial Consulting Group (FCG).
    - AICPA.
    - ASA.
  - Once a year, review:
    - Revenue Ruling 59-60.
    - Ibbotson's SBBI Valuation Edition.
    - Duff & Phelps Risk Premium Report.
    - USPAP.
    - Standards of the BV associations you belong to.
    - How transaction databases you use are constructed.
- Volunteer for committee work.
- Join FCG.

PRACTICE BENCHMARKS FOR PRODUCTIVITY, BILLINGS, REALIZATION, AND THE BOTTOM LINE

The following list is intended to demonstrate basic items that should be considered when a professional firm establishes internal productivity and billing procedures. Some information is based on a best case model.

> - Question to staff: What the heck do you do all day?
> - Answer: If you were around, you'd know.
> - Question to staff: Why didn't you bill at least seven hours today?
> - Answer: Because you have me doing all your unbillable tasks including all this ridiculous admin stuff.

- Productivity:
  - General annual benchmarks depend on practice and type of work.
    - Staff above 90 percent.
    - Managers (nonselling) above 80 percent.
    - Partners above 50 percent.
  - Group must understand that some months are way up and some way down depending on work volume and staff availability.

- Billings:
  - High-end, efficient practice can bill an hourly rate three to four times raw cost hourly rate of staff.
  - Should bill between 90 percent and 100 percent of billable hours generated by staff.
    - May be lower for firms with heavier reliance on fixed-fee engagements.
- Realization:
  - Should collect between 90 percent and 100 percent of what is billed to client.
    - Overruns should be investigated and managed with client before final billing and preferably earlier.
    - Engagement letter language important here.
- Bottom Line:
  - High-end, efficient practice should be over 50 percent profit margin before partner compensation.
  - Over 30 percent acceptable depending on the type of practice and type of work.
- Golden Rule:
  - Seldom really followed.
  - Very easy . . .
  - Tie performance measures DIRECTLY to pay.

FINDING, TRAINING, AND RETAINING THE RIGHT STAFF FOR YOUR PRACTICE

The following list is intended to list basic items that should be considered for a professional firm's workforce.

- Finding Staff:
  - Use your staff to find staff:
    - Provide incentives.
  - Post at the local universities:
    - Full time;
    - Interns.
  - Competition.
  - ASA BVR or E Letter.
  - State CPA Society.
- Training staff:
  - In-house always the best.
    - Staff should constantly be asking questions.
    - Partners should always be asking staff "why" they did what they did.
  - AICPA.
  - ASA.
  - NACVA.
  - IBA.

- Retaining staff:
  - Treat them with respect.
  - Fear-based leadership is not leadership:
    - Only effective in the short term.
    - Learning in a fear-based environment takes an emotional toll.
  - Keep them informed.
    - Team players know what is going on.
  - Pay them above market.
    - Much more expensive to replace staff than to keep them.
    - Don't worry, your competition won't do this.
  - Provide growth opportunities.
    - Transfer existing relationships to staff.
    - Partner/principal can get new clients much easier than staff.
  - Where feasible, flexible work arrangements.

DELEGATE LITIGATION ENGAGEMENTS TO STAFF

The following list is intended to demonstrate partner and staff traits and practices that are critical in delegating litigation engagements.

- What it takes:
  - A change in leadership philosophy:
    - Cannot be control freak.
    - Must want to grow your practice.
    - Type of staff matters but it's you, not the staff.
    - Must have trust but rely on controls and checks.
  - Access to leader:
    - A five-minute conversation with staff can save hours and sometimes even days of work.
    - Must not get annoyed when constantly asked questions and direction from staff.
    - It really takes only one to three hours a day of leader time.
    - Leader can be chargeable through inspection and direction (depends on engagement).
    - Each staff person should have the leader's cell phone.
  - The right staff:
    - Again, leadership is critical, but the right staff members are important.
    - Detail orientation . . . no shooting from the hip.
    - Must feel comfortable asking questions.
    - Cannot be afraid to admit they are puzzled or do not understand what they are doing.
    - Up to leader to set the tone.
    - The model works best with more senior staff but will work with less experienced staff as well.
    - Willingness to ask each other questions as well as the leader.

- Controls and checks:
  - People do what you *inspect*, not what you *expect*.
    - Check each person at least once daily.
    - Effective in smaller groups.
    - Larger organizations: Check direct reports.
    - Rough rule of thumb: Check junior staff at a time interval of two hours or so for each year of experience.
    - Tell them to bring their work and explain the task they are working on, how long they expect to be working on that task, and what their next two tasks are.
    - Make sure they understand the big picture and not just the specific piece they are working on.
    - More senior staff should also check in at least once a day or so.
    - Schedule detailed reviews of work completed to date at reasonable intervals.
    - Where feasible, make staff take notes and tell you what was agreed upon at the meeting before they move on.
    - At the next meeting, make sure they have their notes.
  - Use control sheets where possible.
    - This is a list of who reviewed it and when it was reviewed (Appendix 6.4).
    - Use of cold reviews.
    - It is up to the leader to determine how detailed these control sheets need to be.
  - Summary of findings binder:
    - Standardize it.
    - Everything important summarized with copies of the major backup items.
    - Should point to where everything is and where it came from, including other file binders.
    - Use it to prepare for trial, if necessary.
  - Footing, Proofing, and Comparing:
    - Done by another staff member.
    - Signed off by leader.
    - Recheck changes at end of engagement since such changes are often made under deadline pressure.
- Bottom line:
  - Should go up.
  - Leader must still get into the details, but if engagement is organized properly that will happen.
  - Know the strengths and weaknesses of each staff member.
    - Remember, you can change habits but not personalities.
  - Leader must be disciplined and consistent.

APPENDIX 6.1: SAMPLE FVG E-FLASH COVER SHEET

Welcome to
The FVG Tax Court E-Flash,
easily accessible information on important tax court information.

Please click on the attached PDF file to access news you can use.
We encourage you to forward this E-Flash, with attribution intact, to other
interested parties.
For the full text of this case or more information on FVG, visit our website at
www.fvginternational.com.

* * * * * * * * * *

The Financial Valuation Group of Atlanta, Inc.
provides Business Valuation, Expert Testimony, and Litigation Consulting Services.

* * * * * * * * * *

James R. Hitchner, CPA/ABV, ASA
3340 Peachtree Road, N.E.
Suite 1785, Tower Place
Atlanta, GA 30326
(404) 873–6633
jhitchner@fvginternational.com
www.fvginternational.com

* * * * * * * * * *

To unsubscribe from E-Flash distribution, please respond to this e-mail and
include your e-mail address and the word UNSUBSCRIBE in the subject line.
Thank you.

APPENDIX 6.2: SAMPLE FVG E-FLASH

FINANCIAL VALUATION GROUP

When Results Count

Consulting • Valuations • Expert Testimony

Volume 7-5 / 2005   Edited by John R. Gilbert ABV, ASA - Managing Director

California (Los Angeles)
James S. Rigby ABV, ASA
213.362.9991

California (Oakland)
John J. Mayerhofer
FACHE
510.531.2943

California (Silicon Valley)
Robert T. Lanz
408.777.2914

Florida (Tampa)
Michael J. Mard ABV, ASA
813.985.2232

Steven Hyden ASA
813.985.2232

Florida (Ft. Lauderdale)
Michael A. Crain ABV, ASA,
CFA, CFE
954.382.2201

Georgia (Atlanta)
James R. Hitchner ABV, ASA
404.873.6633

Illinois (Chicago)
Michael J. Mattson
773.769.3045

Iowa (Des Moines)
Terry J. Allen ABV, ASA
515.953.4498

Massachusetts (Boston)
Stephen J. Bravo ABV, ASA
508.872.6060

Missouri (Kansas City)
Terry J. Allen ABV, ASA
816.373.3340

Missouri (St. Louis)
Ralph Ostermueller ABV, ASA
314.965.5921

Montana (Great Falls)
John R. Gilbert ABV, ASA
406.453.1800

Please contact us via email:

info@fvginternational.com

Tax Valuation E-Flash

Estate of Kelley v. Commissioner, T.C. Memo, 2005-235, October 11, 2005

The Tax Court allowed a 32% combined discount for lack of control and marketability for a decedent's 94.83% limited partnership interest in a family limited partnership owning only cash and certificates of deposit. The Court allowed the same discount for decedent's one third interest in the LLC that owned the 1% general partnership interest.

Decedent and his daughter and son-in-law formed KLLP in 1999. Each contributed cash or certificates of deposit in exchange for limited partner interests. KLBP, LLC, owned one-third by decedent and two-thirds by his daughter and son-in-law, held the 1% general partner interest in KLLP. Decedent died a few months after formation and there were no transfers of interests after the initial formation. The taxpayers claimed a 53.5% combined discount for lack of control and marketability while the IRS claimed a 25.2% combined discount.

Taxpayer Expert
The taxpayer appraiser gave an 80% weight to the net asset value and 20% to the income approach. He then applied a discount for lack of control based on general equity closed-end mutual funds. It was his opinion that KLLP was most similar to the closed-end funds with price to net asset value discounts of 21.8% to 25.5% in the 4th quartile. The appraiser then reviewed

> The taxpayers claimed a 53.5% combined discount for lack of control and marketability while the IRS claimed a 25.2% combined discount.

the data from Partnership Profiles that showed the discount to net asset value for 18 publicly registered partnerships was 29% and the data for 100 publicly registered partnerships that had a 27% average discount. He concluded a 25% discount for lack of control was appropriate.

The expert based his discount for lack of marketability on restricted stock studies. The expert also discussed eight factors that provided barriers to marketability for limited partnership interests. Based on this analysis, the expert determined a 38% discount for lack of marketability was appropriate.

Click Here for Full Text of Cases

When <u>Results</u> Count

Consulting • Valuations • Expert Testimony

Volume 7-5 / 2005   Edited by John R. Gilbert ABV, ASA · Managing Director

Services Offered:

- Corporate Transaction Services
- Tax Related Services
- International Valuations
- Employee Stock Ownership Plans
- Litigation Services
- Business Damage Analysis
- Financial Forensics
- Intellectual Property Services
- Financial Reporting (SFAS 141 & 142)
- SEC Review

For a complete listing of our services, please visit:

www.fvginter national.com

Founding Member

FCG

Financial Consulting Group, L.C.

Click Here for Full Text of Cases

IRS Expert

The IRS expert relied solely on the net asset value. He used the arithmetic mean discount to net asset value for closed-end funds of 12% to determine his discount for lack of control. He believed using the mean removed the marketability element in the discounts or premiums.

For the discount for lack of control, the IRS expert relied on a study by Dr. Mukesh Bajaj and

> The Court also believed that the Partnership Profiles data overstates the discount because they contain some element of marketability.

determined a 15% discount for lack of marketability was appropriate considering the low risk of the partnership's investment portfolio.

The Court

The Court relied solely on the net asset value, believing the income approach was not appropriate for a partnership holding only cash and certificates of deposit. For the discount for lack of control, the Tax Court believed that KLLP's lack of similarity to the closed-end mutual funds required the use of more than just the 4th quartile. The Court also believed that the Partnership Profiles data overstates the discount because they contain some element of marketability. The

> The Court also rejected the IRS expert's conclusion, but did conclude that the Bajaj study was an appropriate tool for determining the discount for lack of control.

Court found neither expert particularly persuasive, but determined a 12% discount for lack of control was appropriate.

For the discount for lack of marketability, the Court believed that there are fundamental differences between operating companies used in the discount studies and an entity holding easily valued and liquid interests like cash and certificates of deposit. The Court was also troubled that the taxpayer expert did not analyze the data from the studies and rejected the taxpayer expert's conclusion.

The Court also rejected the IRS expert's conclusion, but did conclude that the Bajaj study was an appropriate tool for determining the discount for lack of control. The Court did not believe

When <u>Results</u> Count

Consulting • Valuations • Expert Testimony

Volume 7-5 / 2005   Edited by John R. Gilbert ABV, ASA - Managing Director

Our National & International Experience Includes:

Aerospace
Agriculture
Automotive
Banking
Chemical
Construction
Dairy Farms
Distribution
Farm Management Companies
Finanancial Services
Flour & Grain Mills
Food Processors
Furniture
Healthcare
Hospitality
Insurance
High-Tech Companies
Manufacturing
Oil and Gas / Mining
Power Generation
Professional Firms
Publishing
Ranching
Service Companies
Software Companies
Telecommunications
Transportation

Founding Member

FCG

Financial Consulting Group, L.C.

Click Here for Full Text of Cases

the expert properly applied the study. The Bajaj study divided the discount into three groups with the middle group having a discount of 20.36%. The Court relied on *McCord v. Commissioner*, 120 T.C. No. 13, which used this middle group, rounded to 20%. The Court further cited the analysis in *Lappo v. Commissioner*, T.C. Memo 2003-258, in which an additional 3% marketability discount was allowed because of characteristics specific to the partnership and added the same 3%, resulting in a total discount for lack of marketability of 23%.

The Court allowed the same discounts for the decedent's 33.33% interest in KLBP, the LLC that owned a one percent general partner interest in KLLP. The discounts were applied directly to the one percent general partner interest without allocation between the limited partnership and LLC ownership interests.

APPENDIX 6.3: SAMPLE FVG ADVERTISEMENT FROM *CURRENT ACCOUNTS*, GSCPA BIMONTHLY PUBLICATION

APPENDIX 6.4: SAMPLE FVG CONTROL SHEET

Valuation Services
Engagement Log Sheet

Client _____	Fee (range) _____
Client Contact _____	
Address _____	Budget _____
_____	
Phone _____	
Facsimile _____	
Subject Company _____	
Nature of Business _____	
Interest Valued _____	
Purpose of Valuation _____	
Date of Valuation _____	

	Initial	Date	W/P Reference
Engagement Selection			
Independence Relationship Check Performed	_____	_____	_____
Proposal Issued	_____	_____	_____
Engagement Letter Issued	_____	_____	_____
Engagement Letter Executed	_____	_____	_____
Indemnification Obtained, if applicable	_____	_____	_____
Engagement Preparation			
Date Report Due	_____	_____	_____
Information Request Sent	_____	_____	_____
Information Received from Client	_____	_____	_____

	Initial	**Date**	**W/P Reference**
Analysis/Report Technical Review			
Staff	_____	_____	_____
Manager	_____	_____	_____
Shareholder	_____	_____	_____
Review Engagement Letter for Changes in Scope	_____	_____	_____
Draft Analysis/Report Reviewed			
Staff	_____	_____	_____
Manager	_____	_____	_____
Shareholder	_____	_____	_____
Draft Analysis/Report Edit	_____	_____	_____
Draft Analysis/Report P&C	_____	_____	_____
Draft Analysis/Report Issued	_____	_____	_____
Final Analysis/Report Reviewed			
Staff	_____	_____	_____
Manager	_____	_____	_____
Shareholder	_____	_____	_____
Cold Review, if applicable	_____	_____	_____
Working Papers Signed Off	_____	_____	_____
Final Analysis/Report Issued	_____	_____	_____

Page 2

CHAPTER 7

Practice Management Workflow Procedures

INTRODUCTION

These procedures will maintain the continuity of the client report and exhibits and will eliminate unnecessary draft files. These procedures are also completely dependent on each firm's internal policies, which can be and often are different than what is presented here. For example, policies concerning notes and drafts can and do differ by firm.

In order to comply with the procedures, e-mails and drafts can be created according to the appropriate templates that exist within the system. Correspondence with the client, including e-mails both sent and received, can be retained in the client folder. Additionally, verbal conversations can be logged on the appropriate form and filed in the client's folder.

If a report draft is created and sent to the attorney, any changes that the attorney recommends may be retained in the client's file and may potentially be used in future litigation. Additionally, drafts sent to the client may be retained both electronically and in the client's file.

For additional information on draft creation and retention and case law relating to draft creation and retention, please see *CPA Expert* (Winter 2004); "Expert Spoliation" by Gregory P. Joseph.

The initial section presents summary flowcharts. The remaining section introduces an example of detailed practice management workflow processes. The process shown here is copyrighted by FVC Holdings, LC and is used with permission.

SECTION I—PRACTICE MANAGEMENT FLOWCHARTS

Practice Management
Workflow Procedures
Summary Flowcharts

1

■ Overall Caveat: Most of the information is presented in a best-case scenario where everything is almost perfect. It will not be possible or relevant to adopt all of the procedures, policies, and ideas. Each professional and firm should choose the resources that fit the firm/group, its philosophy and culture.

■ Caveat: For discussion and educational purposes only. Valuation and litigation services are very much affected by specific facts and circumstances. As such, the views expressed in these written materials do not necessarily reflect the professional opinions or positions that the authors would take in every assignment or practice, or in providing valuation or litigation services in connection with an actual engagement, matter, or practice. Every situation and practice is unique, and differing facts and circumstances may result in variations of the information presented. Jim Hitchner, Mike Mard, and FVG Holdings, LC assume no responsibility for any errors in this information, use of this information, or reliance on the information. Use at your own risk.

■ Process Exposure (PE) points are detailed at the end of the workflow flowchart.

2

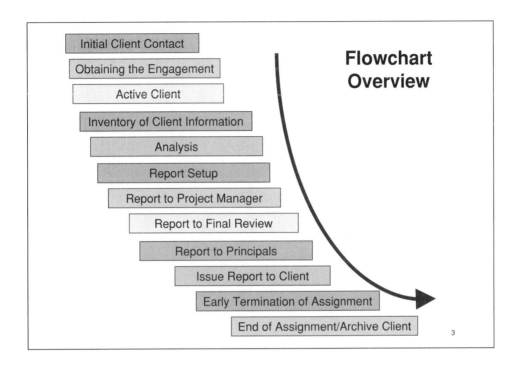

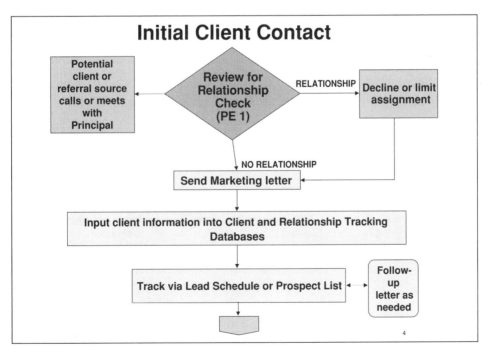

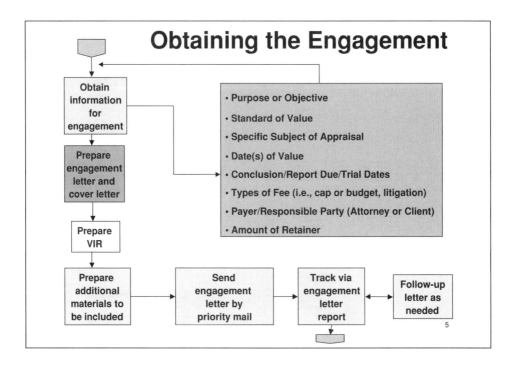

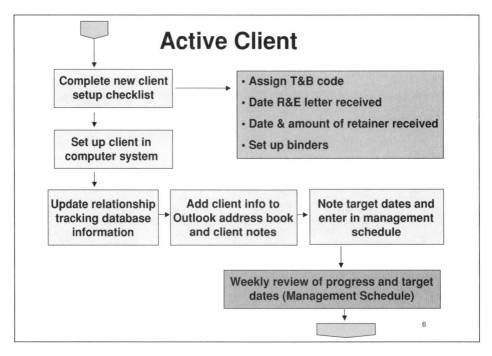

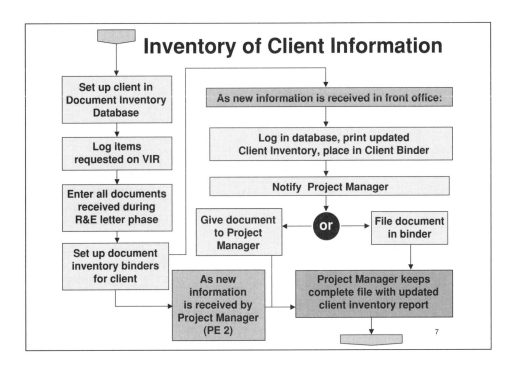

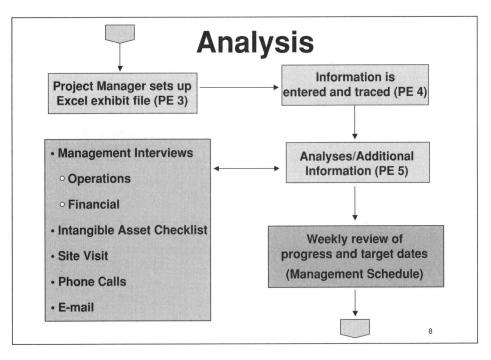

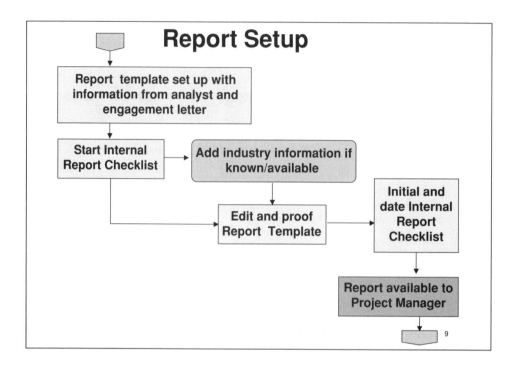

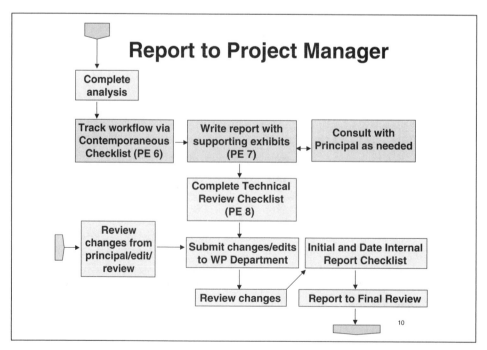

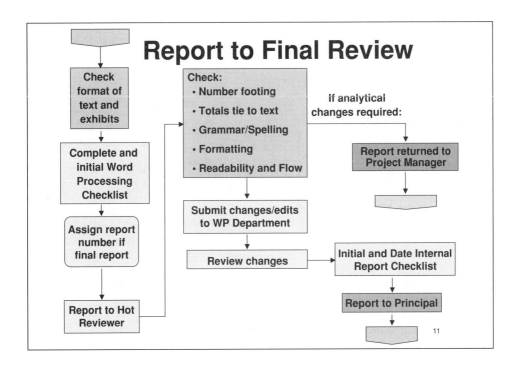

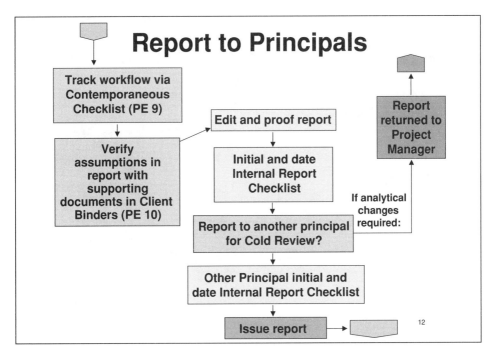

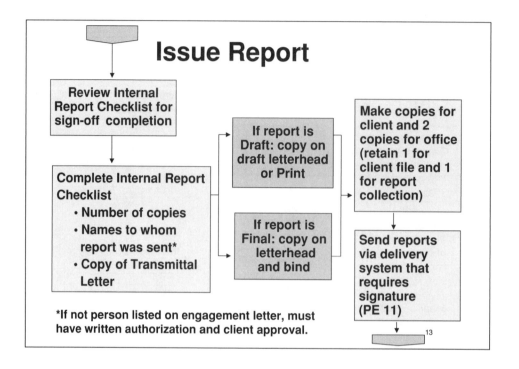

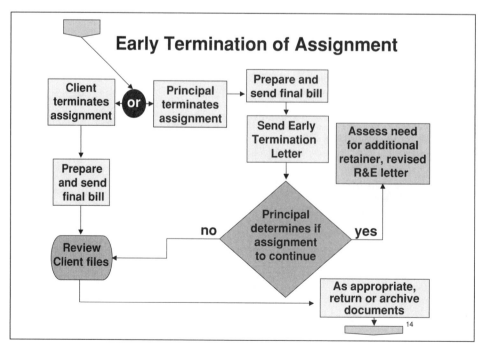

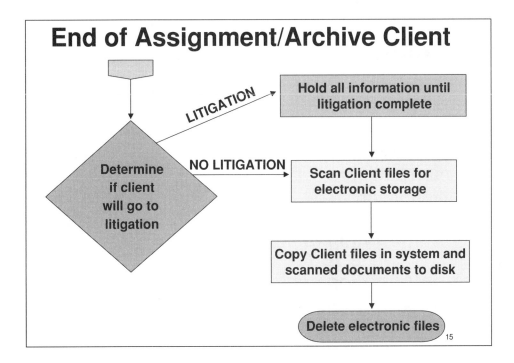

End of Assignment/Archive Client

Determine if client will go to litigation

LITIGATION → **Hold all information until litigation complete**

NO LITIGATION → **Scan Client files for electronic storage**

Copy Client files in system and scanned documents to disk

Delete electronic files

15

Process Exposure 1:

When bypassed:

Review for Relationship

- **Risk of having litigation testimony thrown out due to possible relationship with one of the parties.**

- **May expose company to independence issues established by SEC.**

16

Process Exposure 2:

As new information is received by Project Manager

When Project Manager neglects to notify Document Control personnel of receipt of information:

- **Information is not logged.**

- **Information can be lost (with no record of receipt) or misfiled.**

17

Process Exposure 3:

Project Manager sets up Excel exhibit file

When Project Manager does not use established blank templates or creates more than one set of exhibits:

- **Prior client information retained in footnotes and/or assumptions.**
- **Duplicate files (i.e., various scenarios).**
- **Files that link to external worksheets.**
- **Multiple exhibits files create confusion: Which to use when issuing report?**

18

Process Exposure 4:

Information is entered and traced

When bypassed:

- **Information is incorrectly entered.**

- **Information is not thoroughly traced.**

- **Questionable or uncertain information is not documented.**

19

Process Exposure 5:

Analyses/ Additional Information

When Project Manager speaks to or e-mails client to obtain additional information:

- **Information may not be recorded in the document inventory as supporting information.**

20

Process Exposure 6:

When bypassed:

Track workflow via Contemporaneous Checklist

- **Communication breakdown between Project Manager and Principal.**

- **Unnecessary billable hours or budget overage (due to work having to be redone or more extensive review required by Principal).**

- **Possible write-down on invoice.**

21

Process Exposure 7:

When Project Manager bypasses set procedures and uses shortcuts:

Write report with supporting exhibits

- **Information copied and pasted from old or previous reports (text and exhibits).**
- **Duplicate reports (Save As).**
  Exhibits are hard-coded (no formulas in cells).
- **External workbook links.**
- **Numbers in exhibits are not verified with numbers in text.**

22

Process Exposure 8:

Complete Technical Review Checklist

When bypassed or not done timely:

- Incorrect assumptions/methodologies used.

- Most recent information not used (financial, industry, company).

- Increased billable hours, invoicing due to work involved to correct assumptions/methodologies.

- Inaccurate report issued.

23

Process Exposure 9:

Track workflow via Contemporaneous Checklist

When bypassed:

- **Communication breakdown between Project Manager and Principal.**

- **Unnecessary billable hours or budget overage (due to work having to be redone or more extensive review required by Principal).**

- **Possible write-down on invoice.**

24

Process Exposure 10:

When report and documents in file are not verifiable:

Verify assumptions in report with supporting documents in Client Binders

- **Supporting information from client and/or representative is not documented.**

- **Nonrelevant or nonverifiable information that does not support our conclusion is left in Client Binders.**

25

Process Exposure 11:

When bypassed:

Send reports via delivery system that requires signature (i.e., FedEx)

- **No verification that report was received by appropriate person/firm.**

- **Can jeopardize payment of fees.**

26

SECTION II—PRACTICE MANAGEMENT WORKFLOW PROCESS

Initial Client Contact

Note: All client/prospect information is to be stored in the appropriate folder on the server. Local computer hard drives are not available.

I. Potential Client or Referral Source calls or meets with firm Principal.
  A. Principal completes pink **Contact Information Sheet** (Exhibit 7.1).
  B. Contact Information Sheet is given to Support Staff by Principal for Relationship Review.
II. Support Staff dates receipt of Contact Information Sheet and completes Relationship Review.
  A. Support Staff searches Relationship Tracking Database (or other record-keeping method) to determine if potential relationship exists.
  B. If no potential relationship found in Relationship Tracking Database, Support Staff completes **Relationship Review Checklist** (Exhibit 7.2).
    1. Support Staff e-mails other Company offices with prospective client information to check for potential relationship with other Company offices.
    2. Support Staff follows up with phone calls to those offices that do not respond to e-mail.
    3. Support Staff indicates if there is or is not a potential relationship between other offices and prospective client.
    4. If potential relationship exists, Support Staff indicates reason for potential relationship on Relationship Review Checklist.
    5. Support Staff initials and dates completion of Relationship Review.
    6. Support Staff attaches Relationship Review Checklist to Contact Information sheet.
    7. Results are relayed via e-mail or written documentation to Principal.
  C. If Principal determines relationship exists using either Contact Review Checklist or other means of determination, Principal notifies Client or Referral Source by **Engagement Declination Letter** (Exhibit 7.3) indicating if engagement is declined or limited.
    1. Engagement Declination Letter is stored electronically on server in the client's electronic file.
    2. A copy of the letter is placed in the client's folder.
III. Principal defines potential engagement, including:
  A. Type
  B. Name(s) of Client(s)
  C. Name(s) of Company(ies)
  D. Name(s) of Attorney(ies)
IV. If Principal requests **Marketing Letter** (Exhibit 7.4) be sent to potential client:
  A. Support Staff designated by Principal creates new marketing letter from template.
    1. Support Staff stores the electronic copy of the marketing letter on server.
    2. Support Staff places a copy of the marketing letter in client's folder.
    3. Client's folder is labeled with blue label designating a lead/prospect.

    B. Support Staff mails marketing package via First-Class mail.

    C. Principal follows up with potential client within 10 days.

  V. Schedule Controller inputs information into Client Database (or other Client Management System), including:

    A. Client Name(s)

    B. Contact Name(s)

    C. Company Name(s)

    D. Date of Contact

    E. Type of Engagement

    F. Assigned Principal

  VII. Schedule Controller inputs information in Relationship Tracking Database, including:

    A. Client Name(s)

    B. Contact Name(s)

    C. Company Name(s)

    D. Date of Contact

    E. Type of Engagement

    F. Responsible Company office

  VIII. Weekly on Friday, Schedule Controller generates **Lead Schedule** (Exhibit 7.5), which contains a list of existing leads and new leads generated during the week.

  IX. Weekly on Monday, Lead Schedule is reviewed for follow-up during Monday staff meeting.

    A. Leads marked for follow-up by Principal are contacted via **Lead Follow-up Letter** (Exhibit 7.6) generated by Support Staff. Support staff creating letter communicates with Schedule Controller via e-mail or verbally that letter is sent.

      1. Support Staff enters date of follow-up on Lead Schedule.

      2. Support Staff stores Lead Follow-up Letter on the server.

      3. Support Staff places a copy of the Lead Follow-up Letter in client's folder.

    B. If Lead is marked inactive by Principal:

      1. Schedule Coordinator indicates "Inactive" status in Client Database.

      2. Support Staff moves potential client's marketing folder to inactive file drawer.

Obtaining the Engagement

Note: All client/prospect information is to be stored in the appropriate folder on the server. Local computer hard drives are not available.

  I. Principal obtains information from client.

    A. Such information will include:

      1. Purpose or Objectives of valuation

      2. Standard of Value

      3. Specific Subject of Appraisal

      4. Date(s) of Value

    5. Conclusion/Report Due/Trial Dates

    6. Types of Fee (i.e., cap or budget, litigation)

    7. Payer/Responsible Party (Attorney or Client)

    8. Amount of Retainer required

  B. Verbal Communication

    1. The Principal having the verbal exchange with the client is responsible for documenting pertinent information from the conversation on a "blue" colored **Contact Sheet** (Exhibit 7.7). If it is determined that a new Client Contact exists, Principal will notify Support Staff by indicating same in area on Contact Sheet.

    2. The contact sheet is then given to the Support Staff by the Principal for inclusion into the Client Database and Relationship Tracking Database. Contact sheets may be accumulated by the Principal; however, they must be delivered to the Support Staff frequently.

    3. Blue Contact Sheet is placed in client folder by Support Staff.

  C. Written Correspondence

    1. Written correspondence created or requested by Principal to a client can be copied and filed into the client's folder.

    2. If the correspondence is sent using a form of mail that creates a tracking record, the tracking slip can be filed in the client's folder.

    3. If correspondence was generated by Support Staff, Support Staff notifies Principal that task is complete.

II. Support Staff creates **Representation and Engagement Letter** (See Chapter 6, "Marketing, Managing, and Making Money in Valuation Services") and **Representation and Engagement Letter Cover Letter** (Exhibit 7.8) from Template.

  A. Support Staff stores the electronic Representation and Engagement Letter and the electronic Representation and Engagement Letter Cover Letter on the server.

  B. Support Staff places a copy of the Representation and Engagement Letter in client's folder.

  C. Client's folder is labeled with red label.

  D. Schedule Coordinator updates Client Database with new information.

III. Project Manager prepares initial **Valuation Information Request** (VIR) (See Chapter 8, Checklist 8.3).

  A. Support staff generates the VIR to send to the client based on information received from the Project Manager.

  B. Support Staff stores the electronic Valuation Information Request on the server.

  C. Support Staff places a copy of the Valuation Information Request and the Engagement Letter Cover Letter in client's folder.

  D. Support Staff prepares additional materials to be included as indicated by Principal. Such materials may include:

    1. Firm brochure

    2. Articles

    3. Books

    4. Marketing package

IV. Support Staff sends Representation and Engagement Letter with VIR and additional materials by Priority Mail (for tracking).
  A. Receipt for priority mail is placed in client's folder.
V. Schedule Controller updates information in Client Database, including:
  A. Date of Contact
  B. Date Engagement Letter Sent
  C. Amount of Retainer Requested
  D. Assigned Project Manager
VI. Weekly on Friday, Schedule Controller generates **Engagement Letters Report** (Exhibit 7.9). The Engagement Letters Report lists all outstanding engagement letters that have been sent.
VII. Weekly on Monday, Engagement Letter Report is reviewed for follow-up during Staff Meeting.
  A. If follow-up is required as determined by Principal, Schedule Controller marks follow-up date on Engagement Letter Report.
    1. Engagement Letters marked for follow-up are contacted via **Representation and Engagement Letter Follow-up Letter** (Exhibit 7.10).
      a. Support Staff creates the Representation and Engagement Letter Follow-up Letter (RELFL).
      b. Support Staff stores the electronic copy of the RELFL on the server.
      c. Support Staff places a copy of the RELFL in client's folder.
  B. If engagement is deemed inactive by Principal:
    1. Representation and Engagement Letter, Valuation Information Request, and Representation and Engagement Letter Cover Letter are moved to disk by Support Staff for storage.
    2. Representation and Engagement Letter, Valuation Information Request, and Representation and Engagement Letter Cover Letter are deleted from server by Support Staff.
    3. The client's physical folder is saved for six months.
    4. If requested by the client, information sent by the client relating to the valuation is returned to the client.
    5. After six months, the client's physical folder is thrown out by Support Staff.

Active Client

Note: All client/prospect information is to be stored in the appropriate folder on the server. Local computer hard drives are not available.

I. Project Manager is assigned by Principal (if not already assigned).
II. Client Production Coordinator (CPC) is assigned by Principal.
III. CPC completes **New Client Setup Checklist** (Exhibit 7.11), including:
  A. Assign Time & Billing Code using first 12 characters of client name.
  B. Indicate the date the Representation and Engagement Letter was received.
  C. Indicate amount of retainer and date received.

    D. Set up client binders, including:
1. Labels
2. File Index
3. Blank Contemporaneous Checklist
4. Blank Job Control List
5. Blank Technical Review Checklist
6. Blank Management Questionnaire
7. Copy of Representation and Engagement Letter and VIR sent to client, or blank VIR

    E. Add client to Time and Billing software.

    F. Assign Copier and Phone code if applicable.
1. Update code list on copier.
2. Update phone system.

IV. CPC creates client folder in computer using the following protocol:

    A. A main client folder is created on the server in the following location: F:/Clients/Active/xCLIENTx.

    B. If there is more than one valuation for a client, the file will contain a folder for the year in which the valuation was performed. (Example: F:/Clients/Active/xCLIENTx/2006).

    C. If there is more than one valuation for a client in a particular year, the file will contain a folder for each individual valuation name by type and/or date of valuation within the year folder. (Example: F:/Clients/Active/xCLIENTx/2006/141(or DOV 4–15–06)).

    D. In the final valuation folder created using the previous criteria, create one (1) subfolder for each of the following:
- Correspondence
- Billing
- Analysis
- Report
- Engage

    E. Move all information from Engagement Letter folders and Marketing folder on server to client ENGAGE folder.

V. CPC updates Conflict Tracking Database information with additional information received on VIR, correspondence, and conversations with client as additional information is received by CPC, Project Manager, or Principal.

VI. CPC adds Client information to **Address Book** (Microsoft Outlook or other tracking system).

VII. Target Dates are entered in the Client Database and/or Company Calendar by CPC. Target dates include:

    A. Date report is due

    B. Date(s) of depositions

    C. Date of trial

    D. Date of upcoming meetings, site visits, or phone calls

VIII. Schedule Controller generates **Management Schedule Report** (Exhibit 7.12) weekly on Friday, which includes a list of all Active clients, On-hold clients, and outstanding Engagement Letters. This report shows:

    A. Type of client

    B. Principal and Project Manager(s) assigned to client

      C. Target Dates

      D. General comments about client assignment

      E. Unbilled fees to end of job (backlog)

  IX. Management Schedule Report is reviewed weekly on Monday during Staff meeting.

      A. New Target Dates and other assignment information revealed during management meeting is reviewed and noted as appropriate.

  X. After the weekly Staff meeting, CPC updates Client Database for each assigned client with new information and target dates (Schedule Controller updates unassigned clients).

Inventory of Client Information

Note: All client/prospect information is to be stored in the appropriate folder on the server. Local computer hard drives are not available.

    I. CPC sets up client in Document Control System (or other tracking system) as part of Client Setup Checklist.

   II. DCP records Items requested on the initial VIR in the Document Control System, including:

      A. Description of item requested

      B. Date requested

  III. On a frequent basis, DCP enters items received in the Document Control System, including:

      A. Section and Type of document

      B. Date received

      C. Year of information (ex: 2006 Interim Financial Statements)

      D. Description of information if different from Type

      E. Location of document in binder (if more than one binder or section)

  IV. On a frequent basis, DCP notifies primary Project Manager and Principal that information has been received.

   V. DCP files document in Client Binder, or gives document to Project Manager (per Project Manager's verbal or written request).

  VI. DCP prints updated **Document Control System Report** (Exhibit 7.13) each time new information is received or requested.

      A. DCP files updated Document Control System Report in the front of the client's Administrative binder.

Analysis

Note: All client/prospect information is to be stored in the appropriate folder on the server. Local computer hard drives are not available. Project Manager will not copy previous exhibits. If Project Manager requires a template from a previous exhibit to use on the current client, Project Manager can submit a request to the CPC for template creation by completing the New Client Exhibit Request form.

   I. Project Manager requests MS Excel **Exhibit File** from CPC by completing a **New Client Exhibit Request** (Exhibit 7.14).

      A. If a standard template is requested, the finished template is due in four hours.

      B. If a new template (from previous exhibits) is requested, the finished template is due in the amount of time specified by Project Manager (typically 1–2 days). Once a new template is created, a copy of that new template is maintained for use in the future. Future requests for that same template would be considered standard template requests.

  II. CPC creates new Exhibit File in Client folder in computer from Analysis Template. **Analyses are conducted within this Exhibit File.**

 III. Project Manager enters/processes financial and operational information for assignment.

 IV. Information entered in Exhibit File is traced (verified) by nonprimary Project Manager or staff. The nonprimary Project Manager or staff is assigned by Principal.

      A. Each number in Exhibit File is verified against the source document.

      B. Individual who traces information then initials and dates the Report Sign-off Checklist under "Trace Financial Input."

Note: No staff member is to initiate contact with the client except at the direction of the Project Manager.

  V. During the analysis, the Project Manager may require additional information. This may be obtained through:

      A. Management Interviews

         1. **Operations** (see Chapter 8, Checklist 8.11)

         2. **Financial** (see Chapter 8, Checklist 8.12)

      B. Site Visit (using Management Interview checklists)

      C. E-mails

         1. E-mail correspondence by ANY staff member can be printed by that staff member and filed into the Client's file. This includes both e-mails to and from the staff member. Items can be printed and filed AS THEY ARE RECEIVED AND/OR SENT and not accumulated to be printed at a later date.

            a. Any e-mail that is a request for information from the Client CAN BE COPIED TO THE DOCUMENT CONTROL PERSONNEL (DCP). The e-mail may be blind copied at the Project Manager's request.

               (1) After receiving a copied e-mail that is a request for information, the DCP will enter the request in the Document Control System for tracking.

               (2) The Project Manager is still responsible for copying and filing the e-mail.

         2. Once an e-mail is printed and filed, it can be deleted from electronic storage. Electronic retention of e-mail communications is not allowed—systems can be periodically reviewed during the regularly scheduled review.

      D. Faxes or Letters

         1. Written correspondence created by ANY staff member to a client can be copied and filed into the client's folder.

    2. If an electronic copy of the correspondence is retained, it can be saved into the appropriate client folder on the server.

    3. If the correspondence is sent using a form of mail that creates a tracking record, the tracking slip can be filed in the client's folder.

    4. Support Staff notifies Project Manager that task is complete.

  E. Verbal Communication

    1. The staff member at the direction of the Project Manager (support, project manager, or principal) having the verbal exchange with the client can document pertinent information from the conversation on a "blue" colored **Contact Sheet** (see Exhibit 7.7). If it is determined that a new Client Contact exists, Project Manager will notify CPC by indicating same in area provided on Contact Sheet.

    2. The contact sheet is then given to the CPC by the Project Manager for inclusion into the Client Database, Conflict Tracking Database and Outlook Address List. Contact sheets may be accumulated by the Project Manager; however, they can be delivered to the CPC frequently.

    3. Blue Contact Sheet can be placed in client binder by CPC.

 VI. CPC prints new **Contact Information Summary** (Exhibit 7.15) after each update and places it in the front of the client's Administrative binder.

 VII. Requests for information are given to DCP for entry into Document Control System.

  A. Support Staff mails original request to client.

    1. Project Manager may send request for information directly to client.

    2. Project Manager can copy or blind copy ALL E-mail Information Requests to DCP.

  B. DCP can file copy of Information Request in appropriate client binder.

 VIII. Principal, Project Manager, CPC, and DCP review weekly (during the Staff Meeting) the status of the assignment, including any new target dates.

Report Setup

Note: All client/prospect information is to be stored in the appropriate folder on the server. Local computer hard drives are not available. Project Manager may not copy previous reports. If Project Manager requires a template from a previous report to use on the current client, Project Manager can submit a request to the CPC for template creation by completing the New Client Report Request form.

  I. Project Manager can request MS Word Report framework from CPC by completing a **New Client Report Request** (Exhibit 7.16).

  A. If a standard template is requested, the finished template is due in four hours.

  B. If a new template (from previous report) is requested, the finished template is due in the amount of time specified by Project Manager (typically 1–2 days). Once a new template is created, a copy of that new template can be maintained for use in the future. Future requests for that same template would be considered standard template requests.

  II. CPC creates new **Report Framework** in Client folder in computer from Report Template.

    A. This report framework includes information obtained from the Engagement Letter, such as Company name(s) and Date(s) of value.

    B. If known, CPC includes general and economic industry information in Appendices of report framework.

  III. CPC generates **Internal Report Sign-off Sheet** (Exhibit 7.17), which stays with Report through each phase by performing the following steps:

    A. CPC prints blank form on "goldenrod" colored paper.

    B. CPC completes client and date information on Internal Report Sign-off Sheet.

    C. CPC attaches Internal Report Sign-off Sheet to the front of the Report framework.

  IV. CPC carefully edits and proofs Report template.

   V. CPC initials and dates Initial Report Format task on Internal Report Sign-off Sheet.

  VI. Report is delivered to Project Manager by CPC.

Report to Project Manager

Note: All client/prospect information is to be stored in the appropriate folder on the server. Local computer hard drives are not available. Project Manager will not copy from previous reports. If Project Manager would like to use information from a previous report, Project Manager will print the appropriate section from the previous report's .pdf file and submit to CPC with clear handwritten notes. CPC will incorporate the information into the appropriate section of the client's report and return both original and notes to Project Manager for review.

   I. Project Manager conducts analysis.

  II. Principal, Project Manager, and CPC review weekly (during the Management Meeting) the status of the assignment, including any new target dates.

  III. Project Manager and Principal track workflow via **Contemporaneous Checklist** (see Chapter 8, Checklist 8.33). As each milestone is completed, Project Manager and Principal initial and date the Contemporaneous Checklist.

  IV. Project Manager completes Report with supporting Exhibits, consulting with Principal as needed.

Note: From this point on, unless otherwise indicated, "Report" will refer to the complete hard copy of the report, including exhibits and appendices.

    In order to eliminate the possibility of Project Managers and reviewers editing multiple copies of the same report, hard-copy editing can take place from this point on. The CPC will be responsible for maintaining the status of the report during the Edit and Review Process. The following steps are necessary to ensure that the Edit and Review Process is properly sequenced.

    V. Project Manager gives Report and Internal Report Sign-off Sheet to CPC for hard-copy editing process. Once this process is begun, Project Manager may no longer make changes to the electronic report files or exhibits.

        A. CPC locks electronic files so they cannot be changed.

        B. If Project Manager needs to make further changes to electronic report, Project Manager will notify CPC.

            1. CPC will unlock electronic files for the duration of the editing.

            2. After being notified by the Project Manager that said editing is complete, CPC will relock file.

    VI. CPC prints Report.

    VII. Project Manager completes **Technical Review Checklist** (see Chapter 8, Checklist 8.31), editing hard-copy report as necessary.

        A. Project Manager submits changes and edits to CPC.

        B. CPC makes changes and edits as indicated by Project Manager.

        C. CPC reprints Report.

        D. Edited report and clean report are returned to Project Manager by CPC.

        E. Project Manager reviews changes and edits for accuracy and completion.

        F. In the event that additional edits are necessary, Project Manager will submit changes and edits to CPC and continue with step VII A above.

    VIII. Once all changes and edits are completed, Project Manager initials and dates Internal Report Sign-off Sheet for "Project Manager."

    IX. Project Manager returns Report to CPC.

Report to Final Review

Note: All client/prospect information is to be stored in the appropriate folder on the server. Local computer hard drives are not available. CPC is responsible for monitoring report throughout the review process.

    I. Before Final Review, CPC performs the following tasks:

        A. Checks format of text and exhibits and completes **Word Processing Checklist** (Exhibit 7.18) on electronic Report.

        B. Assigns unique report number (if final report).

        C. Prints clean Report (if necessary).

        D. Prints Report Cover Page using template (Exhibit 7.19) on plain paper with assigned report number in footer.

    II. CPC delivers Report to Hot Reviewer.

    III. Hot Reviewer checks hard-copy Report for:

        A. Number footing

        B. Totals from exhibits agree with report text

        C. Grammar and spelling accuracy

    D. Formatting and Word Processing Checklist items

    E. Readability and flow

  IV. If analytical changes are required, Hot Reviewer meets with Project Manager to review.

   V. Hot Reviewer submits changes and edits to CPC.

    A. CPC completes changes and edits including Exhibits and Appendices.

    B. CPC returns report to Hot Reviewer.

    C. Hot Reviewer reviews report.

    D. In the event that additional changes and/or edits are deemed necessary by Hot Reviewer, Hot Reviewer will submit changes to CPC. The process will continue with step V A. above.

  VI. Hot Reviewer initials and dates Internal Report Sign-off Sheet for "Hot Review."

 VII. Report is delivered to Principal for Review by CPC.

Report to Principals

Note: All client/prospect information is to be stored in the appropriate folder on the server. Local computer hard drives are not available.

    I. Principal tracks workflow via **Contemporaneous Checklist** (see Chapter 8, Checklist 8.33). As each milestone is completed, Principal initials and dates the Contemporaneous Checklist.

   II. Principal verifies assumptions in hard-copy Report with supporting documents in Client binders.

  III. Principal reviews assumptions in hard-copy Report to ensure compliance with appropriate standards.

  IV. Principal edits and proofs hard-copy Report.

    A. If corrections need to be made:

      1. Principal meets with Project Manager.

      2. Project Manager revises Exhibits and Report to ensure accuracy.

      3. Changes on hard-copy Report are conveyed to CPC by Principal or Project Manager.

      4. CPC makes changes and edits.

      5. Project Manager or Principal verifies that edits and changes are correct.

        a. In the event that additional edits and/or changes are necessary, Project Manager or Principal will convey said changes to CPC. The process will continue with step IV above.

      6. Project Manager or Principal returns report to CPC.

      7. Report is sent back to Final Review (see Report to Final Review).

    B. If Report is accurate:

      1. Principal initials and dates Internal Report Sign-off sheet as "Approved by Principal."

   V. Report is delivered to CPC by Principal or Project Manager.

  VI. CPC delivers report to **alternate** Principal for Cold Review, if applicable or requested.

Cold (Concept) Review

Note: All client/prospect information is to be stored in the appropriate folder on the server. Local computer hard drives are not available. All references made to Principal in the following section refer to the alternate Principal listed above.

    I. Principal reviews assumptions in hard-copy Report to ensure compliance with appropriate standards.

   II. Principal reviews:
      A. Text flow
      B. Methodologies
      C. Discounts
      D. Conclusions
      E. Other subjective areas of analysis or assumptions

  III. Principal edits and proofs hard-copy Report.
      A. If corrections need to be made:
        1. Principal meets with Project Manager.
        2. Project Manager revises Exhibits and Report to ensure accuracy.
        3. Changes on hard-copy Report are conveyed to CPC by Cold Reviewer or Project Manager.
        4. CPC makes changes and edits.
        5. Project Manager or Cold Reviewer verifies that edits and changes are correct.
          a. In the event that additional edits and/or changes are necessary, Project Manager or Cold Reviewer will submit said changes to CPC. The process will continue with step 4 above.
        6. Project Manager or Cold Reviewer returns report to CPC.
        7. Report is sent back to Final Review (see Report to Final Review).
      B. If Report is accurate:
        1. Principal initials and dates Internal Report Sign-off Sheet as "Cold Review–Principal."

  IV. Report is delivered to CPC by Principal or Project Manager.

Issue Report to Client*

Note: All client/prospect information is to be stored in the appropriate folder on the server. Local computer hard drives are not available.

    I. CPC reviews Internal Report Sign-off Sheet for completion. Each item is initialed and dated prior to issuance of Report.

   II. If items on Internal Report Sign-off Sheet are not initialed and dated:
      A. CPC verbally notifies Principal and Project Manager.
      B. Report is returned to Project Manager or Principal for completion of Sign-off Sheet item(s).

  III. If all items on Internal Report Sign-off Sheet are initialed and dated:
      A. CPC finalizes Internal Report Checklist, including:

---

*These procedures depend on each firm's draft and report retention policies, and, if appropriate and applicable, jurisdictional rules.

      1. Number of copies
      2. Names to whom report was (is to be) sent (individuals, entities, corporations)
      3. Copy of Transmittal Letter
  IV. CPC creates **Report Cover Letter** (Exhibit 7.20).
   V. If a Preliminary written report is to be issued to the client or attorney:
     A. CPC prints report on Draft paper.
     B. CPC sends one copy of unbound Draft report to client via delivery system that requires signature (i.e., FedEx).
      1. Copy of tracking slip is placed in client's binder.
     C. CPC retains one copy of unbound Draft report in client's binder.
     D. If Draft report is returned:
      1. Report is sent back to Project Manager (see Report to Project Manager).
  VI. If a Final report is to be issued to the client or attorney:
     A. CPC prints copies of report for client as indicated on Internal Report Checklist.
     B. CPC sends copies of bound report to client via delivery system that requires signature.
      1. Copy of tracking slip is placed in client's binder.
     C. CPC retains one copy of bound report in client's binder.
     D. CPC stores one copy of Report in the appropriate **Report Collection** drawer.

Early Termination of Assignment

Note: Client/prospect information is to be stored in the appropriate folder on the server. Local computer hard drives are not available. Regardless of reason for early termination of assignment, no work product is released to the client. All work product is proprietary to OUR COMPANY NAME. Only that information provided by the client is returned to the client.

   I. Termination by client
     A. Client indicates end of assignment via letter or verbal notification (from attorney) that case has settled.
     B. Principal notifies staff to stop all work on assignment and authorizes final bill.
     C. Accounts Payable prepares final bill.
      1. If final bill exceeds retainer received, invoice is created for client.
      2. If retainer exceeds final bill, Accounts Payable submits a request to Administration for refund check to be sent to client.
     D. Accounts Payable sends final bill/refund check to responsible party.
     E. Principal reviews client file. As appropriate:
      1. Client's documents are returned to sender.
      2. Client files (work product) are archived.
  II. Termination by COMPANY
     A. During management meeting, Principal indicates client is to be notified of termination.
     B. Principal notifies staff to stop all work on assignment and authorizes final bill.

    C. Accounts Receivable prepares final bill.
        1. If final bill exceeds retainer received, invoice is created for client.
        2. If retainer exceeds final bill, Accounts Receivable submits a request to Administration for refund check to be sent to client.
    D. CPC sends **Early Termination Letter** (Exhibit 7.21) to client with final bill/refund check.
    E. Principal will review file and authorize collection or write-off of any outstanding balance.
    F. If at any time Principal determines assignment is to continue, Principal:
        1. Ensures account is current.
        2. Assesses need for a revised R&E Letter and additional retainer.

End of Assignment/Archive Client

Note: All client/prospect information is to be stored in the appropriate folder on the server. Local computer hard drives are not available.

     I. If litigation client, maintain client's active status.
    II. CPC prints one copy of Report and Exhibits to .pdf format.
    A. CPC places .pdf report and exhibits in server file.
   III. CPC moves client folder on server to INACTIVE CLIENTS folder
    A. Use same naming structure as that used in the CLIENTS folder.
   IV. Inactive Client files will be maintained in the Inactive Clients folder for one quarter.
    A. During the third week of the quarter, inactive client folders from the previous quarter will be copied onto a CD-ROM by the CPC (two copies).
    B. CPC deletes the Inactive Client files from the computer.
    V. CPC stores one CD-ROM in Client Archive file.
   VI. Administration stores one CD-ROM in off-site storage location.
  VII. CPC archives hard-copy documents.

Exhibit 7.1 Contact Information Sheet

CONTACT INFORMATION

CLIENT NAME: _____

DATE: _____

EMPLOYEE: _____

CONTACTED BY:

NAME _____ TITLE: _____

COMPANY _____

ADDRESS _____

CITY, STATE, ZIP _____

TELEPHONE _____

FAX _____

EMAIL _____

WHAT IS CONNECTION TO ASSIGNMENT (I.E., OPPOSING EXPERT, ACCOUNTANT, ETC.) BE SPECIFIC.

_____

_____

_____

_____

_____

_____

PLACE SHEET IN CLIENT PRODUCTION COORDINATOR TOP TRAY

SUPPORT STAFF USE (DATE AND INITIAL WHERE INDICATED)

Date Received: _____ Relationship Check Complete: _____ /_____ Response to Principal: _____ /_____

ATTACH COMPLETE RELATIONSHIP REVIEW CHECKLIST

Exhibit 7.2 Relationship Review Checklist

RELATIONSHIP REVIEW CHECKLIST

I   Email Relationship Information to all offices.
II Follow-up with phone call to those who do not respond to email. NOTE: Only one response per office is required.
III Indicate if relationship exists.
   A. If relationship exists, state reason for relationship.
IV. Attach this form to Contact Information sheet.

Office Contact Information:

Office	Contact	Email	Phone	EMAIL		PHONE		RELATIONSHIP	
Atlanta				Y	N	Y	N	Y	N
Boston				Y	N	Y	N	Y	N
Chicago				Y	N	Y	N	Y	N
Great Falls				Y	N	Y	N	Y	N
Kansas City				Y	N	Y	N	Y	N
Los Angeles				Y	N	Y	N	Y	N
Oakland				Y	N	Y	N	Y	N
Saratoga				Y	N	Y	N	Y	N
St. Louis				Y	N	Y	N	Y	N
Tampa				Y	N	Y	N	Y	N

Reason for Relationship

_____

_____

Exhibit 7.3   Engagement Declination Letter

Date

Name
Firm
Address
City, State   Zip

Re: Matter

Dear Name:

I am returning the information you sent in connection with the above matter. Regrettably, we
have a business relationship which precludes our involvement.

Sincerely,

PRINCIPAL
TITLE

Enclosures

Exhibit 7.4   Marketing Letter

DATE

CONTACT NAME
FIRM/COMPANY
ADDRESS
CITY, STATE ZIP

Dear CONTACT NAME,

It was a pleasure talking with you yesterday. As you requested, I have enclosed a couple packets that include the following information:

- Curriculum Vitae for my partner PARTNER NAME and myself;
- Firm brochure describing our business valuation and merger and acquisition advisory services and;
- An article I wrote on valuation standards.

Briefly, OUR COMPANY is a business valuation and consulting firm that in eighteen years has provided valuation services for hundreds of clients. Corporate clients come in all sizes from small companies to large, closely held and public companies exceeding one billion dollars in revenues. Our firm has been retained to provide independent valuation opinions for many purposes. Among them are:

1. Appraisals for financial reporting, which include the valuation of intangible assets such as customer lists, technology and depositor relationships;

2. Intellectual property appraisals including trademarks, copyrights, and patents;

3. Litigation support testimony, including dissenting minority shareholders cases, corporate disputes, and marital dissolution;

4. Tax compliance, including family limited partnerships and other gift and estate tax purposes; and

5. Mergers, acquisitions and other forms of corporate sales and reorganizations.

Our fees are based on our standard staff rates, which are $000 to $000 per hour for principals, $000 to $000 per hour for technical analysts and $00 to $000 per hour for paraprofessionals. The fee usually averages around $000 per hour.

(continues)

Exhibit 7.4 *continued*

Please call if you have any questions. In the meantime, please visit our website at WEB ADDRESS.

Sincerely,

PRINCIPAL
TITLE

Enclosures

Exhibit 7.5 Lead Schedule

LEAD SCHEDULE

CompanyNm	MajorContact	Purpose	Employee	InitalContactDt	MarketingSent	FollowupSent
COMPANY	CONTACT NAME	EQUITABLE DIST	PRINCIPAL	01/01/2006	01/01/2006	01/16/2006
COMPANY	CONTACT NAME	DIVORCE	PRINCIPAL	01/15/2006	01/16/2006	
COMPANY	CONTACT NAME	141/142	PRINCIPAL	02/01/2006	02/01/2006	
COMPANY	CONTACT NAME	BUSINESS VALUATION	PRINCIPAL	02/15/2006	02/16/2006	
COMPANY	CONTACT NAME	LITIGATION	PRINCIPAL	03/01/2006	03/01/2006	03/24/2006

Exhibit 7.6   Lead Follow-up Letter

Date

RE:

Dear ,

On DATE, I spoke with you about the possible need for our services in connection with the above referenced matter. I realize these matters take time to develop.
Please keep me informed if you think our services will be needed and feel free to call me at (_ _ _) _ _ _-_ _ _ _ if you have any questions.

I appreciate your consideration and hope to hear from you soon.

Sincerely,

PRINCIPAL
TITLE

Exhibit 7.7 Contact Sheet

<u>**CONTACT SHEET**</u>

Client or Contact: _____

Date of Contact: _____ Phone: _____

In Reference To: _____

Contacted By: _____

If new contact, complete this information and give sheet to Client Production Coordinator

NAME _____ TITLE: _____

COMPANY _____

ADDRESS _____

CITY, STATE, ZIP _____

TELEPHONE _____

FAX _____

EMAIL _____

Additional Comments: _____

_____

_____

_____

_____

_____

_____

_____

_____

_____

_____

_____

_____

SUPPORT STAFF USE (DATE AND INITIAL WHERE INDICATED)

Date/Time Received: _____/_____ Response to Principal: _____/_____

Disclaimer Excluding Any Warranties: This checklist is designed to provide guidance to analysts, auditors, and management but is not to be used as a substitute for professional judgment. These procedures must be altered to fit each assignment. The practitioner takes sole responsibility for implementation of this guide. The implied warranties of merchantability and fitness of purpose and all other warranties, whether expressed or implied, are excluded from this transaction and shall not apply to this guide. The Financial Valuation Group shall not be liable for any indirect, special, or consequential damages.

Exhibit 7.8   Representation and Engagement Letter Cover Letter

Date

Name
Company
Address
City, State   ZIP

Re:

Dear CONTACT;

It was a pleasure talking with you DAY and I look forward to working with you. Enclosed as you requested are:

-       Representation and Engagement Letter; and
-       Retainer invoice for $X,000.

If you decide to retain us, please read and sign both copies of the Representation and Engagement Letter returning one copy to OUR COMPANY NAME. Additionally, please send as soon as possible the following items so we can begin our analysis:

- Federal and State Corporate Income Tax Returns for the last five years;
- Financial (audited or reviewed) statements for the last five years; and
- Corporate Charter, Articles of Incorporation and/or Bylaws.

As the assignment progresses, additional information will be necessary. We will send a detailed Valuation Information Request (VIR) for those items at that time.

Also enclosed are a couple of packets which include:

-       My current Curriculum Vitae;
-       Our firm brochure; and
-       An article my partner and I wrote on valuation standards.

Briefly, OUR COMPANY NAME is a business valuation and consulting firm that in eighteen years has provided valuation services for hundreds of clients. Our corporate clients come in all sizes from small companies to large, closely held and public companies exceeding one billion dollars in revenues. Our firm has been retained to provide independent valuation opinions for many purposes. Among them are:

(continues)

Exhibit 7.8   *continued*

1.   Intangible asset appraisals, including customer relationships, software depositor relationships, mortgage loan pools;

2.   Intellectual property appraisals including trademarks, copyrights, patents, and technology;

3.   Litigation services, including dissenting minority shareholders cases, corporate disputes, and marital dissolution;

4.   Tax compliance, including family limited partnerships and other gift and estate tax purposes; and

5.   Mergers, acquisitions and other forms of corporate sales and reorganizations.

Our fees are based on our standard staff rates which are $000 to $000 per hour for principals, $000 to $000 per hour for technical analysts and $00 to $000 per hour for paraprofessionals. The fee usually averages around $000 per hour.

If you have any questions, please give me a call.

Sincerely,

PRINCIPAL
TITLE

Enclosures

Exhibit 7.9 Engagement Letters Report

ENGAGEMENT LETTERS

ClientProspect	Employee	Type	InitalContactDt	EnglLettSent	EngLettF/U	Retainer	MajorContact	MCPhone	Comments
COMPANY	PRINCIPAL	DIVORCE	04/02/2006	04/02/2006		$5,000.00	CONTACT NAME	(123) 456-7890	DEPO UPCOMING
COMPANY	PRINCIPAL	CP	03/25/2006	03/25/2006		$10,000.00	CONTACT NAME	(123) 456-7890	COURT APPOINTED–JOINT HIRE
COMPANY	PRINCIPAL	PPA	03/17/2006	03/17/2006		$15,000.00	CONTACT NAME	(123) 456-7890	ATTYS DISOLVE PARTNERSHIP-JOINT HIRE
COMPANY	PRINCIPAL	LIT	03/01/2006	03/09/2006		$5,000.00	CONTACT NAME	(123) 456-7890	
COMPANY	PRINCIPAL	LIT	03/01/2006	03/09/2006		$20,000.00	CONTACT NAME	(123) 456-7890	
COMPANY	PRINCIPAL	PPA	03/01/2006	03/09/2006		$15,000.00	CONTACT NAME	(123) 456-7890	
COMPANY	PRINCIPAL	LIT	03/01/2006	03/09/2006		$25,000.00	CONTACT NAME	(123) 456-7890	

Exhibit 7.10   Representation and Engagement Letter Follow-up Letter

Date

RE:

Dear :

On DATE we sent you a Representation and Engagement Letter in connection with the above matter. We have not received the signed Representation & Engagement Letter. Please respond whether the case is still active and if our services will be needed.

If we can be of any assistance or if you have any questions or comments, please feel free to call.

Sincerely,

PRINCIPAL
TITLE

Exhibit 7.11 New Client Setup Checklist

CLIENT _____   DATE _____

TIME & BILLING CODE _____
COPY CODE   _____   INITIAL

                                        Circle One
ENGAGEMENT LETTER RECEIVED?:   Yes   No
    Date Received _____   ____

RETAINER CHECK RECEIVED?:   Yes   No
    Amount $ _____
    Date _____

NEW BINDER SETUP:
    Print Binder Labels/Divider Tabs   ____
    FORMS:
        Engagement Review Checklist   ____
        Management Questionnaire   ____
        Valuation Information Request   ____

CODES:
    Add Client to Time & Billing   ____
    Update Copier Codes (Print List for Copier)   ____

ADDITIONAL:
    Copy Signature Page of R&E for Client Folder   ____
    Client Folder Created in System and All Info Moved   ____
    Address Info Entered into Outlook and Database(s)   ____
    Update Info and Generate Client Build Sheet   ____
    Principle Initial and Assign Client on Build Sheet   ____
    Inventory Any Information Recieved and File in Binder   ____
    Deliver Binder to Analyst Assigned
                                                              ____
**Attach Signed Build Sheet to This Sheet with Original
R&E Letter and File in "New Client Setup" Binder**   ____

Exhibit 7.12 Management Schedule

MANAGEMENT SCHEDULE

Status: Active

	Type	Target Date	Event Date	Event Date	Event Date	Event Date	Event Date	Unbilled Fees to End of Job
COMPANY	141	REPORT DUE DATE	ACTIVITY DATE	ACTIVITY DATE	ACTIVITY DATE	ACTIVITY DATE	ACTIVITY DATE	$10,000
PRINCIPAL								
PROJECT MANAGER								
JR ANALYST								
COMMENTS								
COMPANY	LIT	DEPOSITION DATE	ACTIVITY DATE	ACTIVITY DATE	ACTIVITY DATE	ACTIVITY DATE	ACTIVITY DATE	$25,000
PRINCIPAL								
PROJECT MANAGER								
JR ANALYST								
COMMENTS								
COMPANY	CP		ACTIVITY DATE	ACTIVITY DATE	ACTIVITY DATE	ACTIVITY DATE	ACTIVITY DATE	$15,000
PRINCIPAL								
PROJECT MANAGER								
JR ANALYST								
COMMENTS								
COMPANY	DIV		ACTIVITY DATE	ACTIVITY DATE	ACTIVITY DATE	ACTIVITY DATE	ACTIVITY DATE	$5,000
PRINCIPAL								
PROJECT MANAGER								
JR ANALYST								
COMMENTS								

Disclaimer Excluding Any Warranties: This checklist is designed to provide guidance to analysts, auditors, and management but is not to be used as a substitute for professional judgment. These procedures must be altered to fit each assignment. The practitioner takes sole responsibility for implementation of this guide. The implied warranties of merchantability and fitness of purpose and all other warranties, whether expressed or implied, are excluded from this transaction and shall not apply to this guide. The Financial Valuation Group shall not be liable for any indirect, special, or consequential damages.

Exhibit 7.13 Document Control System Report

Document Inventory Report for:					Billing Code	1234	Valuation Date	09/30/2005
zzz Sample Inventory zzz					Internal Code	zzzSample 0	Hire Date	06/01/2006
					Client Type	SFAS 141/142		
					Description			

Year	Type	Date Received	Date of Document	Description	Exhibit	Binder	Page	ID
ADMINISTRATIVE								
	ENGAGEMENT LETTER	07/03/2006	06/01/2006			1		2327
	INFORMATION REQUEST	07/03/2006				1		2328
FINANCIAL INFORMATION								
2005	FINANCIAL PROJECTIONS	07/03/2006				2		2331
2006	INTERIM STATEMENTS	07/03/2006		CURRENT AND PRIOR YEAR		2		2330
2005	TAX RETURN	07/03/2006				2		2332
OPERATIONS								
	FRANCHISE AGREEMENTS	07/03/2006				2		2333
FACILITIES								
	FIXED ASSET APPRAISALS	07/03/2006				3		2335
PERSONNEL/BENEFITS								
	PAYROLL/SALARIES	07/03/2006		PAST TWO YEARS		2		2336
STOCK								
	STOCK LEDGER	07/03/2006		CURRENT		2		2338
LEGAL								
	DEPOSITIONS	07/03/2006				4		2340
OPPOSITION EXPERTS								
	REPORT	07/03/2006				5		2341

Disclaimer Excluding Any Warranties: This checklist is designed to provide guidance to analysts, auditors, and management but is not to be used as a substitute for professional judgment. These procedures must be altered to fit each assignment. The practitioner takes sole responsibility for implementation of this guide. The implied warranties of merchantability and fitness of purpose and all other warranties, whether expressed or implied, are excluded from this transaction and shall not apply to this guide. The Financial Valuation Group shall not be liable for any indirect, special, or consequential damages.

Exhibit 7.14 New Client Exhibit Request

NEW CLIENT EXHIBIT REQUEST

In order to control workflow, it is necessary that the Analyst request client files be set-up by the CPC. Requests for new files from templates can be submitted on this form.

This form is to be given *directly* to CPC.

Name of Client: _____

Note: Typical turn-around time for standard templates is 2-4 hours.

STANDARD TEMPLATES	MODIFICATIONS TO TEMPLATE
_____ 1 Year Analysis	_____ Black Scholes
_____ 2 Year Analysis	_____ Blockage Discount
_____ 3 Year Analysis	_____ Discount Rate Summary
_____ 4 Year Analysis	_____ Double Black Scholes
_____ 5 Year Analysis	_____ Growth Rate
	_____ Lifing
_____ CPR Only	_____ Options
	_____ QM Discount
	_____ RMA
	_____ Software
	_____ Tax
	_____ Voting Premium Analysis

NEW TEMPLATE

Please create a new template from previous client _____

NOTE: New template turn-around time is 1-2 days.

Analyst: _____   Date: _____

Needed by: _____

CPC Received (Date/Time): _____

Completed (Date/Time): _____

Analyst notified: Y N   CPC Initials: _____

CPC will retain this form on file until Final Report has been issued to client.

Exhibit 7.15 Contact Information Summary

CONTACT INFORMATION SUMMARY

Plaintiff

Atty: _____

Company _____
Address _____
Tel/Fax/Em _____

Plaintiff: _____

Company _____
Address _____
Tel/Fax/Em _____

Experts: _____

Company _____
Address _____
Tel/Fax/Em _____

Experts: _____

Company _____
Address _____
Tel/Fax/Em _____

Other Contacts: _____

Company _____
Address _____
Tel/Fax/Em _____

Other Contacts: _____

Company _____
Address _____
Tel/Fax/Em _____

Defendant:

Atty: _____

Company _____
Address _____
Tel/Fax/Em _____

Defendant: _____

Company _____
Address _____
Tel/Fax/Em _____

Experts: _____

Company _____
Address _____
Tel/Fax/Em _____

Experts: _____

Company _____
Address _____
Tel/Fax/Em _____

Other Contacts: _____

Company _____
Address _____
Tel/Fax/Em _____

Other Contacts: _____

Company _____
Address _____
Tel/Fax/Em _____

IF YOU HAVE UPDATED INFORMATION, COMPLETE A CONTACT SHEET AND PLACE IN TOP TRAY OF CPC

Which side retained us, or for which side were we contacted?   P   D

Exhibit 7.16   New Client Report Request

NEW CLIENT REPORT REQUEST

In order to control workflow, it is necessary that the Analyst request client files be set-up by the CPC. All requests for new files from templates can be submitted on this form.

This form is to be given *directly* to CPC.

Name of Client: _____

Note: Typical turn-around time for standard templates is 2-4 hours.

STANDARD TEMPLATES

_____ Blockage Discount	_____ Patent
_____ Calculation	_____ Practice
_____ Fractional Interest	_____ Preliminary Value Letter
_____ FRCP 26	_____ SFAS 141
_____ Limited Appraisal	_____ SFAS 142
_____ Mediation Fair Value	_____ Short
_____ Mediation Fair Market Value	_____ Standard
_____ Multicompanies	_____ Stock Option
_____ Multi-Dates	_____ Supplemental Analysis Letter
_____ Offering Memorandum	

ADDITIONAL NARRATIVE TEMPLATES

_____ Additional Fair Value New Ventures 142	_____ Hypothetical Appriasal Blurb
_____ Adjusted Net Worth	_____ Income Approach
_____ Asset Valuation	_____ Intangibles
_____ Black-Scholes Narrative	_____ Option Valuation
_____ Black-Scholes with Graph	_____ Practice Goodwill
_____ Estimation of Blockage Discount	_____ Qualification Language
_____ Gikbert S Corp Language	_____ S Corp Considerations

APPENDICES

Standard:

_____ Statement of Limiting Conditions	
_____ Economic Outlook	
_____ Year _____, Qtr _____	
_____ CV	

Additional:

_____ Controlling Interest
_____ Guideline Companies
_____ Key Person
_____ Lack of Marketability/Studies
_____ Minority Interest/Lack of Control
_____ REITS
_____ S Corp Issues
_____ Voting Premium

NEW TEMPLATE

Please create a new template from previous client _____

NOTE: New template turn-around time is 1-2 days.

Analyst: _____   Date: _____

Needed by: _____

CPC Received (Date/Time): _____

Completed (Date/Time): _____

Analyst notified: Y   N   CPC Initials: _____

CPC can **retain this form on file until Final Report has been issued to client.**

Exhibit 7.17   Internal Report Sign-Off

Draft _____   Final _____

CLIENT: _____

REPORT DUE: _____

REPORT LOCATION: _____

EXHIBIT LOCATION: _____

	Target Date	**Date Completed**	**Initial**
INITIAL REPORT FORMAT	_____	_____	_____
TRACE FINANCIAL INPUT	_____	_____	_____
ANALYST #1	_____	_____	_____
ANALYST #2	_____	_____	_____
TECHNICAL REVIEW CHECKLIST	_____	_____	_____
APPROVED BY PRINCIPAL	_____	_____	_____
COLD REVIEW - PRINCIPAL	_____	_____	_____
FINAL APPROVAL	_____	_____	_____
BOUND COPY REVIEW	_____	_____	_____
BILLING TO CLIENT (if applicable)	_____	_____	_____
REPORT SENT TO CLIENT	_____	_____	_____

(# or Electronic)   _____   Copies sent to: _____

_____

Date Sent: _____

_____

Report Tracking #:   _____

_____

Exhibit 7.18   Word Processing Checklist

CLIENT: _____

Exact Company Name, Client Name spelled correctly - Same as Engagement Letter
Spell Check   _____
Cover Page information agrees with Transmittal Letter   _____
Date consistent in Transmittal Letter, Header and Appraisal Summary   _____
Transmittal Letter and Certification Page – Signature(s) at bottom of page   _____
Certification - Single or Plural   _____
Table of Contents:
    Text Titles
    Page Numbers   _____
    Exhibits Names & Numbers and Page Numbers (if Litigation)   _____
    Appendices: Titles and Letter Designation   _____
Appraisal Summary:
    Correct Number of Pages
    Date of Issue   _____
    Date of Valuation   _____
    Value Conclusion   _____
Statement of Contingent and Limiting Conditions - Same as Engagement Letter   _____
For Text, Exhibits, and Appendices:
    Check Margins
    Review Spacing   _____
    Consecutive Page Numbers (include Exhibits if Litigation assignment)   _____
    Consistent Style & Fonts   _____
Conclusion - Same in Transmittal Letter (1st page), Conclusion Page,
    and Valuation Summary Exhibit   _____
Exhibit Names & Numbers - Text agrees with Exhibits   _____
SIC/NAICS Number - Text to Exhibit   _____
SIC/NAICS Description - Text to Exhibit   _____
Value Indicators Agree, Text to Exhibits:
    Asset Approach
    Market Approach   _____
    Income Approach   _____
Exhibits - Source Dates agree with Top Dates   _____
Appendices:
    Correct Economic Outlook, prior to Date of Valuation
    Check DLOM/DLOC-agrees with Text and Exhibit   _____
    C.V. for each Signature   _____
FINAL REPORT IN CORRECT ORDER (Check on number of reports needed)   _____

_____   _____
Word Processor   Date

Exhibit 7.19   Cover Page for Report

**FAIR MARKET VALUE
OF
COMPANY NAME
AS OF
VALUATION DATE**

T-XXX-06-1###

Exhibit 7.20 Report Cover Letter

DATE

CLIENT NAME
FIRM/COMPANY
ADDRESS
CITY, STATE ZIP

Dear CLIENT,

Enclosed is/are a copy/copies of the draft/final valuation report of the fair market value of
_____. A copy of the report has
been forwarded to NAME.

I look forward to receiving your comments so we can finalize the report. All draft reports
must be returned to this office in their entirety before the final report will be issued. If you
have any questions, please call.

Sincerely,

Principal, Credentials
Title

Enclosure(s)

Exhibit 7.21   Early Termination Letter

DATE

CLIENT NAME
COMPANY
ADDRESS
CITY, STATE ZIP

**Re: NAME OF ENGAGEMENT/CASE INFORMATION (FROM
        ENGAGEMENT LETTER)**

Dear CLIENT:

To date, we have sent numerous billings in connection with the above matter. The only payment we have received is the retainer of $X,XXX on DATE. Due to the sensitive nature of the assignment, I have proceeded on good faith without further payments. The balance due as of DATE DUE was $X,XXX, and I do not know if the billings are being processed or when I can expect payment. To bring the billing current, enclosed is the invoice, in summary and detail, for work performed through DATE END. The balance due is now $X,XXX.

Pursuant to the Representation & Engagement Letter dated ENG DATE, FEE AND BILLING, I am considering exercising paragraph 9, which reads:

   9.   The Financial Valuation Group reserves the right to withdraw from or stop work
        on this engagement if fees have not been paid as agreed;

Please expedite full payment immediately so that work interruption does not occur.

Sincerely,

PRINCIPAL
TITLE

cc: OTHER CONTACT

Checklists

Chapter 8 presents the checklists that can be used by analysts to run a valuation process. Not all analysts use checklists. However, for those that do, these checklists should be very helpful.

CHECKLIST 8.1: BUSINESS VALUATION OR REAL ESTATE APPRAISAL?

This checklist helps determine which discipline—business valuation or real estate appraisal—is the pertinent discipline when valuing an entity.

YES	NO	IS THE ENTITY:
❏	❏	A commercial, industrial, or service organization pursuing an economic activity?
❏	❏	An equity interest (such as a security in a corporation or partnership interest)?
❏	❏	A fractional interest, minority interest—that is, less than 100 percent of the entity?
❏	❏	Difficult to split up (perhaps because the owners do not have a direct claim on the assets)?

YES	NO	DOES THE ENTITY:
❏	❏	Derive its revenues from providing goods or services?
❏	❏	Primarily use assets such as machinery, equipment, employee skill, and talent in providing goods or services?
❏	❏	Depend on assets other than or in addition to real estate to generate earnings?
❏	❏	Conduct an economic activity that is more important than the location of the real estate where the economic activity is being conducted?
❏	❏	Have a value that fluctuates with conditions in its industry (as opposed to fluctuations in the real estate market)?

YES	NO	DOES THE ENTITY HAVE:
❏	❏	Intangible assets, such as patents, trademarks, copyrights, franchises, licenses, customer lists, employment contracts, noncompete covenants, and goodwill that the entity uses to generate earnings?
❏	❏	Substantial assets that can be moved?
❏	❏	A variety of tangible and intangible assets that interact to produce economic activity?
❏	❏	Significant operating expenses such as marketing, advertising, research, and transportation?
❏	❏	Substantial labor expenses?
❏	❏	Management that substantially adds to the profit of the company?

Yes answers in the majority—Business Valuation
No answers in the majority—Real Estate Appraisal
Mix of yes and no answers—May need both disciplines

CHECKLIST 8.2:   KEY INFORMATION REQUIREMENTS

Financial

- ❏ Historical and prospective financial information on:
  - ❏ Turnover
  - ❏ Contribution
  - ❏ Marketing
  - ❏ Manufacturing/production
  - ❏ R&D/marketing/capital expenditure
- ❏ Unusual, nonrecurring events
- ❏ Accounting principles and methods
- ❏ Contingent assets/liabilities
- ❏ Details of acquisition of assets
- ❏ Licensing arrangements
- ❏ Serious offers received for the asset

Industry Structure

- ❏ Structure of industry
- ❏ Nature of competition
- ❏ Barriers to entry
- ❏ Availability of substitutes
- ❏ Bargaining leverage of buyers
- ❏ Availability of supply
- ❏ Distribution arrangements
- ❏ Major industry trends
- ❏ Social, political, regulatory, environmental, and economic factors

Market Characteristics

- ❏ Product/service awareness:
  - ❏ Spontaneous
  - ❏ Prompted
- ❏ Market share/position
- ❏ Consumer loyalty
- ❏ Image/esteem
- ❏ Geographical coverage
- ❏ Extension potential (products, markets, channels)
- ❏ Product history and life cycle
- ❏ Buyer purchase criteria
- ❏ Marketing mix
- ❏ Demographics

Legal

- ❏ Registered or statutory rights
  - ❏ Categories of goods or services
  - ❏ Jurisdictions
  - ❏ Pending applications
- ❏ Common law or similar rights (including assessment of legal protection)
- ❏ Duration of property rights
- ❏ Details of licensing arrangements
- ❏ Legal matters outstanding (e.g., infringements)

CHECKLIST 8.3:   VALUATION INFORMATION REQUEST (VIR)
GENERAL

Business Name: _____

Valuation Date: _____

This is a generalized information request. Some items may not pertain to your company, and some items may not be readily available to you. In such cases, indicate N/A or notify us if other arrangements can be made to obtain the data. Items already provided are indicated.

Provided   **N/A**

Financial Information

❑ ❑ 1. Financial statements for fiscal years ending FIVE YEARS (order of preference: audited, reviewed, compiled, and internal).

❑ ❑ 2. Interim financial statements for the month-end DATE OF VALUATION and one year prior.

❑ ❑ 3. Financial projections, if any, for the current year and the next three years. Include any prepared budgets and/or business plans.

❑ ❑ 4. Federal and State Corporate Income Tax Returns and supporting schedules for fiscal years ending FIVE YEARS.

❑ ❑ 5. Explanation of significant nonrecurring and/or nonoperating items appearing on the financial statements in any fiscal year if not detailed in footnotes.

❑ ❑ 6. Accounts payable aging schedule or summary as of DATE OF VALUATION.

❑ ❑ 7. Accounts receivable aging schedule or summary and management's general evaluation of quality and credit risk as of DATE OF VALUATION.

❑ ❑ 8. Restatement of inventories and cost of goods sold on a FIFO basis for each of the past five fiscal years if LIFO accounting is used for inventory reporting purposes.

❑ ❑ 9. Fixed asset and depreciation schedule as of DATE OF VALUATION.

❑ ❑ 10. Amortization schedules of mortgages and notes payable; and terms of bank notes, credit lines, and/or debt agreements as of DATE OF VALUATION.

❑ ❑ 11. Current financial statements for any ESOP, profit-sharing, pension, or other employee benefit trust at DATE OF VALUATION.

❑ ❑ 12. Current level of over- (under-) funding for any defined benefit plan at DATE OF VALUATION.

❑ ❑ 13. Description of any compensation, salaries, dividends, or distributions received by persons not active in the operations of the business, including the year and respective compensation.

❑ ❑ 14. Estimated total revenue, gross profit, and net income for the current fiscal year.

❑ ❑ 15. Explanation of fluctuations, growth, or decline in revenue of the business during the past five years.

❑ ❑ 16. Explanation of expected failure of the business to meet this year's budget based on the year-to-date financial data, if applicable.

❏ ❏ 17. Description of any anticipated significant rate increases in the cost of labor or materials.

❏ ❏ 18. Estimate revenues, gross profits, and earnings before interest and tax (EBIT) for the next five years if revenue growth, gross margins, or net margins are expected to be significantly different as compared to the past five years.

❏ ❏ 19. Explanation of expected changes in the amount of capital expenditures during the next five years if expectations differ from those incurred during the past five years, including the anticipated new levels of capital expenditures.

❏ ❏ 20. Average borrowing rate for the business and financial ratios that must be maintained to comply with lenders' credit terms.

❏ ❏ 21. Description of any assets with stated net book value on the balance sheet that differ significantly from the fair market value that could be realized if the business were liquidated (i.e., appreciated real estate, obsolete inventory, or equipment).

❏ ❏ 22. Description of any assets owned by the business that are not being used in the operations of the business (i.e., excess land, investments, excess cash, unused equipment, etc.).

Products and Markets

❏ ❏ 1. List of the major products, services, or product lines of the business and copies of marketing materials, including sales brochures, catalogs, or other descriptive sales materials.

❏ ❏ 2. Sales and profit contributions analysis by product, product line, service category, customer, subsidiary, and/or location (whichever is applicable).

❏ ❏ 3. Unit volume analyses for existing product lines for the past five years.

❏ ❏ 4. Description of major products or services added in the last two years (or anticipated) and current expectations as to sales potential.

❏ ❏ 5. Description of the features, if any, that distinguish the business's products or services from the competition.

❏ ❏ 6. Causes for the cost of products and services supplied to your business to fluctuate, and list of alternative suppliers available at similar rates, if any.

❏ ❏ 7. Description of new products under development with expectations as to potential.

❏ ❏ 8. List of the top 10 customers of the business, indicating sales (or sales on which commissions were earned) and unit volumes for each of the past three fiscal years if customers are consolidated.

❏ ❏ 9. Summary of major accounts gained (lost) in the last year indicating actual sales in the current year and beyond.

❏ ❏ 10. List of major competitors (full name, location, size, and estimated market share of each).

❏ ❏ 11. List of trade association memberships and industry publications of interest to management.

❏ ❏ 12. Classification of the business's industry (SIC No. or NAICS No.).

❏ ❏ 13. Description of any significant business operations that have been discontinued in recent years or are expected to be discontinued in the future (i.e., sale of facility or business line, closed-out product line, etc.), including date of discontinuation and impact on revenues and profits.

(continues)

Provided

N/A

Products and Markets *(continued)*

❑ ❑ 14. Description of any significant business operations that have been added in recent years or are expected to be added in the near future (i.e., purchase of facility, business acquisition, introduction of new product line, etc.), including date of addition and financial impact.

❑ ❑ 15. List of the names of all principal suppliers accounting for over 10 percent of total purchases.

❑ ❑ 16. Summary of terms of any existing purchase agreements with principal suppliers.

❑ ❑ 17. Summary of importance of research and development to the success of the business.

❑ ❑ 18. Characteristics of customers (i.e., industries served, demographics).

❑ ❑ 19. Approximate number of customers that the business has and percentage that are repeat clientele.

❑ ❑ 20. Approximate time the average customer has been purchasing from the business.

❑ ❑ 21. Description of customers that account for over 10 percent of annual revenue or gross profit of the business.

❑ ❑ 22. Summary of any contractual agreements with customers and/or distributors.

❑ ❑ 23. Description of any contracts or agreements with customers, suppliers, or distributors that would be nontransferable if the business were sold.

❑ ❑ 24. Number of clients that would discontinue relations with the business if the business were sold, including reason(s) and the estimated impact on revenues.

❑ ❑ 25. Summary of factors that stimulate demand for the business's products or services.

❑ ❑ 26. Description of seasonal or cyclical factors, if any.

❑ ❑ 27. Reason for increases or decreases of major competitors during the past five years, including their respective market share.

❑ ❑ 28. Approximate percentage of the market the subject business holds.

❑ ❑ 29. Description of level of difficulty to enter into the market or industry by potential competitors.

❑ ❑ 30. Description of the differences of the subject business from its competitors, including price, quality, strengths, and weaknesses.

❑ ❑ 31. List any publicly held companies or subsidiaries known to operate in your industry.

❑ ❑ 32. Name, address, and phone number of contact at industry organization that assists with market data, if any.

Operations

❑ ❑ 1. In a paragraph or so, complete this statement: "Our company is in the business of . . ."

❑ ❑ 2. Name and description of the operations of all major operating entities, whether divisions, subsidiaries, or departments.

❑ ❑ 3. List of the top 10 suppliers (or all accounting for 5 percent or more of total purchases) and the level of purchases in each of the past two years (include total purchases by the business in each year).

❑ ❑ 4. List of product(s) on which the business is single-sourced or suppliers on which the business is otherwise dependent.

❏ ❏   5. Dividend policy, dividend history, and prospect for future dividends.

❏ ❏   6. Copy of any existing employee stock ownership plan (ESOP).

❏ ❏   7. Copies of all other stock option plans or option agreements, or any other plan providing vested benefits in business stock. Also list number of options granted and to whom, and the stated exercise price(s) and expiration date(s).

❏ ❏   8. Basis for business contributions (contribution policy), contributions in each of the past five years, and projection for future contributions to the ESOP, pension plan, and/or profit-sharing plan.

❏ ❏   9. The most recent projection of emerging ESOP repurchase liability. If no study has been done, list known ESOP liquidity requirements during the next three years (e.g., known retirements during periods).

❏ ❏   10. Description of any services performed for, or by, a related party or business, including services provided, dollar amounts, nonmonetary benefits, and if transactions are at market rates.

Facilities

❏ ❏   1. Location, age, and approximate size of each facility. Provide or estimate business volume by major facility.

❏ ❏   2. Ownership of each facility and other major fixed assets. If leased, include name of lessor and lease terms or agreements. If owned by the business, include:

       • Date purchased;

       • Purchase price;

       • Recent appraisals;

       • Insurance coverage; and

       • Book values.

❏ ❏   3. Estimated depreciation of all assets on a straight-line depreciation basis if accelerated depreciation is used for financial statement purposes.

❏ ❏   4. Copies of any appraisals of real estate or personal property owned by the business.

❏ ❏   5. Copies of any appraisals of any company-owned real property or personal property performed during the last three years.

❏ ❏   6. Comparison of rates of leases to market rates if facilities are rented from a related party.

❏ ❏   7. Description of the terms of the real estate lease including date of expiration, anticipated lease rate changes, and whether it is renewable.

❏ ❏   8. Estimate of the cost to relocate business operations including lost profits from business interruption.

❏ ❏   9. Percentage of total capacity (expressed as percentage of total revenue) of the current business operations.

❏ ❏   10. Description of changes in total operating capacity during the past five years (i.e., physical expansion, technological improvement), including related expenditures.

❏ ❏   11. Based on future expected growth, description of when additional facilities or expansion (if foreseeable) will be needed, including approximate cost.

(continues)

Provided	N/A	

Facilities (*continued*)

❑ ❑ 12. Approximate current and historical backlog (in revenues) or waiting list (number of customers).

Personnel

❑ ❑ 1. Current organization chart.

❑ ❑ 2. Number of employees (distinguish full-time and part-time) at year-end for the last six years including current employee classifications, general wage scales, and approximate rate.

❑ ❑ 3. List all union relationships including name of union, date of current agreement, workers and facilities covered.

❑ ❑ 4. Number of part-time and full-time business-employed salespersons including compensation arrangements or schedules. If there are none, describe how sales are obtained and by whom.

❑ ❑ 5. Description of the management team, including current title, age, length of service, background, annual salary, and bonus for the current year and each of the last two years.

❑ ❑ 6. Full names of the board of directors, including occupation of outside members.

❑ ❑ 7. Summary of employee turnover (i.e., below average, average, or above average) compared to your industry.

❑ ❑ 8. Adequacy of supply of labor.

❑ ❑ 9. Summary of employee compensation (i.e., below average, average, or above average) compared to your industry.

❑ ❑ 10. Description of any significant staffing changes or increases anticipated during the next three to five years.

❑ ❑ 11. Description of terms of any contracts with personnel, such as noncompete agreements or employment contracts.

❑ ❑ 12. Description of significant adverse effect on the operating performance of the business due to the loss of a key employee or manager, including potential revenue losses.

❑ ❑ 13. Specify succession of management, if determined.

❑ ❑ 14. Description of staff members who would not be retained if the business were sold, including their respective current compensation and position with the business.

Corporate Documents and Records

❑ ❑ 1. Corporate charter, articles of incorporation, and/or bylaws.

❑ ❑ 2. Minutes of board of directors and shareholders' meetings for the most recent three years (may be reviewed by us on-site).

❑ ❑ 3. Summary of major covenants or agreements binding on the business (e.g., union contracts, capital leases, employment contracts, service contracts, product warranties, etc.).

❑ ❑ 4. Description of any pending litigation including parties involved, date of filing, description and nature of the lawsuit or claim, current status, expected outcome, and financial impact.

❑ ❑ 5. List of all subsidiary companies and the percentage ownership in each.

❑ ❑ 6. Name of any "related" companies (common ownership, common shareholders, etc.) and brief description of the relationship(s).

❑ ❑ 7. Stock ledger.

☐ ☐   8. All closing statements and purchase agreements related to all purchases of the business's stock over the history of the business.

☐ ☐   9. All closing statements and purchase agreements related to all mergers or acquisitions by the business up to the valuation date.

☐ ☐ 10. Copies of any appraisals of the stock of the business made during the last three years.

☐ ☐ 11. State(s) and year of incorporation or registration.

☐ ☐ 12. Form of ownership (C corporation, S corporation, general partnership, limited partnership, sole proprietorship).

☐ ☐ 13. List of the largest ownership interests in the business including name of owner, percentage of shares held and position with business or inactive in business, total shares authorized, total shares issued, and total shares outstanding.

☐ ☐ 14. Description of any unusual stock features (i.e., voting or nonvoting, preferred or convertible, class A and class B).

☐ ☐ 15. Description of any restrictions on the sale or transfer of ownership interests (buy-sell agreement, lettered stock option to buy, stock options, etc.).

☐ ☐ 16. Description of familial or other relationships among owners.

☐ ☐ 17. Description of sales or transfers of any ownership interests in the business in the past five years, including how the price or value was determined.

☐ ☐ 18. Description of any bona fide offers to purchase the business during the past five years.

☐ ☐ 19. Analysis of adequacy of the current business insurance.

☐ ☐ 20. Description of any subsidiaries, joint ventures, or investments of a material nature in other companies.

CHECKLIST 8.4:   VALUATION INFORMATION REQUEST (VIR) BANK/HOLDING COMPANY

Company Name: _____

Valuation Date: _____

This is a generalized information request. Some items may not pertain to your company, and some items may not be readily available to you. In such cases, indicate N/A or notify us if other arrangements can be made to obtain the data. Items already provided are indicated. If you have any questions on the development of this information, please call.

Provided   N/A

Financial Statements (Banks Only)

☐ ☐   1. Financial statements for fiscal years ending FIVE YEARS (order of preference: audited, reviewed, compiled, and internal).

☐ ☐   2. Federal and State Corporate Tax Returns (if not consolidated) for fiscal years ending FIVE YEARS at DATE OF VALUATION.

☐ ☐   3. Call Reports (include all schedules) as of DATE OF VALUATION.

☐ ☐   4. Uniform Bank Performance Reports as of DATE OF VALUATION.

☐ ☐   5. Internally prepared financial statements. (Audits are sometimes presented in abbreviated form and with supplementary schedules. Please provide copies with supplementary schedules. Also, please provide copies of auditors' management letters for most recent two years.)

Financial Statements (Holding Company If Applicable)

☐ ☐   1. Financial statements for fiscal years ending FIVE YEARS (order of preference: audited, reviewed, compiled, and internal).

☐ ☐   2. Federal and State Corporate Tax Returns (if not consolidated) for fiscal years ending FIVE YEARS at DATE OF VALUATION.

☐ ☐   3. Holding Company Form Y-9 filed with Federal Reserve as of DATE OF VALUATION.

☐ ☐   4. Holding Company Performance Reports as of DATE OF VALUATION.

☐ ☐   5. Internally prepared financial statements as of DATE OF VALUATION, including shareholder reports, 10-Ks and 10-Qs if they are prepared. Parent Company Only and Consolidated.

Employee Stock Ownership Plan/Trust (If Applicable)

☐ ☐   1. DATE OF VALUATION Financial Statement (unaudited) or most recent if DATE OF VALUATION Statement not yet prepared.

☐ ☐   2. Accountant's Report for DATE OF VALUATION.

☐ ☐   3. If ESOP is leveraged, name lender, amount, and terms of debt.

Other Financial Documents

☐ ☐   1. Bank budget as of DATE OF VALUATION.

☐ ☐   2. Holding company budget as of DATE OF VALUATION.

❑　❑　3. Any multi-year projection or business plan available for the bank and/or the holding company.

❑　❑　4. If you are a "public reporting company" with the SEC or the FDIC, copies of all documents filed with the SEC or FDIC during YEAR OF VALUATION.

❑　❑　5. Copies of any offering materials prepared in conjunction with any offering of equity or debt securities during YEAR or PRIOR YEAR OF VALUATION.

❑　❑　6. Directors' examination reports.

❑　❑　7. Letters from outside auditors.

Corporate Documents and Records

❑　❑　1. Summary shareholder list (for the entity being valued) showing names and number of shares owned and detailing:
- Directors and officers;
- Employee stock ownership plan; and
- All other 5 percent (or more) shareholders by name. If a family controls more than 5 percent even though no individual does, please note this.

❑　❑　2. If there is a controlling group of shareholders, please provide:
- The complete list of shareholders with their holdings;
- Copy of any Voting Trust Agreement between the controlling parties;
- Copy of any restrictive legends applicable to the institution's shares; and
- Copy of documentation regarding any hybrid equity securities at either the bank or holding company level, including:
  - Stock options;
  - Warrants (to purchase shares); and
  - Other convertible securities (convertible debentures, convertible preferred stock, etc.).

❑　❑　3. Board of directors' minutes: Provide copies of bank and/or holding company minutes during YEAR OF VALUATION, or excerpts pertaining to discussions of these topics:
- Merger with or acquisition by another banking institution;
- Purchase or sale of branch facilities;
- Purchase, sale, or creation of nonbank subsidiaries;
- Response to report of regulatory examination;
- Declaration or payment of dividends or establishment of dividend policy;
- Plans to raise capital in any form, including the refinancing of capital notes or holding company debt;
- Plans to renovate existing facilities or to build new facilities;
- Discussions of or approval of any off-balance sheet hedging activities;
- Discussions of nonroutine charges to the allowance for loan losses or provisions to the allowance for loan losses; and
- Business planning or financial projections for YEAR OF VALUATION and beyond.

❑　❑　4. ESOP Documentation:
- Copy of ESOP document provisions related to repurchase of employee shares specifying obligation to repurchase, terms or repurchase, and other material factors;
- Specify ESOPs repurchase obligation and terms of repurchase;

(continues)

Provided

N/A

Corporate Documents and Records *(continued)*

- If the holding company has a repurchase option or obligation related to ESOP shares, please specify;
- Copy of any ESOP study of its repurchase liability. If there is no study, please list known liquidity requirements for next three years from anticipated retirements or other commitments to repurchase shares;
- Current ESOP contribution policy or basis for determining annual contributions;
- Provide estimated ESOP contribution for YEAR OF VALUATION, VALYEAR+1 and VALYEAR+2; and
- Accounting treatment of leveraged ESOP if not noted in financial statements.

❑ ❑ 5. Documentation of transactions on known stock transactions during the last year(s) in this form:
- Date;
- Purchaser;
- Seller;
- Price/Director/Explanatory; and
- Shares Share Officer? Comments.

Banking Facilities

❑ ❑ 1. List of all banking branch facilities, indicating for each:
- Branch name/location;
- Actual (or approximate) deposit and loan volumes;
- Whether full service or specific limited services;
- Number of (FTE) employees at branch;
- Whether facility owned or leased (if lease, from whom on what terms?);
- Approximate square footage of the facility;
- Book value of facility on institution's books; and
- Approximate fair market value of the facility.

❑ ❑ 2. If the bank is holding improved or unimproved real estate for future expansion (or which is otherwise not presently occupied), provide:

- Description;

- Date acquired and acquisition cost; and

- Estimated (or appraised) current fair market value.

Other Assets

❑ ❑ 1. Current list of equity securities (including convertible and preferred stocks) owned by the bank or holding company as of the DATE OF VALUATION, including:
- Name of security;
- Original (or current carrying) cost; and
- Current market value.

❑ ❑ 2. List of all mutual fund investments owned, including:
- Name of fund(s);
- Original cost(s); and
- Current carrying cost and the amount of any equity allowance related to the mutual funds.

❑ ❑ 3. Bond portfolio printout summary page(s) detailing book value, market value, weighted average rate, and weighted average maturity by each major category of the bond portfolio:
- U.S. Government and Agencies;
- Tax-exempt securities; and
- Other securities.

❑ ❑ 4. Summarize the bank's present investment portfolio positioning strategy in a paragraph or so.

❑ ❑ 5. Any additional assets that may be considered temporary (debt repossessions) or not directly related to the bank's normal course of business.

Data Processing Facilities

❑ ❑ 1. Description of the current data processing system in use by the bank and discussion of its adequacy for the current level of operations.

❑ ❑ 2. If the system is an in-house system, when did the bank go on it?

❑ ❑ 3. If using a data center, list its name and the date use began.

❑ ❑ 4. Are there currently any plans for changing data centers or purchasing an in-house system? If so, please discuss briefly.

Nonbank Subsidiaries of the Bank or Bank Holding Company, Whether Controlled or Not

❑ ❑ 1. Name and description of the business of any operating nonbank subsidiaries.

❑ ❑ 2. Year-end financials for the subsidiaries if not in audited statements or in consolidating financial statements.

Trust Department Activities

❑ ❑ 1. Brief description of trust activities, including services rendered, number of employees, assets under management, revenues for last three years.

❑ ❑ 2. Summarize future plans for this department.

Liquidity and Asset/Attainability Management

❑ ❑ 1. State the bank's Liquidity Policy (or operating practice) in a paragraph or so in terms of objectives, target ratios, or other terms you use to track and monitor liquidity.

❑ ❑ 2. GAP (Asset/Liability Management) Policy.

❑ ❑ 3. State the bank's GAP policy in a paragraph or so.

❑ ❑ 4. Who are the management and board members of ALCO Committee (or equivalent)?

❑ ❑ 5. If available, provide a recent printout from your asset/liability system or planning model providing:

- Projected balance sheets and income statements over projection horizon GAP reports; and

- A brief statement of the bank's positioning relative to its objectives.

Loan Portfolio Information—Determining the Adequacy of the Allowance for Loan Losses (i.e., the loan loss reserve)

❑ ❑ 1. Description of the method used and the frequency of the determination.

❑ ❑ 2. If a written report is developed, please provide a copy (or a summary of results) for the most recent determination.

(continues)

Provided

N/A

Loan Portfolio Information *(continued)*

❏ ❏ 3. Description of the system or process of loan review in use at the bank.

Lending Policy and Practice

❏ ❏ 4. List the major types of loans routinely made by type and describe typical pricing and maturities for each type.

❏ ❏ 5. Summarize (or provide a copy of the Loan Policy) the bank's:
  • Stated lending limit authorities "effective Lending Limits in Practice Policy" for out-of-territory loans.
  • Number and dollar volume of loans outside your CRA (Community Reinvestment Act) territory, including any loan participations purchased.

❏ ❏ 6. What is the bank's legal lending limit? What is the in-house lending limit?

Lending Concentrations

❏ ❏ 7. List all loans at the lending limit. If credits to related borrowers constitute a concentration of 50 percent of the lending limit or more, include the relationship totals.

❏ ❏ 8. Does the bank have any known industry concentrations or exposures in its loan portfolio? If so, discuss briefly.

Regulation and Regulatory Compliance

❏ ❏ 1. Dates of the two most recent regulatory examinations by appropriate category.

	BANK BY STATE AGENCY	BANK BY FDIC (OCC IF NAT'L BANK)	HOLDING COMPANY BY FEDERAL RESERVE
Most Recent	_____	_____	_____
Next Most Recent	_____	_____	_____

❏ ❏ 2. Is the bank and/or the holding company operating under a formal, written agreement with any regulatory body? If so, provide:
  • Agency;
  • Data and Type of Agreement (Memorandum of Understanding, Cease and Desist, Other);
  • Basic reasons for its issuance;
  • General description of its requirements; and
  • State of the institution's compliance with the order.

Management and the Directorate

❏ ❏ 1. Management compensation: for the top five officers of the bank and holding company:
  • Name/title;
  • Annual compensation, including bonuses, for VALYEAR and FOLLOWINGYEAR; and
  • Beneficial stock ownership in bank or bank holding company.

❏ ❏ 2. Senior management (key officers of the bank or holding company):
- Name/title/age/years of service with bank;
- Current operating responsibilities;
- Prior jobs with bank;
- Prior banking experience;
- Other relevant experience;
- If bank carries life insurance on key executives, provide coverage amounts and annual premiums; and
- If executive is working under an employment agreement, please summarize its terms.

❏ ❏ 3. Board of Directors: Please summarize this information for the bank/holding company:
- For bank: name/board title/age/board tenure in years/occupation;
- For holding company: name/board title/age/board tenure in years/occupation (for significant overlaps between bank and holding company, provide entire list and indicate for each individual whether bank, holding company, or both);
- Please name and describe membership and functions of major board committees; and
- How are outside board members compensated?

Background and History

❏ ❏ 1. For the bank:
- Date of formation and name(s) of principal founder(s);
- Type of charter;
- If applicable, approximate dates of acquisitions of other banks or branches since formation;
- Name changes, if any, since formation;
- If there is a current control group, the date this group obtained control;
- Other significant historical events; and
- If a written history exists, provide a copy.

❏ ❏ 2. For the holding company:
- Date of formation and name(s) of principal founder(s);
- Description of process of gaining control of the bank; and
- Date control acquired.

Competition and the Local Economy

❏ ❏ 1. List major competitors (bank, thrift, or credit union). If a market share study exists, provide a copy of the most recent study.

❏ ❏ 2. Include background information available on the economy of city/county/region (e.g., from Chamber of Commerce and local university economics departments).

CHECKLIST 8.5:   VALUATION INFORMATION REQUEST (VIR)
EMINENT DOMAIN

Business Name: _____

Valuation Date: _____

This is is a generalized information request. Some items may not pertain to your company, and some items may not be readily available to you. In such cases, indicate N/A or notify us if other arrangements can be made to obtain the data. Items already provided are indicated. If you have any questions on the development of this information, please call.

Provided   **N/A**

Financial Information

❑   ❑   1. Financial statements for fiscal years ending FIVE YEARS (order of preference: audited, reviewed, compiled, and internal).

❑   ❑   2. Financial projections for the DAMAGE year and the next three years.

❑   ❑   3. Federal and state Corporate Income Tax Returns and supporting schedules for fiscal years ending FIVE YEARS.

Products and Markets

❑   ❑   1. Major product services or product lines of the company.

❑   ❑   2. Top 10 customers of the company indicating sales and unit volume for each of the past three fiscal years.

❑   ❑   3. Major competitors (full name, location, size and estimated market share of each).

❑   ❑   4. Trade association memberships and brochures of the company.

Operations

❑   ❑   1. In a paragraph or so, please complete this statement: "The company is in the business of . . ."

❑   ❑   2. List the top 10 suppliers.

❑   ❑   3. Dividend policy, dividend history, and prospects for future dividends.

❑   ❑   4. Copies of any appraisals of the stock of the company made during the last three years.

Facilities

❑   ❑   1. Location, age, and approximate size of each facility.

❑   ❑   2. Ownership of each facility and other major fixed assets. If leased, include name of lessor and lease terms or agreements.

❑   ❑   3. Real estate appraisal, which should include a fair market value of price per square foot.

❑   ❑   4. Copies of appraisals of any company-owned real property or personal property performed during the last three years.

Personnel

❑   ❑   1. Current organizational chart.

❑   ❑   2. Number of employees (distinguish between full time and part time).

❏   ❏   3. Description of the management team, include current title, age, length of company service, and background.

❏   ❏   4. Full names of the board of directors.

Corporate Documents and Records

❏   ❏   1. Corporate Charter, Articles of Incorporation, and/or Bylaws.

❏   ❏   2. Minutes of board of directors and shareholders' meetings for the most recent three years.

❏   ❏   3. Stock ledger.

❏   ❏   4. All closing statements and purchase agreements related to all purchases of the company's stock over the history of the company.

❏   ❏   5. All closing statements and purchase agreements related to all mergers or acquisitions by the company up to the valuation date.

Engineering Data

Engineering report should include:

❏   ❏   1. Actual square footage of the taking;

❏   ❏   2. Effect of the taking on parking and maneuverability;

❏   ❏   3. Actual square footage of the building loss due to the taking;

❏   ❏   4. Suggestions of possible cures, if any; and

❏   ❏   5. Cost associated to items lost on the property, such as sign, etc.

Disclaimer Excluding Any Warranties: This checklist is designed to provide guidance to analysts, auditors, and management but is not to be used as a substitute for professional judgment. These procedures must be altered to fit each assignment. The practitioner takes sole responsibility for implementation of this guide. The implied warranties of merchantability and fitness of purpose and all other warranties, whether expressed or implied, are excluded from this transaction and shall not apply to this guide. The Financial Valuation Group shall not be liable for any indirect, special, or consequential damages.

CHECKLIST 8.6: VALUATION INFORMATION REQUEST (VIR) GAS AND OIL RIGHTS

Business Name: _____

Valuation Date: _____

This is a generalized information request. Some items may not pertain to your company, and some items may not be readily available to you. In such cases, indicate N/A or notify us if other arrangements can be made to obtain the data. Items already provided are indicated. If you have any questions on the development of this information, please call.

Provided

    N/A

Financial Information

❑ ❑   1. Financial statements for fiscal years ending FIVE YEARS (order of preference: audited, reviewed, compiled, and internal).

❑ ❑   2. Federal and State Corporate Income Tax Returns and supporting schedules for fiscal years ending FIVE YEARS.

❑ ❑   3. Provide division orders or other documents showing the subject interests, property identification, and legal description for all producing properties.

❑ ❑   4. All reserve studies related to the producing properties.

❑ ❑   5. All remittance advices, cancelled checks, and statements from banks and statements from entities controlling distributions related to the oil and gas rights.

❑ ❑   6. Names, addresses, and phone numbers of operators and purchasers related to the producing properties.

❑ ❑   7. Joint interest bills for the past 12 months.

Operations

❑ ❑   8. Unit agreements.

❑ ❑   9. Operating agreements.

❑ ❑   10. Field descriptions including geologic data and well logs, core analyses or studies, pressure data, fluid analyses, drill stem tests, completion reports, gravity information, and other geologic information related to the producing properties.

❑ ❑   11. Proposed drilling activities, timing related to the proposed drilling activities, estimated costs, and other activities proposed.

❑ ❑   12. Gas contracts, gathering and transportation agreements, gas balancing and processing agreements.

❑ ❑   13. Severance and ad valorem tax rates.

❑ ❑   14. Gas BTU content including shrinkage data.

❑ ❑   15. Production histories.

❑ ❑   16. Decline curves and projections.

❑ ❑   17. Future oil contracts.

❑ ❑   18. Posted field prices for oil, gas, condensate, or other minerals or metals.

❏   ❏   19. Amounts of bonuses or delay rentals for nonproducing properties.

Disclaimer Excluding Any Warranties: This checklist is designed to provide guidance to analysts, auditors, and management but is not to be used as a substitute for professional judgment. These procedures must be altered to fit each assignment. The practitioner takes sole responsibility for implementation of this guide. The implied warranties of merchantability and fitness of purpose and all other warranties, whether expressed or implied, are excluded from this transaction and shall not apply to this guide. The Financial Valuation Group shall not be liable for any indirect, special, or consequential damages.

CHECKLIST 8.7:   VALUATION INFORMATION REQUEST (VIR) HIGH-TECH BUSINESS

Business Name: _____

Valuation Date: _____

This is a generalized information request. Some items may not pertain to your company, and some items may not be readily available to you. In such cases, indicate N/A or notify us if other arrangements can be made to obtain the data. Items already provided are indicated. If you have any questions on the development of this information, please call.

Provided

N/A

Financial Information

Provided	N/A	
❏	❏	1. Financial statements for fiscal years ending FIVE YEARS (order of preference: audited, reviewed, compiled, and internal).
❏	❏	2. Interim financial statements to date as of DATE OF VALUATION and one year prior.
❏	❏	3. Federal and State Corporate Income Tax Returns and supporting schedules for fiscal years ending FIVE YEARS.
❏	❏	4. Financial projections for a minimum of five years. Projections should include balance sheets, income statements, cash flow statements, and identification of any adjustments of assets to fair market value. Assumptions supporting the projections must be provided.
❏	❏	5. Summary of agings of current accounts receivables and payables.

Products and Markets

❏	❏	1. A complete market study. This market study must include potential users by market (geographic and service). The study should also include current and expected competition and current and expected market share.
❏	❏	2. Analysis of actual or perceived competition. Should include discussion of alternative sources of information service or product that would be used if the business did not exist.
❏	❏	3. Complete Web site statistical analysis.
❏	❏	4. Copies of any relevant industry studies you have purchased, produced, or obtained.
❏	❏	5. Description of all strategic alliances and/or partnerships.
❏	❏	6. Description of and a strength and weaknesses analysis of your information technology infrastructure (software, hardware, bandwidth, etc.).
❏	❏	7. Copies of sales materials or other promotional literature.
❏	❏	8. History of company and major competitors.

Operations

❏	❏	1. List of all stock options and warrants including owner, date granted number of shares, option period, and exercise price.
❏	❏	2. List of all venture funding including investor, date of investment, number of shares, and type of shares (if preferred).
❏	❏	3. Notification of any discussions held or planned to be held with potential investors, buyers, investment bankers, or underwriters.

❑ ❑ 4. Copies of latest two versions of company's business plan.
❑ ❑ 5. Copies of all prior appraisals of the company.
❑ ❑ 6. List of five largest customers and their percentage of total sales (if applicable).
❑ ❑ 7. List of five major suppliers including amounts paid (if relevant).

Facilities

❑ ❑ 1. Detailed real property information, including any recent appraisals.
❑ ❑ 2. Detailed fixed asset information, including brand, type, age, serial number, and condition of fixed assets (if available).
❑ ❑ 3. Addresses and descriptions of all facilities.

Personnel

❑ ❑ 1. Officers' compensation for last five years.
❑ ❑ 2. Detail of company ownership and any recent transactions involving company stock or stock options.
❑ ❑ 3. List of five largest customers and their percentage of total sales (if applicable).
❑ ❑ 4. List of five major suppliers including amounts paid (if relevant).

Corporate Documents and Records

❑ ❑ 1. Corporate charter, articles of incorporation, and/or bylaws.
❑ ❑ 2. Minutes of board of directors and shareholders' meetings for the most recent three years (may be reviewed by us on-site).
❑ ❑ 3. Summary of major covenants or agreements binding on the business (e.g., union contracts, capital leases, employment contracts, service contracts, product warranties, etc.).
❑ ❑ 4. Description of any pending litigation including parties involved, date of filing, description and nature of the lawsuit or claim, current status, expected outcome, and financial impact.
❑ ❑ 5. List of all subsidiary companies and the percentage ownership in each.
❑ ❑ 6. Name of any "related" companies (common ownership, common shareholders, etc.) and brief description of the relationship(s).
❑ ❑ 7. Stock ledger.
❑ ❑ 8. All closing statements and purchase agreements related to all purchases of the business's stock over the history of the business.
❑ ❑ 9. All closing statements and purchase agreements related to all mergers or acquisitions by the business up to the valuation date.
❑ ❑ 10. Copies of any appraisals of the stock of the business made during the last three years.
❑ ❑ 11. State(s) and year of incorporation or registration.
❑ ❑ 12. Form of ownership (C corporation, S corporation, general partnership, limited partnership, sole proprietorship).
❑ ❑ 13. List of the largest ownership interests in the business including name of owner, percentage of shares held and position with business or inactive in business, total shares authorized, total shares issued, and total shares outstanding.
❑ ❑ 14. Description of any unusual stock features (i.e., voting or nonvoting, preferred or convertible, class A and class B).
❑ ❑ 15. Description of any restrictions on the sale or transfer of ownership interests (buy-sell agreement, lettered stock option to buy, stock options, etc.).

(continues)

Provided

N/A

Corporate Documents and Records *(continued)*

- ❑ ❑ 16. Description of familial or other relationships among owners.
- ❑ ❑ 17. Description of sales or transfers of any ownership interests in the business in the past five years, including how the price or value was determined.
- ❑ ❑ 18. Description of any bona fide offers to purchase the business during the past five years.
- ❑ ❑ 19. Analysis of adequacy of the current business insurance.
- ❑ ❑ 20. Description of any subsidiaries, joint ventures, or investments of a material nature in other companies.

CHECKLIST 8.8: VALUATION INFORMATION REQUEST (VIR) PROFESSIONAL PRACTICE

Practice Name: _____

Valuation Date: _____

This is a generalized information request. Some items may not pertain to your company, and some items may not be readily available to you. In such cases, indicate N/A or notify us if other arrangements can be made to obtain the data. Items already provided are indicated. If you have any questions on the development of this information, please call.

Provided   **N/A**

Financial Information

Provided	N/A	
❑	❑	1. Financial statements for fiscal years ending FIVE YEARS (order of preference: audited, reviewed, compiled, and internal).
❑	❑	2. Interim financial statements as of DATE OF VALUATION and one year prior.
❑	❑	3. Financial projections for the current year and the next three years. Include any prepared budgets and/or business plans.
❑	❑	4. Federal and State Corporate Income Tax Returns and supporting schedules for fiscal years ending FIVE YEARS. Include State Intangible Personal Property Tax Returns.
❑	❑	5. Explanation of significant nonrecurring and/or nonoperating items appearing on the financial statements in any fiscal year if not detailed in footnotes.
❑	❑	6. Accounts payable aging schedule or summary at DATE OF VALUATION.
❑	❑	7. Accounts receivable aging schedule or summary at DATE OF VALUATION.
❑	❑	8. A listing of work-in-process, including fees earned but not billed.
❑	❑	9. The fee schedule in effect at the valuation date for each staff member, plus each average realization rate (percentage) for the last year.
❑	❑	10. Fixed asset and depreciation schedule at DATE OF VALUATION.
❑	❑	11. Amortization schedules of mortgages and notes payable; and terms of bank notes, credit lines, and/or ESOP debt agreement(s).
❑	❑	12. Current financial statements for the ESOP, profit-sharing, pension, or other employee benefit trust.
❑	❑	13. Current level of over/(under) funding for any defined benefit plan.

Services and Markets

Provided	N/A	
❑	❑	1. List the major services of the practice and provide copies of marketing materials including sales brochures, catalogs, or other descriptive sales materials.
❑	❑	2. Sales and profit contributions analysis by service category.
❑	❑	3. Unit volume analyses for existing services for the past five years.
❑	❑	4. Major services added in the last two years (or anticipated) and current expectations as to sales potential.
❑	❑	5. New services under development with expectations as to potential.

(continues)

Provided

N/A

Services and Markets *(continued)*

☐ ☐   6. List the top 10 customers of the practice, indicating sales (or sales on which commissions were earned) and unit volumes for each of the past three fiscal years.

☐ ☐   7. Major accounts gained (lost) in the last year indicating actual sales in the current year and beyond.

☐ ☐   8. Major competitors (full name, location, size, and estimated market share of each).

☐ ☐   9. Trade association memberships.

☐ ☐   10. Majority industry publications of interest to management.

Operations

☐ ☐   1. In a paragraph or so, complete this statement: "The practice is in the business of . . ."

☐ ☐   2. Briefly name and describe the operations of all major operating entities, whether divisions, subsidiaries, or departments.

☐ ☐   3. List the top 10 suppliers (or all accounting for 5 percent or more of total purchases) and the level of purchases in each of the past two years (include total purchases by the practice in each year).

☐ ☐   4. Identify services on which the practice is single-sourced, or suppliers on which the practice is otherwise dependent.

☐ ☐   5. Dividend policy, dividend history, and prospect for future dividends.

☐ ☐   6. Copy of any existing Employee Stock Ownership Plan (ESOP).

☐ ☐   7. Copies of all other stock option plans or option agreements, or any other plan providing vested benefits in practice stock. Also list number of options granted and to whom, and the stated exercise price(s) and expiration date(s).

☐ ☐   8. For the ESOP, pension plan, and/or profit-sharing plan: basis for practice contributions (contribution policy), contributions in each of the past five years, and projection for future contributions.

☐ ☐   9. The most recent projection of emerging ESOP repurchase liability. If no study has been done, list known ESOP liquidity requirements during the next three years (e.g., known retirements during periods).

☐ ☐   10. Copies of any appraisals of the stock of the practice made during the last three years.

Facilities

☐ ☐   1. Location, age, and approximate size of each facility. Provide or estimate business volume by major facility.

☐ ☐   2. Ownership of each facility and other major fixed assets. If leased, include name of lessor and lease terms or agreements. If owned by the practice, include date purchased, purchase price, recent appraisals, insurance coverage, and book values.

☐ ☐   3. If accelerated depreciation is used for financial statement purposes, provide estimated depreciation as if all assets were on a straight-line depreciation basis. If not readily available, please call so we can discuss how to obtain a reasonable estimate with minimal effort.

❏ ❏ 4. Copies of appraisals of any company-owned real property or personal property performed during the last three years.

Personnel

❏ ❏ 1. Current organization chart.

❏ ❏ 2. Number of employees (distinguish full time and part time) at year-end for the last six years including current employee classifications, general wage scales, and approximate rate.

❏ ❏ 3. List all union relationships including name of union, date of current agreement, workers and facilities covered.

❏ ❏ 4. Number of part-time and full-time practice-employed salespersons, including compensation arrangements or schedules. If there are none, describe how sales are obtained and by whom.

❏ ❏ 5. Description of management team including current title, age, length of practice service and background. Also annual salary and bonus of each person for the current year and each of the last two years.

❏ ❏ 6. Full names of the board of directors. For outside members, provide occupation.

Corporate Documents and Records

❏ ❏ 1. Corporate Charter, Articles of Incorporation, Bylaws, and/or Partnership Agreements.

❏ ❏ 2. Minutes of board of directors' and shareholders' meetings for the most recent three years (may be reviewed by us on-site).

❏ ❏ 3. Summary of major covenants or agreements binding on the practice (e.g., union contracts, capital leases, employment contracts, service contracts, product warranties, etc.).

❏ ❏ 4. Description of any pending litigation including parties involved, date of filing, description and nature of the lawsuit or claim, current status, and expected outcome and financial impact.

❏ ❏ 5. List all subsidiary companies and the percentage ownership in each.

❏ ❏ 6. Name any "related" companies (common ownership, common shareholders, etc.) and brief description of the relationship(s).

❏ ❏ 7. Stock ledger.

❏ ❏ 8. All closing statements and purchase agreements related to all purchases of the practice's stock over the history of the practice.

❏ ❏ 9. All closing statements and purchase agreements related to all mergers or acquisitions by the practice up to the valuation date.

CHECKLIST 8.9: VALUATION INFORMATION REQUEST (VIR) MEDICAL PRACTICE

Practice Name: _____

Valuation Date: _____

This is a generalized information request. Some items may not pertain to your company, and some items may not be readily available to you. In such cases, indicate N/A or notify us if other arrangements can be made to obtain the data. Items already provided are indicated. If you have any questions on the development of this information, please call.

Provided

N/A

Financial Information

❑ ❑   1. Financial statements for fiscal years ending FIVE YEARS (order of preference: audited, reviewed, compiled, and internal).

❑ ❑   2. Interim financial statements for the month-end DATE OF VALUATION and one year prior.

❑ ❑   3. Financial projections, if any, for the current year and the next three years. Include any prepared budgets and/or business plans.

❑ ❑   4. Federal and State Corporate Income Tax Returns and supporting schedules for fiscal years ending FIVE YEARS.

❑ ❑   5. Additional financial information:
- Assets included in the financial records not related to the practice;
- A description of the classes of corporate stock (if more than one);
- A list of ownership of stock at DATE OF VALUATION; and
- A description of any recent transactions in stock. If none, please so indicate.

❑ ❑   6. Copies of buy-sell or other restrictive agreements.

❑ ❑   7. Copies of any prior real estate and business appraisals, if any.

❑ ❑   8. Reconciliation of amounts distributed to the practice from an Independent Practice Association or similar entity, if applicable.

❑ ❑   9. Copy of fee schedule with allowables from insurers.

❑ ❑   10. Data from billing system for the current year and two years prior, by provider and for the entire practice, including:
- Most recent aged accounts receivable by payor class with credit balance amounts;
- Annual patient encounter statistics (type [CPT code or similar description] by units of service, gross charge, and receipts); and
- Charges/Receipts by payor class and self-pay.

Operations

❑ ❑   11. Blank Encounter form.

❑ ❑   12. A fixed asset schedule, including all furniture, fixtures, and equipment utilized in the office. This schedule should include the date of purchase, original cost, approximate condition, and estimated remaining useful life.

❑ ❑   13. Copies of profit-sharing, pension, or 401 plans.

❑ ❑   14. List of inventory and whether it is valued LIFO, FIFO, or specific identification.

Other Documents and Records

❏ ❏ 1. Corporate Charter, Articles of Incorporation, and/or Bylaws.

❏ ❏ 2. Minutes of board of directors' and shareholders' meetings for the most recent three years (may be reviewed by us on-site).

❏ ❏ 3. Summary of major covenants or agreements binding on the professional practice, such as capital leases, employment contracts, service contracts, etc.

❏ ❏ 4. Description of any pending litigation including parties involved, date of filing, description and nature of the lawsuit or claim, current status, and expected outcome and financial impact.

❏ ❏ 5. Name of any "related" companies or professional associations (common ownership, common shareholders, etc.) and the relationship(s). Include percentage of ownership in each.

❏ ❏ 6. Stock ledger.

❏ ❏ 7. Leases.

Facilities

❏ ❏ 1. Location, age and approximate size of each facility. Please provide or estimate business volume by major facility.

❏ ❏ 2. Ownership of each facility and other major fixed assets. If leased, include name of lessor and lease terms or agreements. If owned by the practice, include:
- Date purchased;
- Purchase price;
- Recent appraisals;
- Insurance coverage; and
- Book value.

❏ ❏ 3. If accelerated depreciation is used for financial statement purposes, please provide estimated depreciation as if all assets were on a straight-line depreciation basis.

Personnel

❏ ❏ 1. Current organization chart.

❏ ❏ 2. Number of employees (distinguish full time and part time) at year-end for the last six years including current employee classifications, general wage scales, and approximate rate.

❏ ❏ 3. Description of the management team including current title, age, length of practice service, and background. Also list the annual salary and bonus of each person for the current year and each of the last two years.

❏ ❏ 4. Full names of the board of directors. For outside members, please provide outside occupation.

CHECKLIST 8.10: VALUATION INFORMATION REQUEST (VIR) CONSTRUCTION INDUSTRY

Business Name: _____

Valuation Date: _____

This is a generalized information request. Some items may not pertain to your company, and some items may not be readily available to you. In such cases, indicate N/A or notify us if other arrangements can be made to obtain the data. Items already provided are indicated. If you have any questions on the development of this information, please call.

Provided   **N/A**

Financial Information

❑ ❑ 1. Financial statements for fiscal years ending FIVE YEARS (order of preference: audited, reviewed, compiled, and internal).

❑ ❑ 2. Job schedule (listing of completed and in-process jobs) for fiscal years ending FIVE YEARS (order of preference: audited, reviewed, compiled, and internal).

❑ ❑ 3. Interim financial statements for the month-end DATE OF VALUATION and one year prior.

❑ ❑ 4. Interim job schedule (listing of completed and in process jobs) for the month-end DATE OF VALUATION and one year prior.

❑ ❑ 5. Financial projections, if any, for the current year and the next three years. Include any prepared budgets and/or business plans.

❑ ❑ 6. Federal and State Corporate Income Tax Returns and supporting schedules for fiscal years ending FIVE YEARS.

❑ ❑ 7. Explanation of significant nonrecurring and/or nonoperating items appearing on the financial statements in any fiscal year if not detailed in footnotes.

❑ ❑ 8. Accounts payable aging schedule or summary as of DATE OF VALUATION, including retentions payable.

❑ ❑ 9. Accounts receivable aging schedule or summary and management's general evaluation of quality and credit risk as of DATE OF VALUATION, including retentions receivable.

❑ ❑ 10. Restatement of inventories and cost of goods sold on a FIFO basis for each of the past five fiscal years if LIFO accounting is used for inventory reporting purposes.

❑ ❑ 11. Fixed asset and depreciation schedule as of DATE OF VALUATION.

❑ ❑ 12. Amortization schedules of mortgages and notes payable; and terms of bank notes, credit lines, and/or debt agreements as of DATE OF VALUATION.

❑ ❑ 13. Current financial statements for any ESOP, profit-sharing, pension, or other employee benefit trust at DATE OF VALUATION.

❑ ❑ 14. Current level of over (under) funding for any defined benefit plan at DATE OF VALUATION.

❑ ❑ 15. Description of any compensation, salaries, dividends, or distributions received by persons not active in the operations of the business, including the year and respective compensation.

❏ ❏ 16. Estimated total revenue, gross profit, and net income for the current fiscal year.

❏ ❏ 17. Explanation of fluctuations, growth, or decline in revenue of the business during the past five years.

❏ ❏ 18. Explanation of expected failure of the business to meet this year's budget based on the year-to-date financial data, if applicable.

❏ ❏ 19. Description of any anticipated significant rate increases in the cost of labor or materials.

❏ ❏ 20. Estimate revenues, gross profits, and earnings before interest and tax (EBIT) for the next five years if revenue growth, gross margins, or net margins are expected to be significantly different as compared to the past five years.

❏ ❏ 21. Explanation of expected changes in the amount of capital expenditures during the next five years if expectations differ from those incurred during the past five years, including the anticipated new levels of capital expenditures.

❏ ❏ 22. Average borrowing rate for the business and financial ratios that must be maintained to comply with lenders' credit terms.

❏ ❏ 23. Description of any assets with stated net book value on the balance sheet that differ significantly from the fair market value that could be realized if the business were liquidated (i.e., appreciated real estate, obsolete inventory or equipment).

❏ ❏ 24. Description of any assets owned by the business that are not being used in the operations of the business (i.e., excess land, investments, excess cash, unused equipment, etc.).

Products and Markets

❏ ❏ 1. List of the major products, services, or product lines of the business and copies of marketing materials, including sales brochures, catalogs, or other descriptive sales materials.

❏ ❏ 2. Sales and profit contributions analysis by product, product line, service category, customer, subsidiary, and/or location (whichever is applicable).

❏ ❏ 3. Unit volume analyses for existing product lines for the past five years.

❏ ❏ 4. Description of major products or services added in the last two years (or anticipated) and current expectations as to sales potential.

❏ ❏ 5. Description of the features, if any, that distinguish the business's products or services from the competition.

❏ ❏ 6. Causes for the cost of products and services supplied to the business to fluctuate, and list of alternative suppliers available at similar rates, if any.

❏ ❏ 7. Description of new products under development with expectations as to potential.

❏ ❏ 8. List of the top 10 customers of the business, indicating sales (or sales on which commissions were earned) and unit volumes for each of the past three fiscal years if customers are consolidated.

❏ ❏ 9. Summary of major accounts gained (lost) in the last year indicating actual sales in the current year and beyond.

❏ ❏ 10. List of major competitors (full name, location, size, and estimated market share of each).

❏ ❏ 11. List of trade association memberships and industry publications of interest to management.

(continues)

Provided

N/A

Products and Markets *(continued)*

❑ ❑ 12. Classification of the business's industry (SIC No. or NAICS No.).

❑ ❑ 13. Description of any significant business operations that have been discontinued in recent years or expected to be discontinued in the future (i.e., sale of facility or business line, closed out product line, etc.), including date of discontinuation and impact on revenues and profits.

❑ ❑ 14. Description of any significant business operations that have been added in recent years or expected to be added in the near future (i.e., purchase of facility, business acquisition, introduction of new product line, etc.), including date of addition and financial impact.

❑ ❑ 15. List of the names of all principal suppliers accounting for over 10 percent of total purchases.

❑ ❑ 16. Summary of terms of any existing purchase agreements with principal suppliers.

❑ ❑ 17. Characteristics of customers (i.e., industries served, demographics).

❑ ❑ 18. Approximate number of customers that the business has and percentage that are repeat clientele.

❑ ❑ 19. Approximate time the average customer has been purchasing from the business.

❑ ❑ 20. Description of customers that account for over 10 percent of annual revenue or gross profit of the business.

❑ ❑ 21. Summary of any contractual agreements with customers and/or distributors.

❑ ❑ 22. Description of any contracts or agreements with customers, suppliers, or distributors that would be nontransferable if the business were sold.

❑ ❑ 23. Number of clients that would discontinue relations with the business if the business were sold, including reason(s) and the estimated impact on revenues.

❑ ❑ 24. Summary of factors that stimulate demand for the business's products or services.

❑ ❑ 25. Description of seasonal or cyclical factors, if any.

❑ ❑ 26. Reason for increases or decreases of major competitors during the past five years, including their respective market share.

❑ ❑ 27. Approximate percentage of the market the subject business holds.

❑ ❑ 28. Description of level of difficulty to enter into the market or industry by potential competitors.

❑ ❑ 29. Description of the differences of the subject business to its competitors, including price, quality, strengths, and weaknesses.

❑ ❑ 30. List any publicly held companies or subsidiaries known to operate in your industry.

❑ ❑ 31. Name, address, and phone number of contact at industry organization that assists with market data, if any.

Operations

❑ ❑ 1. In a paragraph or so, complete this statement: "Our company is in the business of . . ."

❑ ❑ 2. Name and description of the operations of all major operating entities, whether divisions, subsidiaries, or departments.

❏ ❏   3. List of the top 10 suppliers (or all accounting for 5 percent or more of total purchases) and the level of purchases in each of the past two years (include total purchases by the business in each year).

❏ ❏   4. List of product(s) on which the business is single-sourced or suppliers on which the business is otherwise dependent.

❏ ❏   5. Dividend policy, dividend history, and prospect for future dividends.

❏ ❏   6. Copy of any existing employee stock ownership plan (ESOP).

❏ ❏   7. Copies of all other stock option plans or option agreements, or any other plan providing vested benefits in business stock. Also list number of options granted and to whom, and the stated exercise price(s) and expiration date(s).

❏ ❏   8. Basis for business contributions (contribution policy), contributions in each of the past five years, and projection for future contributions to the ESOP, pension plan, and/or profit sharing plan.

❏ ❏   9. The most recent projection of emerging ESOP repurchase liability. If no study has been done, list known ESOP liquidity requirements during the next three years (e.g., known retirements during periods).

❏ ❏   10. Copies of any appraisals of the stock of the business made during the last three years.

❏ ❏   11. State(s) and year of incorporation or registration.

❏ ❏   12. Form of ownership (C corporation, S corporation, general partnership, limited partnership, sole proprietorship).

❏ ❏   13. List of the largest ownership interests in the business including name of owner, percentage of shares held and position with business or inactive in business, total shares authorized, total shares issued, and total shares outstanding.

❏ ❏   14. Description of any unusual stock features (i.e., voting or nonvoting, preferred or convertible, class A and class B).

❏ ❏   15. Description of any restrictions on the sale or transfer of ownership interests (buy-sell agreement, lettered stock option to buy, stock options, etc.).

❏ ❏   16. Description of familial or other relationships between owners.

❏ ❏   17. Description of sales or transfers of any ownership interests in the business in the past five years, including how the price or value was determined.

❏ ❏   18. Description of any bona fide offers to purchase the business during the past five years.

❏ ❏   19. Analysis of adequacy of the current business insurance.

❏ ❏   20. Description of any subsidiaries, joint ventures, or investments of a material nature in other companies.

❏ ❏   21. Description of any services performed for, or by, a related party or business, including services provided, dollar amounts, nonmonetary benefits, and if transactions are at market rates.

Facilities

❏ ❏   1. Location, age, and approximate size of each facility. Provide or estimate business volume by major facility.

❏ ❏   2. Ownership of each facility and other major fixed assets. If leased, include name of lessor and lease terms or agreements. If owned by the business, include:
- Date purchased;
- Purchase price;
- Recent appraisals;
- Insurance coverage; and
- Book values.

(continues)

Provided   **N/A**

Facilities *(continued)*

❑ ❑ 3. Estimated depreciation of all assets on a straight-line depreciation basis if accelerated depreciation is used for financial statement purposes.

❑ ❑ 4. Copies of any appraisals of real estate or personal property owned by the business.

❑ ❑ 5. Copies of any appraisals of any company-owned real property or personal property performed during the last three years.

❑ ❑ 6. Comparison of rates of leases to market rates if facilities are rented from a related party.

❑ ❑ 7. Description of the terms of the real estate lease including date of expiration, anticipated lease rate changes, and whether it is renewable.

❑ ❑ 8. Estimate of the cost to relocate business operations, including lost profits from business interruption.

❑ ❑ 9. Percentage of total capacity (expressed as percentage of total revenue) of the current business operations.

❑ ❑ 10. Description of changes in total operating capacity during the past five years (i.e., physical expansion, technological improvement), including related expenditures.

❑ ❑ 11. Based on future expected growth, description of when additional facilities or expansion (if foreseeable) will be needed, including approximate cost.

❑ ❑ 12. List of current backlog including the name of the job, the contract price, the estimated gross profit, and the estimated starting date.

Personnel

❑ ❑ 1. Current organization chart.

❑ ❑ 2. Number of employees (distinguish full time and part time) at year-end for the last six years including current employee classifications, general wage scales, and approximate rate.

❑ ❑ 3. List all union relationships including name of union, date of current agreement, workers and facilities covered.

❑ ❑ 4. Number of part-time and full-time business-employed salespersons including compensation arrangements or schedules. If there are none, describe how sales are obtained and by whom.

❑ ❑ 5. Description of the management team, including current title, age, length of service, background, annual salary, and bonus for the current year and each of the last two years.

❑ ❑ 6. Full names of the board of directors, including occupation of outside members.

❑ ❑ 7. Summary of employee turnover (i.e., below average, average, or above average) compared to your industry.

❑ ❑ 8. Adequacy of supply of labor.

❑ ❑ 9. Summary of employee compensation (i.e., below average, average, or above average) compared to your industry.

❑ ❑ 10. Description of any significant staffing changes or increases anticipated during the next three to five years.

❑ ❑ 11. Description of terms of any contracts with personnel such as noncompete agreements or employment contracts.

❏ ❏ 12. Description of significant adverse effect on the operating performance of the business due to the loss of a key employee or manager, including potential revenue losses.

❏ ❏ 13. Specify succession of management, if determined.

❏ ❏ 14. Description of staff members who would not be retained if the business were sold, including their respective current compensation and position with the business.

Corporate Documents and Records

❏ ❏ 1. Corporate charter, articles of incorporation, and/or bylaws.

❏ ❏ 2. Minutes of board of directors' and shareholders' meetings for the most recent three years (may be reviewed by us on-site).

❏ ❏ 3. Summary of major covenants or agreements binding on the business (e.g., union contracts, capital leases, employment contracts, service contracts, product warranties, etc.).

❏ ❏ 4. Copy of current bonding contracts.

❏ ❏ 5. Description of any pending litigation including parties involved, date of filing, description and nature of the lawsuit or claim, current status, expected outcome, and financial impact.

❏ ❏ 6. List of all subsidiary companies and the percentage ownership in each.

❏ ❏ 7. Name of any "related" companies (common ownership, common shareholders, etc.) and briefly describe the relationship(s).

❏ ❏ 8. Stock ledger.

❏ ❏ 9. All closing statements and purchase agreements related to all purchases of the business's stock over the history of the business.

❏ ❏ 10. All closing statements and purchase agreements related to all mergers or acquisitions by the business up to the valuation date.

❏ ❏ 11. Terms of any offers to purchase the business.

Disclaimer Excluding Any Warranties: This checklist is designed to provide guidance to analysts, auditors, and management but is not to be used as a substitute for professional judgment. These procedures must be altered to fit each assignment. The practitioner takes sole responsibility for implementation of this guide. The implied warranties of merchantability and fitness of purpose and all other warranties, whether expressed or implied, are excluded from this transaction and shall not apply to this guide. The Financial Valuation Group shall not be liable for any indirect, special, or consequential damages.

CHECKLIST 8.11: MANAGEMENT INTERVIEW— OPERATIONS

Exact Business Name _____   Date of Valuation _____

Address _____   Phone _____

_____

Analyst/Interviewer _____   Date of Interview _____

The objective of this management interview is to provide us with operational information that will aid us in the valuation of your business. We will keep the information confidential. Describe the following to the best of your ability. If necessary, use a separate sheet of paper, with reference to each item number. If some items are not applicable, please indicate N/A. Items already provided are indicated.

Provided

N/A

Interviewee(s)

☐ ☐ 1. Name   Title

                 _____   _____

                 _____   _____

                 _____   _____

Purpose and Objective of the Valuation

☐ ☐ 2. The activity or transaction giving rise to the valuation.

Other Information Regarding the Transaction

☐ ☐ 3. Number of shares being valued (each class).
☐ ☐ 4. Total number of shares issued (each class).
☐ ☐ 5. Total number of shares outstanding (each class).
☐ ☐ 6. Date of the valuation.
☐ ☐ 7. State of incorporation.
☐ ☐ 8. Standard of value.

Corporate Information

☐ ☐ 9. Name, address, and telephone number of the business attorney.
☐ ☐ 10. Name, address, and telephone number of the business accountant or bookkeeper.

Description of the Business

☐ ☐ 11. Type of business.
☐ ☐ 12. Products/services sold.
☐ ☐ 13. Type of customers/clients.
☐ ☐ 14. Location of sales/services.
☐ ☐ 15. Business code (see tax return).

❑ ❑ 16. SIC number or NAICS number.
❑ ❑ 17. Type of industry(ies).
❑ ❑ 18. Important industry trends.
❑ ❑ 19. Date business started.
❑ ❑ 20. Fiscal year-end date
❑ ❑ 21. Factors you consider most important to your business's success.

History of the Business

❑ ❑ 22. From founding to the present, history including people, date, places, new products, markets, and physical facilities.

Ownership

❑ ❑ 23. Shareholder list as of the date of valuation.
❑ ❑ 24. Transactions in the common stock and basis for price (parties, dates, shares, and prices).
❑ ❑ 25. Offers to purchase the company, if any. Discuss price, dates, terms, and current status of negotiations.
❑ ❑ 26. Prior appraisals.

Management

❑ ❑ 27. Current organizational chart.
❑ ❑ 28. List key management personnel with title, length of service, age, and annual compensation.
❑ ❑ 29. Key management positions open at this time.
❑ ❑ 30. Plans for succession if key-man dependency exists.
❑ ❑ 31. Adverse impact on business if sudden loss or withdrawal of any key employee.
❑ ❑ 32. Amount and description of key-person life insurance policy, if any.

Products and Services

❑ ❑ 33. Business mix.
❑ ❑ 34. Changes in business mix.
❑ ❑ 35. New products/services.
❑ ❑ 36. Development procedure(s) of new products/services.
❑ ❑ 37. Expected performance of new products/services.
❑ ❑ 38. Percent of output manufactured by company.
❑ ❑ 39. Percentage of manufactured products for resale.
❑ ❑ 40. Proportion of sales that are replacement parts.
❑ ❑ 41. Note any important differences in profit margins by product line.

Markets and the Economy

❑ ❑ 42. Market area.
❑ ❑ 43. Determination of market area by market segment, geography, or customer type.
❑ ❑ 44. Important characteristics of the relevant economic base (obtain information of local Chamber of Commerce if needed).
❑ ❑ 45. Business sensitivity to economic cycles or seasonal influences.
❑ ❑ 46. Industry(ies) of market concentration.
❑ ❑ 47. Approximate percentage of foreign sales, and, if any, total dollar amount of foreign sales.
❑ ❑ 48. Difference in profit margins of foreign sales to domestic sales, if any.
❑ ❑ 49. New product lines or services under consideration.

(continues)

Provided

N/A

Customers

❑ ❑ 50. Major customers and the annual sales to each.
❑ ❑ 51. Length of relationships and customer turnover.
❑ ❑ 52. Company dependency, if any, on small group of large customers or large group of small customers.

Marketing Strategy

❑ ❑ 53. Sales and marketing strategy.
❑ ❑ 54. Sales procedures.
❑ ❑ 55. Sales personnel.
❑ ❑ 56. Basis of sales personnel compensation.
❑ ❑ 57. Risks of obsolescence or replacement by new or similar products.

Operations

❑ ❑ 58. Corporate organization structure (divisions, departments, etc.).
❑ ❑ 59. Flow of operations that produce the product or service.

Production

❑ ❑ 60. Operating leverage of business (high or low level).
❑ ❑ 61. Relationship of variable costs and fixed costs to total revenue.
❑ ❑ 62. Difficulty obtaining liability insurance, if any.
❑ ❑ 63. Insurance rates.
❑ ❑ 64. OSHA or EPS concerns in the work environment, if any, including the prospective cost of compliance.
❑ ❑ 65. Concerns over environmental hazards due to location or previous uses of land or facility.
❑ ❑ 66. Dependency in the production process on patents, licenses, or other contracts not controlled by the company.
❑ ❑ 67. Major suppliers and for what production inputs.
❑ ❑ 68. Raw material suppliers that are manufacturers.
❑ ❑ 69. Raw material suppliers that are wholesalers.
❑ ❑ 70. Dependency for critical components of the product or service on any one supplier.
❑ ❑ 71. Name of union, if any.
❑ ❑ 72. Status of union contract or future organizing activities.
❑ ❑ 73. Number of past union strikes.
❑ ❑ 74. Number of full- and part-time employees.
❑ ❑ 75. Number of employees by division or department.
❑ ❑ 76. General experience, skill, and compensation levels of employees.

Real Property

❑ ❑ 77. List real estate and equipment used by the company including name of owner, affiliated parties (if leased), and market terms (if leased).
❑ ❑ 78. Size, age, condition, and capacity of the facilities.
❑ ❑ 79. Adequacy of facilities or plans for future expansion.
❑ ❑ 80. Plant/office facilities, including:
  • Owners;
  • Real estate taxes;
  • Land:
    • Acreage;

> - Cost;
> - Assessed value; and
> - Fair market value, if known.
> - Buildings:
>   - Type of construction;
>   - Age condition;
>   - Location on the property;
>   - Assessed value;
>   - Fair market value, if known;
>   - Fire insurance amount; and
>   - Square feet.
> - Machinery and equipment:
>   - Description;
>   - Age and condition;
>   - Efficiency utilization (older equipment or state of the art); and
>   - Future plant, machinery, and equipment requirements, including estimated repairs.

❏ ❏ 81. Current value of the real estate and equipment.
❏ ❏ 82. Appraisals of real estate and equipment, or estimates.

Description of the Capital Structure

❏ ❏ 83. Classes of securities.
❏ ❏ 84. Common stock restrictions (such as a buy-sell agreement or charter restrictions), if any.
❏ ❏ 85. Preferred stock terms of issue and protective covenants.
❏ ❏ 86. Subordinated debt terms of issue and protective covenants.
❏ ❏ 87. Outstanding stock options or warrants.
❏ ❏ 88. Obtain and attach copies of the option agreement.

Other

❏ ❏ 89. Dividend policy and dividend history.
❏ ❏ 90. Anticipated future dividend payments.
❏ ❏ 91. Pending litigation and potential impact on the company.
❏ ❏ 92. Existing buy-sell or other restrictive agreements.
❏ ❏ 93. Prenuptial agreement, if any.
❏ ❏ 94. Profit-sharing, ESOP, or other retirement plans.
❏ ❏ 95. Copy of the ESOP plan, if not already provided.
❏ ❏ 96. Copies of provisions related to shareholder liquidity in the plan.
❏ ❏ 97. Company's regulators (e.g., public service commissions, bank regulators).
❏ ❏ 98. Copies of regulatory orders, if any.
❏ ❏ 99. General outlook (if not covered elsewhere).
❏ ❏ 100. Other pertinent information about the business.

CHECKLIST 8.12:   MANAGEMENT INTERVIEW— FINANCIAL REVIEW

Exact Business Name _____   Date of Valuation _____

Address _____   Phone _____

_____

Analyst/Interviewer _____   Date of Interview _____

The objective of this management interview is to provide us with financial information that will aid us in the valuation of your business. We will keep the information confidential. Describe the following to the best of your ability. If necessary, use a separate sheet of paper, with reference to each item number. If some items are not applicable, please indicate N/A. Items already provided are indicated.

Remember that the objective of the interview is not only to identify changes in numbers but also to *ascertain the reasons* for the changes.

Provided

N/A

Interviewee(s)

❏   ❏   1. Name   Title

            _____   _____

            _____   _____

            _____   _____

Financial Statement Review

❏   ❏   2. Quality of the financial statements.
❏   ❏   3. Reason(s) for qualifications of audited and qualified statements, if applicable.
❏   ❏   4. Consistency of accounting principles of company-prepared interim statements with accountant-prepared statements.

Balance Sheet Review

❏   ❏   5. Approximate total asset book value.
❏   ❏   6. Approximate net book value.
❏   ❏   7. Cash.
❏   ❏   8. Minimum level of cash required to operate the company.
❏   ❏   9. Accounts receivable:
            • Normal terms of sale;
            • Comparison of collection period to industry norms and history;
            • History of bad debts; and
            • Receivables concentration by customer.
❏   ❏   10. Inventory:
            • Accounting method used to calculate inventories;
            • Trend in level of inventories and turnover rate; and
            • Obsolete inventory and the amount paid for it.

❏ ❏ 11. Other current assets:
- List of current assets; and
- Current assets not related to the business, if any.

❏ ❏ 12. Fixed assets:
- Major fixed assets;
- Depreciation calculations for book and tax purposes;
- Capital budget for the coming years;
- Types of fixed assets needed in the future; and
- List of excess assets.

❏ ❏ 13. Notes receivable:
- Names and terms (if due from officers and affiliates, comparison of terms to market rates).

❏ ❏ 14. Other assets:
- Long-term.

❏ ❏ 15. Notes payable:
- Names and terms of vendors.

❏ ❏ 16. Accounts payable:
- General terms of purchase of goods and services; and
- Trend in payables and turnover ratios.

❏ ❏ 17. Taxes payable and deferred taxes.

❏ ❏ 18. Other accrued expenses.

❏ ❏ 19. Long-term debt:
- Names and terms (if secured, state asset(s) used as security).

❏ ❏ 20. Mortgage notes payable:
- Terms and collateral.

❏ ❏ 21. Any contingent liabilities.

Income Statement

❏ ❏ 22. Approximate annual sales volume.

❏ ❏ 23. Sales:
- Reason for changes in sales over the past five years;
- Attribution of growth in sales:
  - Unit volume; and
  - Inflation.
- Comparison of growth rate in sales to other items on the income statement;
- Projections for the current year and beyond; and
- Basis for projections.

❏ ❏ 24. Costs of goods sold:
- Key factors that affect cost of goods sold; and
- Changes in accounting procedures, if any.

❏ ❏ 25. Gross profit margin (GPM):
- Changes in GPM for the last five years (price increases, cost increases, inventory write-downs, etc.).

❏ ❏ 26. General and administrative expenses:
- Major expense items of the company;
- Fluctuations in expenses over the last five years; and
- Nonrecurring expenses included in the totals.

❏ ❏ 27. Other income/expense:
- Sources.

❏ ❏ 28. Taxes:
- Federal tax rate; and
- State tax rate.

❏ ❏ 29. Hidden or intangible assets, such as:
- Patents;

(continues)

Provided

N/A

Income Statement *(continued)*

- Favorable leases;
- Favorable financing arrangements;
- Number of recurring, stable customers;
- Employment contracts;
- Copyrights;
- Long-term customers' contracts;
- Trademark;
- Unique research and development;
- Highly trained staff in place; and
- Undervalued securities or other investments.

❑   ❑   30. Key liabilities
- Commitments for new buildings or machinery; and
- Long-term loans outstanding and terms.

Disclaimer Excluding Any Warranties: This checklist is designed to provide guidance to analysts, auditors, and management but is not to be used as a substitute for professional judgment. These procedures must be altered to fit each assignment. The practitioner takes sole responsibility for implementation of this guide. The implied warranties of merchantability and fitness of purpose and all other warranties, whether expressed or implied, are excluded from this transaction and shall not apply to this guide. The Financial Valuation Group shall not be liable for any indirect, special, or consequential damages.

CHECKLIST 8.13:   MANAGEMENT INTERVIEW— INSURANCE AGENCY

Exact Agency Name _____   Date of Valuation _____

Address _____   Phone _____

_____

Analyst/Interviewer _____   Date of Interview _____

The objective of this management interview is to provide us with operational information that will aid us in the valuation of your business. We will keep the information confidential. Describe the following to the best of your ability. If necessary, use a separate sheet of paper, with reference to each item number. If some items are not applicable, please indicate N/A. Items already provided are indicated.

Provided

N/A

Interviewee(s)

❑ ❑ 1. Name   Title

_____   _____

_____   _____

_____   _____

History of the Business

❑ ❑ 2. Brief but complete description of the start-up of business.
❑ ❑ 3. Date business started.
❑ ❑ 4. Purchases of other businesses during the development of agency.

Corporate Information

❑ ❑ 5. Name, address, and telephone number of the business accountant or bookkeeper.

Owners

❑ ❑ 6. List all owners by class of stock and percentage owned.
❑ ❑ 7. Job history and experience (i.e., resumes) of the owners.
❑ ❑ 8. Ages and health of the owners.
❑ ❑ 9. Recent transactions in the common stock of the company.
❑ ❑ 10. Ownership and management perquisites.

Personnel

❑ ❑ 11. List all personnel with title, length of service, age, and annual compensation.
❑ ❑ 12. Are there any part-time employees?
❑ ❑ 13. Describe licenses and designations of key personnel, including the year earned.

(continues)

Provided

N/A

Personnel (*continued*)

❑ ❑ 14. Would losing a key employee affect the business drastically?

❑ ❑ 15. Provide copies of all noncompete agreements, if any.

Real Property

❑ ❑ 16. Describe the office facilities.

❑ ❑ 17. Is owned or leased? Provide a copy of the lease, if applicable.

Furniture and Equipment

❑ ❑ 18. Describe the furniture and equipment.

❑ ❑ 19. Is owned or leased? Provide a copy of the lease(s), if applicable.

❑ ❑ 20. For all owned furniture and equipment, please provide a fixed asset schedule.

Insurance Carriers

❑ ❑ 21. List any EDP terminals owned by insurance carriers that are utilized in the agency.

❑ ❑ 22. Provide copies of all insurance carrier contracts.

❑ ❑ 23. Have any new carrier contracts been applied for?

❑ ❑ 24. List all carriers that have terminated contracts, the dates terminated, and the amounts and types of coverage formerly provided in the last full year of representation.

❑ ❑ 25. Provide the amount of the limit to settle claims, if any.

Book of Business

❑ ❑ 26. Describe the amounts of direct billed and agency billed.

❑ ❑ 27. Describe the amounts of property/casualty, life, and health premiums.

❑ ❑ 28. Describe the amounts of commercial and personal lines premiums.

Policy Holders

❑ ❑ 29. If available, please attach a list of all policy holders by product line, the original years of coverage, and if applicable, the years of termination.

❑ ❑ 30. List the five largest policyholders, the amounts of premium, and descriptions of coverage, including the original issue date.

❑ ❑ 31. Provide the amount of written premium and commissions earned by carrier.

❑ ❑ 32. Provide the amount of contingency commissions, the applicable carrier, and the year earned.

Financial Statements

❑ ❑ 33. Provide complete financial statements of the business for the last five years.

❑ ❑ 34. Provide corporate tax returns for the last five years.

❑ ❑ 35. Provide all production reports for the last five years (or all years available).

❑ ❑ 36. Provide all photocopies of any buy-sell or other restrictive agreements.

❑   ❑   37. Describe any hidden assets or liabilities. These would be items or benefit (or liability) to the agency that may not have been fully reflected in the financial statements. They would include such things as long-term policyholder contracts, lawsuits, or undervalued securities.

❑   ❑   38. Have there been any extraordinary or highly unusual downturns or upturns to the business?

❑   ❑   39. Have there been any unusual or nonrecurring or credits not evident on the income statements?

❑   ❑   40. List any nonoperating assets that are included on recent balance sheets. These would include assets not necessary in the day-to-day operations of the business.

Other

❑   ❑   41. General outlook (if not covered elsewhere).

❑   ❑   42. Is there anything else we should know about the business that we have not already discussed?

CHECKLIST 8.14: MANAGEMENT INTERVIEW— PROFESSIONAL PRACTICE

Exact Practice Name _____   Date of Valuation _____

Address _____   Phone _____

_____

Analyst/Interviewer _____   Date of Interview _____

The objective of this management interview is to provide us with operational information that will aid us in the valuation of your business. We will keep the information confidential. Describe the following to the best of your ability. If necessary, use a separate sheet of paper, with reference to each item number. If some items are not applicable, please indicate N/A. Items already provided are indicated.

Provided　**N/A**

Interviewee(s)

❑　❑　1. Name　　　　　　　　　　　Title

　　　　　　_____　　_____

　　　　　　_____　　_____

　　　　　　_____　　_____

Purpose and Objective of the Valuation

❑　❑　2. The activity or transaction giving rise to the valuation.

Partners

❑　❑　3. List key personnel with title, and approximate annual compensation (with bonuses listed separately).

❑　❑　4. Provide an abbreviated curriculum vitae of each partner, including age, education, board certification, and unusual experience.

❑　❑　5. Would the health of all partners be considered excellent? If not, describe any limitations due to health.

❑　❑　6. Describe life insurance in which the firm is the beneficiary.

❑　❑　7. Describe a typical week for the average partner, including the percentage of time spent in these areas:
- Directly billable;
- Administrative;
- Promotion; and
- Civic affairs.

Practice

❑　❑　8. If not correct above, what is the exact name of the practice?

❑　❑　9. When was the practice established? Provide a brief history of the development of the practice, including past partners, important dates, previous locations, and so on.

❑　❑　　10. Provide a current organizational chart. Describe the management team including current title, age, length of service, and background. Also, include the annual salary and bonus of each person for the current year and the last two years.

❑　❑　　11. Attach a list of all personnel (other than partners and the management team), stating the title/function and compensation of each.

❑　❑　　12. List the board of directors by name and title. For outside members, please provide occupation.

❑　❑　　13. Describe the growth trends and revenue and operating capacity (billable hours).

❑　❑　　14. Are any changes in services offered being considered?

❑　❑　　15. Is the firm responsive to seasonal fluctuations? Please explain.

❑　❑　　16. How have services been marketed or advertised?

Facilities

❑　❑　　17. Describe any land owned, including:
- Acreage;
- Original cost; and
- Approximate fair market value.

❑　❑　　18. Describe any building owned, including:
- Age and condition;
- Original cost;
- Approximate fair market value;
- Fire insurance amount; and
- Square feet.

❑　❑　　19. Furniture, fixtures, and equipment (FF&E). Since the FF&E schedule has been requested in our valuation information request, there will be no need to duplicate the listing here. What is requested is a discussion of the future plans for significant purchases of FF&E.

❑　❑　　20. Library:
- Description by major service and/or groups of works;
- Original cost;
- Replacement cost; and
- Unique volumes, if any.

❑　❑　　21. Please describe anything else that should be known about the practice for valuation purposes. Any information that will add to (or detract from) the reputation of the practice or the individual practitioners will have a similar effect on the valuation.

CHECKLIST 8.15: MANAGEMENT INTERVIEW— MEDICAL PRACTICE

Exact Practice Name _____   Date of Valuation _____

Address _____   Phone _____

_____

Analyst/Interviewer _____   Date of Interview _____

The objective of this management interview is to provide us with operational information that will aid us in the valuation of your business. We will keep the information confidential. Describe the following to the best of your ability. If necessary, use a separate sheet of paper, with reference to each item number. If some items are not applicable, please indicate N/A. Items already provided are indicated.

Provided

N/A

Interviewee(s)

❑ ❑   1. Name   Title

              _____   _____

              _____   _____

              _____   _____

Purpose and Objective of the Valuation

❑ ❑   2. The activity or transaction giving rise to the valuation.

Description of the Practice

❑ ❑   3. What is the full name of the P.A.?
❑ ❑   4. What date was the business established?
❑ ❑   5. Discuss the history of the practice, from founding to present, including past physicians, important dates, past locations, and so on.
❑ ❑   6. If incorporated, why was the practice incorporated?

Corporate Contacts

❑ ❑   7. Provide the name, address, and telephone number of the practice's attorney(s).
❑ ❑   8. Provide the name, address, and telephone number of the practice's accountant(s).

Physicians

❑ ❑   9. Provide a curriculum vitae for each doctor in the practice, including age, education (undergraduate school, medical school, residency), special license requirements, board certification, number of years experience, articles written, and lectures delivered.

❏ ❏   10. Is the general health of each doctor excellent, good, or poor?

❏ ❏   11. Describe the life insurance for each doctor if the beneficiary is the practice.

❏ ❏   12. Describe the typical work week for each doctor, including:
- Average number of patients per day;
- Nature of treatment;
- Average time per patient/treatment; and
- Hours worked per day.

❏ ❏   13. For each doctor, estimate the percentage of time spent in:
- Office visits/treatments;
- Surgery—hospital;
- Surgery—in office;
- Administration;
- Promotion; and
- Civic affairs.

❏ ❏   14. Indicate for each doctor if they will continue employment with the present practice.

Coverage

❏ ❏   15. List the physicians on the call schedule.

❏ ❏   16. Indicate which physicians take calls at the hospital emergency room (ER) as well as for established patients.

❏ ❏   17. If no ER service is provided, indicate when it was discontinued, if applicable.

❏ ❏   18. For each physician on call, estimate the percentage of time:
- Evenings per week on call; and
- Weekends per month on call.

❏ ❏   20. Do physicians make any payments to one another for coverage?

Personnel

❏ ❏   21. Attach a current organizational chart.

❏ ❏   22. Attach a list of employees, other than physicians, at year-end for last year, including current employee classifications, general wage scales, and approximate rate (distinguish full time and part time).

❏ ❏   23. List management personnel with title, length of service, age, and annual compensation (including bonuses) for the current year and past two years.

❏ ❏   24. Is there a board of directors? List and describe. For outside members, provide occupation.

The Practice

❏ ❏   25. How is marketing conducted (e.g., professional referral, patient referral, direct mail, yellow pages, other)?

❏ ❏   26. Who/what is your competition (specialized, general, mini-hospitals)?

❏ ❏   27. If there are other practices at the same location as the practice, list their name(s) and the medical specialties they practice.

❏ ❏   28. Who are the primary referral sources for the practice?

❏ ❏   29. Discuss past and projected growth trends, revenue, and operating capacity.

❏ ❏   30. Are there any limited factors to future growth?

❏ ❏   31. Are any new products/services being considered?

❏ ❏   32. Have there been any recent sales of stock (or interests) or offers to buy (or sell)?

❏ ❏   33. Are there any comparable sales of similar practices?

(continues)

Provided

N/A

Patient Demographics

❑ ❑ 34. What geographic area do patients come from?

❑ ❑ 35. Estimate the percentage of patients by age group, gender, and socioeconomic status.

Office

❑ ❑ 36. Estimate the number of hospital and office consultations by physician.

❑ ❑ 37. What types of procedures are performed in the office?

❑ ❑ 38. Does the practice utilize a recall system for getting patients to return for follow-up visits or post-ops?

❑ ❑ 39. How is hazardous waste disposed of?

❑ ❑ 40. Are there HIPAA issues?

Hospital

❑ ❑ 41. At what hospital(s) do the practice's physicians have privileges?

❑ ❑ 42. What day(s) do the physicians have surgical block time at the hospital?

❑ ❑ 43. Are there other days when operations are performed?

❑ ❑ 44. Do the physicians operate in any freestanding ambulatory surgery centers?

❑ ❑ 45. How many inpatients does the practice have at a given time?

❑ ❑ 46. Are the physicians members of a hospital PHO (physican hospital organization) or any IPAs (independent practice association)?

Patient Mix/Billing System

❑ ❑ 47. What type of billing software is used in the practice?

❑ ❑ 48. How recently was it upgraded?

❑ ❑ 49. Does the practice use an outside service bureau to do its billing? If so, indicate the name of the company and how they charge the practice for the service.

❑ ❑ 50. Does the practice file claims electronically? When was this service started or discontinued?

❑ ❑ 51. How are co-pays collected?

❑ ❑ 52. Does the practice accept Medicare assignment?

Property and Equipment

❑ ❑ 53. Describe the office facilities, including number of locations, square feet, number of examining rooms, number of operating rooms, and number of X-ray rooms.

❑ ❑ 54. If facilities are leased, what is the amount of the monthly payment and from whom are the facilities leased?

❑ ❑ 55. If facilities are owned, provide the age, condition, assessed value, and fair market value, if known.

❑ ❑ 56. Describe any specialized equipment.

❑ ❑ 57. If specialized equipment is leased, what is the amount of the monthly payment?

❑ ❑ 58. If specialized equipment is owned, provide the age, condition, assessed value, and fair market value, if known.

❑ ❑ 59. List and discuss company-owned vehicles.

❑   ❑   60. Describe the library, including:
- Original cost;
- Replacement cost; and
- Unique volumes.

Other

❑   ❑   61. Do the physicians in the practice have outside income (such as from medical directorships or consulting fees)?

❑   ❑   62. General outlook (if not covered elsewhere).

❑   ❑   63. Is there anything else we should know about the business that we have not already discussed?

Disclaimer Excluding Any Warranties: This checklist is designed to provide guidance to analysts, auditors, and management but is not to be used as a substitute for professional judgment. These procedures must be altered to fit each assignment. The practitioner takes sole responsibility for implementation of this guide. The implied warranties of merchantability and fitness of purpose and all other warranties, whether expressed or implied, are excluded from this transaction and shall not apply to this guide. The Financial Valuation Group shall not be liable for any indirect, special, or consequential damages.

CHECKLIST 8.16: MANAGEMENT INTERVIEW— CONSTRUCTION INDUSTRY

Exact Business Name _____   Date of Valuation _____

Address _____   Phone _____

_____

Analyst/Interviewer _____   Date of Interview _____

The objective of this management interview is to provide us with financial information that will aid us in the valuation of your business. We will keep the information confidential. Describe the following to the best of your ability. If necessary, use a separate sheet of paper, with reference to each item number. If some items are not applicable, please indicate N/A. Items already provided are indicated.

Provided

N/A

Interviewee(s)

❏ ❏ 1. Name   Title

_____   _____

_____   _____

_____   _____

Purpose and Objective of the Valuation

❏ ❏ 2. The activity or transaction giving rise to the valuation.

Other Information Regarding the Transaction

❏ ❏ 3. Number of shares being valued (each class).
❏ ❏ 4. Total number of shares issued (each class).
❏ ❏ 5. Total number of shares outstanding (each class).
❏ ❏ 6. Date of the valuation.
❏ ❏ 7. State of incorporation.
❏ ❏ 8. Standard of value.

Corporate Information

❏ ❏ 9. Name, address, and telephone number of the business attorney.
❏ ❏ 10. Name, address, and telephone number of the business accountant or bookkeeper.

Description of the Business

❏ ❏ 11. Type of business:
    • General contractor;
    • Subcontractor.
❏ ❏ 12. Products/services sold.
❏ ❏ 13. Type of customers/clients.
❏ ❏ 14. Location of sales/services.
❏ ❏ 15. Business code (see tax return).

❏ ❏ 16. SIC number or NAICS number.
❏ ❏ 17. Type of industry(ies).
❏ ❏ 18. Important industry trends.
❏ ❏ 19. Date business started.
❏ ❏ 20. Fiscal year-end date.
❏ ❏ 21. Factors you consider most important to your business's success.

History of the Business

❏ ❏ 22. From founding to the present, history including people, dates, places, new products, markets, and physical facilities.

Ownership

❏ ❏ 23. Shareholder list as of the date of valuation.
❏ ❏ 24. Transactions in the common stock and basis for price (parties, dates, shares, and prices).
❏ ❏ 25. Offers to purchase the company, if any. Discuss price, dates, terms, and current status of negotiations.
❏ ❏ 26. Prior appraisals.

Management

❏ ❏ 27. Current organizational chart.
❏ ❏ 28. List key management personnel with title, length of service, age, and annual compensation.
❏ ❏ 29. Key management positions open at this time.
❏ ❏ 30. Plans for succession if key-person dependency exists.
❏ ❏ 31. Adverse impact on business if sudden loss or withdrawal of any key employee.
❏ ❏ 32. Effectiveness of job cost estimators.
❏ ❏ 33. Amount and description of key-person life insurance policy, if any.

Products and Services

❏ ❏ 34. Business mix.
❏ ❏ 35. Changes in business mix.
❏ ❏ 36. New products/services.
❏ ❏ 37. Development procedure(s) of new products/services.
❏ ❏ 38. Expected performance of new products/services.
❏ ❏ 39. Note any important differences in profit margins by product line.

Markets and the Economy

❏ ❏ 40. Market area.
❏ ❏ 41. Determination of market area by market segment, geography, or customer type.
❏ ❏ 42. Important characteristics of the relevant economic base (obtain information of local Chamber of Commerce if needed).
❏ ❏ 43. Business sensitivity to economic cycles or seasonal influences.
❏ ❏ 44. Industry(s) of market concentration.
❏ ❏ 45. Approximate percentage of foreign sales, and, if any, total dollar amount of foreign sales.
❏ ❏ 46. Difference in profit margins of foreign sales to domestic sales, if any.
❏ ❏ 47. New product lines or services under consideration.

Customers

❏ ❏ 48. Major customers and the annual sales to each.
❏ ❏ 49. Length of relationships and customer turnover.

(continues)

Provided **N/A**

Customers *(continued)*

❑ ❑ 50. Company dependency, if any, on small group of large customers or large group of small customers.

❑ ❑ 51. Company dependency on bid contracts versus no-bid contracts.

Bonding

❑ ❑ 52. Surety agent.

❑ ❑ 53. Length of time they have provided bonding credit.

❑ ❑ 54. Amount of bonding credit extended.

❑ ❑ 55. Manner in which the amount of bonding credit is computed.

❑ ❑ 56. Multiple used by the surety agent to compute bonding credit.

Marketing Strategy

❑ ❑ 57. Sales and marketing strategy.

❑ ❑ 58. Sales procedures.

❑ ❑ 59. Sales personnel.

❑ ❑ 60. Basis of sales personnel compensation.

❑ ❑ 61. Risks of obsolescence or replacement by new or similar products.

Operations

❑ ❑ 62. Corporate organization structure (divisions, departments, etc.).

❑ ❑ 63. Flow of operations that produce the product or service.

Production

❑ ❑ 64. Operating leverage of business (high or low level).

❑ ❑ 65. Relationship of variable costs and fixed costs to total revenue.

❑ ❑ 66. Difficulty obtaining liability insurance, if any.

❑ ❑ 67. Insurance rates.

❑ ❑ 68. OSHA or EPS concerns in the work environment, if any, including the prospective cost of compliance.

❑ ❑ 69. Concerns over environmental hazards due to location or previous uses of land or facility.

❑ ❑ 70. Dependency in the production process on patents, licenses, or other contracts not controlled by the company.

❑ ❑ 71. Major suppliers and for what production inputs.

❑ ❑ 72. Raw material suppliers that are manufacturers.

❑ ❑ 73. Raw material suppliers that are wholesalers.

❑ ❑ 74. Dependency for critical components of the product or service on any one supplier

❑ ❑ 75. Name of union, if any.

❑ ❑ 76. Status of union contract or future organizing activities.

❑ ❑ 77. Number of past union strikes.

❑ ❑ 78. Number of full- and part-time employees.

❑ ❑ 79. Number of employees by division or department.

❑ ❑ 80. General experience, skill, and compensation levels of employees.

Real Property

❑ ❑ 81. List real estate and equipment used by the company including name of owner, affiliated parties (if leased), and market terms (if leased).

❑ ❑ 82. Size, age, condition, and capacity of the facilities.

❑ ❑ 83. Adequacy of facilities or plans for future expansion.

❏   ❏   84. Plant/office facilities, including:
- Owners;
- Real estate taxes;
- Land:
  - Acreage;
  - Cost;
  - Assessed value; and
  - Fair market value, if known.
- Buildings:
  - Type of construction;
  - Age condition;
  - Location on the property;
  - Assessed value;
  - Fair market value, if known;
  - Fire insurance amount; and
  - Square feet.
- Machinery and equipment:
  - Description;
  - Age and condition;
  - Efficiency utilization (older equipment or state of the art); and
  - Future plant, machinery, and equipment requirements, including estimated repairs.

❏   ❏   85. Current value of the real estate and equipment.
❏   ❏   86. Appraisals of real estate and equipment, or estimates.

Description of the Capital Structure

❏   ❏   87. Classes of securities.
❏   ❏   88. Common stock restrictions (such as a buy-sell agreement or charter restrictions), if any.
❏   ❏   89. Preferred stock terms of issue and protective covenants.
❏   ❏   90. Subordinated debt terms of issue and protective covenants.
❏   ❏   91. Outstanding stock options or warrants.
❏   ❏   92. Obtain and attach copies of the option agreement.

Other

❏   ❏   93. Dividend policy and dividend history.
❏   ❏   94. Anticipated future dividend payments.
❏   ❏   95. Pending litigation and potential impact on the company.
❏   ❏   96. Existing buy-sell or other restrictive agreements.
❏   ❏   97. Prenuptial agreement, if any.
❏   ❏   98. Profit sharing, ESOP, or other retirement plans.
❏   ❏   99. Copy of the ESOP plan, if not already provided.
❏   ❏   100. Copies of provisions related to shareholder liquidity in the plan.
❏   ❏   101. Company's regulators (e.g., public service commissions, bank regulators).
❏   ❏   102. Copies of regulatory orders, if any.
❏   ❏   103. General outlook (if not covered elsewhere).
❏   ❏   104. Other pertinent information about the business.

Financial Statement Review

❏   ❏   105. Quality of the financial statements.
❏   ❏   106. Reason(s) for qualifications of audited and qualified statements, if applicable.
❏   ❏   107. Consistency of accounting principles of company prepared interim statements with accountant-prepared statements.

(continues)

Provided

N/A

Financial Statement Review *(continued)*

❑   ❑   108. Method of accounting for long-term contracts.

Balance Sheet Review

❑   ❑   109. Approximate total asset book value.
❑   ❑   110. Approximate net book value.
❑   ❑   111. Cash.
❑   ❑   112. Minimum level of cash required to operate the company.
❑   ❑   113. Minimum level of cash required to satisfy bonding requirements.
❑   ❑   114. Marketable securities and other investments:
            • Normal terms of sale.
❑   ❑   115. Accounts receivable:
            • Normal terms of sale;
            • Comparison of collection period to industry norms and
              history;
            • History of bad debts;
            • Receivables concentration by customer; and
            • Typical retention percentage.
❑   ❑   116. Costs and estimated earnings in excess of billings (underbillings):
            • Management's billing policy on uncompleted jobs.
❑   ❑   117. Inventory:
            • Accounting method used to calculate inventories;
            • Trend in level of inventories and turnover rate; and
            • Obsolete inventory and the amount paid for it.
❑   ❑   118. Other current assets:
            • List of current assets; and
            • Current assets not related to the business, if any.
❑   ❑   119. Fixed assets:
            • Major fixed assets;
            • Depreciation calculations for book and tax purposes;
            • Capital budget for the coming years;
            • Types of fixed assets needed in the future; and
            • List of excess assets.
❑   ❑   120. Notes receivable:
            • Names and terms (if due from officers and affiliates,
              comparison of terms to market rates).
❑   ❑   121. Other assets:
            • Long term.
❑   ❑   122. Notes payable:
            • Names and terms of vendors.
❑   ❑   123. Accounts payable:
            • General terms of purchase of goods and services;
            • Trend in payables and turnover ratios; and
            • Typical retentions percentage.
❑   ❑   124. Billings in excess of costs and estimated earnings (overbillings).
❑   ❑   125. Taxes payable and deferred taxes.
❑   ❑   126. Other accrued expenses.
❑   ❑   127. Long-term debt:
            • Names and terms (if secured, state asset(s) used as security).
❑   ❑   128. Mortgage notes payable:
            • Terms and collateral.
❑   ❑   129. Any contingent liabilities.

Income Statement

❏ ❏ 130. Approximate annual sales volume.
❏ ❏ 131. Sales:
- Reason for changes in sales over the past five years;
- Attribution of growth in sales:
  - Unit volume;
  - Inflation.
- Comparison of growth rate in sales to other items on the income statement;
- Projections for the current year and beyond;
- Amount of bonding credit compared to projections; and
- Basis for projections.

❏ ❏ 132. Costs of goods sold:
- Key factors that affect cost of goods sold; and
- Changes in accounting procedures, if any.

❏ ❏ 133. Gross profit margin (GPM):
- Changes in GPM for the last five years (price increases, cost increases, inventory write-downs, etc.).

❏ ❏ 134. General and administrative expenses:
- Major expense items of the company;
- Fluctuations in expenses over the last five years; and
- Nonrecurring expenses included in the totals.

❏ ❏ 135. Other income/expense:
- Sources.

❏ ❏ 136. Taxes:
- Federal tax rate; and
- State tax rate.

❏ ❏ 137. Hidden or intangible assets, such as:
- Patents;
- Favorable leases;
- Favorable financing arrangements;
- Number of recurring, stable customers;
- Employment contracts;
- Copyrights;
- Long-term customers' contracts;
- Trademark;
- Unique research and development;
- Highly trained staff in place; and
- Undervalued securities or other investments.

❏ ❏ 138. Key liabilities:
- Commitments for new buildings or machinery; and
- Long-term loans outstanding and terms.

Schedules of Completed and Uncompleted Contracts (Job Schedule)

❏ ❏ 139. Approximate annual volume of contracts.
❏ ❏ 140. Comparison of gross profit margins of completed contracts with the same contract on the prior year's uncompleted jobs.
❏ ❏ 141. Comparison of gross profit margins on uncompleted contracts with completed contracts and other uncompleted.

CHECKLIST 8.17: VALUATION INFORMATION REQUEST (VIR) COPYRIGHTS

Business Name: _____

Valuation Date: _____

This is a generalized information request. Some items may not pertain to your company, and some items may not be readily available to you. In such cases, indicate N/A or notify us if other arrangements can be made to obtain the data. Items already provided are indicated. If you have any questions on the development of this information, please call.

Provided   **N/A**

Copyrights

Provided	N/A	
❑	❑	1. Provide a list of all copyrighted registrations.
❑	❑	2. Provide a list of works (articles, books, paintings, etc.).
❑	❑	3. Identify copyright names that are associated with products and/or services (such as software or report templates).
❑	❑	4. Identify historical sale of products and/or services employing the works for the last five years.
❑	❑	5. Provide projection of products and/or services that will employ the works for the next five years.
❑	❑	6. Are any copyrighted works being licensed in or out? If yes, provide details.

Disclaimer Excluding Any Warranties: This checklist is designed to provide guidance to analysts, auditors, and management but is not to be used as a substitute for professional judgment. These procedures must be altered to fit each assignment. The practitioner takes sole responsibility for implementation of this guide. The implied warranties of merchantability and fitness of purpose and all other warranties, whether expressed or implied, are excluded from this transaction and shall not apply to this guide. The Financial Valuation Group shall not be liable for any indirect, special, or consequential damages.

CHECKLIST 8.18: VALUATION INFORMATION REQUEST (VIR) CUSTOMER RELATIONSHIPS

Business Name: _____

Valuation Date: _____

This is a generalized information request. Some items may not pertain to your company, and some items may not be readily available to you. In such cases, indicate N/A or notify us if other arrangements can be made to obtain the data. Items already provided are indicated. If you have any questions on the development of this information, please call.

Provided **N/A**

Customer Relationships

❑ ❑ 1. Provide customer sales history for the last five years for the top 10 customers.

❑ ❑ 2. Provide complete customer history for the last five years (this would be for lifing).

❑ ❑ 3. Provide financial data representing annual costs for the last five years associated with developing/soliciting new customers.

❑ ❑ 4. Provide schedule of new customers gained in each of the last five years with sales.

❑ ❑ 5. For the last five years, how many customers in a given year failed to purchase in the following year? Provide those customers' sales for the prior year.

Disclaimer Excluding Any Warranties: This checklist is designed to provide guidance to analysts, auditors, and management but is not to be used as a substitute for professional judgment. These procedures must be altered to fit each assignment. The practitioner takes sole responsibility for implementation of this guide. The implied warranties of merchantability and fitness of purpose and all other warranties, whether expressed or implied, are excluded from this transaction and shall not apply to this guide. The Financial Valuation Group shall not be liable for any indirect, special, or consequential damages.

CHECKLIST 8.19: VALUATION INFORMATION REQUEST (VIR) IN-PROCESS RESEARCH AND DEVELOPMENT

Business Name: _____

Valuation Date: _____

This is a generalized information request. Some items may not pertain to your company, and some items may not be readily available to you. In such cases, indicate N/A or notify us if other arrangements can be made to obtain the data. Items already provided are indicated. If you have any questions on the development of this information, please call.

Provided

N/A

In-Process Research and Development

❑ ❑ 1. Describe the in-process research and development.

❑ ❑ 2. Describe competitive advantages and disadvantages of the in-process research and development.

❑ ❑ 3. Describe industry trends and competitive pressures that may affect the useful life of the in-process research and development.

❑ ❑ 4. In light of 2 and 3 above, what is the current percent complete and the estimated useful life of the in-process research and development?

❑ ❑ 5. If available, please provide cost records documenting development of the in-process research and development:
- Person-hours to develop;
- Various technical levels of persons working on the assignment;
- Pay scales for individuals at each technical review; and
- Information to determine overhead rate.

❑ ❑ 6. In the absence of cost records, estimate effort to create the in-process research and development:
- Who would work on the assignment (employees and consultants);
- Pay rates for individuals in above; and
- Information to determine overhead rate.

❑ ❑ 7. What products or services will employ the in-process research and development?

❑ ❑ 8. Provide projections of products and/or services that will employ the in-process research and development for the next five years:
- Project revenues including licensing income for the lifespan of the in-process research and development;
- Project direct expenses associated with producing revenue including the costs to complete the IPR&D; and
- Obtain or develop indirect expenses (i.e., overhead).

CHECKLIST 8.20: VALUATION INFORMATION REQUEST (VIR) KNOW-HOW

Business Name: _____

Valuation Date: _____

This is a generalized information request. Some items may not pertain to your company, and some items may not be readily available to you. In such cases, indicate N/A or notify us if other arrangements can be made to obtain the data. Items already provided are indicated. If you have any questions on the development of this information, please call.

Provided

N/A

Know-How

❏	❏	1. Describe know-how, including competitive advantages and disadvantages.
❏	❏	2. Describe industry trends and competitive pressures that may affect the useful life of the know-how.
❏	❏	3. In light of 1 and 2 above, what is the estimated useful life of the know-how?
❏	❏	4. What products or services employ the know-how?
❏	❏	5. If available, provide historical cost records documenting development of the know-how: • Person-hours to develop; • Various technical levels of persons working on the assignment; • Pay scales for individuals in 5b at each technical level; and • Information to determine overhead rate.
❏	❏	6. In the absence of historical cost records, estimate corporate effort to recreate the know-how if it were to be developed from scratch: • Who would work on the assignment (employees and consultants); • Pay rates for individuals in 6a above; and • Information to determine overhead rate.
❏	❏	7. Identify historical sale of revenues for products and/or services employing know-how for the last five years.
❏	❏	8. Know-how associated with products and/or services: • Provide projection of products and/or services that employ the know-how for the next five years; • Project direct expenses associated with producing revenue; and • Obtain or develop indirect expenses (i.e., overhead).
❏	❏	9. Are you licensing in or out any know-how? If yes, provide details.

Disclaimer Excluding Any Warranties: This checklist is designed to provide guidance to analysts, auditors, and management but is not to be used as a substitute for professional judgment. These procedures must be altered to fit each assignment. The practitioner takes sole responsibility for implementation of this guide. The implied warranties of merchantability and fitness of purpose and all other warranties, whether expressed or implied, are excluded from this transaction and shall not apply to this guide. The Financial Valuation Group shall not be liable for any indirect, special, or consequential damages.

CHECKLIST 8.21:   VALUATION INFORMATION REQUEST (VIR) PATENTS

Business Name: _____

Valuation Date: _____

This is a generalized information request. Some items may not pertain to your company, and some items may not be readily available to you. In such cases, indicate N/A or notify us if other arrangements can be made to obtain the data. Items already provided are indicated. If you have any questions on the development of this information, please call.

Provided   **N/A**

Patent

Provided	N/A	
❏	❏	1. Provide a summary of patents held by the company.
❏	❏	2. Provide copies of patent applications and patent abstracts.
❏	❏	3. Distinguish which patents have commercial applications (i.e., are producing or are reasonably forecast to produce revenue in the future).
❏	❏	4. If available, provide historical cost records documenting development of the patent(s): • Person hours to develop; • Various technical levels of persons working on the assignment; • Pay scales for individuals at each technical level; and • Information to determine overhead rate.
❏	❏	5. Identify patents and associated products that now have or are expected to have commercial viability: • Prepare forecast or projection of revenues related to patent over the life of the patent; and • Project direct expenses associated with producing revenue.
❏	❏	6. Comment on the possibility of extending patent protection beyond statutory life of patent.
❏	❏	7. Are you licensing in or out any patents? If yes, provide details.

CHECKLIST 8.22: VALUATION INFORMATION REQUEST (VIR) SOFTWARE

Business Name: _____

Valuation Date: _____

This is a generalized information request. Some items may not pertain to your company, and some items may not be readily available to you. In such cases, indicate N/A or notify us if other arrangements can be made to obtain the data. Items already provided are indicated. If you have any questions on the development of this information, please call.

Provided

N/A

Software

☐ ☐ 1. Describe the function of the software.

☐ ☐ 2. If available, provide historical cost records documenting development of the software:
 • Person-hours to develop;
 • Various technical levels of persons working on the assignment;
 • Pay scales for individuals at each technical level; and
 • Information to determine overhead rate.

☐ ☐ 3. In the absence of historical cost records, estimate effort to recreate the software if it were to be developed from scratch:
 • Who would work on the assignment (employees and consultants);
 • Pay rates for individuals above; and
 • Information to determine overhead rate.

☐ ☐ 4. What was the expected useful life at inception and at valuation date? Obtain support for estimate:
 • When was software actually placed in use?
 • Describe internal development that may extend life;
 • Describe internal development of replacement software that might shorten life; and
 • Describe external factors that may affect life.

☐ ☐ 5. Obtain historical revenues applicable to software.

☐ ☐ 6. Provide projection of revenues applicable to the software for the next five years:
 • Project revenues including licensing income for lifespan of software;
 • Project direct expenses associated with producing revenue; and
 • Obtain or develop indirect expenses (i.e., overhead).

Disclaimer Excluding Any Warranties: This checklist is designed to provide guidance to analysts, auditors, and management but is not to be used as a substitute for professional judgment. These procedures must be altered to fit each assignment. The practitioner takes sole responsibility for implementation of this guide. The implied warranties of merchantability and fitness of purpose and all other warranties, whether expressed or implied, are excluded from this transaction and shall not apply to this guide. The Financial Valuation Group shall not be liable for any indirect, special, or consequential damages.

CHECKLIST 8.23:   VALUATION INFORMATION REQUEST (VIR) PROPRIETARY PROCESS/PRODUCTS TECHNOLOGY

Business Name: _____

Valuation Date: _____

This is a generalized information request. Some items may not pertain to your company, and some items may not be readily available to you. In such cases, indicate N/A or notify us if other arrangements can be made to obtain the data. Items already provided are indicated. If you have any questions on the development of this information, please call.

Provided

N/A

Proprietary Processes/Products Technology

❑   ❑   1. Describe the proprietary process/product technology.

❑   ❑   2. Describe competitive advantages and disadvantages of the proprietary process/product technology.

❑   ❑   3. Describe industry trends and competitive pressures that may affect the useful life of the proprietary process/product technology.

❑   ❑   4. In light of 2 and 3 above, what is the estimated useful life of the proprietary process/product technology support?

❑   ❑   5. If available, please provide historical cost records documenting development of the process/product technology:
- Person-hours to develop;
- Various technical levels of persons working on the assignment;
- Pay scales for individuals at each technical level; and
- Information to determine overhead rate.

❑   ❑   6. In the absence of historical cost records, estimate effort to recreate the process/product technology if it were to be developed from scratch:
- Who would work on the assignment (employees and consultants)?
- Pay rates for individuals above; and
- Information to determine overhead rate.

❑   ❑   7. Identify historical sale of products and/or services employing process/product technology for the last five years.

❑   ❑   8. What products or services employ the proprietary process/product technology?

❑   ❑   9. Provide projection of products and/or services that employ the process/product technology for the next five years.
- Project revenues including licensing income for the life span of process/product technology;
- Project direct expenses associated with producing revenue; and
- Obtain or develop indirect expenses (i.e., overhead).

❑   ❑   10. Is any technology being licensed in or out? If yes, provide details.

CHECKLIST 8.24: VALUATION INFORMATION REQUEST (VIR) TRADEMARK/TRADE NAME

Business Name: _____

Valuation Date: _____

This is a generalized information request. Some items may not pertain to your company, and some items may not be readily available to you. In such cases, indicate N/A or notify us if other arrangements can be made to obtain the data. Items already provided are indicated. If you have any questions on the development of this information, please call.

Provided

N/A

Trademark/Trade Name

❑ ❑   1. Provide a list of all trademark/trade name registrations.

❑ ❑   2. Provide a list of trademark/trade names that are not registered.

❑ ❑   3. Identify trademarks/trade names that are associated with products and/or services.

❑ ❑   4. Identify historical sale of products and/or services employing trademarks/trade names for the last five years.

❑ ❑   5. Provide projection of products and/or services that employ the trademarks/trade names for the next five years.

❑ ❑   6. Are any trademarks/trade names being licensed in or out? If yes, provide details.

Disclaimer Excluding Any Warranties: This checklist is designed to provide guidance to analysts, auditors, and management but is not to be used as a substitute for professional judgment. These procedures must be altered to fit each assignment. The practitioner takes sole responsibility for implementation of this guide. The implied warranties of merchantability and fitness of purpose and all other warranties, whether expressed or implied, are excluded from this transaction and shall not apply to this guide. The Financial Valuation Group shall not be liable for any indirect, special, or consequential damages.

CHECKLIST 8.25: PROCEDURES FOR THE VALUATION OF INTANGIBLE ASSETS

Business Name: _____

Valuation Date: _____

An intangible asset is an asset (excluding financial instruments) that lacks physical substance. An intangible asset acquired in a business combination shall be recognized as an asset apart from goodwill if that asset arises from contractual or other legal rights. If an intangible asset does not arise from contractual or other legal rights, it shall be recognized as an asset apart from goodwill only if it is separable, that is, it is capable of being separated or divided from the acquired enterprise and sold, transferred, licensed, rented, or exchanged (regardless of whether there is an intent to do so). For GAAP purposes, an intangible asset that cannot be sold, transferred, licensed, rented, or exchanged individually is considered separable if it can be sold, transferred, licensed, rented, or exchanged with a related contract, asset, or liability. However, the value of an assembled workforce of at-will employees acquired in a business combination shall be included in the amount recorded as goodwill regardless of whether it meets the criteria for recognition apart from goodwill.

The purpose of this checklist is to guide the analyst in the valuation of intangible assets. For each item, the analyst should indicate completion, or check the item N/A.

Completed **N/A**

Valuation

❑ ❑ 1. Determine the standard of value:
- Fair market value;
- Fair value;
- Investment value;
- Intrinsic value or fundamental value; and
- Other: _____.

❑ ❑ 2. State the purpose of the valuation.

❑ ❑ 3. Determine the premise of value:
- Value in use, as part of a going concern. (This premise contemplates the contributory value to an income-producing enterprise of the intangible asset as part of a mass assemblage of tangible and intangible assets.)
- Value in place, as part of an assemblage of assets. (This premise contemplates that the intangible asset is fully functional, is part of an assemblage of assets that is ready for use but is not currently engaged in the production of income.)
- Value in exchange, in an orderly disposition. (This premise contemplates that the intangible asset will be sold in its current condition, with normal exposure to its appropriate secondary market, but without the contributory value of any associated tangible or intangible assets.)
- Value in exchange, in a forced liquidation. (This premise contemplates that the intangible asset is sold piecemeal, in an auction environment, with an artificially abbreviated exposure to its secondary market.)

Intangible Asset Description

❑ ❑ 4. Is the intangible asset subject to specific identification or a recognizable description?

❑ ❑ 5. Categorize the intangible asset as:
   • Marketing related;
   • Customer related;
   • Artistic related;
   • Contract related; and
   • Technology related.

❑ ❑ 6. Determine and list the intangible assets eligible for appraisal.

❑ ❑ 7. Describe fully the intangible asset identified. Attach necessary contracts, drawings, patents, listings, and so on to fully identify the intangible asset.

History of the Asset

❑ ❑ 8. Describe the legal existence and protection associated with the intangible asset.

❑ ❑ 9. Is the transferability of the ownership restricted? Explain.

❑ ❑ 10. Describe the susceptibility of the asset being destroyed.

❑ ❑ 11. Describe the inception of the intangible asset (attach a list providing start dates for all customer or client lists).

❑ ❑ 12. To what degree is the revenue associated with these intangible assets due to the day-to-day efforts of the owner? Explain.

❑ ❑ 13. Provide isolated financial results directly related to the asset, such as:
   • Historical cost to create the asset;
   • Annual cost to maintain the asset; and
   • Specific cash flow related to the asset.

❑ ❑ 14. Provide a description of the history of the asset, including year(s) created.

❑ ❑ 15. Provide all contracts or agreements.

❑ ❑ 16. Provide all strategic, marketing, and business plans related to the asset.

Industry and Market

❑ ❑ 17. Provide all market or industry surveys or studies related to the asset.

❑ ❑ 18. Describe the competitive environment related to the asset.

❑ ❑ 19. Describe the general economic environment related to the asset.

Financial Information

❑ ❑ 20. Describe the specific industry environment related to the asset.

❑ ❑ 21. Provide all previous valuation reports related to the asset.

❑ ❑ 22. Provide all financial projections including unit sales.

❑ ❑ 23. Provide all budgets/forecasts.

❑ ❑ 24. Determine associated cost of capital related directly to the asset.

Life Cycle

❑ ❑ 25. At what stage in its life cycle is the asset?

❑ ❑ 26. Please describe the product life cycle.

Valuation Approaches

❑ ❑ 27. Determine valuation approach:
   • *Cost Approach*—The cost approach is based on the principle of substitution. A prudent investor would not pay more for an intangible asset than it would cost to replace that intangible asset with a ready-made comparable substitute. Some

(continues)

Completed

N/A

Valuation Approaches *(continued)*

intangible assets likely to be valued using the cost approach include computer software, automated databases, technical drawings and documentation, blueprints and engineering drawings, laboratory notebooks, technical libraries, chemical formulations, food and other product recipes, and so on.

- *Market Approach*—The market approach compares the subject intangible asset with similar or comparable intangible assets that have been sold or listed for sale in the appropriate primary or secondary market. Correlations must be extrapolated.
- *Income Approach*—The income approach measures future economic benefits, discounted to a present value. Different measures of economic income may be relevant to the various income approach methodologies. Given the different measures of economic income that may be used in the income approach, an essential element in the application of this valuation approach is to ensure that the discount rate or the capitalization rate used is derived on a basis consistent with the measure of economic income used.

Cost Approach

❑ ❑ 28. Determine the appropriate cost method:
- Reproduction cost (the cost at current prices to construct an exact duplicate or replica of the subject intangible asset. This duplicate would be created using the same materials, standards, design, layout and quality of workmanship used to create the original intangible asset).
- Replacement cost (the cost to create at current prices an asset having equal utility to the intangible asset. Replacement cost utilizes modern methods and standards, state of the art design and layout and the highest available quality of workmanship).

❑ ❑ 29. Determine the appropriate adjustment for obsolescence:
- Physical deterioration (the reduction from cost due to physical wear and tear resulting from continued use).
- Functional obsolescence (the reduction due to the inability to perform the function or yield the periodic utility for which the asset was originally designed).
- Technological obsolescence (the reduction due to improvements in technology that make an asset less than an ideal replacement for itself, generally resulting in improvements in design or engineering technology and resulting in greater standardized measure of utility production).
- Economic obsolescence (the reduction due to the effects, events or conditions that are not controlled by, and thus external to, the current use or condition of the subject asset).

❑ ❑ 30. Determine the number of employees involved in creating the intangible asset.

❑ ❑ 31. Categorize the employees by salary level.

❑ ❑ 32. Capture the associated employer cost related to each hour of salary level.

❑ ❑ 33. Determine the number of hours per employee salary level utilized to develop the asset.

❏ ❏ 34. Extend the number of hours per salary level by the salary and associated employer cost for an estimate of reproduction costs new.

❏ ❏ 35. Adjust reproduction cost new for associated deterioration or obsolescence.

❏ ❏ 36. Compare net result of reproduction cost with replacement cost new.

❏ ❏ 37. Complete the cost approach analysis.

Market Approach

❏ ❏ 38. Determine the market served by the guideline or comparable asset.

❏ ❏ 39. Complete a primary and secondary market search for similar guideline assets, including an analysis of available public data specific to royalty rates and intellectual property transactions.

❏ ❏ 40. Determine the historical return on the investment earned by the subject intangible asset.

❏ ❏ 41. Determine the income-generating capacity of the subject intangible asset.

❏ ❏ 42. Determine the expected prospective return on the investment earned by the guideline asset.

❏ ❏ 43. Determine the expected prospective return by the subject intangible asset.

❏ ❏ 44. Determine the historical age and expected remaining useful life of the guideline or comparable intangible asset.

❏ ❏ 45. Determine the historical age and the remaining useful life of the subject intangible asset.

❏ ❏ 46. Analyze the terms of the sale of the guideline or the comparable intangible asset including:
   • The time of the sale;
   • The price paid;
   • The payout terms; and
   • Other related terms (including special seller financing and earn out agreement, non-compete agreement, etc.).

❏ ❏ 47. Determine the degree of adjustment necessary to the guideline or comparable intangible asset related to:
   • Physical deterioration;
   • Functional obsolescence;
   • Technological obsolescence; and
   • Economic obsolescence.

❏ ❏ 48. Determine the degree of adjustment necessary to the subject intangible asset related to:
   • Physical deterioration;
   • Functional obsolescence;
   • Technological obsolescence; and
   • Economic obsolescence.

❏ ❏ 49. Complete extrapolation of market approach correlation.

Income Approach

❏ ❏ 50. Determine the economic income related to the identified intangible asset for the following:
   • Net income before tax;
   • Net income after tax;
   • Net operating income;
   • Gross rental income;
   • Gross royalty or license income (actual or hypothetical if a relief from royalties method is employed, in which case should

(continues)

Completed

N/A

Income Approach (continued)

include an analysis of available public data specific to royalty rates and intellectual property transactions);
- Gross or operating cash flow; and
- Net or free cash flow.

☐ ☐ 51. Determine the direct cost associated with maintaining the identified intangible asset. These costs should include cost of operating the asset, storing the asset (facilities), and managing a return from the asset (staff expenses). Pay particular attention to any anticipated unusual costs (such as renewing a patent).

☐ ☐ 52. Determine specific cash flow to the intangible asset by taking an economic return on contributory assets that are part of the initial cash flow stream. Contributory assets include:
- Working capital;
- Fixed assets; and
- Other intangible assets.

☐ ☐ 53. Determine an appropriate discount rate reflecting a fair return on the investment by considering:
- The opportunity cost of capital;
- The term period of the investment (including consideration of the expected remaining life of the subject intangible asset);
- The systematic risk of the investment;
- The unsystematic risk of the investment;
- The time value of money; and
- Growth (utilized for computing terminal value).

☐ ☐ 54. Obtain the necessary data to complete the actuarial retirement rate methodology including:
- Inception dates for all active files; and
- Inception dates and retirement dates for all inactive files comprising the subject intangible asset (5-year history desirable).

☐ ☐ 55. In absence of hard data for No. 54, obtain management's representations as to:
- Average age of all active files;
- Average remaining life of all active files; and
- Estimated number of visits per file.

☐ ☐ 56. Complete the actuarial retirement rate methodology by:
- Observing the data; and
- Determining the curve fitting using appropriate statistical tools (S-curve, O-curve, L-curve, R-curve).

☐ ☐ 57. Match the actuarial retirement rate curve with the actual data.
☐ ☐ 58. Determine the probable life curve.
☐ ☐ 59. Determine the remaining useful life and survivorship percentages.
☐ ☐ 60. Apply the survivorship percentages to the discounted cash flow.
☐ ☐ 61. Complete income approach methodology.

Relief from Royalties Method

☐ ☐ 62. How is the licensed product unique? What are the competitive advantages of the licensed product including the scope and remaining life of any patents related to the products?

☐ ☐ 63. Analyze the markets in which the licensee will sell the licensed products, including:
- Market size;

- Growth rates;
- Extent of competition; and
- Recent developments.

❑ ❑ 64. Determine the degree of complexity in the sale of the licensed product.

❑ ❑ 65. Determine the extent of customization in customer-specific applications. (Note: Royalty rates are generally inversely related to the level of complexity and licensee customization.)

❑ ❑ 66. Determine the size of the licensed territory, including any restrictions or exclusivity. (Note: Exclusivity is directly correlated to higher royalty rates.)

❑ ❑ 67. Determine the length of the initial license term and provisions for renewal. (Note: Royalty rates will increase if the provisions for renewal are favorable for licensing.)

❑ ❑ 68. What are the provisions for termination? (Note: The conditions for unilateral license termination generally protect the licensor from a material breach committed by the licensee. These terms should be identified.)

❑ ❑ 69. Does a minimum royalty rate exist?

❑ ❑ 70. Analyze the licensee's ability to assign the license to a third party, either directly or indirectly (e.g., through the purchase of stock ownership).

❑ ❑ 71. What is the licensor's presence within its own markets?

❑ ❑ 72. What is the licensor's financial viability?

❑ ❑ 73. What is the licensor's size and market share?

❑ ❑ 74. What is the licensor's depth of senior management and stability?

❑ ❑ 75. What is the licensor's depth of technical knowledge?

❑ ❑ 76. What is the licensor's business plan related to the licensed products, including R&D funding and market analysis?

❑ ❑ 77. To what extent and timeliness does the licensor offer to support the licensee including:
- Technical product advice;
- Assisting the licensee with sales; and
- Assisting the licensee with marketing efforts in the defined territory.

❑ ❑ 78. Determine the licensee's available profit percentage available for the royalty (e.g., 25%?, 50%?) depending on:
- Available profitability as compared with the industry;
- The nature of the long-term competitive advantage of the product;
- The degree the license terms are favorable to the licensee;
- The degree of support and market share offered by the licensor;
- The degree of any noncash value offered by the licensee to the licensor;
- The degree the licensee is required to purchase certain components used in the manufacturing of licensed products from the licensor (mandatory supply arrangement); and
- The degree of foreign exchange risk borne by either the licensee or the licensor (the risk of future devaluation).

CHECKLIST 8.26: ROYALTY FACTORS

Exact Business Name _____

Date of Valuation _____

The objective of this checklist is to provide the analyst with a list of those items generally needed for the valuation of royalty rates (patent example here). The analyst should initial as each item is obtained. Items not needed may be marked N/A.

Obtained	N/A	
❑	❑	1. The royalties received by the patentee for the licensing of the patent in suit, proving or tending to prove an established royalty.
❑	❑	2. The rates paid by the licensee for the use of other patents comparable to the patent in suit.
❑	❑	3. The nature and scope of the license, as exclusive or nonexclusive; or as restricted or nonrestricted in terms of territory or with respect to whom the manufactured product may be sold.
❑	❑	4. The licensor's established policy and marketing program to maintain his patent monopoly by not licensing others to use the invention or by granting licenses under special conditions designed to preserve that monopoly.
❑	❑	5. The commercial relationship between the licensor and licensee, such as whether they are competitors in the same territory in the same line of business or whether they are inventor and promoter.
❑	❑	6. The effect of selling the patented specialty in promoting sales of other products of the licensee; the existing value of the invention to the licensor as a generator of sales of his non-patented items; and the extent of such derivative or convoyed sales.
❑	❑	7. The duration of the patent and the term of the license.
❑	❑	8. The established profitability of the product made under the patent, its commercial success, and its current popularity.
❑	❑	9. The utility and advantages of the patent property over the old modes or devices, if any, that had been used for working out similar results.
❑	❑	10. The nature of the patented invention, the character of the commercial embodiment of it as owned and produced by the licensor, and the benefits to those who have used the invention.
❑	❑	11. The extent to which the infringer has made use of the invention and any evidence probative of the value of that use.
❑	❑	12. The portion of the profit or of the selling price that may be customary in the particular business or in comparable businesses to allow for the use of the invention or analogous inventions.
❑	❑	13. The portion of the realizable profit that should be credited to the invention as distinguished from non-patented elements, the manufacturing process, business risks, or significant features or improvements added by the infringer.[1]

---

[1] Business appraisers may wish to compare *Georgia-Pacific* (318 Federal Supplement 1116 (1970)) Factor 13 to traditional excess-earnings approaches.

❑   ❑   14. The opinion testimony of qualified experts.

❑   ❑   15. The amount that a licensor (such as the patentee) and the licensee (such as the infringer) would have agreed on (at the time the infringement began) if both had been reasonably and voluntarily trying to reach an agreement; that is, the amount that a prudent licensee—who desired, as a business proposition, to obtain a license to manufacture and sell a particular article embodying the patented invention—would have been willing to pay as a royalty and yet be able to make a reasonable profit and which amount would have been acceptable by a prudent patentee who was willing to grant a license.[2]

Disclaimer Excluding Any Warranties: This checklist is designed to provide guidance to analysts, auditors, and management but is not to be used as a substitute for professional judgment. These procedures must be altered to fit each assignment. The practitioner takes sole responsibility for implementation of this guide. The implied warranties of merchantability and fitness of purpose and all other warranties, whether expressed or implied, are excluded from this transaction and shall not apply to this guide. The Financial Valuation Group shall not be liable for any indirect, special, or consequential damages.

---

[2] Compare to business appraisal concept of "fair market value."

CHECKLIST 8.27: MANAGEMENT INTERVIEW— PATENT VALUATION

Exact Business Name _____ Date of Valuation _____

Address _____ Phone _____

_____

Analyst/Interviewer _____ Date of Interview _____

The objective of this management interview is to provide us with operational information that will aid us in the valuation of your business. We will keep the information confidential. Describe the following to the best of your ability. If necessary, use a separate sheet of paper, with reference to each item number. If some items are not applicable, please indicate N/A. Items already provided are indicated.

Completed

N/A

Interviewee(s)

❑ ❑ 1. Name   Title

_____   _____

_____   _____

_____   _____

Purpose and Objective of the Valuation

❑ ❑ 2. The activity or transaction giving rise to the valuation.

Patent

❑ ❑ 3. List of patents to be valued, including copy of complete application.

❑ ❑ 4. Provide descriptions of the products and processes encompassed by the patents.

❑ ❑ 5. Describe how the patent will be utilized in a products(s).

❑ ❑ 6. Describe the firm's R&D facilities.

❑ ❑ 7. Identify the portion of time spent on R&D by each member of the group.

❑ ❑ 8. What has company done to exploit patent and what are the results?

❑ ❑ 9. Describe the marketplace for the patent including potential uses, current uses, size of market, and so on.

❑ ❑ 10. If there are competing patents, what market share does each of the patents have?

❑ ❑ 11. Have there been any market studies performed related to the patent?

❑ ❑ 12. How will the lack of additional registrations affect the size of the marketplace for the products and the market penetration in other parts of the world?

❏ ❏   13. How defendable is the patent?

❏ ❏   14. Why was it not registered in additional countries?

❏ ❏   15. Has there been any actual, threatened, or potential litigation involving the patent?

❏ ❏   16. What is the estimated time until the patent becomes technically obsolete?

❏ ❏   17. What alternatives (real or perceived) are there for the patents for potential users?

❏ ❏   18. How does the patent benefit the user?

❏ ❏   19. What is the cost to upgrade technology for necessary enhancements to keep it competitive?

❏ ❏   20. What are the untapped uses of the patent?

❏ ❏   21. Has the patent ever been offered (or planned to be) for license? If so, on what terms?

❏ ❏   22. Has the patent ever been (or planned to be) offered for sale? If so, at what price?

❏ ❏   23. Has the patent ever been valued by internal or external parties?

❏ ❏   24. If the company is gifting the patent, why does the company want to get rid of the patent? Why was it developed if it is not necessary?

❏ ❏   25. If applicable, why do you believe the tax benefit of a charitable donation is more valuable to the company than exploiting the patent?

Disclaimer Excluding Any Warranties: This checklist is designed to provide guidance to analysts, auditors, and management but is not to be used as a substitute for professional judgment. These procedures must be altered to fit each assignment. The practitioner takes sole responsibility for implementation of this guide. The implied warranties of merchantability and fitness of purpose and all other warranties, whether expressed or implied, are excluded from this transaction and shall not apply to this guide. The Financial Valuation Group shall not be liable for any indirect, special, or consequential damages.

CHECKLIST 8.28:   REVENUE RULING 59-60

Business Name _____

Date of Valuation _____

Revenue Ruling 59-60 contains a wealth of information. It has also stood the test of time and is often quoted in valuation situations, whether tax, divorce, litigation, ESOPs, and so on.

This valuation checklist has been created to assist in a quick review of the key points as well as for the practical application of this ruling to an actual valuation. The analyst should indicate for each item if it has been reviewed or considered or if it is not applicable. The primary information concerning discounts and premiums is highlighted by an asterisk (*).

Reviewed	N/A		
			Purpose
❏	❏		Estate tax.
❏	❏		Gift tax.
❏	❏		Income tax (as amplified by Revenue Ruling 65-192).
❏	❏	*	Value of closely held corporations.
❏	❏	*	Value of thinly traded stock.
❏	❏		Value of other business entities such as partnerships, proprietorships, etc. (as amplified by Revenue Ruling 65-192).

Background Definitions

		Dates of Valuation:
❏	❏	Date of death.
❏	❏	Alternate date (6 months after date of death).

Definition of Fair Market Value

❏	❏	" . . . the price at which the property would change hands between a willing buyer and a willing seller when the former is not under any compulsion to buy and the latter is not under any compulsion to sell, both parties having reasonable knowledge of relevant facts."
❏	❏	" . . . the hypothetical buyer and seller are assumed to be able, as well as willing, to trade and to be well informed about the property and concerning the market for such property."

Approach to Valuation

❏	❏	Facts and circumstances.
❏	❏	No general formula applicable.
❏	❏	Wide difference of opinion as to fair market value.
❏	❏	Valuation is not an exact science.
❏	❏	Sound valuation: ❏ Relevant facts; ❏ Common sense; ❏ Informed judgment; and ❏ Reasonableness.
❏	❏	Future outlook: ❏ Value varies as general economic conditions change; ❏ Optimism versus pessimism; ❏ Uncertainty as to the stability or continuity of future income;

        ❑ Risk of loss of earnings and value;
        ❑ Highly speculative value to very uncertain future prospects; and
        ❑ Valuation is a prophecy as to the future.

❑   ❑   Use of guideline public companies.

Factors to Consider

The nature of the business and the history of the enterprise from its inception

❑	❑		Past stability or instability.
❑	❑		Growth or lack of growth.
❑	❑	*	Diversity or lack of diversity of its operations.
❑	❑	*	Degree of risk in the business.
❑	❑		Study of gross and net income.
❑	❑	*	Dividends history.
❑	❑		Nature of the business.
❑	❑		Products or services.
❑	❑		Operating and investment assets.
❑	❑	*	Capital structure.
❑	❑		Plant facilities.
❑	❑		Sales records.
❑	❑	*	Management.
❑	❑		Due regard for recent significant changes.
❑	❑		Events of the past that are unlikely to recur in the future should be discounted.
❑	❑		Value has a close relation to future expectancy.
❑	❑		Recent events are of greatest help in predicting the future.

The economic outlook in general and the condition and outlook of the specific industry in particular

❑	❑		Current and prospective economic conditions.
❑	❑		National economy.
❑	❑		Industry or industries.
❑	❑		More or less successful than its competitors; stable with competitors.
❑	❑		Ability of industry to compete with other industries.
❑	❑		Prospective competition.
❑	❑		Price trends in the markets for commodities and securities.
❑	❑	*	Possible effects of a key person or thin management/lack of succession.
❑	❑		Effect of the loss of the manager on the future expectancy of the business.
❑	❑	*	Key person life insurance could be partially offsetting.

The book value of the stock and the financial condition of the business

❑	❑		Two historical, fiscal year-end balance sheets.
❑	❑		Balance sheet as of the end of the month preceding the valuation date.
❑	❑	*	Liquid position (ratio of current assets to current liabilities).
❑	❑		Gross and net book value of principal classes of fixed assets.
❑	❑		Working capital.
❑	❑		Long-term indebtedness.
❑	❑	*	Capital structure.
❑	❑		Net worth.
❑	❑	*	Nonoperating assets, such as investments in securities and real estate, should be revalued on the basis of their market price.
❑	❑		Generally, nonoperating assets command lower rate of return.
❑	❑		Acquisitions of production facilities or subsidiaries.

(continues)

Reviewed

N/A

Factors to Consider *(continued)*

☐ ☐   Improvements in financial position.
☐ ☐ * Recapitalizations.
☐ ☐ * Changes in capital structure.
☐ ☐ * Classes of stock.
☐ ☐ * Examine charter or certificate of incorporation to examine the rights and privileges of the various stock issues including:
    ☐ Voting powers;
    ☐ Preference as to dividends; and
    ☐ Preference as to assets in the event of liquidation.

The earning capacity of the company

☐ ☐   Preferably five or more years of detailed profit-and-loss statements.
☐ ☐   Gross income by principal items.
☐ ☐   Principle deductions from gross income:
    ☐ Operating expenses;
    ☐ Interest and other expense on each item of long-term debt;
    ☐ Depreciation and depletion;
    * ☐ Officers' salaries in total if reasonable and in detail if they appear excessive:
    ☐ Contributions based on nature of business and its community position; and
    ☐ Taxes.
☐ ☐ * Net income available for dividends.
☐ ☐ * Rates and amounts of dividends paid on each class of stock.
☐ ☐   Remaining amount carried to surplus.
☐ ☐   Adjustments to, and reconciliation with, surplus as stated on the balance sheet.
☐ ☐   Separate recurrent from nonrecurrent items of income and expense.
☐ ☐ * Distinguish between operating income and investment income.
☐ ☐   Ascertain whether any line of business is operating consistently at a loss and might be abandoned with benefit to the company.
☐ ☐ * Percentage of earnings retained for business expansion should be noted when dividend-paying capacity is considered.
☐ ☐   Since potential future income is a major factor in many valuations, all information concerning past income that will be helpful in predicting the future should be secured.
☐ ☐   Prior earnings records are usually the most reliable guide as to future earnings expectancy.
☐ ☐   The use of arbitrary 5- or 10-year averages without regard to current trends or future prospects will not produce a realistic valuation.
☐ ☐   If a record of progressively increasing or decreasing net income is found, then greater weight may be accorded the most recent years' profits in estimating earning power.
☐ ☐   Look at margins and percentages of sales to assess risk:
    ☐ Consumption of raw materials and supplies for manufacturers, processors, and fabricators;
    ☐ Cost of purchased merchandise for merchants;
    ☐ Utility services;
    ☐ Insurance;
    ☐ Taxes;

❏ Depreciation and depletion; and

❏ Interest.

The dividend-paying capacity

❏ ❏ * Primary consideration to dividend-paying capacity rather than dividends actually paid.

❏ ❏ * Recognition of the necessity of retaining a reasonable portion of profits to meet competition.

❏ ❏ * When valuing a controlling interest, the dividend factor is not a material element, since the payment of such dividends is discretionary with the controlling stockholders.

❏ ❏ * The individual or group in control can substitute salaries and bonuses for dividends, thus reducing net income and understating the dividend-paying capacity of the company.

❏ ❏ * Dividends are a less reliable factor for valuation.

Whether the enterprise has goodwill or other intangible value

❏ ❏ Goodwill is based on earning capacity.

❏ ❏ Goodwill value is based on the excess of net earnings over and above a fair return on the net tangible assets.

❏ ❏ Factors to consider to support intangible value:

❏ Prestige and renown of the business;

❏ Trade or brand name; and

❏ Record of success over a prolonged period in a particular locality.

❏ ❏ In some instances it may not be possible to make a separate valuation of tangible and intangible assets.

❏ ❏ Intangible value can be measured by the amount that the value of the tangible assets exceeds the net book value of such assets.

Sales of the stock and the size of the block of stock to be valued

❏ ❏ Prior sales should be arm's length.

❏ ❏ Forced or distressed sales do not reflect fair market value.

❏ ❏ Isolated sales in small amounts may not control as a measure of value.

❏ ❏ * Blockage is not an issue since the stock is not publicly traded.

❏ ❏ * The size of the block of stock is a relevant factor.

❏ ❏ * A minority interest in an unlisted corporation's stock is more difficult to sell than a similar block of listed stock.

❏ ❏ * Control of a corporation, either actual or in effect, may justify a higher value for a specific block of stock since it is an added element of value.

The market price of stocks of corporations engaged in the same or a similar line of business having their stocks actively traded in a free and open market, either on an exchange or over the counter

❏ ❏ * Must be evidence of an active free public market for the stock as of the valuation date to be used as a comparable company.

❏ ❏ Use only comparable companies.

❏ ❏ The lines of business should be the same or similar.

❏ ❏ A comparable with one or more issues of preferred stock, bonds, or debentures in addition to its common stock should not be considered to be directly comparable to one having only common stock outstanding.

❏ ❏ A comparable with a declining business and decreasing markets is not comparable to one with a record of current progress and market expansion.

(continues)

Reviewed

N/A

Weight to Be Accorded Various Factors

❑ ❑ Certain factors carry more weight than others because of the nature of the company's business.

❑ ❑ Earnings may be the most important criterion of value in some cases, whereas asset value will receive primary consideration in others.

❑ ❑ Primary consideration to earnings when valuing stocks of companies that sell products or services to the public.

❑ ❑ Greatest weight to the assets underlying the security to be valued for investment or holding-type companies.

❑ ❑ Closely held investment or real estate holding company:
  ❑ Value is closely related to the value of the assets underlying the stock.
  ❑ The appraiser should determine the fair market values of the assets of the company.
  * ❑ Operating expenses of such a company and the cost of liquidating it, if any, merit consideration.
  ❑ The market values of the assets give due weight to potential earnings and dividends of the particular items of property underlying the stock, capitalized at rates deemed proper by the investing public at the valuation date.
  ❑ Adjusted net worth should be accorded greater weight in valuing the stock of a closely held investment or real estate holding company, whether or not family owned, than any of the other customary yardsticks of appraisal, such as earnings and dividend-paying capacity.

Capitalization Rates

❑ ❑ It is necessary to capitalize the average or current results at some appropriate rate.

❑ ❑ One of the most difficult problems in valuation.

❑ ❑ That there is no ready or simple solution will become apparent by a cursory check of the rates of return and dividend yields in terms of the selling price of corporate shares listed on the major exchanges.

❑ ❑ Wide variations will be found even for companies in the same industry.

❑ ❑ The ratio will also fluctuate from year to year depending on economic conditions.

❑ ❑ No standard tables of capitalization rates applicable to closely held corporations can be formulated.

❑ ❑ Important factors to consider:
  ❑ Nature of the business;
  ❑ Risk; and
  ❑ Stability or irregularity of earnings.

Average of Factors

❑ ❑ Valuations cannot be made on the basis of a prescribed formula.

❑ ❑ There are no means whereby the various applicable factors in a particular case can be assigned mathematical weights in deriving the fair market value.

❑ ❑ No useful purpose is served by taking an average of several factors (e.g., book value, capitalized earnings, and capitalized dividends) and basing the valuation on the result.

❏   ❏   Such a process excludes active consideration of other pertinent factors, and the end result cannot be supported by a realistic application of the significant facts in the case except by mere chance.

Restrictive Agreements

❏   ❏   *   Where shares of stock were acquired by a decedent subject to an option reserved by the issuing corporation to repurchase at a certain price, the option price is usually accepted as the fair market value for estate tax purposes.

❏   ❏   *   The option price is not determinative of fair market value for gift tax purposes.

❏   ❏   *   Where the option, or buy and sell agreement, is the result of voluntary action by the stockholders and is binding during the life as well as at the death of the stockholders, such agreement may or may not, depending on the circumstances of each case, fix the value for estate tax purposes.

❏   ❏   *   Such agreements are a factor to be considered, with other relevant factors, in determining fair market value.

❏   ❏   *   Where the stockholder is free to dispose of his or her shares during life and the option is to become effective only upon his or her death, the fair market value is not limited to the option price.

❏   ❏   *   Determine whether the agreement represents a bona fide business arrangement or is a device to pass the decedent's shares for less than an adequate and full consideration in money or money's worth:
    ❏ Relationship of the parties;
    ❏ Relative number of shares held by the decedent; and
    ❏ Other material facts.

CHECKLIST 8.29:   REVENUE RULING 77-287:
VALUATION CHECKLIST

Business Name _____

Date of Valuation _____

Revenue Ruling 77-287 deals with the valuation of restricted securities. These types of securities are also referred to as unregistered securities, investment letter stock, control stock, or private placement stock. A thorough understanding of this revenue ruling will also assist in determining DLOM in closely held companies.

This valuation checklist has been created to assist in a quick review of the key points as well as for the practical application of this ruling to an actual valuation. The analyst should indicate for each item if it has been reviewed or considered or if it is not applicable.

Reviewed

N/A

Purpose

❑   ❑   Amplifies Revenue Ruling 59-60.

❑   ❑   Valuation of securities that cannot be immediately resold because they are restricted from resale pursuant to federal securities laws.

Nature of the Problem

❑   ❑   Valuation of stock that has not been registered for public trading when the issuing company has stock of the same class that is actively traded in the securities markets.

❑   ❑   Determine the difference between the fair market value of the registered actively traded shares versus the unregistered shares of the same company.

❑   ❑   Encountered in estate and gift tax as well as when unregistered shares are issued in exchange for assets or the stock of an acquired company.

Background and Definitions

❑   ❑   Restricted securities cannot lawfully be distributed to the general public until a registration statement relating to the corporation underlying the securities has been filed, and has also become effective under the rules of the SEC and Federal securities laws.

❑   ❑   *Restricted securities*—Defined in Rule 144 as "securities acquired directly or indirectly from the issuer thereof, or from an affiliate of such issuer, in a transaction or chain of transactions not involving any public offering."

❑   ❑   *Unregistered securities*—Securities where a registration statement, providing full disclosure by the issuing corporation, has not been filed with the SEC pursuant to the Securities Act of 1933. The registration statement provides the prospective investor with a factual basis to make an investment decision.

❑   ❑   *Investment letter stock*—Also called letter stock. Shares of stock issued without SEC registration. The stock is subject to resale and transfer restrictions set forth in a letter agreement requested by the issuer and signed by the buyer. Such stock may be found in the hands of individual or institutional investors.

❑ ❑ *Control stock*—The stock is held by an officer, director, or other person close to corporate management. These people are subject to certain requirements pursuant to SEC rules upon resale of shares they own in such corporations.

❑ ❑ *Private placement stock*—The stock has been placed with an institution or other investor who will presumably hold it for a long period and ultimately arrange to have the stock registered if it is to be offered to the general public. This stock may or may not be subject to a letter agreement. Private placements are exempted from the registration and prospectus provisions of the Securities Act of 1933.

❑ ❑ *Exempted securities*—Expressly excluded from the registration provisions of the Securities Act of 1933 and the distribution provisions of the Securities Exchange Act of 1934.

❑ ❑ *Exempted transactions*—Certain sales or distributions that do not involve a public offering and are excluded from the registration and prospectus provisions of the 1933 and 1934 Acts. It is unnecessary for issuers to go through the registration process.

Securities Industry Practice in Valuing Restricted Securities

❑ ❑ Investment company valuation practices.

❑ Open-end investment companies must publish the valuation of their portfolios on a regular basis.

❑ Many own restricted and unrestricted securities of the same companies.

❑ Valuation methods:
  ❑ Market price of unrestricted publicly traded stock less a constant percentage discount based on purchase discount;
  ❑ Market price of unrestricted publicly traded stock less a constant percentage discount different from purchase discount;
  ❑ Market price of unrestricted publicly traded stock less a discount amortized over a fixed period;
  ❑ Market price of the unrestricted publicly traded stock; and
  ❑ Cost of the restricted stock until it is registered.

❑ The SEC stated that there are no automatic formulas.

❑ The SEC has determined that it is the responsibility of the board of directors of the particular investment company to determine the "fair value" of each issue of restricted securities in good faith.

❑ ❑ *Institutional Investors Study*
  ❑ SEC undertook an analysis of the purchases, sales, and holding of securities by financial institutions.
  ❑ Published in March 1971.
  ❑ Includes an analysis of restricted securities.
  ❑ Period of study is January 1, 1966 through June 30, 1969.
  ❑ Characteristics of the restricted securities purchasers and issuers.
  ❑ The size of transactions in both dollars and shares.
  ❑ Marketability discounts on different trading markets.
  ❑ Resale provisions.
  ❑ The amount of discount allowed for restricted securities from the freely traded public price of the unrestricted securities was generally related to these factors:

(continues)

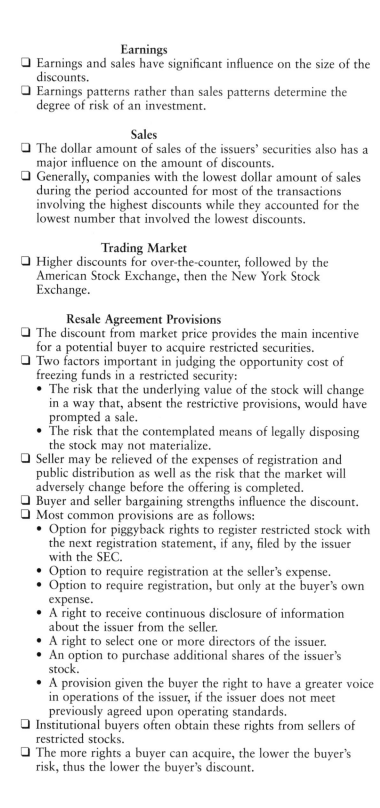

Earnings
❑ Earnings and sales have significant influence on the size of the discounts.
❑ Earnings patterns rather than sales patterns determine the degree of risk of an investment.

Sales
❑ The dollar amount of sales of the issuers' securities also has a major influence on the amount of discounts.
❑ Generally, companies with the lowest dollar amount of sales during the period accounted for most of the transactions involving the highest discounts while they accounted for the lowest number that involved the lowest discounts.

Trading Market
❑ Higher discounts for over-the-counter, followed by the American Stock Exchange, then the New York Stock Exchange.

Resale Agreement Provisions
❑ The discount from market price provides the main incentive for a potential buyer to acquire restricted securities.
❑ Two factors important in judging the opportunity cost of freezing funds in a restricted security:
  • The risk that the underlying value of the stock will change in a way that, absent the restrictive provisions, would have prompted a sale.
  • The risk that the contemplated means of legally disposing the stock may not materialize.
❑ Seller may be relieved of the expenses of registration and public distribution as well as the risk that the market will adversely change before the offering is completed.
❑ Buyer and seller bargaining strengths influence the discount.
❑ Most common provisions are as follows:
  • Option for piggyback rights to register restricted stock with the next registration statement, if any, filed by the issuer with the SEC.
  • Option to require registration at the seller's expense.
  • Option to require registration, but only at the buyer's own expense.
  • A right to receive continuous disclosure of information about the issuer from the seller.
  • A right to select one or more directors of the issuer.
  • An option to purchase additional shares of the issuer's stock.
  • A provision given the buyer the right to have a greater voice in operations of the issuer, if the issuer does not meet previously agreed upon operating standards.
❑ Institutional buyers often obtain these rights from sellers of restricted stocks.
❑ The more rights a buyer can acquire, the lower the buyer's risk, thus the lower the buyer's discount.

❑ Small buyers may not be able to negotiate the large discounts or the rights and options that the volume buyers are able to negotiate.

Summary

❑   ❑ A variety of methods have been used by the securities industry to value restricted securities.

        ❑ The SEC rejects all automatic or mechanical solutions to the valuation of restricted securities.

        ❑ The SEC prefers to rely on good-faith valuations by the board of directors of each company.

        ❑ The study made by the SEC found that restricted securities generally are issued at a discount from the market value of freely traded securities.

Facts and Circumstances Material to the Valuation of Restricted Securities

❑   ❑ Often a company's stock cannot be traded because of securities statutes as in the case of investment letter restrictions.

❑   ❑ Stock may also be restricted from trading because of a corporate charter restriction or a trust agreement restriction.

❑   ❑ These documents and facts, when used in conjunction with those discussed in Section IV of Revenue Ruling 59-60, will be useful in the valuation of restricted securities:

    ❑ A copy of any declaration of trust agreement or any other agreements relating to the shares of restricted stock;

    ❑ A copy of any documents showing any offers to buy or sell or indications of interest in buying or selling the restricted shares;

    ❑ The latest prospectus of the company;

    ❑ Three to five years of annual reports;

    ❑ Trading prices and trading volume and the related class of traded securities one month preceding the valuation date;

    ❑ The relationship of the parties to the agreements concerning the restricted stocks, such as whether they are members of the immediate family or perhaps whether they are officers or directors of the company; and

    ❑ Whether the interest being valued represents a majority or minority ownership.

Weighing Facts and Circumstances Material to Restricted Stock Valuation

❑   ❑ Depending on the circumstances of each case, certain factors may carry more weight than others.

❑   ❑ Earnings, net assets, and net sales must be given primary consideration.

❑   ❑ In some cases, one element may be more important than others.

❑   ❑ For manufacturing, producing, or distributing companies, primary weight must be accorded earnings and net sales.

❑   ❑ For investment or holding companies, primary weight must be given to the net assets.

❑   ❑ Careful review of resale provisions found in restricted agreements.

❑   ❑ The two elements of time and expense should be reflected in a discount.

(continues)

Reviewed	N/A	
❑	❑	The longer the buyer of the shares must wait to liquidate the shares, the greater the discount.
❑	❑	If the provisions make it necessary for the buyer to bear the expense of registration, the greater the discount.
❑	❑	If the provisions of the restricted stock agreement make it possible for the buyer to piggyback shares of the next offering, the smaller the discount.
❑	❑	The relative negotiating strengths of the buyer and seller of restricted stock.
❑	❑	A tight money situation may cause a buyer to have the greater balance of negotiating strength.
❑	❑	In some cases the relative strengths may tend to cancel each other out.
❑	❑	The market experience of freely tradable securities of the same class as restricted securities is also significant.
❑	❑	Whether the shares are privately held or publicly traded.
❑	❑	Securities traded on a public market generally are worth more to investors than those that are not traded on a public market.
❑	❑	The type of public market in which the unrestricted securities are traded is to be given consideration.

CHECKLIST 8.30: REVENUE RULING 93-12: VALUATION CHECKLIST

Business Name _____

Date of Valuation _____

The IRS revoked Revenue Ruling 81-253, which applied family attribution to determine control when valuing minority interests in closely held companies. Since Revenue Ruling 81-253 was issued, the IRS lost a majority of the court cases concerning this issue.

Revenue Ruling 93-12 states that a minority discount on transferred stock to a family member will not be challenged solely because the transferred interest, when aggregated with interest held by family members, will be part of a controlling interest. This ruling arose from a gift tax case.

This valuation checklist has been created to assist in a quick review of the key points as well as for the practical application of this ruling to an actual valuation. The analyst should indicate for each item if it has been reviewed or considered or if it is not applicable.

Reviewed	N/A	
Issue		
❏	❏	If a donor transfers shares in a corporation to each of the donor's children, is the factor of corporate control in the family to be considered in valuing each transferred interest?
Facts		
❏	❏	Taxpayer owned all the shares of stock of a corporation.
❏	❏	Taxpayer made simultaneous gifts of 20 percent blocks of stock to each of five children.
Law and Analysis		
❏	❏	The value of the property at the date of the gift shall be considered the amount of the gift.
❏	❏	The value of the property is the price at which the property would change hands between a willing buyer and a willing seller, neither being under any compulsion to buy or to sell, and both having reasonable knowledge of relevant facts.
❏	❏	Fair market value on the date of the gift.
❏	❏	The degree of control of the business being represented by the block of stock to be valued is among the factors to be considered.
❏	❏	Revenue Ruling 81-253, 1981-1C.B. 187 holds that, ordinarily, no minority shareholder discount is allowed with respect to transfers of shares of stock between family members if, based on a composite of the family members' interests at the time of the transfer, control (either majority voting control or de facto control through family relationships) of the corporation exists in the family unit.
❏	❏	Revenue Ruling 81-253 states that the IRS will not follow the decision in the 1981 case *Est. of Bright v. United States.*

(continues)

Reviewed

N/A

Law and Analysis *(continued)*

❑ ❑   In *Bright* the court allowed a 27.5 percent interest to be valued as a minority interest, even though the shares were to be held by the decedent's surviving spouse.

❑ ❑   There is mention of *Propstra v. United States* (1982), *Est. of Andrews v. Comm* (1982), and *Est. of Lee v. Comm* (1978). These cases held that the corporations' share owned by other family members cannot be attributed to an individual family member for determining whether the individual family member's share should be valued as a controlling interest of the corporation.

❑ ❑   The IRS has concluded, in the case of a corporation with a single class of stock, notwithstanding the family relationship of the donor, the donee, and other shareholders, the shares of other family members will not be aggregated with the transferred shares to determine whether the transferred shares should be valued as part of a controlling interest.

❑ ❑   The five 20 percent interests that were gifted should be valued without regard to the family relationship of the parties.

Holding

❑ ❑   If a donor transfers shares in a corporation to each of the donor's children, the factor of corporate control in the family is not considered in valuing each transferred interest.

❑ ❑   The IRS will follow *Bright, Propstra, Andrews,* and *Lee* in not assuming that all voting power held by family members may be aggregated as part of a controlling interest.

❑ ❑   A minority discount will not be disallowed solely because a transferred interest, when aggregated with interests held by family members, will be part of a controlling interest.

❑ ❑   This will be the case whether the donor held 100 percent or some lesser percentage of the stock immediately before the gift.

Effect on Other Documents

❑ ❑   Revenue Ruling 81-253 is revoked.

CHECKLIST 8.31: TECHNICAL REVIEW CHECKLIST

Business Name _____

Valuation Purpose_____ Valuation Date _____

Valuation Premise _____

Valuation Standard of Value _____

Valuation Level of Value _____

This general checklist has been developed for the purpose of providing a convenient method of indicating the completion of a valuation and establishing that review procedures have been completed. This is one way of assuring the working papers support valuation conclusions. The reviewer(s) should check in the appropriate space below to indicate completion of the various phases of review.

Name _____ Title _____ Date of Review _____

Reviewer No. 1: Analyst _____

Reviewer No. 2: Report Signer_____

Math Reviewer _____

Rev. 1	Rev. 2	Math		
❑	❑	n/a	1.	Check that the scope of our work has been unrestricted. If the scope has been restricted, sufficient data must be available to support the valuation conclusion. Such restrictions should be clearly stated in the reports.
			2.	Check that the terms of the report match the terms of the Representation and Engagement letter and include:
❑	❑	n/a		Valuation Client/Entity Name;
❑	❑	n/a		Valuation Purpose; and
❑	❑	n/a		Valuation Date.
❑	❑	n/a	3.	Verify if the scope of the work has been restricted. If it has been restricted, sufficient data must be available to support the valuation conclusion. Such restrictions should be clearly stated in the report.
			4.	Check that the valuation standard and premise and value being considered have been properly defined:
❑	❑	n/a		If the valuation concerns a business enterprise or equity interest, consider any buy-sell agreements, investment

(continues)

Rev. 1	Rev. 2	Math	
			letter stock restrictions, restrictive corporate charter, or partnership agreement clauses, and any similar features or factors that may have an influence on value.
❏	❏	n/a	If the valuation concerns assets, the valuator must consider whether the assets are: • Valued independently; or • Valued as parts of a going concern.
❏	❏	n/a	If the valuation concerns equity interests in a business enterprise, consider whether the interests are valued on a majority or minority basis, and document the appropriate adjustments.
❏	❏	n/a	If the equity interest is valued on a majority basis, investigate and document the possibility that the business enterprise may have a higher value in liquidation than for continued operation as a going concern. If liquidation is the indicated basis of valuation, any real estate or personal property to be liquidated must be valued under the appropriate standard.
			5. Review all work programs for completeness, including:
❏	❏	n/a	Data Request; and
❏	❏	n/a	Management Interview Notes.
			6. Check the source data, management interview, and site visit for:
❏	❏	n/a	The nature and history of the business;
❏	❏	n/a	Financial and economic conditions affecting the business enterprise, its industry, and the general economy;
❏	❏	n/a	Past results, current operations, and future prospects of the business enterprise, including a thorough analysis of tax return or financial statement information;
❏	❏	n/a	Past sales of capital stock or partnership interests in the business enterprise being valued;
❏	❏	n/a	Sales of similar businesses or capital stock of publicly held similar businesses;
❏	❏	n/a	Prices, terms, and conditions affecting past sales of similar business interests; and
❏	❏	n/a	Physical condition, remaining life expectancy, and functional and economic utility or obsolescence of assets.
			7. Review selected financial data by agreeing the report to the source documents including:
❏	❏	❏	Most current total assets at the valuation date;
❏	❏	❏	Most current stockholders' equity at the valuation date;
❏	❏	❏	Most current net income at the valuation date;
❏	❏	❏	Most current sales at the valuation date; and
❏	❏	❏	Most current shares of stock at the valuation date.
❏	❏	n/a	8. Verify the guideline company's selection criteria are clearly defined and acceptable.

❏	❏	n/a	9. Review and assure the subject company is sufficiently comparable to each guideline company in terms of: Business operations (SIC);
❏	❏	n/a	Product or services similarity;
❏	❏	n/a	Method of marketing (internal sales, external brokers, etc);
❏	❏	n/a	Advantages or disadvantages of patents, copyrights, or trademarks;
❏	❏	n/a	Advantages or disadvantages of intangible assets;
❏	❏	n/a	Size (specify revenue, total assets, earnings, etc.);
❏	❏	n/a	Financial risk comparability (liquidity, activity, leverage, performance);
❏	❏	n/a	Years in business;
❏	❏	n/a	Depth of management; and
❏	❏	n/a	Other factors (unions, geographic diversification, etc.).
❏	❏	n/a	10. Are excluded guideline companies that survived the first cut sufficiently explained as to why they were omitted?
❏	❏	n/a	11. Were appropriate adjustments for comparability made to the selected guideline company financial data before computing valuation ratios (such as LIFO/FIFO, depreciation, etc.)?
❏	❏	❏	12. Trace the guideline company stock prices to the source data, assuring adherence to the valuation date.
❏	❏	n/a	13. Assure a satisfactory explanation as to the valuation multiples elected (priced earnings, price to book, invested capital to EBITDA, etc.).
❏	❏	n/a	14. Verify adequate documentation of the weighting of the multiple indicators in order to arrive at the market approach indication of value. This weighting may be specific percentages or a blended judgment within the array.
❏	❏	n/a	15. If the guideline company public company method is used and, based on the adjustments in the assignment (or lack thereof), this method produces a minority, marketable value indicator, is there adequate documentation to adjust for: • Control interest (if necessary); and • Closely held interest.
❏	❏	n/a	16. If the guideline company transaction method (external transactions) was used and if this method based on the facts of the assignment produces a control, marketable indicator, is there adequate documentation to reflect the necessary adjustments for: • Minority interest; and • Closely held interest.
			17. Review the calculations when valuing preferred stock, specifically:
❏	❏	❏	Trace market yields to underlying source documents; and
❏	❏	n/a	Explain the election of the rating of the preferred stock chosen for the subject company.

(continues)

Rev. 1	Rev. 2	Math		
❏	❏	n/a	18.	Assure an adequate explanation as to the election of the rating of the preferred stock elected for the subject company.
			19.	If internal transactions are utilized, trace these to source documents:
❏	❏	❏		Prices;
❏	❏	n/a		Terms;
❏	❏	n/a		Conditions;
❏	❏	❏		Multiples; and
❏	❏	n/a		Dates.
❏	❏	n/a	20.	Review selected computations extending through price for the market approach including preferred stock.
❏	❏	n/a	21.	Review the fair market value calculations necessary to compute preferred stock value and other classes of stock, if any.
			22.	Review each selected guideline company's financial data as of the valuation date by agreeing or tracing the information in the draft valuation report to the original source documents, including:
❏	❏	❏		Revenues;
❏	❏	❏		Net Income;
❏	❏	❏		Total Assets;
❏	❏	❏		Equity;
❏	❏	❏		Shares Outstanding; and
❏	❏	❏		EBIT and EBITDA, if utilized.
❏	❏	n/a	23.	Review the subject company's financial performance and its placement within the guideline group, specifically related to critical financial ratios such as liquidity, performance, activity, and leverage ratios. The election of specific ratios within these categories will be different for each assignment.
❏	❏	n/a	24.	Review the market price for each guideline company and the computation of market multiples. Agree the data indicated in the report to source documents.
❏	❏	n/a	25.	Check that the selection of the discount for lack of marketability, if any, is appropriate.
❏	❏	n/a	26.	Check the appropriateness of the adjustment for control premium or minority discount.
			27.	Check that all work papers serve a valuation purpose and are completed properly. This includes:
❏	❏	n/a		The search for guideline company transactions should be clearly documented.
❏	❏	n/a		Guideline company financial results should be adjusted properly for accounting consistency.

❑ ❑ n/a   All adjustments necessary to develop an economic balance sheet should be supported by adequate documentation.

❑ ❑ n/a   All adjustments to earnings should be adequately documented. This includes substantiation of nonrecurring items.

❑ ❑ n/a   28. Projections should have reasonable assumptions supported by current or anticipated events, such as new customer contracts.

❑ ❑ n/a   29. The derivation of the discount or capitalization rate as of the valuation date should be detailed.

                          30. Review the report for grammar and technical consistency. Each valuation report issued must have these sections:

❑ ❑ n/a   Title Page;

❑ ❑ n/a   Transmittal Letter;

❑ ❑ n/a   Certification of Appraiser(s);

❑ ❑ n/a   Table of Contents;

❑ ❑ n/a   Valuation Summary, including:
- A description of the subject being valued;
- A clear definition of the value estimated;
- A statement of the objectives of the valuation including the valuation date; and
- A clear statement of the scope of the valuation.

❑ ❑ n/a   A description and explanation of the information considered and the valuation methodology utilized;

❑ ❑ n/a   Statement of Contingent and Limiting Conditions (including hypothetical, fractional, or preliminary labeling);

❑ ❑ n/a   Economic Outlooks—National and Local to project;

❑ ❑ n/a   Industry Outlook; and

❑ ❑ n/a   Curriculum Vitae (for primary appraised involved on the assignment).

❑ ❑ n/a   31. Check that generally accepted valuation standards, including the Uniform Standards of Professional Appraisal Practice, have been observed.

Disclaimer Excluding Any Warranties: This checklist is designed to provide guidance to analysts, auditors, and management but is not to be used as a substitute for professional judgment. These procedures must be altered to fit each assignment. The practitioner takes sole responsibility for implementation of this guide. The implied warranties of merchantability and fitness of purpose and all other warranties, whether expressed or implied, are excluded from this transaction and shall not apply to this guide. The Financial Valuation Group shall not be liable for any indirect, special, or consequential damages.

CHECKLIST 8.32: REVIEW CHECKLIST—EMINENT DOMAIN

Business Name _____

Valuation Date _____

This work program checklist has been developed for the purpose of providing a convenient method of establishing that the necessary procedures have been completed, thus assuring the work papers adequately support valuation conclusions in an eminent domain valuation. The reviewer should check in the appropriate space below to indicate completion of the various phases of review.

Completed   **N/A**

❑ ❑ 1. Check that the scope of the work has been unrestricted.

❑ ❑ 2. Obtain and review information gathered during the initial stages of this engagement, including a copy of the right-of-way map and any related memos or notes.

3. Coordinate an initial meeting with the business owner and perform these procedures:

❑ ❑ Verify the history of the business and determine its qualifications for business damages. (The business, not necessarily the same owner, has been at that location for a minimum of four years as of the date of taking; there is a partial taking of property that affects the business on the remainder; the business has been damaged as a result of the taking of property, with due consideration given to any limitation on access to and from the business.)

❑ ❑ As determined necessary, coordinate efforts with other experts including:
• Real estate appraisers;
• Engineers;
• Customer surveys;
• Marketing/site research; and
• Other.

❑ ❑ Discuss the taking with the business owner and determine the general effect to the business. Prepare a memo.

❑ ❑ Obtain a general understanding of the business, its history, and ownership in detail.

❑ ❑ Determine the future plans the owner has for the business and document in detail.

❑ ❑ Obtain copies of the required financial information. (Normally this would include the prior five years' tax returns and financial statements, building leases, and current financial information since the latest year-end.)

❑ ❑ Obtain necessary operational information required.

❏ ❏   4. Immediately after meeting with the business owner, follow up with a letter summarizing the meeting.

❏ ❏   5. If appropriate, initiate engagement letter for signature.

❏ ❏   6. Upon receipt of financial information, submit it with proper instructions to financial analyst for input.

❏ ❏   7. Analyze output of financial data and calculate projections based on historical information. The resultant projections should represent the expected revenues and expenses for the business in the foreseeable future, adjusted for nonrecurring items, owner salaries, use of facilities, and equipment.

        8. Review and verify the material consistency with reports submitted by other experts including:

❏ ❏   Real estate appraisers;

❏ ❏   Engineers;

❏ ❏   Customer surveys;

❏ ❏   Marketing/site research; and

❏ ❏   Other.

❏ ❏   9. Using the financial projections and any other information obtained, including the operational data if applicable, determine the preliminary effect of the taking on the business. This analysis should include any possible reductions in revenues (and gross profits), savings from reduced expenses, required increases in expenses, and other costs to mitigate damages.

❏ ❏ 10. If it does appear economically feasible to continue in operation at the present location, consider a relocation of the business. This analysis would normally include an understanding of the customer base, the competitive nature of the business, the market rent situation, and any other pertinent factors.

❏ ❏ 11. In conjunction with the previous steps, calculate the value of the business.

      12. Conclude business damages as limited to the lesser of:

❏ ❏   Actual damage;

❏ ❏   Relocation; and

❏ ❏   Value of the business.

❏ ❏ 13. Prepare a thorough list of the assumptions and information sources used.

(continues)

Completed

N/A

☐   ☐   14. Prepare a draft of the business damage report.

☐   ☐   15. Review the report draft, and make any necessary changes.

☐   ☐   16. Make arrangements to have the business owner and other pertinent parties review the report draft.

☐   ☐   17. Incorporate agreed-on changes from all reviewers into final report and produce a final draft of the report.

☐   ☐   18. Review the final report and make sure all initials are obtained on a report control sheet.

☐   ☐   19. Coordinate with time and billing personnel to ensure a detailed printout will be available of total time. Have a standard detailed billing prepared.

☐   ☐   20. If necessary, prepare a representation letter and have it signed by the business owner.

☐   ☐   21. Deliver appropriate copies of report and billing.

☐   ☐   22. Review work paper file to make sure all work papers are properly prepared and support the final report.

CHECKLIST 8.33:   REVIEW CHECKLIST— CONTEMPORANEOUS

Business Name _____   Valuation Date _____

Project Manager _____   Due Date _____

Premise of Value _____   Fee Budget _____

Each item on this checklist is to be reviewed contemporaneously with the development of the assignment. As the project manager completes the major section of the appraisal, that portion of the assignment must be forwarded to the partner in charge of that assignment for the partner's immediate review.

Completed **Reviewed**

Planning

❏ ❏ 1. Review and acceptance of the Representation and Engagement Letter.
❏ ❏ 2. Identify the **valuation issues** in consultation with the project manager.
❏ ❏ 3. Determine the **file organization** and sections.
❏ ❏ 4. Request information from client.
❏ ❏ 5. Establish **target dates** for key elements of the assignment, including the target report release date.

Data Received

❏ ❏ 6. Determine if the minimum necessary data has been received.
❏ ❏ 7. **Review inventory**, update information request.
❏ ❏ 8. Update inventory.

Financial Statement Input

❏ ❏ 9. **Spread** financial information.
❏ ❏ 10. Research relevant SIC code and RMA data.
❏ ❏ 11. Verify accuracy of input (**trace** financial spreads to source).
❏ ❏ 12. Perform financial analysis.
❏ ❏ 13. Complete **contemporaneous checklist**.
❏ ❏ 14. Perform management interview.

Market Search

❏ ❏ 15. Research **economic and industry outlooks**.
❏ ❏ 16. Search for guideline companies.
❏ ❏ 17. **Determine acceptance** of guideline companies.
❏ ❏ 18. Gather information on guideline companies.

(continues)

Completed **Reviewed**

Guideline Companies Input and Ratios

❑ ❑ 19. **Spread** guideline company financial information.
❑ ❑ 20. Verify accuracy of input (**trace** financial spreads to source).
❑ ❑ 21. Analyze financial ratios and determine final **pricing ratios.**
❑ ❑ 22. Finalize value indication.

Asset-Based Approach

❑ ❑ 23. Determine **assets and liabilities** to be restated.
❑ ❑ 24. Obtain **appraisals** performed by other appraisers.
❑ ❑ 25. Obtain client representations and so on.
❑ ❑ 26. Finalize value indication.

Income Approach

❑ ❑ 27. Develop the **discount rate** and/or **capitalization rate.**
❑ ❑ 28. **Normalize** the financial statements.
❑ ❑ 29. Develop ongoing **earnings base** and/or projections.
❑ ❑ 30. Finalize value indication.

Conclusion Issues/Valuation Adjustments

❑ ❑ 31. Control premium, discount for lack of marketability, discount rate, and so on.
❑ ❑ 32. Value indicator and weight of each.
❑ ❑ 33. **Determine final conclusion.**

Allocation of Intangible Assets

❑ ❑ 34. Verify **actuarial retirement rate** methodology:
- Number of active customers;
- Number of inactive customers;
- Development of angle adds;
- Determination of the average age of the active customers;
- Statistical verification of the selection of the lifing curve;
- Determination of the remaining useful life; and
- Application of the discounted cash flow methodology.

Report Narrative

❑ ❑ 35. Prepare draft report.
❑ ❑ 36. Review draft report.
❑ ❑ 37. Make changes necessary for final issuance, including exhibits.
❑ ❑ 38. Review final report and complete **review checklist.**

CHECKLIST 8.34: REVIEW CHECKLIST—COMPLIANCE WITH THE UNIFORM STANDARDS OF PROFESSIONAL APPRAISAL PRACTICE (USPAP) STANDARD RULE 9

Business Name _____

Date of Valuation _____

This checklist assists the valuation analyst to ensure his or her work is in compliance with USPAP. All NO answers should be explained.

Yes	No	
❑	❑	1. Has the scope of the work been determined to produce a credible appraisal?
❑	❑	2. Under the scope of work, is there sufficient research and analysis to support a credible appraisal?
❑	❑	3. Did the appraiser identify the client and other intended users, the intended use and the effective date?
❑	❑	4. Has the standard and premise of value been defined?
❑	❑	5. Has the appraiser identified the characteristics of the subject property?
❑	❑	6. Have all buy-sell agreements and/or language and/or investment letter stock restrictions been considered?
❑	❑	7. Have all restrictive corporate charter or partnership agreement clauses been considered?
❑	❑	8. Have elements of control and/or minority been considered?
❑	❑	9. Is the appraiser aware of, does he/she understand and correctly employ recognized approaches, methods, and procedures to produce a credible appraisal?
❑	❑	10. Has marketability and/or liquidity (or lack of) been considered?
❑	❑	11. Have the nature and history of the business or intangible asset been fully considered?
❑	❑	12. Have financial and economic conditions affecting the business been considered?
❑	❑	13. Have general industry conditions been considered?
❑	❑	14. Have general economic conditions been considered?
❑	❑	15. Has there been a thorough analysis of tax returns and/or financial statements reflecting: • Past results; • Current operations; and • Future prospects?
❑	❑	16. Has consideration been given to past sales of capital stock or other ownership interests or intangible asset?
❑	❑	17. Has consideration been given to the sales of similar ownership interests or assets, including: • Prices; • Terms; and • Conditions?

(continues)

Yes	No	
❑	❑	18. Has consideration been given to one or more approaches to value?
❑	❑	19. Has consideration been given to the economic benefit of tangible and intangible assets?
❑	❑	20. Did the appraiser reconcile the quality and quantity of data available and analyzed, and reconcile the applicability or relevance of the approaches, methods, and procedures?
❑	❑	21. Did the appraiser identify any extraordinary assumptions or hypothetical conditions?
❑	❑	22. Did the appraiser consider liquidation value?
❑	❑	23. Have the Uniform Standards of Professional Appraisal Practice been observed?

Explanation of NO Answers:

Item No.   *Explanation*

_____   _____
_____   _____
_____   _____
_____   _____
_____   _____
_____   _____
_____   _____
_____   _____
_____   _____
_____   _____

CHECKLIST 8.35: APPRAISAL REVIEW CHECKLIST

Business Name _____

Valuation Date _____

Check YES if the item described has been adequately considered and reflected in the report (or is not applicable). Check NO if the item should have been considered but was not. All NO items checked should be clarified by the responsible appraiser.

Yes **No**

Description of the Valuation Subject and Purpose

❑ ❑   1. Party retaining the appraiser.
❑ ❑   2. Interest being valued.
❑ ❑   3. Form of organization (C/S corporation, partnership).
❑ ❑   4. State of legal incorporation or registration.
❑ ❑   5. Legal rights and restrictions of ownership, if not obvious.
❑ ❑   6. Value characteristics and physical condition, if applicable.
❑ ❑   7. Description of classes of ownership and distribution of each.
❑ ❑   8. Purpose(s) of the appraisal.
❑ ❑   9. Standard and premise of value with statutory references.
❑ ❑ 10. Meaning attached to the standard of value used.
❑ ❑ 11. Date(s) for which the value applies.
❑ ❑ 12. Statement of contingent and limiting conditions to which the appraisal values are subject (including limitations on the use of hypothetical, fractional, and preliminary appraisals).

Appraiser Qualifications and Independence

❑ ❑ 13. Transmittal letter with signatures of responsible parties and inclusion of dissenting opinions.
❑ ❑ 14. Statement of the appraiser's objectivity in the valuation result.
❑ ❑ 15. Appraiser made a physical inspection and/or visited with management and conducted an interview at the subject's location.
❑ ❑ 16. Appraiser conducted a telephone interview with management.

Overall Appearance of the Report

❑ ❑ 17. Grammar and diction.
❑ ❑ 18. Ambiguous versus well-defined terminology.
❑ ❑ 19. Spelling and typographical errors.
❑ ❑ 20. Completeness.
❑ ❑ 21. Layout, organization, and overall appearance.
❑ ❑ 22. Reasonable balance between "soft" (boilerplate) and "hard" analysis.
❑ ❑ 23. Clear sources of information verifiable by the reader.

Qualitative Factors about the Business

❑ ❑ 24. Nature and history of the enterprise since inception.
❑ ❑ 25. Products and services, and business mix.
❑ ❑ 26. Industries, markets, and customers served.
❑ ❑ 27. Competitors and the competitive environment.
❑ ❑ 28. Description of facilities.
❑ ❑ 29. Flow of operations (discuss vendors if applicable).   *(continues)*

Yes	No	
❑	❑	30. Description of management and key personnel.
❑	❑	31. Organizational structure (including subsidiaries and affiliates).
❑	❑	32. Related parties and entities and extent of relationships.
❑	❑	33. Economic conditions and outlook for the industry.

Financial Position and Performance

Yes	No	
❑	❑	34. Adequate discussion of assets, liabilities, liquidity, and leverage.
❑	❑	35. Book value and financial condition.
❑	❑	36. Existence of goodwill or other intangible value.
❑	❑	37. Adequate discussion of financial performance (revenue and profit margins, including historical, current, and expected future levels) and nonrecurring or extraordinary items.
❑	❑	38. Earning capacity.
❑	❑	39. Dividend paying capacity, history, and prospects.

Valuation Methodology(ies)

Yes	No	
❑	❑	40. Description and explanation of the appraisal method(s) used.
❑	❑	41. Proper support and justification of approaches used.
❑	❑	42. Reasonable, well-documented financial statement adjustments.
❑	❑	43. Sales of stock and the size of the block to be valued.
❑	❑	44. Market prices of similar companies traded publicly.
❑	❑	45. Clear criteria and selection procedures of guideline companies, if used, and sufficient explanation, if not used.
❑	❑	46. Clear and convincing connection between historical and projected performance, if projections are utilized and/or otherwise explained.
❑	❑	47. Reasonable and appropriate capitalization rate/factor, explain if alternate method is used.
❑	❑	48. Consideration of factors relevant to the methodologies used.
❑	❑	49. Proper use of valuation discounts and/or premiums.
❑	❑	50. Appropriate consideration of the marketability of the securities.

Final Analysis

Yes	No	
❑	❑	51. Clear statement of the valuation conclusion(s).
❑	❑	52. Logic and reasonableness of conclusion(s).
❑	❑	53. Proper support and justification of conclusion(s).
❑	❑	54. Reconciliation of valuation methods and approaches.

Explanation of NO Answers:

Item No.	*Explanation*
_____	_____
_____	_____
_____	_____
_____	_____

CHECKLIST 8.36:   NON-APPRAISER'S GUIDE TO REVIEWING BUSINESS VALUATION REPORTS

Check if these items are reflected in the report.

Yes   No

Are the following clearly stated?

☐ ☐ Specific definition of what is being appraised.
☐ ☐ Purpose of appraisal.
☐ ☐ Date of valuation.
☐ ☐ Date of report preparation.
☐ ☐ Standard of value, including reference to statutes if a statutory standard is applicable.

Are the following adequately described (to give you a basic knowledge)

☐ ☐ Form of ownership (corporate, partnership, etc.).
☐ ☐ History of the company.
☐ ☐ Major assets, both tangible and intangible (goodwill, patents, etc.).
☐ ☐ Products or services.
☐ ☐ Markets or customers.
☐ ☐ Competition.
☐ ☐ Management.
☐ ☐ Who owns the company.
☐ ☐ How the company is capitalized.
☐ ☐ Outlook for the economy, industry, and company.
☐ ☐ Past transactional evidence of value (e.g., sale of stock, etc.).
☐ ☐ Sensitivity to seasonal or cyclical factors.
☐ ☐ State of incorporation.
☐ ☐ Sources of information.

Financial Analysis

☐ ☐ Is there a discussion of the firm's financial statements?
☐ ☐ Are there exhibits summarizing balance sheets and income statements for a sufficient period of time?
☐ ☐ Are any adjustments made to the financial statements as explained?
☐ ☐ Are company financial statements compared to those of its industry?
☐ ☐ If discounted future earnings or cash flows are used, are the appropriate statements summarized and key assumptions included?

Valuation Methodology and Report

☐ ☐ Are the methods used identified and the reasons for their selection discussed?
☐ ☐ Are the steps followed in the application of the method(s) understandable, and do they lead you to the value conclusion?
☐ ☐ When applicable, are sales of similar businesses or capital stock of publicly traded similar businesses used for comparison?
☐ ☐ Does the report explain how any discounts, capitalization rates, or valuation multiples were determined or used?
☐ ☐ Is the terminology used in the report defined so that it is understandable?

(continues)

Yes	No	
❏	❏	Does the report identify the appraisers and have the appraisers signed the report?
❏	❏	Does the report contain the statement of certification signed by the appraiser?

Does the appraiser's statement of qualifications present relevant qualifications for this appraisal?

❏	❏	Education.
❏	❏	Technical training.
❏	❏	Professional designations.
❏	❏	Professional appraisal organization memberships and activities.
❏	❏	Type and years of experience.
❏	❏	Does the report contain a statement of confidentiality?

Does the report contain a statement of assumptions and limiting conditions (regarding):

❏	❏	Conflicts of interest.
❏	❏	Reliance on data and information supplied by others without verification.
❏	❏	The valuation only being valid for the valuation date and stated purpose.

Reviewer's Judgment:

❏	❏	Does the report, in your opinion, cover all the material factors that affect the value of the business?
❏	❏	Is the value conclusion reasonable, as a result of all the factors presented in the report?

Disclaimer Excluding Any Warranties: This checklist is designed to provide guidance to analysts, auditors, and management but is not to be used as a substitute for professional judgment. These procedures must be altered to fit each assignment. The practitioner takes sole responsibility for implementation of this guide. The implied warranties of merchantability and fitness of purpose and all other warranties, whether expressed or implied, are excluded from this transaction and shall not apply to this guide. The Financial Valuation Group shall not be liable for any indirect, special, or consequential damages.

CHECKLIST 8.37:   AUDITOR REVIEW OF VALUATION FOR FINANCIAL REPORTING

Business Name _____   Valuation Date _____

Reviewer _____   Valuation Type _____

Each item on this checklist is to be reviewed progressively by the responsible auditor and by category as the appraiser/valuer completes the engagement. Scheduling this progressive review of the valuation engagement will eliminate surprises at the end of the engagement that could cause a delay in issuing the audit. This checklist does not replace the valuation audit program but is intended to facilitate communication between the valuers and the auditors concerning key valuation issues as the valuation progresses. When completed, this review checklist will insure the auditor has completed critical steps in the audit program.

Completed

Are the following clearly stated?

❑   Does the valuer have specialized training in business valuation and intangible assets?
❑   Does the valuer hold the appropriate professional designations in business valuation (for example, CPA/ABV, ASA, CBA, CVA)?
❑   Can the valuer adequately discuss FASB Statements 121, 131, 141, 142, 144, Concepts Statement 7, and the AICPA's "best practices" guide on "In Process Research and Development"?
❑   Does the valuer have adequate experience in valuing intangible assets?
❑   Does the valuer meet the qualifications for a valuation specialist per FASB 73?

Industry and Company Risks

❑   Does the valuer understand your perception of the industry's business and financial risks applicable to the company?
❑   Does the valuer understand your perception of the company's business and financial risks?
❑   If the valuer is not familiar with the industry's business and financial risks, did he or she adequately communicate how he or she would obtain sufficient relevant knowledge about the industry's business and financial risks?

Company Projections

❑   Did the valuer perform a mathematical check of the company projections?
❑   If so, did he or she find any mathematical errors?
❑   Can the valuer adequately explain how he or she tested the underlying assumptions?
❑   Does the valuer have a list of the assumptions that required additional analysis or support?
❑   Does the valuer's risk analysis of the underlying assumptions correspond with the analysis of the underlying assumptions?
❑   If not, can you reconcile the differences?

Guideline Companies Selected

❑   Can the valuer adequately explain the process used in selecting the guideline companies?
❑   Does the valuer have a list of considered but excluded companies?

(continues)

Completed

❑ Are all the guideline companies in the same industry?
❑ If not, can the valuer explain why the guideline companies have the same investment risk characteristics as the subject company?
❑ Do the guideline companies selected appear appropriate?

Discount Rate Development

❑ Did the valuer use the modified or capital asset pricing model?
❑ Did the valuer use the buildup method as a fundamental analysis?
❑ Did the valuer use the weighted average cost capital?
❑ If so, does the equity portion match either the (modified) capital asset pricing model or the buildup method?
❑ If so, can the valuer justify the selection of the interest rate used?
❑ If so, is the tax rate used in determining the after-tax interest rate appropriate for the subject company?
❑ If so, can the valuer justify the weighting between the equity and the debt portions of the weighted average cost of capital model?
❑ Does the valuer have supporting documentation for the input items in the various discount rate development models?

Economic Adjustments

❑ Has the company or valuer identified all the appropriate nonrecurring economic events or costs?
❑ Can the valuer justify any other economic adjustments made to the income statements?
❑ If using an adjusted balance sheet method, did the valuer provide appropriate documentation for the economic adjustments made to the balance sheet?

Allocation of Income to Identifiable Intangible Assets

❑ Has the valuer made a list of identifiable intangible assets applicable to the subject company?
❑ Does the schedule of income allocation and returns on contributory assets have appropriate supporting documentation?
❑ Does the schedule of income allocation reconcile to total company income?
❑ Are there any reasons to disagree with the income allocation schedule?
❑ If so, have these issues been discussed with the valuer?

Royalty Rates

❑ Does the valuer have a list of royalty rates applicable to each identifiable intangible asset?
❑ Were the royalty rates derived from a royalty rate survey?
❑ If so, did the valuer present any analysis related to the quality or the survey?
❑ Did the valuer use the 25 percent rule in determining the royalty rate?
❑ Were the royalty rates derived from a study of actual licensing transactions?
❑ Can the valuer adequately explain the selection process used in determining the guideline licensing transaction?
❑ Can the valuer explain any adjustments to the guideline royalty rate transactions?